Posttraumatic Stress Disorder

ISSUES AND CONTR

Posttraumatic Stress Disorder

ISSUES AND CONTROVERSIES

Edited by

GERALD M. ROSEN

University of Washington and Private Practice, Seattle, USA

John Wiley & Sons, Ltd

Other Wiley Editorial Offices

John Wiley & Sons Inc., 111 River Street, Hoboken, NJ 07030, USA

Jossey-Bass, 989 Market Street, San Francisco, CA 94103-1741, USA

Wiley-VCH Verlag GmbH, Boschstr. 12, D-69469 Weinheim, Germany

John Wiley & Sons Australia Ltd, 33 Park Road, Milton, Queensland 4064, Australia

John Wiley & Sons (Asia) Pte Ltd, 2 Clementi Loop #02-01, Jin Xing Distripark, Singapore 129809

John Wiley & Sons Canada Ltd, 22 Worcester Road, Etobicoke, Ontario, Canada M9W 1L1

Wiley also publishes its books in a variety of electronic formats. Some content that appears in print may not be available in
electronic books.

Library of Congress Cataloging-in-Publication Data

Posttraumatic stress disorder : issues and controversies / edited by Gerald Rosen.
    p.   cm.
  Includes bibliographical references and index.
  ISBN 0-470-86284-X (cloth : alk. paper)—ISBN 0-470-86285-8 (pbk. : alk. paper)
  1. Post-traumatic stress disorder.   I. Rosen, Gerald, 1939–
RC552.P67P669   2004
616.85′21—dc22   2004006446

British Library Cataloguing in Publication Data

A catalogue record for this book is available from the British Library

ISBN 0-470-86284-X (hbk)
ISBN 0-470-86285-8 (pbk)

Typeset in 10/12pt Times by SNP Best-set Typesetter Ltd., Hong Kong
Printed and bound in Great Britain by TJ International Ltd, Padstow, Cornwall
This book is printed on acid-free paper responsibly manufactured from sustainable forestry
in which at least two trees are planted for each one used for paper production.

Contents

About the Editor

Gerald M. Rosen has a private practice in Clinical Psychology, and holds an appointment as Clinical Professor in the Department of Psychology at the University of Washington, Seattle. He is on the Editorial Board of *The Scientific Review of Mental Health Practice*, and has published peer-reviewed articles on professional issues in the treatment and assessment of Posttraumatic Stress Disorder.

Contributors

Joyce N. Bittenger, Graduate student with Dr Zoellner, Department of Psychology, University of Washington, Seattle, Washington, USA

Marilyn L. Bowman, Professor and Director of Clinical Training, Department of Psychology, Simon Fraser University, Burnaby, British Columbia, Canada

Richard A. Bryant, Professor, School of Psychology, University of New South Wales, Sydney, Australia

Jon D. Elhai, Assistant Professor, Disaster Mental Health Institute, University of South Dakota, Vermillion, South Dakota, USA

Oliver Fassler, Graduate student with Dr Lynn, Department of Psychology, Binghamton University, Binghamton, New York, USA

B. Christopher Frueh, Associate Professor, Department of Psychiatry and Behavioral Sciences, Medical University of South Carolina and Ralph H. Johnson Veterans Affairs Medical Center, Charleston, South Carolina, USA

James D. Herbert, Associate Professor and Director of Clinical Training, Department of Psychology, Drexel University, Philadelphia, Pennsylvania, USA

Danny G. Kaloupek, Associate Professor, Department of Psychiatry and Behavioral Neuroscience, Boston University School of Medicine; Deputy Director, Behavioral Science Division, National Center for PTSD, VA Boston Healthcare System, Boston, Massachusetts, USA

Joshua A. Knox, Graduate student with Dr Lynn, Department of Psychology, Binghamton University, Binghamton, New York, USA

Scott O. Lilienfeld, Associate Professor, Department of Psychology, Emory University, Atlanta, Georgia, USA

Elizabeth F. Loftus, Distinguished Professor, Department of Psychology and Social Behavior, Department of Criminology, Law and Society, and Department of Cognitive Sciences, University of California, Irvine, California, USA

Steven J. Lynn, Professor, Department of Psychology, Binghamton University, Binghamton, New York, USA

Richard J. McNally,   Professor, Department of Psychology, Harvard University, Cambridge, Massachusetts, USA

Scott P. Orr,   Associate Professor of Psychology, Department of Psychiatry, Harvard Medical School, Boston, Massachusetts; Coordinator for Research and Development, VA Medical Center, Manchester, New Hampshire, USA

Gerald M. Rosen,   Private practice; Clinical Professor, Department of Psychology, University of Washington, Seattle, Washington, USA

Marc Sageman,   Private practice; Clinical Associate Professor, Department of Psychiatry, University of Pennsylvania, Philadelphia, Pennsylvania, USA

Arieh Y. Shalev,   Professor, Department of Psychiatry, Hadassah University Hospital, Jerusalem, Israel

Ben Shephard,   Historian and author, Bristol, UK

Derek Summerfield,   Honorary Senior Lecturer, Institute of Psychiatry, Kings College, London; Research Associate, Refugee Studies Centre, University of Oxford, London, UK

Rachel Yehuda,   Professor of Psychiatry and Director, Division of Traumatic Stress Studies, Mount Sinai School of Medicine and Bronx Veterans Affairs, Bronx, New York, USA

Allan Young,   Professor, Department of Social Studies of Medicine, Department of Anthropology, and Department of Psychiatry, McGill University, Montreal, Quebec, Canada

Lori A. Zoellner,   Associate Professor, Department of Psychology, University of Washington, Seattle, Washington, USA

Preface

Recognizing that psychiatric impairment can follow particularly horrific and life-threatening events, in 1980 the American Psychiatric Association established the diagnosis of Posttraumatic Stress Disorder (PTSD). This new diagnosis rested on several assumptions: first, that a specific class of traumatic events (known as the stressor criterion) was linked to a particular set of reactions (the symptom criteria). Second, and consistent with the "adversity-stress" model of adjustment, it was assumed that characteristics of the events themselves, rather than factors of individual vulnerability, were the primary determinants of post-incident morbidity. The diagnosis of PTSD also was based on theories that postulated the role of dissociative processes, unique mechanisms behind the formation of traumatic memories, and unique physiological or anatomical markers that could distinguish PTSD from other psychiatric conditions. Additional assumptions guided the development of treatments for both the immediate aftermath and long-term sequelae of trauma.

It is the rare moment when most every assumption and theoretical underpinning of a psychiatric disorder comes under attack, or is found to lack empirical support. Yet, this is the situation faced by PTSD. After nearly 25 years of research and clinical experience, there is little about the diagnosis that has gone unchallenged. Experts have questioned if the symptom criterion of PTSD constitute a unique disorder, or instead represent an amalgam of already known problems with depression and anxiety. Controversy surrounds the stressor criterion, and the assumption that a unique class of events results in PTSD. Research has challenged the adversity-stress model, finding that characteristics of the individual, rather than the event, best predict posttraumatic morbidity. Multiple concerns persist regarding the assessment of posttraumatic reactions, both in terms of the adequacy of available assessment methods and the adequacy of the construct itself. Many of the most contentious debates have concerned the nature of traumatic memory, an issue thought by many to be central to our understanding of posttraumatic reactions. Controversies surrounding PTSD are not limited to the diagnosis itself: they extend to debate over appropriate treatment, and to concerns that a Westernized construct that medicalizes human emotions has been exported to other cultures.

This text explores these issues, and provides an overview of the leading controversies in posttraumatic studies. The aim in bringing these chapters together is to stimulate discussion and analysis; to clarify the merits of the diagnosis and its appropriate applications. For better or for worse, PTSD has changed our vocabulary and shaped our views on human resilience and coping in the face of adversity. It is time to step back and consider where we are, and where this diagnosis is taking us.

Each chapter stands on its own, although there is an overall organization that takes the reader from general concerns with defining criteria (Chapter 1), through problems with the adversity-stress model (Chapters 2 and 3), to issues with assessment (Chapters 4 through 6), the nature of traumatic memory (Chapters 7 through 9), and concerns regarding treatment and the medicalization of human suffering (Chapters 10 through 12). The authors provide a historical context to current debates, scholarly reviews of the literature, and recommendations for the practicing clinician who must apply the best we know to help those who experience trauma. Accordingly, this text provides invaluable reading for clinicians, researchers, and students who work in the area of traumatic stress studies. Professionals in allied health fields and the law, as well as the interested public, also will find the chapters informative.

Gerald M. Rosen

Acknowledgments

The idea for a text on issues and controversies surrounding Posttraumatic Stress Disorder originated at the 2002 annual conference of the Association for Advancement of Behavior Therapy. Throughout the development of this book, Richard McNally provided invaluable guidance and support for which I am deeply grateful. I thank Chris Frueh for switching roles and serving as editor on the chapter I authored. Finally, I extend my sincere gratitude to the authors who contributed their expertise, insights, and considerable expenditures of time, to make this text possible.

1 Conceptual Problems with the DSM-IV Criteria for Posttraumatic Stress Disorder

RICHARD J. McNALLY

Department of Psychology, Harvard University, USA

Controversy has haunted the diagnosis of posttraumatic stress disorder (PTSD) ever since its appearance in the third edition of the *Diagnostic and Statistical Manual of Mental Disorders* (DSM-III; American Psychiatric Association [APA], 1980). At the outset, psychiatrists opposed to the inclusion of the diagnosis in DSM-III argued that the problems of trauma-exposed people were already covered by combinations of existing diagnoses. Ratifying PTSD would merely entail cobbling together selected symptoms in people suffering from multiple disorders (e.g., phobias, depression, personality disorder) and then attributing these familiar problems to a traumatic event. Moreover, the very fact that the movement to include the diagnosis in DSM-III arose from Vietnam veterans' advocacy groups working with anti-war psychiatrists prompted concerns that PTSD was more of a political or social construct, rather than a medical disease discovered in nature. Although the aforementioned two concerns have again resurfaced in contemporary debates about PTSD, additional issues have arisen as well. For example, the concept of a *traumatic stressor* has broadened to such an extent that today the vast majority of American adults have been exposed to PTSD-qualifying events. This state of affairs is drastically different from the late 1970s and early 1980s when the concept of *trauma* was confined to catastrophic events falling outside the perimeter of everyday experience. As the chapters in this volume illustrate, early twenty-first-century scholars are raising fresh questions about the syndromic validity of PTSD.

Many traumatologists regard skepticism about the syndromic validity of PTSD as motivated by either a malicious agenda to silence the voices of survivors, or by sheer ignorance of the psychiatric consequences of overwhelmingly horrific experience. In contrast, scholars working outside mainstream traumatology do not consider the diagnosis as exempt from critique. They write from diverse perspectives, and hail from varied disciplines, such as anthropology (e.g., Antze & Lambek, 1996; Young, 1995, 2001, 2002), sociology (e.g., Lembcke, 1998), history (e.g., Burkett, 2001; Burkett & Whitley, 1998; Dean, 1997; Shephard, 2001, 2002), psychiatry (e.g., Bracken & Petty, 1998; Reisner, 2003; Satel, 2003; Summerfield, 1999, 2000, 2001), and philosophy (e.g., Hacking, 1998, 1999, pp. 125–162). Rather than review these wide-ranging critiques of PTSD, this chapter focuses on several conceptual problems arising from the diagnostic criteria themselves.

Posttraumatic Stress Disorder: Issues and Controversies. Edited by G. M. Rosen.
© 2004 John Wiley & Sons, Ltd.   ISBN 0-470-86284-X/0-470-86285-8.

As previously observed, the diagnosis of PTSD emerged in the wake of the Vietnam War. Advocates for the diagnosis claimed that extant diagnostic categories failed to capture the unique psychiatric symptomatic profile arising from exposure to a catastrophic stressor. This profile, embodied in the criteria themselves, has evolved since DSM-III. According to DSM-IV (APA, 1994), PTSD is a syndrome comprising three clusters of signs and symptoms: (1) repeatedly reexperiencing the trauma (Criterion B: e.g., intrusive recollections of the event, nightmares); (2) avoidance of activities and stimuli associated with the trauma and emotional numbing (Criterion C: e.g., difficulty experiencing positive emotions); and (3) heightened arousal (Criterion D: e.g., irritability, exaggerated startle reflex). The disorder can only be diagnosed if a person has been exposed to an event that qualifies as a "traumatic" stressor (Criterion A). The symptoms must persist for at least one month (Criterion E) and must cause distress or impairment (Criterion F).

CRITERION A: THE TRAUMATIC STRESSOR CRITERION

PTSD is unusual among DSM-IV disorders in that its diagnosis requires a specific etiologic event: exposure to a traumatic stressor. If a person has not been exposed to a stressor that qualifies as "traumatic," then one cannot assign the diagnosis, regardless of how symptomatic the person might be. A great deal rides on how we define the concept of traumatic stressor, and how we distinguish traumatic stressors from the ordinary stressors of everyday life. The prevalence of the disorder, characterization of its psychobiological correlates, its assessment and treatment, all depend on how we define what counts as a traumatic stressor.

According to DSM-III (1980), a qualifying stressor was one "that would evoke significant symptoms of distress in almost everyone" (p. 238). Qualifying stressors, such as rape, combat, torture, and earthquakes, were those deemed to fall "generally outside the range of usual human experience" (APA, 1980, p. 236). The authors of DSM-III-R changed Criterion A (APA, 1987, p. 250). The concept of traumatic stressor now included witnessing or learning about one's family or friends being exposed to serious dangers as well as being directly exposed to such dangers oneself.

The DSM-IV PTSD Committee, on which this author was a member, debated the merits of further changes in Criterion A. Some members believed that an excessively stringent definition of what counts as a traumatic stressor would exclude many people from receiving the diagnosis and the treatment they deserve. If an event is subjectively perceived as traumatic, then would this not determine whether a person becomes symptomatic? Accordingly, some members believed that subjective appraisal ought to figure in the definition of what counts as a traumatic stressor.

The committee also discussed the possibility of abolishing Criterion A altogether. Removing reference to an etiologic event and diagnosing the disorder on the basis of signs and symptoms, as well as duration and impairment, would have brought PTSD in line with most other DSM syndromes that do not specify a causal event in the diagnostic criteria (e.g., panic disorder, obsessive-compulsive disorder).

Other committee members worried that either abolishing Criterion A or liberalizing the definition of a traumatic stressor would result in overdiagnosis of PTSD, thereby causing both scientific and forensic problems. Broadening the definition would make it difficult to specify the psychobiological mechanisms underlying symptoms arising from extremely diverse events. For example, attempts to elucidate the physiological correlates (e.g., heart rate, activation in specific brain regions) of recollecting a traumatic event would be difficult if definitional broadening resulted in highly heterogeneous groups of individuals being studied. The psychobiology of someone remembering a minor car accident will likely differ from someone remembering a brutal rape. Moreover, if *any* event could qualify as a PTSD-inducing stressor, as long as it was perceived as traumatic, then the diagnosis would invite abuse in the courtroom.

As it turns out, the committee did alter Criterion A (APA, 1994, pp. 427–428). Although a traumatic stressor had been defined as "an event that is outside the range of usual human experience" (DSM-III-R; APA, 1987, p. 250), this requirement was dropped in DSM-IV for two main reasons (Davidson & Foa, 1991). First, it was unclear what constituted "usual" human experience. Stressors outside this boundary for an affluent American might well be within the boundary of usual experience for someone in an impoverished, war-torn country in the developing world. Second, many events triggering PTSD, such as automobile accidents and criminal assaults, were far from uncommon.

The DSM-IV committee changed the definition of Criterion A in other ways, too. A trauma-exposed person was now one who "experienced, witnessed, or was confronted with an event or events that involved actual or threatened death or serious injury, or a threat to the physical integrity of self or others," as long as "the person's response involved intense fear, helplessness, or horror."

This two-part definition of a traumatic stressor warrants several comments. First, the concept of a traumatic stressor was no longer defined solely by criteria external to the person. Indeed, the event now was defined partly by the emotional response of the person. Second, like DSM-III-R, witnessing or learning about another's misfortune counted as a trauma for the witness or recipient of this information. But the DSM-IV criteria no longer required that the direct victim be among the family or friends of the witness. Third, "threats to the physical integrity of self" (p. 427) allowed "developmentally inappropriate sexual experiences without threatened or actual violence or injury" (p. 424) to count as traumatic stressors. This revision enabled nonviolent childhood sexual molestation to qualify as a PTSD-level stressor. Fourth, if a person failed to experience intense fear, helplessness, or horror peritraumatically (i.e., during the trauma), then the diagnosis could not be applied. This stipulation would seemingly bar anyone who "dissociated" during the trauma from receiving the diagnosis. Dissociation supposedly blunts the emotional response to trauma. Yet scholars have adduced evidence that peritraumatic dissociation is among the best predictors of subsequent PTSD (Ozer, Best, Lipsey, & Weiss, 2003).

CONCEPTUAL BRACKET CREEP IN THE DEFINITION OF TRAUMA

DSM-IV introduced changes in Criterion A that have accelerated a conceptual bracket creep in the definition of trauma (McNally, 2003a). Despite a textual emphasis on perception of serious physical threat, these changes have broadened what counts as a PTSD-level stressor. For example, a person who reacts with horror upon learning about another person's exposure to a threat would qualify as having been exposed to a Criterion A traumatic stressor. That is, one no longer need directly be exposed to life threat, nor even vicariously exposed to danger. To qualify as a trauma survivor, one need only respond with fright to learning about the misfortunes of others, including strangers.

Breslau and Kessler (2001) conducted an important empirical study documenting how conceptual bracket creep in the definition of trauma has altered the epidemiologic profile of PTSD. By applying the DSM-IV stressor criterion, they found that 89.6% of adults in the Detroit metropolitan area had been exposed to at least one traumatic event—yet only 9.2% developed PTSD. Breslau and Kessler found that the rate of exposure to traumatic stressors increased from 270 events per 100 persons to 430 events per 100 persons. That is, "the population's total life experiences that can be used to diagnose PTSD has increased materially by 59.2%" (Breslau & Kessler, 2001, p. 703). Events now qualifying as traumatic under the broadened stressor criterion accounted for 37.8% of the total number of cases of PTSD identified in the community.

Attending closely to the details of DSM-IV, Avina and O'Donohue (2002) argued that repeatedly overhearing off-color jokes in the workplace may qualify, under some circumstances, as a Criterion A stressor sufficiently traumatic to produce PTSD. More specifically, exposure to sexual jokes and other, more severe forms of sexual harassment may provide the basis for lawsuits to obtain "appropriate monetary compensation" (Avina & O'Donohue, 2002, p. 74) for work-related PTSD.

Although Avina and O'Donohue (2002) were merely presenting the theoretical and clinical rationale for suing employers who permit employees to tell offensive sexual jokes, others have confirmed that such successful suits have begun to occur. For example, a Michigan woman filed suit against her employer after claiming she developed PTSD from repeatedly hearing foul language and being exposed in the workplace to practical jokes having sexual connotations (McDonald, 2003). To compensate her for PTSD and claims of depression, the court awarded $21 million.

The expanding definition of trauma is relevant to surveys conducted after the September 11, 2001, terrorist attacks. For example, a person horrified by watching television footage of the carnage at the World Trade Center would qualify as having been exposed to a Criterion A stressor (e.g., being "confronted with" an event that threatened others), thereby enabling the classification of any reactions (e.g., dreams, sleep problems, irritability) as "symptoms" of PTSD. Consider the RAND Corporation study. Telephone interviewers assessed a representative sample of 560 adults throughout the United States on the weekend after 9-11, concluding that 44% of Americans "had substantial symptoms of stress" (Schuster et al., 2001, p. 1507), and ominously predicting that the psychiatric effects of terrorism "are unlikely to disappear soon" (p. 1511). Schuster et al. (2001) said that "clinicians should anticipate that even people far from the attacks will have trauma-related symptoms" (p. 1512).

How did Schuster et al. arrive at these dire conclusions? Interviewers asked respondents whether they had experienced any of five symptoms since the attacks on September 11, with each symptom rated on a five-point scale ranging from one ("not at all") to five ("extremely"). A respondent qualified as "substantially stressed" if he or she assigned a rating of at least four ("quite a bit") to one of the five symptoms. Thus, respondents who said they had experienced "quite a bit" of anger at Osama bin Laden were classified as substantially stressed.

Several authors have expressed concerns about the medicalizing of these emotional reactions by calling them *symptoms* reflective of presumed psychiatric illness (e.g.,

Reisner, 2003; Wakefield & Spitzer, 2002). Moreover, many of the "symptoms" of PTSD may reflect nonspecific distress. Consider a New Yorker who was working downtown on 9-11, and who later mentions problems with falling asleep, difficulty concentrating, and irritability. Although each of these might be a "PTSD symptom," each may arise for unrelated reasons. Similarly, it would be misleading to refer to nonspecific physical symptoms, such as fatigue and cough, as "symptoms" of bacterial pneumonia in the absence of verifying evidence (e.g., a culture; McNally, Bryant, & Ehlers, 2003).

CRITERION A AND THE CENTRAL PARADOX OF PTSD

The central paradox of PTSD is that psychologically traumatizing events—as distinct from physically traumatizing ones—must be cognitively appraised for their impact to be felt. A force delivered to the skull can damage the brain irrespective of one's appraisal of the experience. But a psychic trauma carries its force through the meaning the event has for the person. For example, a person threatened with a gun can only be psychically traumatized if he or she knows what a gun is.

In fact, the proximal cause of PTSD may be how the person interprets the meaning of the stressor (McNally, 2003b, pp. 96–100). And how one interprets the event may, in turn, be influenced by historical and cultural factors. For example, although witnessing the violent death of another person is currently deemed a Criterion A stressor, attending public executions has often been a popular form of family entertainment throughout history (Domino & Boccaccini, 2000). Shocking nearly everyone in the West, many African girls eagerly await traditional coming-of-age ceremonies in which their genitalia are carved up by older women (Obermeyer, 1999; Shweder, 2000). Conversely, compelling Hindus to violate religious taboos by forcing them to eat pork and beef is a common method of torture in Bhutan (Shrestha et al., 1998).

If subjective appraisal of the event is the proximal determinant of its stressfulness, does this imply that whatever a person regards as highly threatening or stressful counts as a traumatic event? Is conceptual bracket creep inevitable?

Not necessarily. Merely because all psychological stressors are cognitively mediated does not entail that reality does not constrain appraisal. Indeed, stressors that are appraised as highly threatening *are* often highly threatening. Problems arise only when seemingly trivial stressors are appraised as highly traumatic (e.g., repeatedly overhearing foul language in the workplace). When appraisal closely tracks reality, it becomes redundant with objective features of the event. When appraisal overestimates threat, vulnerability factors are likely to account for more of the variance than properties of the event itself. If PTSD is to remain in DSM-V, then it might be wise to tighten up the definition and conceptual underpinnings of criterion A.

CRITERION A AND THE DOSE-RESPONSE MODEL

The dose-response model of PTSD holds that symptom severity increases as the magnitude of the stressor increases (March, 1993). Many scientists interpret this model in Pavlovian fear conditioning terms (e.g., Keane, Zimering, & Caddell, 1985). They regard traumatic stressors as akin to unconditioned stimuli that evoke unconditioned responses of terror, thereby establishing neutral cues as conditioned stimuli that elicit the conditioned responses integral to PTSD. Therefore, they hold that a laboratory rat's response to inescapable shock mimics at least some aspects of the human response to trauma (Foa, Zinbarg, & Rothbaum, 1992; van der Kolk, Greenberg, Boyd, & Krystal, 1985). Within limits, the dose-response model has its merits. All things being equal, extreme stressors are more likely to produce PTSD symptoms than are mild stressors. Yet many studies fail to support a straightforward dose-response relation between measures of trauma severity and resultant psychopathology.

The dose-response construal of PTSD suffers from conceptual as well as empirical problems. For example, calibrating stressor magnitude is much more complicated in traumatology than it is in the Pavlovian conditioning laboratory. Scientists can measure laboratory stressors (unconditioned stimuli) in purely physical terms that are independent of the rat's behavior (e.g., number of shocks, shock amperage). Yet in traumatology, scientists often must rely solely on the retrospective self-reports of trauma victims themselves for measuring stressor magnitude. That is, researchers presuppose that psychiatrically disturbed persons can provide reliable, objective accounts of stressor magnitude undistorted by their clinical state.

In striking contrast to this presupposition, several longitudinal studies have shown that current clinical state affects how trauma-exposed people remember both the objective (e.g., exposure to danger) and subjective (e.g., one's emotional reaction to danger) features of past trauma events (Harvey & Bryant, 2000; Roemer, Litz, Orsillo, Ehlich, & Friedman, 1998; Schwarz, Kowalski, & McNally, 1993; Southwick, Morgan, Nicolaou, & Charney, 1997). The more distressed a survivor is at follow-up assessment, the more severe the survivor recalls the original traumatic stressor to have been, relative to the original assessment. Because so many studies consistent with the dose-response model depend on a correlation between current self-reported symptoms and self-reported recollection of traumatic stressors (e.g., Friedman, Schneiderman, West, & Corson, 1986), one must question how strong the relation really is between objectively defined stressors and resultant psychopathology.

PROBLEMS WITH THE SYMPTOMATIC CRITERIA

Although many of the most contentious issues regarding PTSD concern DSM-IV's Criterion A, specific difficulties with several symptomatic criteria have become apparent. Consider the reexperiencing symptoms (Criterion B), in which remembering the trauma as if it were occurring in the present is the hallmark of PTSD. The focus on past threat is what sets PTSD apart from the other anxiety disorders, in which threat lies in the future (e.g., generalized anxiety disorder, panic disorder).

The reexperiencing cluster comprises five items (APA, 1994, p. 428): (1) "recurrent and intrusive distressing recollections of the event, including images, thoughts, or perceptions;" (2) "recurrent distressing dreams of the events;" (3) "acting or feeling as if the traumatic event were recurring," including illusions, hallucinations, flashbacks, and a sense of reliving the experience; (4) "intense psychological distress at exposure to internal or external cues that symbolize or resemble an aspect of the traumatic event;" and (5) "physiological reactivity on exposure to internal or external cues that symbolize or resemble an aspect of the traumatic event."

There is surprisingly little prospective data on these symptoms. Most of what we know about intrusive recollections and nightmares, for example, is based on asking patients to think back and reflect on the frequency of intrusive thoughts and nightmares (for a review, see McNally, 2003b, pp. 105–124). Researchers have almost never had patients track the frequency of these symptoms in structured diaries. Asking patients to estimate how often they have suffered from intrusive thoughts, nightmares, and flashbacks during the past month—let alone, say, since the Vietnam War—amounts to relying heavily on fallible autobiographical memory.

Retrospective accounts of reexperiencing symptoms can produce misleading results. For example, van der Kolk, Blitz, Burr, Sherry, and Hartmann (1984) popularized the notion that traumatic nightmares are often exact replicas—instant replays—of the sensory aspects of traumatic experiences. But as Brenneis (1994) pointed out, van der Kolk et al. "based their 'exact replica' conclusion on the dreamers' statements of equivalence without collecting any dreams" (p. 432). Instead of having patients prospectively record their nightmares in a dream diary shortly after awakening, van der Kolk et al. simply asked their PTSD patients during an interview whether their nightmares matched the combat events the patients had experienced in Vietnam.

Mellman and his colleagues have been among the few investigators who have asked trauma patients to record their reexperiencing symptoms (nightmares) prospectively (Esposito, Benitez, Barza, & Mellman, 1999; Mellman, David, Bustamante, Torres, & Fins, 2001). They found that many of the recorded distressing dreams were related to trauma, and a minority were experienced as replicas of the trauma.

Yet nightmares cannot literally replay the sensory aspects of the traumatic experience. An instant replay would require a quasi-photographic mechanism that accurately preserves the sensory details of the trauma on a mental videotape that gets replayed during sleep. But because autobiographical memory does not operate like a video recorder during waking life, there is no reason to expect it does so during sleep. Moreover, to claim that a nightmare is an exact replica of a traumatic event, the person must compare the nightmare, recollected after awakening, to the trauma as recollected during ordinary waking life. But the standard against which the dream is compared—the trauma as recalled by the dreamer when awake—is itself a fallible reconstruction of the event. Because the standard of comparison is itself a reconstruction, how can anyone be sure that the dream replicates what actually happened? Although the occasional "replicative" nightmare is a striking feature of psychological trauma, it is nothing more than a memory illusion.

Inspection of the reexperiencing criteria raises other questions. Each of the five criteria supposedly picks out a distinct mode of reexperiencing the trauma. But how distinct are these phenomena? Symptom B1 includes "images" and "perceptions" of the event in addition to "thoughts" about it. How is an "image" or a "perception" distinguishable from the "hallucination" or "flashbacks" listed under symptom B3? Are flashbacks merely especially vivid images or perceptions (or thoughts)? Although Brewin (2001) has suggested that flashbacks may be mediated by neurobiological mechanisms distinct from those mediating intrusive thoughts, his theory awaits further empirical scrutiny.

Historians have recently adduced evidence seemingly inconsistent with Brewin's theory about a special mechanism subserving flashbacks (Jones et al., 2003). Scrutinizing British medical military archives, they found that psychiatrically traumatized soldiers in World War I and World War II almost never reported anything akin to the flashback experiences mentioned by trauma survivors much later in the twentieth century. If the flashback amounts to an idiom of distress bound to a certain cultural and historical niche, then one must question whether an evolved neurobiological system mediating a timeless, acultural response to trauma truly exists.

In fact, Frankel's (1994) historical survey of the flashback experience suggests that it is anything but a timeless response to trauma. The concept originated in the motion picture industry, migrated to psychiatry as a term referring to the reactivation of sensory disturbances in hallucinogenic drug users, and finally emerged in traumatology to denote an especially vivid form of reliving traumatic experiences in Vietnam veterans (Frankel, 1994).

On the other hand, Kardiner (1941) described cases of American World War I veterans who reported symptoms strikingly similar to later descriptions of flashbacks (p. 82). Kardiner's cases raise the possibility that the scrutinizing of British military archives by Jones et al. (2003) only demonstrated that British doctors simply failed to ask the right questions of their patients, thus leading to the near-absence of flashbacks from the military medical records (Jones et al., 2003; see also Kimbrell, Myers, & Freeman, 2003).

One thing is certainly clear. For reasons sketched above, flashbacks cannot literally be a replaying of the sensory events that occurred during the trauma. The mind does not operate like a videotape machine, regardless of how compelling these sensory reenactments seem to be. In fact, like vivid "flashbulb memories" (Brown & Kulik, 1977), flashbacks often depart from what the patient knows actually happened (McNally, 2003b, pp. 53–57, 113–117). For example, Mayer and Pope (1997) described a Vietnam veteran whose flashbacks of his combat injury differed from the way he knew it had actually occurred. People have reported flashbacks of the homicide of loved ones even though they were not present at the murder scene (Rynearson & McCreery, 1993). And vivid obsessional images have been mistaken for flashbacks (Lipinski & Pope, 1994).

Among the reexperiencing symptoms, psychophysiologic reactivity to reminders of the trauma have been extensively studied in the laboratory. Depending on one's criteria, between 50% and 67% of people with PTSD exhibit heightened physiological reactivity (e.g., skin conductance, heart rate) while listening to audiotaped descriptions of their traumatic event (Orr, Metzger, & Pitman, 2002). Trauma-exposed people without PTSD are seldom physiologically reactive while listening to audiotaped descriptions of their traumatic experiences. Still, many people who qualify for PTSD according to structured diagnostic interviews are nonreactive for reasons that are not fully understood. Finally, complicating matters somewhat, nonpsychotic people who believe they have been abducted by space aliens also exhibit heightened reactivity to audiotaped descriptions of their traumatic "abduction memories" (McNally et al., in press). Taken together, psychophysiologic reactivity in the script-driven imagery paradigm reflects emotional intensity of a memory, regardless of whether it is accurate or not.

Problems with symptomatic criteria are not confined to the reexperiencing cluster. Indeed, probably no PTSD symptom has caused as much confusion or mischief as that of "psychogenic amnesia" (McNally, 2004). The original conception of PTSD emphasized that traumatic experiences were all too memorable, an assertion fully consistent with the scientific literature (Pope, Oliva, & Hudson, 1999). DSM-III (1980) did acknowledge that memory trauma survivors complain about ordinary forgetfulness in everyday life, as embodied in the symptom of "memory impairment or trouble concentrating" (p. 238). Contrary to the misconceptions of some psychotherapists (e.g., Brown, Scheflin, & Whitfield,

1999), this symptom has nothing whatsoever to do with "repressed" memories of trauma, a concept that refers to an inability to access dissociated traumatic experiences. Such authors confuse everyday forgetfulness occurring after a trauma with an inability to remember the trauma itself.

As reports of repressed (or dissociated) and recovered memories of trauma began to gain currency among some therapists in the 1980s, certain traumatologists reconceptualized PTSD as entailing an inability to remember trauma (or least parts of it) as well as a syndrome marked by intrusive remembering. This view was incorporated in DSM-III-R, and retained in DSM-IV, whereby everyday forgetfulness was quietly replaced by a new symptom: an "inability to recall an important aspect of the trauma (psychogenic amnesia)" (p. 250).

The meaning of this symptom is ambiguous. Inferences about amnesia, or an inability to remember, presuppose that the information got encoded in the first place. Yet this is often not true. Because the mind is not a video recorder, not every aspect of a traumatic experience will get encoded into memory: this is especially true when an event is rapidly unfolding as in an automobile accident or a sudden assault. Accordingly, failure to encode every aspect of a traumatic experience—including an "important" one—must not be confused with an inability to recall an aspect that has been encoded. As another example, many people robbed at gunpoint fail to encode the face of their assailant because their attention was focused on the assailant's weapon. Their inability to recall what the robber looked like does not count as amnesia because the face of the robber never made it into long-term memory. The DSM-V Committee should seriously consider replacing this criterion with the original DSM-III symptom of memory and concentration problems.

WHATEVER HAPPENED TO DELAYED ONSET PTSD?

Despite its reputation as a uniquely traumatizing conflict, the Vietnam War was notable for its *low* rate of psychiatric casualties (Dean, 1997, p. 40). The rate of psychiatric breakdown was 12 per 1,000 men, whereas it was 37 per 1,000 during the Korean War, and as high as 101 per 1,000 during World War II. Moreover, most of the psychiatric cases in Vietnam were unrelated to combat trauma.

Not only was the rate of breakdown rare in-country, research on those returning to the United States also failed to uncover much psychopathology. In a seldom-cited prospective study of 577 returning combat veterans, assessed seven months after their return from Vietnam, Borus (1974) found no significant difference in indices of maladjustment relative to a control group of 172 non-veterans. Indeed, only 1.1% (6 out of 577) of the combat veterans experienced adjustment problems, including either psychiatric or antisocial, that warranted a premature discharge from the military. Yet anti-war psychiatrists, such as Lifton (1973), claimed that the effects of the war emerged only months or years after the combatant returned from the service. Indeed, the main argument for the inclusion of PTSD in DSM-III was that the syndrome typically emerged long after the trauma (Scott, 1993, p. 43).

Strikingly, however, the syndrome of delayed onset PTSD has nearly vanished from the psychiatric landscape. Studies on trauma survivors since 1980 have overwhelmingly indicated that people who develop PTSD exhibit their symptoms within hours or days after the trauma—not years later (e.g., Rothbaum & Foa, 1993). Indeed, the realization that PTSD symptoms, if they occur at all, erupt immediately following exposure to trauma was an important reason for including acute stress disorder in DSM-IV. Almost all cases of apparent delayed onset PTSD turn out to involve either delayed help-seeking or subsyndromic PTSD intensified by exposure to another stressor (Solomon, Kotler, Shalev, & Lin, 1989). Pure cases of delayed onset—exposure to trauma followed by a long period of good adjustment that precedes full-blown emergence of the disorder—are rare to nonexistent.

Delayed onset PTSD remains on the books as a relic from the Vietnam era (APA, 1994, p. 429). It may constitute an instance of a "transient mental illness" (Hacking, 1998)—a psychiatric disease that flourishes in a certain cultural and historical niche, and then later disappears when circumstances change.

CONCLUSION

For a PTSD diagnosis, DSM-IV requires that symptoms be present for at least one month (Criterion E) and produce impairment or distress (Criterion F). These criteria reflect an oblique attempt to demarcate "normal" stress reactions from "disordered" ones. Attempts to mark a distinction between genuine mental disorders and ordinary unhappiness is a vexing conceptual problem for psychopathology in general, not just traumatology (e.g., Lilienfeld & Marino, 1995; McNally, 2001; Wakefield, 1992).

Advocates of the PTSD diagnosis seem to believe that it constitutes a *natural kind*, not a culture-bound, socially constructed idiom of distress. Natural kinds are entities discovered in nature that exist independently of our attempts to describe them (see Dupré, 2002; Wilson, 1999). For example, scientists believe that any successful chemistry would ultimately result in discovery of the same elements represented in the periodic table. The elements were there to be discovered by chemists; they were not invented or constructed by them. Likewise, medical scientists discover diseases, such as AIDS, cancer, and bacterial pneumonia. These are natural kinds, not socially constructed kinds. With the increasing medicalization of psychopathology, advocates for the reality of a PTSD diagnosis often claim biological support for the syndrome as a natural kind. As Yehuda and McFarlane (1997) argued:

> biological findings have provided objective validation that PTSD is more than a politically or socially motivated conceptualization of human suffering. Indeed, biological observations have delineated PTSD from other psychiatric disorders and have allowed a more sophisticated description of the long-term consequences of traumatic stress. (p. xi)

Yehuda and McFarlane (1997) further argue that biological data provide

> concrete validation of human suffering and a legitimacy that does not depend on arbitrary social and political forces. Establishing that there is a biological basis for psychological trauma is an essential first step in allowing the permanent validation of human suffering. (p. xv)

Although one might take issue with the claim that acknowledgment of human suffering requires the results of biological validation, Yehuda and McFarlane apparently believe that researchers in traumatic stress have managed to "carve nature at its joints" by discovering a discrete syndrome that differs in kind, not merely in degree, from the normal stress response. That is, they appear to suggest that PTSD was discovered in nature by astute clinical scientists; it was not created by them.

Yet it is likely that PTSD is neither a natural kind nor a purely socially constructed kind. There is a third possibility. PTSD may count as an *interactive kind* (Hacking, 1999, pp. 100–124). Unlike natural kinds discovered in nature, interactive kinds are affected by the very process of classification itself. For example, given that flashbacks are now part of the cultural lore of trauma, people experience their trauma as photographic reenactments, whereas this would not have been possible before. Thus, according to this perspective, PTSD is not "discovered" in nature, but co-created via the interaction of psychobiology and the cultural context of classification.

In conclusion, despite nearly 25 years of research, the PTSD diagnosis remains contentious (McNally, 2003a). Many, if not most, traumatologists believe that PTSD is a timeless, acultural psychobiological response to overwhelming trauma—a natural kind. One purpose of this chapter, and other contributions to this text, is to encourage scholars and clinicians to revisit their assumptions and to reexamine them with an open mind.

REFERENCES

American Psychiatric Association (1980). *Diagnostic and statistical manual of mental disorders* (3rd edn). Washington, DC: Author.

American Psychiatric Association (1987). *Diagnostic and statistical manual of mental disorders* (3rd edn, rev.). Washington, DC: Author.

American Psychiatric Association (1994). *Diagnostic and statistical manual of mental disorders* (4th edn). Washington, DC: American Psychiatric Association.

Antze, P., & Lambek, M. (eds) (1996). *Tense past: Cultural essays in trauma and memory.* New York: Routledge.

Avina, C., & O'Donohue, W. (2002). Sexual harassment and PTSD: Is sexual harassment diagnosable trauma? *Journal of Traumatic Stress*, *15*, 69–75.

Borus, J. F. (1974). Incidence of maladjustment in Vietnam returnees. *Archives of General Psychiatry*, *30*, 554–557.

Bowman, M. (1997). *Individual differences in posttraumatic response: Problems with the adversity-distress connection.* Mahwah, NJ: Erlbaum.

Bowman, M. (1999). Individual differences in posttraumatic distress: Problems with the DSM-IV model. *Canadian Journal of Psychiatry*, *44*, 21–33.

Bracken, P. J., & Petty, C. (eds) (1998). *Rethinking the trauma of war.* London: Free Association Books.

Brenneis, C. B. (1994). Can early childhood trauma be reconstructed from dreams? On the relation of dreams to trauma. *Psychoanalytic Psychology*, *11*, 429–447.

Breslau, N., & Kessler, R. C. (2001). The stressor criterion in DSM-IV posttraumatic stress disorder: An empirical investigation. *Biological Psychiatry*, *50*, 699–704.

Brewin, C. R. (2001). A cognitive neuroscience account of posttraumatic stress disorder and its treatment. *Behaviour Research and Therapy*, *39*, 373–393.

Brown, D., Scheflin, A. W., & Whitfield, C. L. (1999). Recovered memories: The current weight of the evidence in science and in the courts. *Journal of Psychiatry and Law*, *27*, 5–156.

Brown, R., & Kulik, J. (1977). Flashbulb memories. *Cognition*, *5*, 73–99.

12   POSTTRAUMATIC STRESS DISORDER

Burkett, B. G. (2001). Stolen valor: The "history" that never was. In J. N. Moore & R. F. Turner (eds), *The real lessons of the Vietnam War: Reflections twenty-five years after the fall of Saigon* (pp. 249–265). Durham, NC: Carolina Academic Press.

Burkett, B. G., & Whitley, G. (1998). *Stolen valor: How the Vietnam generation was robbed of its heroes and its history.* Dallas, TX: Verity.

Davidson, J. R. T., & Foa, E. B. (1991). Diagnostic issues in posttraumatic stress disorder: Considerations for the *DSM-IV*. *Journal of Abnormal Psychology, 100*, 346–355.

Dean, E. T., Jr (1997). *Shook over hell: Post-traumatic stress, Vietnam, and the Civil War.* Cambridge, MA: Harvard University Press.

Domino, M. L., & Boccaccini, M. T. (2000). Doubting Thomas: Should family members of victims watch executions? *Law and Psychology Review, 24*, 59–75.

Dupré, J. (2002). *Humans and other animals.* Oxford: Oxford University Press.

Esposito, K., Benitez, A., Barza, L., & Mellman, T. (1999). Evaluation of dream content in combat-related PTSD. *Journal of Traumatic Stress, 12*, 681–687.

Foa, E. B., Zinbarg, R., & Rothbaum, B. O. (1992). Uncontrollability and unpredictability in post-traumatic stress disorder: An animal model. *Psychological Bulletin, 112*, 218–238.

Frankel, F. H. (1994). The concept of flashbacks in historical perspective. *International Journal of Clinical and Experimental Hypnosis, 42*, 321–336.

Friedman, M. J., Schneiderman, C. K., West, A. N., & Corson, J. A. (1986). Measurement of combat exposure, posttraumatic stress disorder, and life stress among Vietnam combat veterans. *American Journal of Psychiatry, 143*, 537–539.

Hacking, I. (1998). *Mad travelers: Reflections on the reality of transient mental illness.* Charlottesville, VA: University Press of Virginia.

Hacking, I. (1999). *The social construction of what?* Cambridge, MA: Harvard University Press.

Harvey, A. G., & Bryant, R. A. (2000). Memory for acute stress disorder symptoms: A two-year prospective study. *Journal of Nervous and Mental Disease, 188*, 602–607.

Jones, E., Hodgins-Vermaas, R., McCartney, H., Beech, C., Palmer, I., Hyams, K. et al. (2003). Flashbacks and post-traumatic stress disorder: The genesis of a 20th-century diagnosis. *British Journal of Psychiatry, 182*, 158–163.

Kardiner, A. (1941). *The traumatic neuroses of war.* Washington, DC: National Research Council.

Keane, T. M., Zimering, R. T., & Caddell, J. T. (1985). A behavioral formulation of posttraumatic stress disorder in Vietnam veterans. *Behavior Therapist, 8*, 9–12.

Kimbrell, T., Myers, M., & Freeman, T. (2003). Flashbacks and PTSD in US veterans. *British Journal of Psychiatry, 183*, 263.

Lembcke, J. (1998). *The spitting image: Myth, memory, and the legacy of Vietnam.* New York: New York University Press.

Lifton, R. J. (1973). *Home from the war: Vietnam veterans: neither victims nor executioners.* New York: Touchstone.

Lilienfeld, S. O., & Marino, L. (1995). Mental disorder as a Roschian concept: A critique of Wakefield's "harmful dysfunction" analysis. *Journal of Abnormal Psychology, 104*, 411–420.

Lipinski, J. F., Jr, & Pope, H. G., Jr (1994). Do "flashbacks" represent obsessional imagery? *Comprehensive Psychiatry, 35*, 245–247.

March, J. S. (1993). What constitutes a stressor? The "Criterion A" issue. In J. R. T. Davidson & E. B. Foa (eds), *Posttraumatic stress disorder: DSM-IV and beyond* (pp. 36–54). Washington, DC: American Psychiatric Press.

Mayer, P., & Pope, H. G., Jr (1997). Unusual flashbacks in a Vietnam veteran. *American Journal of Psychiatry, 154*, 713.

McDonald, J. J., Jr (2003). Posttraumatic stress dishonesty. *Employee Relations Law Journal, 28*, 93–111.

McNally, R. J. (2001). On Wakefield's harmful dysfunction analysis of mental disorder. *Behaviour Research and Therapy, 39*, 309–314.

McNally, R. J. (2003a). Progress and controversy in the study of posttraumatic stress disorder. *Annual Review of Psychology, 54*, 229–252.

McNally, R. J. (2003b). *Remembering trauma.* Cambridge, MA: Belknap Press/Harvard University Press.

McNally, R. J. (2004). The science and folklore of traumatic amnesia. *Clinical Psychology: Science and Practice, 11*, 29–33.

McNally, R. J., Bryant, R. A., & Ehlers, A. (2003). Does early psychological intervention promote recovery from posttraumatic stress? *Psychological Science in the Public Interest, 4*, 45–79.

McNally, R. J., Lasko, N. B., Clancy, S. A., Macklin, M. L., Pitman, R. K., & Orr, S. P. (in press). Psychophysiologic responding during script-driven imagery in people reporting abduction by space aliens. *Psychological Science.*

Mellman, T. A., David, D., Bustamante, V., Torres, J., & Fins, A. (2001). Dreams in the acute aftermath of trauma and their relationship to PTSD. *Journal of Traumatic Stress, 14*, 241–247.

Obermeyer, C. M. (1999). Female genital surgeries: The known, the unknown, and the unknowable. *Medical Anthropology Quarterly, 13*, 32–39.

Orr, S. P., Metzger, L. J., & Pitman, R. K. (2002). Psychophysiology of post-traumatic stress disorder. *Psychiatric Clinics of North America, 25*, 271–293.

Ozer, E. J., Best, S. R., Lipsey, T. L., & Weiss, D. S. (2003). Predictors of posttraumatic stress disorder and symptoms in adults: A meta-analysis. *Psychological Bulletin, 129*, 52–73.

Pope, H. G., Jr, Oliva, P. S., & Hudson, J. I. (1999). Repressed memories: The scientific status. In D. L. Faigman, D. H. Kaye, M. J. Saks, & J. Sanders (eds), *Modern scientific evidence: The law and science of expert testimony* (Vol. 1, Pocket Part) (pp. 115–155). St Paul, MN: West Publishing.

Reisner, S. (2003). Trauma: The seductive hypothesis. *Journal of the American Psychoanalytic Association, 51*, 381–414.

Roemer, L., Litz, B. T., Orsillo, S. M., Ehlich, P. J., & Friedman, M. J. (1998). Increases in retrospective accounts of war-zone exposure over time: The role of PTSD symptom severity. *Journal of Traumatic Stress, 11*, 597–605.

Rothbaum, B. O., & Foa, E. B. (1993). Subtypes of posttraumatic stress disorder and duration of symptoms. In J. R. T. Davidson & E. B. Foa (eds), *Posttraumatic stress disorder: DSM-IV and beyond* (pp. 23–35). Washington, DC: American Psychiatric Press.

Rynearson, E. K., & McCreery, J. M. (1993). Bereavement after homicide: A synergism of trauma and loss. *American Journal of Psychiatry, 150*, 258–261.

Satel, S. (2003, May 19). The trauma society [Review of the book *Remembering Trauma*]. *New Republic, 228*, 29–36.

Schuster, M. A., Stein, B. D., Jaycox, L. H., Collins, R. L., Marshall, G. N., Elliott, M. N. et al. (2001). A national survey of stress reactions after the September 11, 2001, terrorist attacks. *New England Journal of Medicine, 345*, 1507–1512.

Schwarz, E. D., Kowalski, J. M., & McNally, R. J. (1993). Malignant memories: Post-traumatic changes in memory in adults after a school shooting. *Journal of Traumatic Stress, 6*, 545–553.

Scott, W. J. (1993). *The politics of readjustment: Vietnam veterans since the war.* New York: Aldine de Gruyter.

Shephard, B. (2001). *A war of nerves: Soldiers and psychiatrists in the twentieth century.* Cambridge, MA: Harvard University Press.

Shephard, B. (2002). The rise of the trauma culture. In J. E. Hovens & G. J. van der Ploeg (eds), *De historie van de psychiatrie als basis voor de toekomst* (pp. 13–30). Rotterdam: Delta Psychitistrisch Ziekenhuis.

Shrestha, N. M., Sharma, B., van Ommeren, M., Regmi, S., Makaju, R., Komproe, I. et al. (1998). Impact of torture on refugees displaced within the developing world: Symptomatology among Bhutanese refugees in Nepal. *JAMA*, *280*, 443–448.

Shweder, R. A. (2000). What about "female genital mutilation"? And why understanding culture matters in the first place. *Daedalus*, *129* (4), 209–232.

Solomon, Z., Kotler, M., Shalev, A., & Lin, R. (1989). Delayed onset PTSD among Israeli veterans of the 1982 Lebanon War. *Psychiatry*, *52*, 428–436.

Southwick, S. M., Morgan, C. A., III, Nicolaou, A. L., & Charney, D. S. (1997). Consistency of memory for combat-related traumatic events in veterans of Operation Desert Storm. *American Journal of Psychiatry*, *154*, 173–177.

Summerfield, D. (1999). A critique of seven assumptions behind psychological programmes in war-affected areas. *Social Science and Medicine*, *48*, 1449–1462.

Summerfield, D. (2000). War and mental health: A brief overview. *British Medical Journal*, *321*, 232–235.

Summerfield, D. (2001). The invention of post-traumatic stress disorder and the social usefulness of a psychiatric category. *British Medical Journal*, *332*, 95–98.

van der Kolk, B., Blitz, R., Burr, W., Sherry, S., & Hartmann, E. (1984). Nightmares and trauma: A comparison of nightmares after combat with lifelong nightmares in veterans. *American Journal of Psychiatry*, *141*, 187–190.

van der Kolk, B., Greenberg, M., Boyd, H., & Krystal, J. (1985). Inescapable shock, neurotransmitters, and addiction to trauma: Toward a psychobiology of posttraumatic stress. *Biological Psychiatry*, *20*, 314–325.

Wakefield, J. C. (1992). The concept of mental disorder: On the boundary between biological facts and social values. *American Psychologist*, *47*, 373–388.

Wakefield, J. C., & Spitzer, R. L. (2002). Lowered estimates—but of what? *Archives of General Psychiatry*, *59*, 129–130.

Wilson, R. A. (ed.). (1999). *Species: New interdisciplinary essays*. Cambridge, MA: MIT Press.

Yehuda, R., & McFarlane, A. C. (1997). Introduction. In R. Yehuda & A. C. McFarlane (eds), *Psychobiology of posttraumatic stress disorder* (pp. xi–xv). New York: New York Academy of Sciences.

Young, A. (1995). *The harmony of illusions: Inventing post-traumatic stress disorder*. Princeton, NJ: Princeton University Press.

Young, A. (2001). Our traumatic neurosis and its brain. *Science in Context*, *14*, 661–683.

Young, A. (2002). The self-traumatized perpetrator as a "transient mental illness." *L'Evolution Psychiatrique*, *67*, 630–650.

2 Risk Factors and the Adversity-Stress Model

MARILYN L. BOWMAN
Department of Psychology, Simon Fraser University, BC, Canada

RACHEL YEHUDA
Mount Sinai School of Medicine and Bronx Veterans Affairs, New York, USA

Human history is a story of achievement and joy, of premature death and suffering. Natural disasters and wars, along with smaller-scale threats to life and well-being, have been ubiquitous, and humans always have had the task of managing responses to horror and fear. Religious beliefs and propitiatory rituals traditionally had specific functions of offering thanks for well-being and achievement, and of seeking relief from suffering. Throughout history, events have often been framed in terms of individuals conquering adversity and surviving with resilience, triumph, and progress.

More recently, threatening experiences have been re-framed in a mental health model that views adverse events as contributing to emotional disorder. Increasingly, emotional disorder is considered an inevitable response to adversity. Popular culture has readily adopted the proposition that adversity results in mental illness, and posttraumatic stress disorder (PTSD) has been embraced as a condition which occurs in response to traumatic events. So pervasive is the expectation of emotional disorder following trauma that the provision of instant "trauma teams" to treat exposed individuals is now regarded as essential after an extreme event.

PTSD as defined in the fourth *Diagnostic and Statistical Manual of Mental Disorders* (DSM: American Psychiatric Association, 1994) is an anxiety disorder in which an event's "severity, duration, and proximity" (p. 426) "are the most important factors affecting the likelihood of developing the disorder." While other factors "may" influence the disorder, it "can develop in individuals without any predisposing conditions, particularly if the stressor is especially extreme" (p. 427). This is consistent with a classical animal, biological stress model in which "dose" determines response. In this model both physical and temporal proximity should be correlated with greater disorder.

PTSD first entered the DSM in 1980, although definitions for the crucial factor of the index event have changed over time. The earliest criterion specified extreme events outside normal human experience; by 1994 this had broadened to include awareness of events that threatened others and elicited responses of fear, helplessness, or horror. The current model is fraught with assumptions about what may or may not be traumatic, and is not fully consistent with human experience across time and cultures. For example, in a recent news story, an Iraqi father was furiously angry after his daughter died, shot by soldiers who accurately inferred that she carried grenades and was a suicide bomber. Her father was not angry that she had been shot and killed, but that she left his house without permission, thus violating his tribal code of family honor. "Had she returned home I would have killed her myself and drunk her blood," he reported (Faramarzi, 2003). Kurdish parents told a reporter they like having lots of sons (among their typical 12–18 children) because, "If you have five boys in the family, when one dies it won't change anything" (Boscarino, 1996).

Not only do events vary in their meaning, so do the signs and symptoms of event-focused disorder. DSM-IV defines three main symptom clusters in PTSD, including re-experiencing, avoidance, and increased arousal. Some of these symptoms appear to be time- and culture-bound. For example, an historical study of combat stress disorders in Germany in World War I showed a pattern of symptoms different from today's typical reactions (Lerner, 1996). The German soldiers mostly showed sensory-motor symptoms such as deafness, mutism, shaking, blindness, stuttering, limping, and tics. In contrast, flashbacks, anger, and other symptoms in the current definition were not seen. Similarly, a historical study of the symptom patterns in British veterans with combat-related disability pensions discovered that flashbacks represent a modern phenomenon significantly absent among soldiers in the Boer War, or in World Wars I and II (Jones et al., 2003). Thus, while armies often recognized a combat-distress syndrome under varying names, the signs and symptoms vary with time and place.

Cultural and individual variations in defining and responding to challenging events raise a general question about whether mental disorder or resilience is the more "natural" or normal. Answering this question requires an examination of the data on patterns of response, and the risk factors that affect the probability of PTSD after exposure to threatening events.

EPIDEMIOLOGICAL STUDIES OF TRAUMA EXPOSURE AND PTSD

Events are often described as "traumatic," but this descriptor confounds objective event qualities with subjective response features through backward reasoning. Nonetheless, to review the literature effectively, we will refer to traumatic or "toxic" events (TEs) as intended in DSM-IV. Overall, the lifetime prevalence of adults' exposure to TEs is high, even in modern affluent, peacetime democracies. Data from a representative sample of nearly 6,000 adults in the United States (the National Comorbidity Survey, NCS) showed that 61% of men and 51% of women had experienced one or more from a list of 12 severe TEs (Kessler, Sonnega, Bromet, Hughes, & Nelson, 1995). A large representative study in Detroit found a higher rate of 89.6% (92% in men and 87% in women) across ages 18–45, with a lifetime average of 4.8 TEs (Breslau et al., 1998). Similar lifetime data were reported in Canada, with 81% of men and 74% of women experiencing TEs (Stein, Walker, Hazen, & Forde, 1997b).

The lifetime prevalence of PTSD in the general population is significantly lower than the high TE exposure rates. The best US data (NCS) report a lifetime overall PTSD rate of 7.8%, with 5% in men and 10% in women (Kessler et al., 1995); one-year prevalence was 3.6% (Kessler et al., 1994). A Detroit study of 1,007 adults found a lifetime PTSD rate of 9.2% in adults, with 6.2% in men and 13% in women (Breslau, Davis, Andreski, & Peterson, 1991). A Canadian study found "past-month" rates of 1.2% in men and 2.7% in women (Stein, Koverola, Hanna, Torchia, & McClarty, 1997a). A highly inclusive sample in Iceland revealed lifetime rates of zero in men, and 1.3% in women (Lindal & Stefansson, 1993). A sample of young adults in Munich reported 26% of males with TE exposures but only 1% with PTSD; in women, 18% were exposed and 2.2% met criteria (Perkonigg, Kessler, Storz, & Wittchen, 2000). These data show that overall lifetime prevalence of PTSD is quite low, varying across cultures and gender.

Conditional risk is the incidence of PTSD within those exposed to TEs. It varies widely in different samples for the same kind of exposure, and within similar samples for different kinds of events. In the general population exposed to any TE, the NCS found the PTSD rate after exposure was 8.2% in men and 20% in women (Kessler et al., 1995). Within the Detroit sample the conditional risk was 6.2% in males and 13% in females, for an overall rate of 9.2% (Breslau et al., 1998).

EVENT TYPE AND THE STRESSOR-DOSE MODEL

The current PTSD model includes an implicit assumption that a greater TE "dose" will elicit the disorder at a higher rate, with dose usually construed in terms of different kinds of events. Yet characteristics of events that confer risk for PTSD are not a simple function of "severity." For example, studies often contrast impersonal events such as natural disasters, with events designed to inflict interpersonal violence. The latter are considered to represent greater threat (Green, 1990), yet the objective harms are similar.

Combat should represent a severe TE in that life-threatening exposure is direct and prolonged; thus, high PTSD rates should be expected. Some data support the dose-response model (e.g., Goldberg et al., 1990; Vukšíc-Mihaljević, Mandíc, Benšíc, & Mihaljević, 2000). Other data suggest significant variations in rates of PTSD, including 0.7% in one World War II veteran group (Lee, Vaillant, Torrey, & Elder, 1995); 8% two years after participating in the first Gulf War (Wolfe, Erickson, Sharkansky, King, & King, 1999); and 15% in the National Vietnam Veterans Readjustment study (NVVRS; Kulka et al., 1990a). Within a large sample of Vietnam veterans, 76% of those in the war theater and exposed to high combat did not develop PTSD (Boscarino, 1996). Participation by British soldiers in both the first Gulf War and peacekeeping in Bosnia was associated with very low PTSD rates of 1–3% (Ismail et al., 2002).

Civilians living under combat conditions may show dose-response correlation, as in a sample of nearly 700 in the Gaza Strip. Here the conditional risk of PTSD was 36% in those exposed to a specific TE, compared to a baseline level of 29% (Afana, Steffen, Bjertness, Grunefeld, & Hauff, 2002). However, other data for war effects on civilians contradict the dose-response model. Among Israeli children living near the Jordanian border and regularly shelled, as compared to children distant and unshelled, there were no differences in anxiety (Ziv & Israeli, 1973). Civilians in Northern Ireland showed no increase in hospital admission rates for mental disorders across 20 and 30 years of terrorist violence (Curran, 1988; Summerfield, Loughrey, Nikapota, & Parry-Jones, 1997).

Events unrelated to combat have also been widely studied, including serious motor vehicle accidents, harrowing medical procedures, diagnoses of grave disease, natural disasters, and assaults. The best-designed studies on motor vehicle accidents have reported rates of PTSD no greater than 10% (Brom, Kleber, & Hofman, 1993), especially if participants are truly random (Malt, 1988). A well-designed longitudinal Swiss study of severely injured accident victims found a one-month PTSD rate of 4.7%, dropping to 1.9% at one year (Schnyder, Moergeli, Klaghofer, & Buddeberg, 2001). In studies that assertively recruit subjects from the public and thus obtain biased samples, PTSD rates are often higher (e.g., Blanchard, Hickling, Taylor, & Loos, 1995).

Great variations in rates of PTSD have also been reported after impersonal events such as natural disasters. Comparing Nicaraguan adolescents in three cities after Hurricane Mitch, there was a dose-response relationship between objective events and PTSD severity (Goenjian, Molina, & Steinberg, 2001), suggesting homogeneity within that culture. In contrast, there were significant ethnic differences in PTSD rates after a hurricane in Florida (ranging from 15% in Caucasians to 38% in Spanish-preferring Hispanics) and these could not be accounted for by exposure differences or other risk factors (Perilla, Norris, & Lavizzo, 2002). Some 10% of a community sample met PTSD criteria three months after an earthquake in China (Wang, Zhao, & Naotaka, 1999), while after an earthquake in Turkey, rates ranged from 31% to 43% (Basoglu, Salcioglu, & Livanou, 2002). Among the best studies of TEs that do not represent personally intended threat are the longitudinal samples described by Australian psychiatrist Alexander McFarlane. Since the 1980s he has assessed functioning before and after the repetitive giant bush fires that regularly threaten lives and property. Overall, he has found that PTSD or other emotional disorders are a minority phenomenon not related to the severity of exposure (McFarlane, 1990).

Deliberate attacks often yield higher PTSD rates than impersonal disasters, and dose-response variations may correlate with the severity of the assault. Among 157 victims of violent assaults, 20% met PTSD criteria at six months (Brewin, Andrews, & Rose, 1999). In a large community sample of female crime victims, PTSD rates were 13% in those who had experienced low-stress crime, compared to 35% in those experiencing high-stress crime (Resnick, Kilpatrick, Best, & Kramer, 1992). However, even after intentional harm events, individuals show significant variations in response. Studies on Turkish torture victims report that most did not develop PTSD (Basoglu et al., 1994; Basoglu & Paker, 1995).

MULTIPLE EVENTS: ADAPTATION OR SENSITIZATION?

Previous multiple TEs, in particular, assaultive violence, represent the strongest risk factors for PTSD in the community (Breslau, Chilcoat, Kessler, & Davis, 1999), in veterans (Bremner, Southwick, Johnson, Yehuda, & Charney, 1993), in raped women (Yehuda, Resnick, Schmeidler, Yang, & Pitman, 1998b), and among those responding with PTSD to the events of September 11, 2001, in New York (Galea, Ahern, & Resnick, 2002). The literature is rich with other examples of increasing risk with increasing numbers of TE exposures. At the same time, there are findings not consistent with the sensitization model. American undergraduates demonstrated no differences in rates of PTSD or depression arising from a single or multiple crime events (Falsetti & Resick, 1995). When American and Canadian firefighters were compared for PTSD risk factors, documented TE exposures were not a significant factor in either group (Corneil, Beaton, Murphy, Johnson, &

Pike, 1999). Among assaulted psychiatric nurses, those with previous assaults sorted into two distinct groups, with either very high or significantly low distress responses (Wykes & Whittington, 1998). The authors speculated the low-distress group had become "violence-habituated;" another interpretation could be that they had shown adaptation, developing cognitive and emotional skills to manage their experiences.

These multiple-event data suggest that while some individuals show adaptive responses to events, others show sensitization. An event-focused model could explain this as a function of differences in the severity of early traumatic events. There are biological analogies wherein early environmental severity generates either adaptation or sensitization to later exposure. Total system shock (anaphylaxis) can occur when an organism is confronted twice with large doses of an alien substance; the sensitization that develops between doses may even bring death (Haas, 2001). In contrast, Portier and Richet (1902) discovered that repeated small doses of toxic substances develop an organism's adaptive capacity to respond to later challenges from a large exposure. This developed resilience became the basis for immunization programs against infectious diseases, and is consistent with a human learning model of mastery and adaptation. Consistent with the immunization model, 90% in a community sample reported that coping with stressful events was aided by previous experience with stressors, from which developed confidence and coping skills (Aldwin, Sutton, & Lachman, 1996).

SUMMARY: THE EPIDEMIOLOGY OF TE EXPOSURE AND PTSD

Rates of exposure to extremely threatening events are commonly quite high in adult populations, even in modern industrialized democracies in peacetime, yet rates of PTSD are quite low. Conditional rates among those exposed vary significantly, approaching close to zero even in some combat groups. Clearly, most people do not develop PTSD or other emotional disorders, even with direct and prolonged exposure to threatening events. Thus, trauma exposure appears to be a necessary but not sufficient condition for the development of PTSD, with distinct features of individuals determining who develops the disorder (McFarlane, 1999; Shalev, 1996; Yehuda, McFarlane, & Shalev, 1998a). This compels attention to the risk factors that dispose some individuals to develop and maintain PTSD. Risk factors operate before, during, and after events to affect how different individuals respond to trauma (Bowman, 1997; Yehuda & McFarlane, 1995).

The present chapter focuses on findings that pertain to pre-incident risk factors, thereby highlighting various challenges to the stress-adversity model of PTSD. The task of identifying these pre-incident risk factors should not be construed as blaming the victim who develops PTSD. Blame is moral language appropriately used in theology and law courts. Science uses the language of risk factors to understand the etiology of disorders without any moralistic implications.

PRE-EVENT TRAITS AND PSYCHIATRIC STATUS

Before reviewing risk factor data, it is necessary to note that PTSD research often suffers from methods problems. Most studies use clinical samples to look at individuals only after an event has taken place, often failing to include exposed individuals who do not seek treatment, while including those who do not meet diagnostic criteria, and those who volunteer. Many studies fail to verify the index event(s), fail to use broadly standardized measures of personality and formal diagnostic criteria, or only examine correlates of the disorder at one time. Such cross-sectional studies with biased subject selection and correlational data limit the interpretation of results. These research design problems are significant when trying to understand risk factors contributing to PTSD. Harvey and Yehuda (1999) have outlined tactics for good research designs with a gold standard of community-based, representative, longitudinal, prospective studies that employ standardized instruments.

PERSONALITY TRAITS AND COPING STYLES

Long-standing dispositions are studied in personality research to discover the consistency of individual differences, the relations between traits and behaviors, and the reliability of traits across different populations. Researchers even within the cognitive-behavioral tradition (e.g., Clark, Watson, & Mineska, 1994; Mischel & Shoda, 1995) have accrued evidence that some traits are reliable individual attributes that contribute meaningful variance to observed behavior across situations.

Although "neurosis" was removed from the DSM as a mental disorder, the trait of neuroticism has emerged as a major dimension in studies of the structure of personality. Neuroticism (N) is one of five robust, central traits (Costa & McCrae, 1992); it refers to the long-standing disposition to respond to events with negative affect (McCrae & Costa, 1987), including anxiety and depression (Clark et al., 1994). The disposition to respond to life events with negative affect is a temperament style identifiable in children (Chess, 1977), and is longitudinally stable across childhood (e.g., Kagan, 1989; Schwartz, Snidman, & Kagan, 1999) and adulthood (Costa & McCrae, 1994; Lee et al., 1995; McCrae & Costa, 1987). Qualities that represent a contrast with N show similar longitudinal consistency and have been studied under the rubrics of hardiness (Kobasa, 1979), resilience (Garmezy, 1991), and happiness (Brebner, 1998; Diener, Suh, Lucas, & Smith, 1999).

Trait N is correlated with PTSD (Davidson, Kudler, & Smith, 1987; Kuhne, Orr, & Barage, 1993), and is a risk factor for PTSD after exposure (Breslau, Davis, & Andreski, 1995). Such findings arise in studies of combat and civilian events. In a study of 100 Vietnam veterans with combat-attributed PTSD, the most striking finding was an extremely high trait N score that was independent of combat exposure (Talbert, Braswell, Albrecht, Hyer, & Boudewyns, 1993). Trait N or anxiety contributed more variance to post-combat PTSD symptoms than did combat (Casella & Motta, 1990; Hyer et al., 1994; Sutker, Bugg, & Allain, 1991; Sutker, Davis, Uddo, & Ditta, 1995). An Australian study of randomly selected veterans with and without PTSD found that enlistment scores on an index of N were a risk factor for later PTSD (O'Toole, Marshall, Schureck, & Dobson, 1998). Similar to findings on high N, low hardiness in Vietnam veterans contributed more variance to PTSD than did TEs and other variables (King, King, Fairbank, Keane, & Adams, 1998). Low hardiness characterized Gulf War veterans with PTSD, with one component (commitment) accounting for 26% of the variance (Sutker et al., 1995).

Studies of civilians show a similar relationship between N or trait anxiety and post-trauma reactions for a variety of events including Hurricane Hugo (Lonigan, Shannon,

Taylor, Finch, & Sallee, 1994), severe burns (Fauerbach, Lawrence, Schmidt, Munster, & Costa, 2000), parental response to childhood cancer (Kazak et al., 1998), and traumatic distress after Australian bushfires (McFarlane, 1989, 1990). In a large community sample, trait emotionality accounted for 47% of emotional disorder symptoms ten years later, while stressful life events only accounted for 38% of these symptoms (Aldwin et al., 1996).

PSYCHIATRIC HISTORY AND PERSONALITY DISORDERS

In addition to the major risk factor of temperament, other individual attributes associated with posttrauma morbidity include prior problems, psychiatric history, and personality disorder. Individuals with PTSD thus have high rates of pre-event psychiatric disorders (Kessler et al., 1995). A history of a pre-event anxiety disorder was the strongest risk predictor of PTSD among Vietnam veterans (Kulka et al., 1990b), while having any Axis I disorder almost doubled the rate of PTSD following the Oklahoma City bombing (North et al., 1999). In a large Australian group of Vietnam veterans, PTSD was associated with other diagnoses whose onset tended to pre-date PTSD (O'Toole et al., 1998).

Long-standing personality disorders may also increase the risk of developing PTSD after TEs. Among Vietnam veterans with PTSD, a lifetime history or current diagnosis of anti-social personality disorder correlated with developing PTSD in the war theater (Kulka et al., 1990a). For male Vietnam veterans, a history of childhood anti-social behavior was one of several risk factors for PTSD (King, King, Foy, & Gudanowski, 1996). A huge twin study of Vietnam Era males found that a history of childhood conduct disorder was a risk factor both for exposure to TEs and for the risk of developing PTSD upon exposure (Koenen et al., 2002). In the 1995 National Comorbidity Survey, where 59% of those with PTSD had three or more additional psychiatric disorders, the authors observed that PTSD "usually occurs subsequent to at least one previous DSM-III-R disorder" (Kessler et al., 1995, p. 1058). A later calculation of the temporal order of diagnoses showed that a prior history of other psychiatric disorders was associated with increased risk of subsequent PTSD (Kessler et al., 1999).

Low intelligence is a risk factor for future exposure to TEs (Green, Grace, Lindy, Gleser, & Leonard, 1990), and for PTSD after exposure. Prospective longitudinal studies of children in high-risk environments have found that higher IQ reduced the risk of psychiatric disorder (Cederblad & Dahlin, 1995; Fergusson & Lynskey, 1996), including PTSD (Silva, Alpert, & Munoz, 2000). Pre-combat mental ability has been negatively associated with combat PTSD in veterans in the United States (Macklin et al., 1998; McNally & Shin, 1995; Pitman, Orr, Lowenhagen, & Macklin, 1991), and Israel (Kaplan et al., 2002). Education is strongly correlated with IQ, and low educational level increases risk for PTSD (Afana et al., 2002; Engdahl, Harkness, Eberly, Page, & Bielinski, 1993; Englehard, van den Hout, Kindt, Arntz, & Schouten, 2003; Gold et al., 2000; Kaplan et al., 2002).

PRE-EVENT BELIEFS AND ATTRIBUTIONS

Beliefs, thoughts, attributions, cognitive schemas, and general attitudes all provide meaning to life events and contribute to emotional arousal. The role of these factors in the development of PTSD is illustrated by a case in which several people were hit by a car and developed PTSD. Their symptoms did not relate to the accident. Instead, these individuals were terrified by religious fears that arose after members of their church told them they "deserved" the accident because they weren't sufficiently faithful to Jesus (D. Hartman, personal communication, March 3, 2002).

Beliefs structure meaning and affect emotion. At the individual level, a shared event can lead to significantly varying emotional responses when framed in terms of different meanings. Classic laboratory studies in the 1960s showed that emotional and bodily responses to a film of bloody aboriginal circumcision rites varied depending on the cognitive set provided to subjects through narrative voice-overs (Speisman, Lazarus, Mordkoff, & Davison, 1964). In one condition emphasizing pain and the risk of infection, watchers responded with significant arousal, while a different group hearing an intellectualized explanation emphasizing the cultural importance of the ritual responded with little arousal. In everyday life as well, the influence of beliefs can be found. An event such as the sudden death of a spouse is not reliably associated with the development of PTSD symptoms unless it has additional meaning, such as arising from violence (Kaltman & Bonanno, 2003).

In the case of PTSD, four cognitive or belief aspects have been suggested as central to the disorder: (1) the appraisal of an event that it is harmful; (2) general beliefs about personal vulnerability; (3) attempts to assign meaning to the event; and (4) beliefs about the amount of individual control (Parrot & Howes, 1991). Ehlers and Clark (2000) have outlined a broad model of the role of cognition in PTSD. They identified the thoughts, appraisals, and beliefs that contribute to dysfunction at every stage during and after a traumatic event, and proposed features that seem amenable to treatment. Research using this model has found that key cognitive features present early after assault (e.g., negative beliefs about self and world) are risk factors for PTSD severity at six and nine months, with effects beyond those of event severity (Dunmore, Clark, & Ehlers, 2001). Pre-event beliefs about self-worth, safety, and the trustworthiness of others were protective factors against PTSD following an assault (Ali, Dunmore, Clark, & Ehlers, 2002).

Additional studies have found positive relationships between several beliefs and post-trauma morbidity. These beliefs include:

1 Self-evaluations of vulnerability and limited resources to meet challenge (Carlier, Lambers, & Gersons, 2000; Dutton, Burghardt, Perrin, & Chrestman, 1994).
2 Low self-efficacy (Benight et al., 1997; Ferren, 1999).
3 Appraisals of harm and frightening meanings (Alvarez-Conrad, Zoellner, & Foa, 2001; Ehlers, Mayou, & Bryant, 2003; Smith & Bryant, 2000).
4 Anxiety viewed as being harmful, as in the construct of anxiety sensitivity (Asmundson, Bonin, & Frombach, 2000; Fedoroff, Taylor, Asmundson, & Koch, 2000).
5 Harmful appraisals of other symptoms such as intrusive thoughts (Ehlers, Mayou, & Bryant, 1998; Englehard, Macklin, & McNally, 2001; Englehard, van den Hout, Arntz, & McNally, 2002; Kazak et al., 1998; Mayou, Ehlers, & Bryant, 2002; Reynolds & Brewin, 1998).

Other beliefs appear to serve as buffers, providing resilience in the face of adverse events. Religious and political beliefs served such functions among Turkish victims of torture, as demonstrated by low PTSD rates in this group (Basoglu et al., 1994; Basoglu & Paker, 1995). The belief that the world operates in meaningful and coherent ways also has been shown to buffer posttraumatic reactions (Antonovsky, 1979; Frommberger et al., 1999; Kaiser, Sattler, Bellack, & Dersin, 1996; Vickberg, Duhamel, & Smith, 2001).

One important feature in appraising meaning of a TE is attribution of responsibility or Locus of Control (LOC; Rotter, 1966), concepts that concern internal or external attributions of control, responsibility, and blame. Research on these issues has demonstrated complex interactions between beliefs and posttrauma morbidity. PTSD is often correlated with the belief that control is exercised by external forces (external LOC: Solomon, Mikulincer, & Avitzur, 1988). In a giant prospective longitudinal study started in 1947 and followed up in 1988/89, childhood internal LOC was a key predictor of long-term resilience (Cederblad & Dahlin, 1995). Among rape victims, enduring beliefs of internal LOC and self-efficacy were negatively correlated with distress (Regehr, Cadell, & Jansen, 1999).

Much evidence suggests that accepting self-blame (allied to believing in internal LOC) lowers the risk for PTSD. Self-blame predicted good coping among 29 individuals who had been paralyzed in serious accidents (Janoff-Bulman & Wortman, 1977). Acceptance of "moderate guilt" was associated with the greatest treatment improvement in 225 veterans with PTSD (Roberts, 2000). Among people followed at both six and 12 months after a serious MVA, those who continued to show PTSD symptoms were those who attributed more than half the blame to others (Delahanty et al., 1997). Similar results were obtained in another sample in which self-blame was associated with fewer initial symptoms and more rapid recovery (Hickling, Blanchard, & Buckley, 1999). External attributions of blame after a severe head injury also were associated with greater severity of PTSD symptoms in a British community study (Huw, Evans, Needham, & Wilson, 2002).

Other data show more complexity as to whether self-blame or externally-targeted blame represents a greater risk for PTSD. It may be that these beliefs interact with events, because there are data in which internal self-blame is associated with greater disorder in some situations. When internal LOC individuals experience particularly harsh outcomes, they suffer greater losses in well-being (Janoff-Bulman & Brickman, 1982). A "pessimistic" style, in which there is a stable and global internal (self) attribution for negative events, is associated with depression (Peterson & Seligman, 1984). This "learned helplessness" has also been associated with PTSD in veterans (McCormick, Taber, & Kruedelback, 1989) and in adolescents following a disaster (Joseph, Brewin, Yule, & Williams, 1993). A validation study of the Posttraumatic Cognitions Inventory found that self-blame was one of three factors that identified PTSD cases, along with negative thoughts about the self and the world (Foa, Ehlers, & Clark, 1999). The greater PTSD response typical of women has been explained as a possible consequence of increased self-blame (Tolin & Foa, 2002).

What might explain the contradictory findings regarding attributions of responsibility and PTSD? It may be that internal LOC beliefs that are effective for well-being under broadly normal conditions operate differently under extreme conditions. A deeper construct could be operating, involving an individual's capacity to recognize conditions under which internal responsibility is appropriate, and those under which it is not. A decade ago Janoff-Bulman (1992) suggested that individuals are at greatest risk of event-related disorder when customary assumptions and beliefs about the self or the world are "shattered" by intrusive events. This metaphor suggests that the brittleness of beliefs may be the deeper risk factor, and there is some evidence supporting this. Among rape victims, assaults in perceived-safe environments led to more severe PTSD symptoms than assaults in dangerous environments (Cascardi, Riggs, Hearst-Ikeda, & Foa, 1996). This suggests that in part it was the shattering of a belief in a safe environment that added risk for PTSD. It may be that beliefs about the fairness of the world, personal efficacy and safety, and internal LOC, begin to function as risk factors when they are held rigidly in the face of strongly contrary events. Conversely, acceptance of the idea that some events are not consistent with one's basic model may be the response tactic most likely to provide protection when very toxic events intrude. Belief rigidity, rather than any specific belief, may constitute the most important cognitive risk for PTSD.

BIOLOGICAL FACTORS

Biological features that have been studied as risk factors for PTSD include genes, hormones, psychophysiological response styles, and brain anatomy. Genetic factors, for example, play a role in who is exposed to TEs (Loehlin, 1992; True & Lyons, 1999), and determine who carries traits such as neuroticism that affect how individuals respond to adverse events. A twin study found significant heritability in the emotional appraisal given to life events (Wierzbicki, 1989). In 30,000 twin pairs, N showed a heritability of about 50% (Loehlin, 1989), and genetic loading of N contributed to its consistency across life (Bouchard, Lykken, McGue, Segal, & Tellegen, 1990; Costa & McCrae, 1992). Component facets of anxiety (Usala & Hertzog, 1991) and depression (Kendler et al., 1995) show similar patterns of genetic loading and temporal consistency, accounting for more variance in affective symptoms than do severe life events.

Twin studies specific to PTSD also suggest considerable heritability in the disorder. A large twin study of veterans from the Vietnam Era Twin Registry found that "heritability contributed substantially to the susceptibility for nearly all symptoms of PTSD even after taking into account differences in concordance for combat exposure between monozygotic (MZ) and dizygotic (DZ) twin pairs" (True et al., 1993, p. 261). When the main symptom clusters were studied, approximately 30% of the variance in PTSD symptoms was accounted for by genetic factors (True & Lyons, 1999). Another recent large twin study using the Vietnam Era Twin Registry found 38% genetic variance contributed to both PTSD and panic disorder, with an additional 14% genetic contribution specific to PTSD (Chantarujikapong et al., 2001). A large study in civilian twins found similar genetic effects both for exposure to traumatic situations and for PTSD symptoms (Stein, Jang, Taylor, Vernon, & Livesley, 2002).

STRESS HORMONES

The search for biological markers related to PTSD has been based on the logic that if normal stress hormones are activated over prolonged periods, they might effect changes in brain physiology or even anatomy. Studies have examined two main questions: (1) Are there reliable individual physiological, anatomical, or psychophysiological correlates specific to those who develop PTSD? and, (2) If there are such correlates, do they constitute pre-event risk factors or do they arise directly from confronting a TE and developing PTSD?

Hormones released under acute stress are under the control of the hypothalamus–pituitary–adrenal axis (HPA), and have been the focus of much research. Animal models of stress predict that a threatening event should result in higher levels of cortisol release from the adrenal glands, raising the possibility of depletion of this response with repetition. An animal study using genetically-selected animals with congenital learned helplessness found blunting of the HPA-axis hormonal response after exposure to intermittent stress (King, Abend, & Edwards, 2001). Some research on human adults is consistent with this. Within MVA cases, cortisol levels in the early aftermath of trauma were significantly lower in those who later developed PTSD (Delahanty, Raimonde, & Spoonster, 2000; McFarlane, Atchison, & Yehuda, 1997). In a study of multiple assault rape victims, the first rape experience led to cortisol rises, while rape after previous multiple assaults did not (Resnick, Yehuda, Pitman, & Foy, 1995). In another study on rape victims, immediate hormonal response did not predict later PTSD status, but the subset of participants with multiple prior TEs again showed a weakened cortisol response (Yehuda et al., 1998b). Another study found low cortisol response associated with lifetime PTSD within a sample of adults with Holocaust-exposed parents (Yehuda et al., 2000). Cortisol levels in Vietnam veterans with current PTSD were lower than in veterans with past PTSD (Boscarino, 1996).

These data suggest that individual histories with repeated stressors might represent risk for PTSD through altering the production of stress hormones. Multiple TE exposures may engender sensitization to stimuli and overuse of arousal systems that eventually blunt the capacity of the hormonal system to respond. Another possibility is that low cortisol levels seen in PTSD cases represent pre-event hormonal risk features, characterized by an inadequate capacity to respond to any occasion of trauma. Finally, some reviews of the literature have concluded that cortisol levels in PTSD-diagnosed individuals bear no consistent relationship to trauma (e.g., McNally, 2003).

PSYCHOPHYSIOLOGICAL RESPONSES

Another line of research has examined the ways in which individuals with PTSD respond on basic psychophysiological measures, searching for a characteristic response pattern. For example, exaggerated heart rate or startle responses, and generalized reactions to challenging stimuli with failure to modulate responses (habituation), are often correlates of PTSD. In a crucial study that controlled for pre-event risk by examining MZ twin-pairs discordant for TE exposure, heart rate responses to startling tones in those with PTSD did not represent a pre-event risk factor, but rather an acquired sign as the disorder developed (Orr et al., 2003). There are, however, significant variations in observed patterns. In a large and carefully conducted study, Keane et al. (1998) found that about one-third of current PTSD cases did not show any characteristic pattern of psychophysiological responses to trauma cues. Other studies support this finding (see review by Orr, Metzger, & Pitman, 2002).

BRAIN ANATOMY: DOES TRAUMATIC STRESS DAMAGE THE HUMAN BRAIN?

The question of whether trauma and the subsequent development of PTSD are associated with changes in brain anatomy has been the focus of lively debate (Bremner, 1999, 2001; Pitman, 2001; Yehuda, 2001). For a while, evidence suggested that PTSD was correlated with small hippocampi, and data were interpreted as showing that high cortisol served as an agent of hippocampal atrophy. Smaller hippocampal volumes were found in a sample of Vietnam veterans with PTSD compared to no-disorder controls, although hippocampal volumes did not correlate with combat exposure (Bremner et al., 1995). As the hippocampus is centrally involved in memory, and memory processes have been considered central to the development of PTSD, the smaller hippocampal volumes found in studies appeared to provide a plausible connection. The initial study by Bremner and colleagues was flawed, with small sample, statistical problems, lack of pre-combat data, and inadequate controls. Additional studies, however, continued to find a relationship between hippocampal volumes and severity of posttrauma reactions. In a study of Vietnam veterans, smaller hippocampal volumes were found among PTSD-diagnosed individuals, even after controlling for alcohol use (Gurvits et al., 1996). Reduced left hippocampal volume also was found in 21 women with severe abuse histories, compared to a socio-demographically matched group (Stein et al., 1997a). Within a group of women at least three years post-breast-cancer surgery, those reporting distressing cancer-related intrusive memories had a mean left hippocampal volume smaller by 5% than women not reporting these memories (Nakano et al., 2002). Reduced general white matter and left hippocampal volume was reported in a series of 12 PTSD subjects and 10 controls after controlling for alcohol history (Villarreal et al., 2002). Research problems common to these studies include the lack of pre-event hippocampal volume measures, small samples, and issues of comorbidity (McEwan, 1997).

By 2001, negative findings began to appear from longitudinal and twin samples, with several failures to replicate hippocampal volume correlates to PTSD. Schuff et al. (2001) found no significant differences in left and right hippocampal volumes or in a biochemical marker of neurons in the hippocampus, when comparing those with and without PTSD. Similar findings were obtained in other studies with adults (Bonne et al., 2001), and with children (Carrion et al., 2001; De Bellis, Hall, Boring, Frustaci, & Moritz, 2001). A most informative study was provided by Gilbertson et al. (2002); they studied 40 male MZ twin-pairs discordant for Vietnam exposure and found that non-exposed, small hippocampus volume represented a pre-event risk factor, rather than resulting from trauma itself or from subsequent PTSD. These findings highlight a central concern that applies to other biological correlates of PTSD, the issue of causality. To address the issue, additional twin studies and longitudinal prospective studies are needed.

IMPLICATIONS FOR DIAGNOSIS AND TREATMENT

There are numerous additional studies that point to the importance of risk factors in determining an individual's response to adverse life events. Among Australian firefighters only 9% of the variance in distress came from exposure (McFarlane, 1987). In Vietnam veterans with PTSD, 26% of variance in distress came from a personality trait (externalizing coping), while only 9% came from combat exposure (Wolfe, Keane, Kaloupek, Mora, & Wine, 1993). A meta-analysis of factors affecting responses after violence concluded that subjective factors account for twice the variance of that associated with objective event features (Weaver & Clum, 1995). Attributions of positive meaning to military participation among US peacekeepers in Somalia was a negative risk factor about equal to the positive risk associated with exposure to negative events (Litz, Orsillo, Friedman, Ehlich, & Batres, 1997). These are just samples from the numerous studies that find that individual risk factors contribute more variance to the development of PTSD than does exposure to the toxic event. In fact, in the general population of modern democracies, the adversity-dose of toxic life experiences typically accounts for only 10% of subjective symptoms in emotional distress disorders (Byrne, 1984; McFarlane, 1987) or illness (Miller & Ingham, 1979). Combinations of multiple risk factors account for far greater portions of the variance.

The implications of these findings are clear. Most people navigate through threatening life events without developing a mental disorder, while a small proportion respond with disorder associated with the operation of additional risk factors. A fruitful model for PTSD should take into account the natural diathesis in individuals, advancing a diathesis-stress model similar to that found useful for other disorders (Meehl, 1962). This derives from the ancient Greek notion that some individuals, by virtue of their inborn nature, become overexcited and deranged when confronted with unusually exciting events (Monroe & Simons, 1991). In addition, it may be that various risk factors combine to form distinctive clusters of subgroups within PTSD, and these subgroups reflect different routes to the disorder and different symptom weights. A sensitization model, for example, may best apply to a cluster of individuals with high genetic fearful emotionality and its associated dysfunctional beliefs. A different risk constellation may lie in a combination of attributions of external responsibility, early childhood conduct disorder, and later anti-social beliefs that correlate with anger (Granic & Butler, 1998). In this manner, various combinations of beliefs and emotions may represent subsets of risk factors for one PTSD constellation or another. Such differences may be obscured when PTSD-diagnosed individuals are studied only via group means, rather than through alternative research methods that use, for example, cluster techniques.

Individual differences may be considered "nuisance variables" when analyzing mean data from group studies, best understood as error variance. Yet, these individual variations are highly salient features when diagnosing and treating a person with clinical disorder. The inclusion of risk factors in conceptual models of PTSD is likely to advance clinical diagnosis and treatment. Consideration of these variables would allow clinicians to match treatment methods with individual needs, thereby improving treatment compliance and enhancing effectiveness. Conversely, failure to consider risk factors may partly explain the overall muted evidence for treatment efficacy in PTSD outcome studies (Litz, Gray, Bryant, & Adler, 2002; Paunovic, 1998; Rose, Bisson, & Wessely, 2001; Shalev, Bonne, & Eth, 1996; Solomon, Gerrity, & Muff, 1992). Consider, for example, current imaginal exposure methods that attempt to elicit event-related emotions while employing cognitive reframing strategies (Foa & Riggs, 1995; Horowitz, Stinson, & Field, 1991; Rachman, 1980). By focusing on the event, rather than individual factors, constructs like trait N may be ignored, thereby failing to adjust for an individual's ability (or inability) to cope with imaginal exposure methods, and readiness for negative affective arousal. Other individual "risky" cognitions such as anxiety sensitivity (Fedoroff et al., 2000) may mediate an individual's response to exposure-based methods (Ehlers & Clark, 2000). The failure to consider individuals' differences may account for reports that event exposure-intensive therapies have problems with compliance (Scott & Stradling, 1997), are impossible to carry out in some patients (Foa, Keane, & Friedman, 2000), and may even be associated with worsening of symptoms, poor attendance, and less treatment involvement (Tarrier & Humphreys, 2000; Tarrier, Pilgrim, & Sommerfield, 1999).

Overall, research demonstrates that PTSD is best understood as the periodic expression of long-standing dispositions that often are risk factors for both threatening exposures and subsequent dysfunctions. At the very least, pre-event risk factors that include enduring personality features and beliefs have been found to predict PTSD more reliably than event features. Considering these issues in case formulations will help clinicians integrate salient risk and resilience factors into a unique whole, in order to best care for each individual.

REFERENCES

Afana, A.-H., Steffen, O., Bjertness, E., Grunefeld, B., & Hauff, E. (2002). The prevalence and associated socio-demographic variables of Posttraumatic Stress Disorder (PTSD) among patients attending primary care centers in the Gaza Strip. *Journal of Refugee Studies, 15,* 283–295.

Aldwin, C. M., Sutton, K. J., & Lachman, M. (1996). The development of coping resources in adulthood. *Journal of Personality, 64,* 837–871.

Ali, T., Dunmore, E., Clark, D., & Ehlers, A. (2002). The role of negative beliefs in posttraumatic stress disorder: A comparison of assault victims and nonvictims. *Behavioural and Cognitive Psychotherapy, 30,* 249–257.

Alvarez-Conrad, J., Zoellner, L. A., & Foa, E. B. (2001). Linguistic predictors of trauma pathology and physical health. *Applied Cognitive Psychology, 15,* S159–S170.

American Psychiatric Association (1994). *Diagnostic and statistical manual of mental disorders* (4th edn). Washington, DC: Author.

Antonovsky, A. (1979). *Health, stress, and coping.* San Francisco: Jossey-Bass.

Argyle, M. (1987). *The psychology of happiness.* London: Methuen.

Asmundson, G. J. G., Bonin, M. F., & Frombach, I. K. (2000). Evidence of a disposition toward fearfulness and vulnerability to posttraumatic stress in dysfunctional pain patients. *Behaviour Research and Therapy, 38,* 801–812.

Basoglu, M., & Paker, M. (1995). Severity of trauma as predictor of long-term psychological status in survivors of torture. *Journal of Anxiety Disorders, 9,* 339–353.

Basoglu, M., Paker, M., Paker, O., Oxmen, E., Marks, I., Incesu, C. et al. (1994). Psychological effects of torture: A comparison of tortured with nontortured political activists in Turkey. *American Journal of Psychiatry, 151,* 76–81.

Basoglu, M., Salcioglu, E., & Livanou, M. (2002). Traumatic stress responses in earthquake survivors in Turkey. *Journal of Traumatic Stress, 15,* 269–276.

Benight, C. C., Antoni, M. H., Kilbourn, K., Ironson, G., Kumar, M. A., Fletcher, M. A. et al. (1997). Coping self-efficacy buffers psychological and physiological disturbances in HIV-infected men following a natural disaster. *Health Psychology, 16,* 248–255.

Blanchard, E. B., Hickling, E. J., Taylor, A. E., & Loos, W. (1995). Psychiatric morbidity associated with motor vehicle accidents. *Journal of Nervous and Mental Disease, 183,* 495–504.

Bonne, O., Brandes, D., Giboa, A., Gomori, J. M., Shenton, M. E., Pitman, R. K. et al. (2001). Longitudinal MRI study of hippocampal volume in trauma survivors with PTSD. *American Journal of Psychiatry, 158,* 1248–1251.

Boscarino, J. A. (1996). Posttraumatic stress disorder, exposure to combat, and lower plasma cortisol among Vietnam veterans: Findings and clinical implications. *Journal of Consulting and Clinical Psychology, 64,* 191–201.

Boscarino, J. A. (1997). Diseases among men 20 years after exposure to severe stress: Implications for clinical research and medical care. *Psychosomatic Medicine, 59,* 605–614.

Bouchard, T. J., Lykken, D. T., McGue, M., Segal, N. L., & Tellegen, A. (1990). Sources of human psychological differences: The Minnesota study of twins reared apart. *Science*, *250*, 223–228.

Bowman, M. L. (1997). *Individual differences in posttraumatic response: Problems with the adversity-distress connection.* Mahwah, NJ: Lawrence Erlbaum Associates.

Brebner, J. (1998). Happiness and personality. *Personality and Individual Differences*, *25*, 279–296.

Bremner, J. D. (1999). Does stress damage the brain? *Biological Psychiatry*, *45*, 797–805.

Bremner, J. D. (2001). Hypotheses and controversies related to effects of stress on the hippocampus: An argument for stress-induced damage to the hippocampus in patients with posttraumatic stress disorder. *Hippocampus*, *11*, 75–81.

Bremner, J. D., Randall, P., Scott, T. M., Bronen, R. A., Seibyl, J. P., Southwick, S. M. et al. (1995). MRI-based measurement of hippocampal volume in patients with combat-related posttraumatic stress disorder. *American Journal of Psychiatry*, *152*, 973–981.

Bremner, J. D., Southwick, S. M., Johnson, D. R., Yehuda, R., & Charney, D. S. (1993). Childhood physical abuse and combat-related posttraumatic stress disorder in Vietnam veterans. *American Journal of Psychiatry*, *150*, 235–239.

Breslau, N., Chilcoat, H. D., Kessler, R. C., & Davis, G. C. (1999). Previous exposure to trauma and PTSD effects of subsequent trauma: Results from the Detroit area survey of trauma. *American Journal of Psychiatry*, *156*, 902–907.

Breslau, N., Davis, G. C., & Andreski, P. (1995). Risk factors for PTSD-related traumatic events: A prospective analysis. *American Journal of Psychiatry*, *152*, 529–535.

Breslau, N., Davis, G. C., Andreski, P., & Peterson, E. (1991). Traumatic events and posttraumatic stress disorder in an urban population of young adults. *Archives of General Psychiatry*, *48*, 216–222.

Breslau, N., Kessler, R. C., Chilcoat, H. D., Schultz, L. R., Davis, G. C., & Andreski, P. (1998). Trauma and posttraumatic stress disorder in the community: The 1996 Detroit area survey of trauma. *Archives of General Psychiatry*, *55*, 626–632.

Brewin, C. R., Andrews, B., & Rose, S. (1999). Acute stress disorder and posttraumatic stress disorder in victims of violent crime. *American Journal of Psychiatry*, *156*, 360–366.

Brom, D., Kleber, R. J., & Hofman, M. C. (1993). Victims of traffic accidents: Incidence and prevention of post-traumatic stress disorder. *Journal of Clinical Psychology*, *49*, 131–140.

Byrne, D. G. (1984). Personal assessments of life-event stress and the near future onset of psychological symptoms. *British Journal of Medical Psychology*, *57*, 241–248.

Carlier, I. V. E., Lambers, R. D., & Gersons, B. P. R. (2000). The dimensionality of trauma: A multidimensional scaling comparison of police officers with and without posttraumatic stress disorder. *Psychiatry Research*, *97*, 29–39.

Carrion, V. G., Weems, C. F., Eliez, S., Patwardhan, A., Brown, W., Ray, R. D. et al. (2001). Attenuation of frontal asymmetry in pediatric posttraumatic stress disorder. *Biological Psychiatry*, *50*, 943–951.

Cascardi, M., Riggs, D. S., Hearst-Ikeda, D., & Foa, E. B. (1996). Objective ratings of assault safety as predictors of PTSD. *Journal of Interpersonal Violence*, *11*, 65–78.

Casella, L., & Motta, R. W. (1990). Comparison of characteristics of Vietnam veterans with and without Posttraumatic Stress Disorder. *Psychological Reports*, *67*, 595–605.

Cederblad, M., & Dahlin, L. (1995). Intelligence and temperament as protective factors for mental health: A cross-sectional and prospective epidemiology study. *European Archives of Psychiatry and Clinical Neuroscience*, *245*, 11–19.

Chantarujikapong, S. I., Scherrer, J. F., Xian, H., Eisen, S. A., Lyons, M. J., Goldberg, J. et al. (2001). A twin study of generalized anxiety disorder symptoms, panic disorder symptoms and posttraumatic stress disorder in men. *Psychiatry Research*, *103*, 133–146.

Chess, T. A. (1977). *Temperament and development.* New York: Brunner/Mazel.

Clark, L. A., Watson, D., & Mineska, S. (1994). Temperament, personality, and the mood and anxiety disorders. *Journal of Abnormal Psychology*, *103*, 103–116.

Corneil, W., Beaton, R., Murphy, S., Johnson, C., & Pike, K. (1999). Exposure to traumatic incidents and prevalence of posttraumatic stress symptomatology in urban firefighters in two countries. *Journal of Occupational Health Psychology*, *4*, 131–141.

Costa, P. T., & McCrae, R. R. (1992). Four ways five factors are basic. *Personality and Individual Differences*, *13*, 653–665.

Costa, P. T., & McCrae, R. R. (1994). Stability and change in personality from adolescence through adulthood. In C. F. Halverson, G. A. Kohnstamm, & R. P. Martin (eds), *The developing structure of temperament and personality from infancy to adulthood* (pp. 139–150). Hillsdale, NJ: Lawrence Erlbaum Associates.

Curran, P. S. (1988). Psychiatric aspects of terrorist violence: Northern Ireland 1969–1987. *British Journal of Psychiatry*, *153*, 470–475.

Davidson, J., Kudler, H., & Smith, R. (1987). Personality in chronic post-traumatic stress disorder: A study of the Eysenck Inventory. *Journal of Anxiety Disorders*, *1*, 295–300.

De Bellis, M. D., Hall, J., Boring, A. M., Frustaci, K., & Moritz, G. (2001). A pilot longitudinal study of hippocampal volumes in pediatric maltreatment-related posttraumatic stress disorder. *Biological Psychiatry*, *50*, 305–309.

Delahanty, D. L., Herberman, H. B., Craig, K. J., Hayward, M. C., Fullerton, C. S., Ursano, R. J. et al. (1997). Acute and chronic distress and posttraumatic stress disorder as a function of responsibility for serious motor vehicle accidents. *Journal of Consulting and Clinical Psychology*, *65*, 560–567.

Delahanty, D. L., Raimonde, A. J., & Spoonster, E. (2000). Initial posttraumatic urinary cortisol levels predict subsequent PTSD symptoms in motor vehicle accident victims. *Biological Psychiatry*, *48*, 940–947.

Diener, E., Suh, E. M., Lucas, R. E., & Smith, H. E. (1999). Subjective well-being: Three decades of progress. *Psychological Bulletin*, *125*, 276–302.

Dunmore, E., Clark, D., & Ehlers, A. (2001). A prospective investigation of the role of cognitive factors in persistent posttraumatic stress disorder (PTSD) after physical or sexual assault. *Behaviour Research and Therapy*, *39*, 1063–1084.

Dutton, M. A., Burghardt, K. J., Perrin, S. G., & Chrestman, K. R. (1994). Battered women's cognitive schemata. *Journal of Traumatic Stress*, *7*, 237–255.

Ehlers, A., & Clark, D. M. (2000). A cognitive model of posttraumatic stress disorder. *Behaviour Research and Therapy*, *38*, 319–345.

Ehlers, A., Mayou, R. A., & Bryant, B. (1998). Psychological predictors of chronic posttraumatic stress disorder after motor vehicle accidents. *Journal of Abnormal Psychology*, *107*, 508–519.

Ehlers, A., Mayou, R. A., & Bryant, B. (2003). Cognitive predictors of posttraumatic stress disorder in children: Results of a prospective longitudinal study. *Behaviour Research and Therapy*, *41*, 1–10.

Engdahl, B. E., Harkness, A. R., Eberly, R. E., Page, W. F., & Bielinski, J. (1993). Structural models of captivity trauma, resilience, and trauma response among former prisoners of war 20 to 40 years after release. *Social Psychiatry and Psychiatric Epidemiology*, *28*, 109–115.

Englehard, I. M., Macklin, M. L., & McNally, R. J. (2001). Emotion- and intrusion-based reasoning in Vietnam veterans with and without chronic posttraumatic stress disorder. *Behaviour Research and Therapy*, *39*, 1339–1348.

Englehard, I. M., van den Hout, M. A., Arntz, A., & McNally, R. J. (2002). A longitudinal study of "intrusion-based reasoning" and posttraumatic stress disorder after exposure to a train disaster. *Behaviour Research and Therapy*, *40*, 1415–1434.

Englehard, I. M., van den Hout, M. A., Kindt, M., Arntz, A., & Schouten, E. (2003). Peritraumatic dissociation and posttraumatic stress after pregnancy loss: A prospective study. *Behaviour Research and Therapy, 41,* 67–78.

Falsetti, S. A., & Resick, P. A. (1995). Causal attributions, depression, and post-traumatic stress disorder in victims of crime. *Journal of Applied Social Psychology, 25,* 1027–1042.

Faramarzi, S. (2003). Daughter's attack brings shame to family. *Vancouver Sun,* May 31, p. A17.

Fauerbach, J. A., Lawrence, J. W., Schmidt, C. W., Munster, A. M., & Costa, P. T. (2000). Personality predictors of injury-related posttraumatic stress disorder. *Journal of Nervous and Mental Disease, 188,* 510–517.

Fedoroff, I. C., Taylor, S., Asmundson, G. J. G., & Koch, W. J. (2000). Cognitive factors in traumatic stress reactions: Predicting PTSD symptoms from anxiety sensitivity and beliefs about harmful events. *Behavioural and Cognitive Psychotherapy, 28,* 5–15.

Fergusson, D. M., & Lynskey, M. T. (1996). Adolescent resiliency to family adversity. *Journal of Child Psychology and Psychiatry, 37,* 281–292.

Ferren, P. M. (1999). Comparing perceived self-efficacy among adolescent Bosnian and Croatian refugees with and without posttraumatic stress disorder. *Journal of Traumatic Stress, 12,* 405–420.

Foa, E. B., Ehlers, A., & Clark, D. M. (1999). The Posttraumatic Cognitions Inventory (PTCI): Development and validation. *Psychological Assessment, 11,* 303–314.

Foa, E. B., Keane, T. M., & Friedman, M. J. (eds) (2000). *Effective treatments for PTSD.* New York: Guilford Press.

Foa, E. B., & Riggs, D. S. (1995). Posttraumatic stress disorder following assault: Theoretical considerations and empirical findings. *Current Directions in Psychological Science, 4,* 61–65.

Frommberger, U., Stieglitz, R.-D., Straub, S., Nyberg, E., Schlickewei, W., Kuner, E. et al. (1999). The concept of "sense of coherence" and the development of posttraumatic stress disorder in traffic accident victims. *Journal of Psychosomatic Research, 46,* 343–348.

Galea, S., Ahern, J., & Resnick, H. (2002). Psychological sequelae of the September 11 terrorist attacks in New York City. *New England Journal of Medicine, 346,* 982–987.

Garmezy, N. (1991). Resilience and vulnerability to adverse developmental outcomes associated with poverty. *American Behavioral Scientist, 34,* 416–430.

Gilbertson, M. W., Shenton, M. E., Ciszewski, A., Kasai, K., Lasko, N. B., Orr, S. P. et al. (2002). Smaller hippocampal volume predicts pathologic vulnerability to psychological trauma. *Nature Neuroscience, 5,* 1242–1247.

Goenjian, A. K., Molina, L., & Steinberg, A. M. (2001). Posttraumatic stress and depressive reactions among Nicaraguan adolescents after Hurricane Mitch. *American Journal of Psychiatry, 158,* 788–794.

Gold, P. B., Engdahl, B. E., Eberly, R. E., Blake, R. J., Page, W. F., & Frueh, B. C. (2000). Trauma exposure, resilience, social support, and PTSD construct validity among former prisoners of war. *Social Psychiatry and Psychiatric Epidemiology, 35,* 36–42.

Goldberg, J., True, W. R., Eisen, S. A., & Henderson, W. G. (1990). A twin study of the effects of the Vietnam War on posttraumatic stress disorder. *Journal of the American Medical Association, 263,* 1227–1232.

Granic, I., & Butler, S. (1998). The relation between anger and antisocial beliefs in young offenders. *Personality and Individual Differences, 24,* 759–765.

Green, B. L. (1990). Defining trauma: Terminology and generic stressor dimensions. *Journal of Applied and Social Psychology, 20,* 1632–1642.

Green, B. L., Grace, M. C., Lindy, J. D., Gleser, G. C., & Leonard, A. (1990). Risk factors for PTSD and other diagnoses in a general sample of Vietnam veterans. *American Journal of Psychiatry, 147,* 729–733.

Gurvits, T. V., Shenton, M. E., Hokama, H., Ohta, H., Lask, N. B., Gilbertson, M. W. et al. (1996). Magnetic resonance imaging study of hippocampal volume in chronic, combat-related posttraumatic stress disorder. *Biological Psychiatry, 40*, 1091–1099.

Haas, L. F. (2001). Charles Robert Richet (1850–1935). *Journal of Neurology, Neurosurgery and Psychiatry, 70*, 255.

Harvey, A. G., & Bryant, R. A. (1999). Predictors of acute stress following motor vehicle accidents. *Journal of Traumatic Stress, 12*, 519–525.

Harvey, P. D., & Yehuda, R. (1999). Strategies to study risk for the development of PTSD. In R. Yehuda (ed.), *Risk factors for posttraumatic stress disorder* (pp. 1–22). Washington, DC: American Psychiatric Press.

Hickling, E. J., Blanchard, E. B., & Buckley, T. C. (1999). Effects of attribution of responsibility for motor vehicle accidents on severity of PTSD symptoms, ways of coping, and recovery over six months. *Journal of Traumatic Stress, 12*, 345–353.

Horowitz, M. J., Stinson, C., & Field, N. (1991). Natural disasters and stress response syndromes. *Psychiatric Annals, 21*, 556–562.

Huw, W. W., Evans, J. J., Needham, P., & Wilson, B. A. (2002). Neurological, cognitive and attributional predictors of posttraumatic stress symptoms after traumatic brain injury. *Journal of Traumatic Stress, 15*, 397–400.

Hyer, L., Braswell, L., Albrecht, B., Boyd, S., Boudewyns, P., & Talbert, S. (1994). Relationship of NEO-PI to personality styles and severity of trauma in chronic PTSD victims. *Journal of Clinical Psychology, 50*, 699–707.

Ismail, K., Kent, K., Brugha, T., Hotopf, M., Hull, L., Seed, P. et al. (2002). The mental health of UK Gulf war veterans: Phase 2 of a two-phase cohort study. *British Medical Journal, 325*, 576–581.

Janoff-Bulman, R. (1992). *Shattered assumptions: Towards a new psychology of trauma.* New York: Free Press.

Janoff-Bulman, R., & Brickman, P. (1982). Expectations and what people learn from failure. In N. T. Feather (ed.), *Expectations and actions* (pp. 207–237). Hillsdale, NJ: Erlbaum.

Janoff-Bulman, R., & Wortman, C. B. (1977). Attributions of blame and coping in the "real world": Severe accident victims react to their lot. *Journal of Personality and Social Psychology, 35*, 351–363.

Jones, E., Hodgins-Vermaas, R., McCartney, H., Beech, C., Palmer, I., Hyams, K. et al. (2003). Flashbacks and post-traumatic stress disorder: The genesis of a 20th-century diagnosis. *British Journal of Psychiatry, 182*, 158–163.

Joseph, S. A., Brewin, C. R., Yule, W., & Williams, R. (1993). Causal attributions and post-traumatic stress in adolescents. *Journal of Child Psychology and Psychiatry, 34*, 247–253.

Kagan, J. (1989). Temperamental contributions to social behavior. *American Psychologist, 44*, 668–674.

Kaiser, C. F., Sattler, D. N., Bellack, D. R., & Dersin, J. (1996). A conservation of resources approach to a natural disaster: Sense of coherence and psychological distress. *Journal of Social Behavior and Personality, 11*, 459–476.

Kaltman, S., & Bonanno, G. A. (2003). Trauma and bereavement: Examining the impact of sudden and violent deaths. *Journal of Anxiety Disorders, 17*, 131–147.

Kaplan, Z., Weiser, M., Reichenberg, A., Rabinowitz, J., Caspi, A., Bodner, E. et al. (2002). Motivation to serve in the military influences vulnerability to future posttraumatic stress disorder. *Psychiatry Research, 109*, 45–49.

Kazak, A. E., Stuber, M. L., Barakat, L. P., Meeske, K., Guthrie, D., & Meadows, A. T. (1998). Predicting posttraumatic stress symptoms in mothers and fathers of survivors of childhood cancers. *Journal of the American Academy of Child and Adolescent Psychiatry, 37*, 823–831.

Keane, T. M., Kaloupek, D. G., Blanchard, E. B., Hsieh, F. Y., Kolb, L. C., Orr, S. P. et al. (1998). Utility of psychophysiological measurement in the diagnosis of posttraumatic stress disorder: Results from a Department of Veterans Affairs' cooperative study. *Journal of Consulting and Clinical Psychology, 66*, 914–923.

Kendler, K. S., Kessler, R. C., Walters, E. E., MacLean, C., Neale, M. C., Heath, A. C. et al. (1995). Stressful life events, genetic liability, and onset of an episode of major depression in women. *American Journal of Psychiatry, 152*, 833–842.

Kessler, R. C., McGonagle, K., Zhao, S., Nelson, C. B., Hughes, M. et al. (1994). Lifetime and 12-month prevalence of DSM-III-R psychiatric disorder in the United States: Results from the National Comorbidity Study. *Archives of General Psychiatry, 51*, 8–19.

Kessler, R. C., Sonnega, A., Bromet, E., Hughes, M., & Nelson, C. B. (1995). Posttraumatic stress disorder in the National Comorbidity Survey. *Archives of General Psychiatry, 52*, 1048–1060.

Kessler, R. C., Sonnega, A., Bromet, E., Hughes, M., Nelson, C. B., & Breslau, N. (1999). Epidemiological risk factors for trauma and PTSD. In R. Yehuda (ed.), *Risk factors for post-traumatic stress disorder* (pp. 23–59). Washington, DC: American Psychiatric Press.

King, D. W., King, L. A., Foy, D. W., & Gudanowski, D. M. (1996). Prewar factors in combat-related posttraumatic stress disorder: Structural equation modeling with a national sample of female and male Vietnam veterans. *Journal of Consulting and Clinical Psychology, 64*, 520–531.

King, J. A., Abend, S., & Edwards, E. (2001). Genetic predisposition and the development of posttraumatic stress disorder in an animal model. *Biological Psychiatry, 50*, 231–237.

King, L. A., King, D. W., Fairbank, J. A., Keane, T. M., & Adams, G. A. (1998). Resilience-recovery factors in posttraumatic stress disorder among female and male Vietnam veterans: Hardiness, postwar social support, and additional stressful life events. *Journal of Consulting and Clinical Psychology, 74*, 420–432.

Kobasa, S. C. (1979). Stressful life events, personality, and health. *Journal of Personality and Social Psychology, 37*, 1–11.

Koenen, K. C., Harley, R., Lyons, M., Wolfe, J., Simpson, J. C., Goldberg, J. et al. (2002). A twin registry study of familial and individual risk factors for trauma exposure and posttraumatic stress disorder. *Journal of Nervous and Mental Disease, 190*, 209–218.

Kuhne, A., Orr, S. P., & Barage, E. (1993). Psychometric evaluation of post-traumatic stress disorder: The Multidimensional Personality Questionnaire as an adjunct to the MMPI. *Journal of Clinical Psychology, 49*, 218–225.

Kulka, R. A., Schlenger, W. E., Fairbank, J. A., Hough, R. L., Jordan, B. K., Marmar, C. R. et al. (1990a). *Trauma and the Vietnam war generation: Report of findings from the national Vietnam veterans readjustment study.* New York: Brunner/Mazel.

Kulka, R. A., Schlenger, W. E., Fairbank, J. A., Hough, R. L., Jordan, B. K., Marmar, C. R. et al. (1990b). *The national Vietnam veterans readjustment study: Table of findings and technical appendices.* New York: Brunner/Mazel.

Lee, K. A., Vaillant, G. E., Torrey, W. C., & Elder, G. H. (1995). A 50-year prospective study of the psychological sequelae of World War II combat. *American Journal of Psychiatry, 152*, 516–522.

Lerner, P. F. (1996). *Hysterical men: War, neurosis and German mental medicine, 1914–1921.* Ann Arbor, MI: University Microfilms International.

Lindal, E., & Stefansson, J. G. (1993). The lifetime prevalence of anxiety disorders in Iceland as estimated by the National Institute of Mental Health Diagnostic Interview Schedule. *Acta Psychiatrica Scandinavica, 88*, 29–34.

Litz, B. T., Gray, M. J., Bryant, R. A., & Adler, A. B. (2002). Early intervention for trauma: Current status and future directions. *Clinical Psychology: Science and Practice, 9*, 112–134.

Litz, B. T., Orsillo, S. M., Friedman, M., Ehlich, P., & Batres, A. (1997). Posttraumatic stress disorder associated with peacekeeping duty in Somalia for US military personnel. *American Journal of Psychiatry*, *154*, 178–184.

Loehlin, J. C. (1989). Partitioning environmental and genetic contributions to behavioral development. *American Psychologist*, *443*, 1285–1292.

Loehlin, J. C. (1992). *Genes and environment in personality development.* Newbury Park, CA: Sage.

Lonigan, C. J., Shannon, M. P., Taylor, C. M., Finch, A. J., & Sallee, F. R. (1994). Children exposed to disaster: II. Risk factors for the development of post-traumatic symptomatology. *Journal of the American Academy of Child and Adolescent Psychiatry*, *33*, 94–105.

Macklin, M. L., Metzger, L. J., Litz, B. T., McNally, R. J., Lasko, N. B., Orr, S. P. et al. (1998). Lower precombat intelligence is a risk factor for posttraumatic stress disorder. *Journal of Consulting and Clinical Psychology*, *66*, 323–326.

Malt, U. (1988). The long-term psychiatric consequences of accidental injury. A longitudinal study of 107 adults. *British Journal of Psychiatry*, *153*, 810–818.

Mayou, R. A., Ehlers, A., & Bryant, B. (2002). Posttraumatic stress disorder after motor vehicle accidents: 3-year follow-up of a prospective longitudinal study. *Behaviour Research and Therapy*, *40*, 665–675.

McCormick, R. A., Taber, J. I., & Kruedelback, N. (1989). The relationship between attributional style and post-traumatic stress disorder in addicted patients. *Journal of Traumatic Stress*, *2*, 477–487.

McCrae, R. R., & Costa, P. T. (1987). Validation of the five-factor model of personality across instruments and observers. *Journal of Personality and Social Psychology*, *52*, 81–90.

McEwan, B. S. (1997). Possible mechanisms of atrophy of the human hippocampus. *Molecular Psychiatry*, *2*, 255–262.

McEwan, B. S. (2001). Commentary on PTSD discussion. *Hippocampus*, *11*, 82–84.

McFarlane, A. C. (1987). Life events and psychiatric disorder: The role of a natural disaster. *British Journal of Psychiatry*, *151*, 362–367.

McFarlane, A. C. (1989). The aetiology of post-traumatic morbidity: Predisposing, precipitating, and perpetuating factors. *British Journal of Psychiatry*, *154*, 221–228.

McFarlane, A. C. (1990). An Australian disaster: The 1983 bushfires. *International Journal of Mental Health*, *19*, 36–47.

McFarlane, A. C. (1999). Risk factors for the acute biological and psychological response to trauma. In R. Yehuda (ed.), *Risk factors for posttraumatic stress disorder* (pp. 163–190). Washington, DC: American Psychiatric Press.

McFarlane, A. C., Atchison, M., & Yehuda, R. (1997). The acute stress response following motor vehicle accidents and its relation to PTSD. *Annals of the New York Academy of Sciences*, *821*, 482–485.

McNally, R. J. (2003). *Remembering trauma.* Cambridge, MA: Harvard University Press.

McNally, R. J., & Shin, L. M. (1995). Association of intelligence with severity of posttraumatic stress disorder symptoms in Vietnam combat veterans. *American Journal of Psychiatry*, *152*, 936–938.

Meehl, P. E. (1962). Schizotaxia, schizotypy, schizophrenia. *American Psychologist*, *17*, 827–838.

Miller, P. M., & Ingham, J. G. (1979). Reflections on the life-events-to-illness link with some preliminary findings. In I. Sarason & C. Spielberger (eds), *Stress and anxiety* (Vol. 6, pp. 313–336). New York: John Wiley and Sons.

Mischel, W., & Shoda, Y. (1995). A cognitive-affective system theory of personality: Reconceptualizing situations, dispositions, dynamics, and invariance in personality structure. *Psychological Review*, *102*, 246–268.

Monroe, S. M., & Simons, A. D. (1991). Diathesis-stress theories in the context of life stress research: Implications for the depressive disorders. *Psychological Bulletin, 110*, 406–425.

Nakano, T., Wenner, M., Inagaki, M., Kugaya, A., Akechi, T., Matsuoka, Y. et al. (2002). Relationship between distressing cancer-related recollections and hippocampal volume in cancer survivors. *American Journal of Psychiatry, 159*, 2087–2093.

North, C. S., Nixon, S. J., Shariat, S., Mallonee, S., McMillen, J. C., Spitznagel, E. L. et al. (1999). Psychiatric disorders among survivors of the Oklahoma City bombing. *Journal of the American Medical Association, 282*, 755–762.

Orr, S. P., Metzger, L. J., Lasko, N. B., Macklin, M. L., Hu, F. B., Shalev, A. Y. et al. (2003). Physiologic responses to sudden, loud tones in monozygotic twins discordant for combat exposure: Association with posttraumatic stress disorder. *Archives of General Psychiatry, 60*, 283–288.

Orr, S. P., Metzger, L. J., & Pitman, R. K. (2002). Psychophysiology of post-traumatic stress disorder. *Psychiatric Clinics of North America, 25*, 271–293.

O'Toole, B. I., Marshall, R. P., Schureck, R. J., & Dobson, M. (1998). Posttraumatic stress disorder and comorbidity in Australian Vietnam veterans: Risk factors, chronicity and combat. *Australian and New Zealand Journal of Psychiatry, 32*, 32–42.

Parrot, C., & Howes, J. L. (1991). The application of cognitive therapy to posttraumatic stress disorder. In T. M. Vallis, J. L. Howes, & P. C. Miller (eds), *The challenge of cognitive therapy: Applications to nontraditional populations* (pp. 85–109). New York: Plenum.

Paunovic, N. (1998). Cognitive factors in the maintenance of PTSD. *Scandinavian Journal of Behaviour Therapy, 27*, 167–178.

Perilla, J. L., Norris, F. H., & Lavizzo, E. A. (2002). Ethnicity, culture, and disaster response: Identifying and explaining ethnic differences in PTSD six months after Hurricane Andrew. *Journal of Social and Clinical Psychology, 21*, 20–45.

Perkonigg, A., Kessler, R. D., Storz, S., & Wittchen, H.-U. (2000). Traumatic events and posttraumatic stress disorder in the community: Prevalence, risk factors and comorbidity. *Acta Psychiatrica Scandinavica, 101*, 46–59.

Peterson, C., & Seligman, M. E. (1984). Causal explanations as a risk factor for depression: Theory and evidence. *Psychological Review, 91*, 347–374.

Pitman, R. K. (2001). Hippocampal diminution in PTSD: More (or less?) than meets the eye. *Hippocampus, 11*, 73–74.

Pitman, R. K., Orr, S. P., Lowenhagen, M. J., & Macklin, M. L. (1991). Pre-Vietnam contents of posttraumatic stress disorder veterans' service medical and personnel records. *Comprehensive Psychiatry, 32*, 416–422.

Portier, P., & Richet, C. (1902). De l'action anaphylactique de certains venins. [Concerning the anaphylactic action of some venoms] *Comptes Rendus des Séances de la Société de Biologie, 54*, 170–173.

Rachman, S. (1980). Emotional processing. *Behaviour Research and Therapy, 18*, 51–60.

Regehr, C., Cadell, S., & Jansen, K. (1999). Perceptions of control and long-term recovery from rape. *American Journal of Orthopsychiatry, 69*, 110–115.

Resnick, H. S., Kilpatrick, D. G., Best, C. L., & Kramer, T. L. (1992). Vulnerability-stress factors in development of posttraumatic stress disorder. *Journal of Nervous and Mental Disease, 180*, 424–430.

Resnick, H. S., Yehuda, R., Pitman, R., & Foy, D. W. (1995). Effect of previous trauma on acute plasma cortisol level following rape. *American Journal of Psychiatry, 152*, 1675–1677.

Reynolds, M., & Brewin, C. R. (1998). Intrusive cognitions, coping strategies and emotional responses in depression, post-traumatic stress disorder and a non-clinical population. *Behaviour Research and Therapy, 36*, 135–147.

Reynolds, M., & Wells, A. (1999). The Thought Control Questionnaire: Psychometric properties in a clinical sample, and relationships with PTSD and depression. *Psychological Medicine, 29,* 1089–1099.

Roberts, K. A. (2000). Trauma recovery in military veterans with chronic PTSD: An emphasis on the problem of guilt. A treatment outcomes study. *Dissertation Abstracts International, 60*(8-B), 4249.

Rose, S., Bisson, J., & Wessely, S. (2001). Psychological debriefing for preventing post traumatic stress disorder (PTSD). *The Cochrane Library (3).* Oxford: Update Software.

Rotter, J. B. (1966). Generalized expectancies for Internal vs External control of reinforcement. *Psychological Monographs: General and Applied, 80*(1/609), 1–28.

Schnurr, P. P. (1999). Personality as a risk factor for PTSD. In R. Yehuda (ed.), *Risk factors for posttraumatic stress disorder* (pp. 191–222). Washington, DC: American Psychiatric Press.

Schnyder, U., Moergeli, H., Klaghofer, R., & Buddeberg, C. (2001). Incidence and prediction of posttraumatic stress disorder symptoms in severely injured accident victims. *American Journal of Psychiatry, 158,* 594–599.

Schuff, N., Neylan, T. C., Lenoci, M. A., Du, A. T., Weiss, D. S., Marmar, C. R. et al. (2001). Decreased hippocampal N-acetylaspartate in the absence of atrophy in posttraumatic stress disorder. *Biological Psychiatry, 50,* 952–959.

Schwartz, C., Snidman, N., & Kagan, J. (1999). Adolescent social anxiety as an outcome of inhibited temperament in childhood. *Journal of the American Academy of Child and Adolescent Psychiatry, 38,* 1008–1015.

Scott, M. J., & Stradling, S. G. (1997). Client compliance with exposure treatments for posttraumatic stress disorder. *Journal of Traumatic Stress, 10,* 523–526.

Shalev, A. Y. (1996). Stress vs traumatic stress: From acute homeostatic reactions to chronic psychopathology. In B. A. van der Kolk & A. C. McFarlane (eds), *Traumatic stress: The effects of overwhelming experience on mind, body, and society* (pp. 77–101). New York: Guilford Press.

Shalev, A. Y., Bonne, O., & Eth, S. (1996). Treatment of posttraumatic stress disorder: A review. *Psychosomatic Review, 58,* 165–182.

Shalev, A. Y., Peri, T., Brandes, D., Freedman, S., Orr, S. P., & Pitman, R. K. (2000). Auditory startle response in trauma survivors with posttraumatic stress disorder: A prospective study. *American Journal of Psychiatry, 157,* 255–261.

Silva, R. R., Alpert, M., & Munoz, D. M. (2000). Stress and vulnerability to posttraumatic stress disorder in children and adolescents. *American Journal of Psychiatry, 157,* 1229–1235.

Simon, R. I. (2002). Distinguishing trauma-associated narcissistic symptoms from posttraumatic stress disorder: A diagnostic challenge. *Harvard Review of Psychiatry, 10,* 28–36.

Smith, K., & Bryant, R. A. (2000). The generality of cognitive bias in acute stress disorder. *Behaviour Research and Therapy, 3,* 709–715.

Solomon, S. D., Gerrity, E. T., & Muff, A. M. (1992). Efficacy of treatments for posttraumatic stress disorder. *Journal of the American Medical Association, 268,* 633–638.

Solomon, Z., Mikulincer, M., & Avitzur, E. (1988). Coping, locus of control, social support and combat-related posttraumatic stress disorder: A prospective study. *Journal of Personality and Social Psychology, 55,* 279–285.

Southwick, S. M., Morgan, C. A., III, Nicolaou, A. L., & Charney, D. S. (1997). Consistency of memory for combat-related traumatic events in veterans of Operation Desert Storm. *American Journal of Psychiatry, 154,* 173–177.

Speisman, J. C., Lazarus, R. S., Mordkoff, A. M., & Davison, L. (1964). Experiential reduction of stress based on ego-defense theory. *Journal of Abnormal and Social Psychology, 68,* 367–380.

Stein, M. B., Jang, K. L., Taylor, S., Vernon, P. A., & Livesley, W. J. (2002). Genetic and environmental influences on trauma exposure and posttraumatic stress disorder symptoms: A twin study. *American Journal of Psychiatry*, *159*, 1675–1681.

Stein, M. B., Koverola, C., Hanna, C., Torchia, M. G., & McClarty, B. (1997a). Hippocampal volume in women victimized by childhood sexual abuse. *Psychological Medicine*, *27*, 951–959.

Stein, M. B., Walker, J. R., Hazen, A. L., & Forde, D. R. (1997b). Full and partial posttraumatic stress disorder: Findings from a community survey. *American Journal of Psychiatry*, *154*, 1114–1119.

Summerfield, D. A., Loughrey, G., Nikapota, A., & Parry-Jones, W. (1997). Civil violence. In D. Black, M. Newman, J. Harris-Hendriks, & G. Mezey (eds), *Psychological trauma: A developmental approach* (pp. 148–175). London: Gaskell.

Sutker, P. B., Bugg, F., & Allain, A. N. (1991). Psychometric prediction of PTSD among POW survivors. *Psychological Assessment*, *3*, 105–110.

Sutker, P. B., Davis, J. M., Uddo, M., & Ditta, S. R. (1995). War zone stress, personal resources, and PTSD in Persian Gulf War returnees. *Journal of Abnormal Psychology*, *104*, 444–452.

Talbert, F. S., Braswell, L. C., Albrecht, J. W., Hyer, L. A., & Boudewyns, P. A. (1993). NEO-PI profiles in PTSD as a function of trauma level. *Journal of Clinical Psychology*, *49*, 663–669.

Tarrier, N., & Humphreys, L. (2000). Subjective improvement in PTSD patients with treatment by imaginal exposure or cognitive therapy: Session by session changes. *British Journal of Clinical Psychology*, *39*, 27–34.

Tarrier, N., Pilgrim, H., & Sommerfield, C. (1999). A randomized trial of cognitive therapy and imaginal exposure in the treatment of chronic posttraumatic stress disorder. *Journal of Consulting and Clinical Psychology*, *67*, 13–18.

Tarrier, N., Sommerfield, C., Pilgrim, H., & Garagher, B. (2000). Factors associated with outcome of cognitive-behavioural treatment of chronic post-traumatic stress disorder. *Behaviour Research and Therapy*, *38*, 191–202.

Tolin, D. F., & Foa, E. B. (2002). Gender and PTSD: A cognitive model. In R. Kimerling & P. Ouimette (eds), *Gender and PTSD* (pp. 76–97). New York: Guilford Press.

True, W. R., & Lyons, M. J. (1999). Genetic risk factors for PTSD: A twin study. In R. Yehuda (ed.), *Risk factors for posttraumatic stress disorder* (pp. 61–78). Washington, DC: American Psychiatric Press.

True, W. R., Rice, J., Eisen, S. A., Heath, A. C., Goldberg, J., Lyons, M. J. et al. (1993). A twin study of genetic and environmental contributions to liability for posttraumatic stress symptoms. *Archives of General Psychiatry*, *50*, 257–264.

Usala, P. D., & Hertzog, C. (1991). Evidence of differential stability of state and trait anxiety in adults. *Journal of Personality and Social Psychology*, *60*, 471–479.

Vickberg, S. M. J., Duhamel, K. N., & Smith, M. Y. (2001). Global meaning and psychological adjustment among survivors of bone marrow transplant. *Psycho-Oncology*, *10*, 29–39.

Villarreal, G., Hamilton, D. A., Petropoulos, H., Driscoll, I., Rowland, L. M., Griego, J. A. et al. (2002). Reduced hippocampal volume and total white matter volume in posttraumatic stress disorder. *Biological Psychiatry*, *52*, 119–125.

Vukšíc-Mihaljevíc, Ž., Mandíc, N., Benšíc, M., & Mihaljevíc, S. (2000). Posttraumatic stress disorder among Croatian veterans: A causal model. *Psychiatry and Clinical Neurosciences*, *54*, 625–636.

Wang, S., Zhao, C., & Naotaka, S. (1999). Prevalence and predictors of post-traumatic stress disorder after an earthquake: Findings from a randomized community sample in northern China (translated abstract). *Chinese Mental Health Journal*, *13*, 28–30.

Weaver, T. L., & Clum, G. A. (1995). Psychological distress associated with interpersonal violence: A meta-analysis. *Clinical Psychology Review*, *15*, 115–140.

Wierzbicki, M. (1989). Twins' responses to Pleasant, Unpleasant, and Life Events. *Journal of Genetic Psychology*, *150*, 135–145.

Wolfe, J., Erickson, D. J., Sharkansky, E. J., King, D. W., & King, L. A. (1999). Course and predictors of posttraumatic stress disorder among Gulf War veterans: A prospective analysis. *Journal of Consulting and Clinical Psychology*, *67*, 520–528.

Wolfe, J., Keane, T., Kaloupek, D., Mora, C., & Wine, P. (1993). Patterns of positive readjustment in Vietnam combat veterans. *Journal of Traumatic Stress*, *6*, 179–193.

Wortman, C. B., & Silver, R. C. (1992). Reconsidering assumptions about coping with loss: An overview of current research. In L. Montada, S.-H. Filipp, & M. Lerner (eds), *Life crises and experiences of loss in adulthood* (pp. 341–365). Hillsdale, NJ: Lawrence Erlbaum Associates.

Wykes, T., & Whittington, R. (1998). Prevalence and predictors of early traumatic stress reactions in assaulted psychiatric nurses. *Journal of Forensic Psychiatry*, *9*, 643–658.

Yehuda, R. (2001). Are glucocortoids responsible for putative hippocampal damage in PTSD? How and when to decide. *Hippocampus*, *11*, 85–89.

Yehuda, R., Bierer, L. M., Schmeidler, J., Aferiat, D. H., Breslau, I., & Dolan, S. (2000). Low cortisol and risk for PTSD in adult offspring of Holocaust survivors. *American Journal of Psychiatry*, *157*, 1252–1259.

Yehuda, R., & McFarlane, A. C. (1995). Conflict between current knowledge about posttraumatic stress disorder and its original conceptual basis. *American Journal of Psychiatry*, *152*, 1705–1713.

Yehuda, R., McFarlane, A. C., & Shalev, A. Y. (1998a). Predicting the development of posttraumatic stress disorder from the acute response to a traumatic event. *Biological Psychiatry*, *44*, 1305–1313.

Yehuda, R., Resnick, H. S., Schmeidler, J., Yang, R.-K., & Pitman, R. K. (1998b). Predictors of cortisol and 3-Methoxy-4-hydroxy-phenylglycol responses in the acute aftermath of rape. *Biological Psychiatry*, *43*, 855–859.

Ziv, A., & Israeli, R. (1973). Effects of bombardment on the manifest anxiety level of children living in kibbutzim. *Journal of Consulting and Clinical Psychology*, *40*, 287–291.

3 Risk Factors and PTSD: A Historian's Perspective

BEN SHEPHARD

Bristol, UK

I am a military historian. Reading the current PTSD literature, I am first of all traumatized by its prose. When, however, I have mastered my acute symptoms, a second reaction sets in—I feel a sense of *déjà vu*. For—beneath all the jargon about the "adversity-stress model", all the talk of "event" and "risk"—I slowly begin to recognize fairly recent acquaintances like "stressor", then old friends like "vulnerability" and "predisposition", now fashionably decked out as "pre-event traits", come into focus. After a while, I even begin to have flashbacks—not the short subliminal flashes that cinematically illiterate psychiatrists (Jones et al., 2003) call flashbacks; but the real thing—as in Forties *film noir*, where a voice-over from a dying Burt Lancaster triggers the plot: "Waiting for the cops to arrive, my mind went back . . . to when I first saw her . . . that hot day in August . . . coming back from the drug store . . . She seemed like any other dame . . ."; or the more corny 1930s-type, where the wind blows the pages of a calendar backwards. Back, back, back . . . to a time when doctors still wrote in English.

This chapter is a series of such flashbacks, glimpses of the concept of predisposition as it waxed, waned, and then waxed again in the twentieth century. It does not pretend to be comprehensive (for one thing, most French and German writing on the topic has been ignored); but rather, to mix the metaphor, it aims to provide historical snapshots in the hopes that they will give some perspective to current debates. Each profession has its governing illusion; for historians it is the notion that the past will somehow "illuminate" the present. We cling to this mantra, for without it, what social function do we have? Yet experience shows that busy professionals like psychiatrists mostly have a ruthlessly functional approach to history, comparable to that of the Communist Party in the Brezhnev epoch: the medical literature of the past is important and interesting when it buttresses and legitimizes present practice. When it doesn't, forget it.

Having selectively reviewed the history, this chapter will then attempt to answer several questions. What conclusions—if any—can we draw from this story? Are there any broad insights which can help us better to understand the current literature and perhaps (hubristic thought) avoid the mistakes of the past? Is the concept of predisposition that is current today genuinely new or just another turn of the wheel?

Before turning out the lights and getting the projector going, it is worth stressing two basic points. First, although there has been general agreement that "predisposition" means

Posttraumatic Stress Disorder: Issues and Controversies. Edited by G. M. Rosen.
© 2004 John Wiley & Sons, Ltd. ISBN 0-470-86284-X/0-470-86285-8.

an underlying or pre-war weakness, that vulnerability has taken many forms—poor heredity, bad upbringing, broken home, over-dependence on mother, drunken father, nightmares, low intelligence, or simply membership of a particular ethnic or socio-economic group. Second, I shall mainly be reviewing the literature generated by war and the question of predisposition tends to arise in the military context at three specific points: at induction, when a man is being considered for the forces; if he breaks down in the army; and finally, at the end of his service, when his claim to a pension is being considered. In between those three points, the issue of predisposition seldom arises in its pure form because many other variables also come into play—leadership, group morale, patriotic feeling, the behaviour of his wife, and so on.

NATURE VERSUS NURTURE IN THE WORLD WARS

I shall begin, rather arbitrarily, at Maghull Hospital, near Liverpool, England, late in 1917. By then, World War I was entering its fourth year and a paradox had been revealed—that, on the one hand, anyone can break down in war but, on the other, that you shouldn't let just anyone into the army. In other words, numerous young men of impeccable character and social background had developed shell-shock, thus disproving pre-war ideas that only women, "degenerates", weaklings, "neuropaths", and foreigners got mentally ill; while, at the same time, it was becoming clear that the British Army had made an enormous and costly mistake by not giving proper medical vetting to its wartime recruits.

Two members of Maghull's temporary staff, the anatomist and polymath Grafton Elliot Smith and the psychologist Tom Pear, seized on the first of these phenomena. "The war," they wrote in their book *Shell-Shock and Its Lessons*, "has shown us one inescapable fact, that a psychoneurosis may be produced in almost anyone if only his environment be made 'difficult' enough for him." They then drew a wider conclusion:

> It has warned us that the pessimistic, helpless appeal to heredity, so common in the case of insanity must [be abandoned] . . . In the causation of the psychoneuroses, heredity undoubtedly counts, but social and material environment count infinitely more. (Smith & Pear, 1917, pp. 87–88)

Elliot Smith and Pear were deliberately using shell-shock to reopen the pre-war nature–nurture controversy; interfering—as feisty, combative academic outsiders—in one of the great debates within English psychiatry. Before the war, while they had been reading Freud and flirting with hypnosis at Manchester University, their boss at Maghull, R. G. Rows, had been the pathologist in a provincial asylum and a prominent figure in a campaign within the mental health profession to break down the barriers between sanity and madness—between living in society and the "disaster of committal" to an asylum— by removing the stigma attached to mental illness and creating out-patient clinics for "borderline" patients. Now they were taking up the cudgels on his behalf (Shephard, 1996).

The opposite camp was quick to respond. "The great stress laid upon nurture rather than nature shows the authors to be out-and-out-environmentalists," wrote Dr Robert Armstrong-Jones, the Medical Superintendent of Claybury Asylum. Anyway, he said, Elliot Smith and Pear were wrong. In his experience, "a family history of insanity, epilepsy, paralysis, neurasthenia, or parental alcoholism ha[d] been obtained in 33% of all cases of shell-shock". Heredity *was* a great factor and there were few cases of shell-shock which "do not inherit in their nervous system some *locus resistentiae minoris*, which has tended towards a breakdown at some age or other under the necessary stress" (Armstrong-Jones, 1917, p. 2). To reinforce this point, Armstrong-Jones' colleague at Claybury, Frederick Mott, then got a junior doctor to compare the family and personal histories of 100 cases of war psycho-neurosis with those of 100 wounded men. Mott was a pathologist by trade and before the war had been a tireless popularizer of the role of biological factors in mental illness (Mott, 1913); his assistant's results duly showed a "striking difference in the comparative frequency of inborn neuropathic or psychopathic tendency or temperamental timidity in the two groups" (Wolfsohn, 1918; see also Mott, 1919).

Which side was right? Both were of course. In 1931, Millais Culpin, a humane, undogmatic and experienced physician, gave a more temperate account of what had happened during the war. "It was soon realised by those who treated these patients," Culpin wrote, "that a large number had suffered from symptoms before enlistment."

> Mott estimated the percentage at eighty [actually 74]. My figures gave a lower percentage, but I took as my standard of predisposition the consideration whether I would, on psychological grounds, have rejected the man on examination before enlistment, with his previous history, as now known, placed before me. Judged by this standard, 56.8% of my subjects were predisposed to breakdown, and 10% of my own hospital cases had suffered no apparent ill-effects from Army service, but drifted into a shell-shock hospital on the strength of their pre-existing symptoms. When all the cases were classified . . . those with a notable predisposition showed up very badly; they had been bad bargains for the country. (Culpin, 1931, p. 45)

Culpin then tried to quantify the difference. The soldiers whom he did not consider predisposed had, he reckoned, served for an average of 38.2 months in the military, with 19 months overseas service, before breaking down, while those "in which war service aggravated the previous condition" had on average done 27.1 months and 11.5 months abroad. Finally, the patients whose "previous condition was unaltered" had served an average of 22 months, but only 2.7 months abroad. From this he concluded that "although the predisposed most readily fell victims to disabling symptoms, yet any man, if exposed to modern warfare for a sufficiently long period, would eventually reach his breaking point" (Culpin, 1931, pp. 45–47).

SELECTION: THE FIRST ATTEMPT

The fact that the "notably predisposed" were "a bad bargain" for their country was very much taken on board by Thomas W. Salmon, the psychiatric adviser to the American Army, when he visited Britain in 1917. His recommendation that "insane, feebleminded, psychopathic and neuropathic individuals" should be screened out led the US Army to introduce the first serious attempt psychologically to vet recruits to the armed forces (Bailey, Williams, Komora, Salmon, & Fenton, 1929). That programme has attracted a huge historical literature—not least, because it was in part hijacked by the Harvard psychologist Robert Yerkes, to provide data for his own work on the relationship between race and intelligence (Carson, 1993; Gould, 1981; Kevles, 1968; Reed, 1987; Samelson, 1977). A variety of tests of intelligence and personality were used, but the application seems to have been patchy and variable. According to one estimate, 72,000 (2%) of US recruits were rejected on neuropsychiatric grounds, either at boards or in training; according to another, 68,000 (1.4%) were rejected at enlistment and a further 35,000 (0.9%) were discharged from the armed forces with neuropsychiatric disorders (Jones, Hyams, & Wessely, 2003, p. 41). There is certainly evidence that the American screening programme had some impact on casualty levels in France; on the other hand, the fairly brief American involvement in the war produced 69,394 neuropsychiatric casualties; as late as 1927, there were 68,727 American ex-servicemen of World War I in veterans' hospitals with neuropsychiatric disorders (Shephard, 1999b, p. 40). For some reason, this disaster—caused by a very similar brew of veterans' agitation, medical "advocacy", and political mismanagement to that from which PTSD emerged in the 1970s—has been completely ignored by modern psychiatrists and historians (with the exception of Cox, 2001).

PREDISPOSITION RETURNS

Predisposition reappeared in the 1920s, but in a new form. When large numbers of veterans failed to get better and continued drawing pensions for war neurosis, the issue of premorbid weakness returned to the medical literature—couched this time in moralistic, rather than hereditary or environmental, language. For example, Dr George Benton, who had worked with veterans at the US Public Health Service Hospital in Waukesha, Wisconsin, complained in 1921 that "a soldier whose total army life and experience consisted of one night in camp and ninety days in hospital presents a more hopeless picture than many a full-fledged veteran of two or three years of most varied and arduous war experience" (Benton, 1921, p. 360). The prominent Boston psychiatrist Douglas Thom distinguished between active and passive groups of patients. The active group, he argued, sought refuge in neurosis. They were usually inherently unstable individuals "and it is because of this instability that the neurosis develops". Their symptoms were "usually of a crude character and the patient clings to them with great persistence". By contrast, the second or passive group was made up of individuals "who do not seek but are overtaken by this neurosis" (Thom, 1923).

In Britain, the revival of predisposition is best illustrated by the career of the dominant figure in psychiatric war pensions between 1922 and 1945, Francis Prideaux. After working as a colonial doctor in Fiji, Prideaux returned to England in 1916 and, although a newcomer to psychiatry, soon established a reputation as an effective shell-shock therapist, confidently telling medical meetings about the results he was achieving with such techniques as suggestion. But by 1920, he was talking of "failures", and the following year, when researching chronic war neurosis cases for the Medical Research Council, he began to emphasize the role of intelligence, arguing that those who failed to recover were usually of lower intelligence. Later in the decade, as Chief Psychiatrist of the Ministry of Pensions, Prideaux carried out a follow-up study of "neurasthenic pensioners", which established that "57% had served at home only and another 20% broke down after less than 6 months service overseas and 59% had a pre-war history of neurotic illness or tendency". This discovery contributed to a notable hardening of tone evident in a document which the Ministry of Pensions sent out in 1928, which resurrected pre-war terms like "the congenital stigmata of degeneration" and spoke of " 'constitutionally psychopathic inferiors', people who have been since childhood habitually abnormal in their emotional reactions and general conduct and defective in the social and moral sense" (Shephard, 1999a).

Prideaux was very much the moving spirit in an initiative which the British Ministry of Pensions took early in 1939, designed to make sure that "shell-shock" would not be handled as disastrously in the next war (for which Whitehall was by then preparing itself) as it had been in the last, particularly if, as was then widely expected, German bombing produced many thousands of civilian nervous casualties. He secured broad agreement from a group of prominent neurologists and psychiatrists (nearly all of whom had treated "shell-shock" in World War I) that this time around the problem would not be medicalized: quasi-medical words like "shell-shock" would not be used, and the problem of mental breakdown would be treated as a social, not a medical, phenomenon; and that, as far as possible, those who developed psycho-neuroses would not automatically be discharged from the forces and given a pension. However, when Prideaux sought to argue that *all* cases of wartime psycho-neurosis were due to "the constitutional factor, hereditary or acquired"—to assert that there was no such thing as traumatic neurosis—he was pulled up short by the most powerful figure in British psychiatry. Edward Mapother, the medical director of the Maudsley Hospital, was no weak-kneed liberal. He believed, for example, that "public sentimentality" had prevented the "sane treatment" of "shell-shock" a generation earlier and that "a very large number had [been given] pensions who should not have had them". He was also a realist, telling a conference in 1935 that "in war, all else is subordinate to the winning of it". But now, drawing on his wide experience as a front-line surgeon, "shell-shock" doctor, and psychiatric adviser to veterans' charities, he contradicted Prideaux:

> There were a number of cases [said Mapother] which arose solely from war service and showed no indication of previous abnormality. Justice required that adequate provision be made for such men ... To label a man as a constitutional neurotic though you could trace no evidence of it in his past history was unjustifiable. (Shephard, 1999a, p. 507)

Here the British were confronting the central conundrum in the management of war neurosis: how to discourage the mass of the population from developing psychiatric problems while simultaneously behaving fairly and humanely to those who *do* break down; reconciling the needs of the genuinely traumatized veteran with the over-riding necessity to deny secondary gain. After some argument, it was decided in 1939 to withhold all pensions during hostilities but to pay them to deserving cases afterwards. This line was more or less stuck to for the rest of the war, though it ran into political opposition and was bitterly criticized by some young doctors. Whatever one thinks of it morally, it was undeniably effective in reducing civilian casualties in the 1940–1941 Luftwaffe Blitz (Shephard, 1999a).

Prideaux's committee also discussed, but did not resolve, another issue raised by the war—that of personnel selection. The case for vetting recruits to the military had been given fresh weight, many now argued, by changes in the nature of warfare itself; so that, with trenches and cannon fodder giving way to tanks and aeroplanes, a new breed of soldier was needed, more intelligent and specialized. Was it not now possible to use the techniques of medicine, psychology, and psychiatry to eliminate the vulnerable from the battlefield, leaving war to those who could handle it, and thus avoid the crippling inter-war pensions bill? Could not the tests for industrial skills and aptitudes developed between the wars be adapted for the military?

The Chiefs of Staff were not convinced. The British Army did not test its recruits at all until 1941, when a progressively-minded general, Sir Ronald Adam, was made Adjutant-General and seized on the issue of testing largely for political reasons. Adam realized that after being buffeted by *Blitzkrieg* in France, Norway, and Crete, the army needed to appear rational, modern, scientific, and, above all, democratic, and so he allowed a group of psychiatrists from London's Tavistock Clinic to bring in intelligence and aptitude testing of ordinary soldiers and more ambitious tests of character for officers. The psychiatrists privately admitted, however, that they had "no test for courage" (Shephard, 2001).

THE "NEUROTIC CONSTITUTION"

The two-year delay in introducing testing had one important side effect: it produced a fresh wave of literature on "predisposition". Because of Churchill's reluctance to invade Europe, many British soldiers spent four years exposed to nothing worse than the "chickenshit" of service life; yet large numbers of the unsuitable men admitted before 1941 broke down, thus providing the grand psychiatrists now in uniform with data on "the neurotic personality". Few of the soldiers studied by Eliot Slater at Sutton or J. A. Hadfield at Bath had been involved in combat; the anxiety, hysteria, depression, and hypochondria of which they complained had rather been caused by "separation from home and family, home worries, a life of relative hardship, army discipline, the pressure of tasks physically, intellectually or temperamentally beyond them". Their neurosis was "not so much an illness as a simple failure to adapt to army routine and discipline, in part an incapacity to adapt, and a response to this incapacity" (Slater, 1943, p. 1).

The psychiatrists noticed how attitudes had changed since World War I; how, for example, men now seldom bothered to cloak their fears in hysterical symptoms as they had a generation earlier. Hadfield, a prominent shell-shock doctor in the earlier war, was struck by the number of patients (47%) who now "volunteered the statement: 'I have been nervous all my life; I have had depressed turns ever since I can remember.'" (Hadfield, 1942, p. 283). Slater noted that "the psychopaths were as anxious as the hysterics to earn their discharge from the army by fair means or foul". The psychiatrists could scarcely disguise their contempt for these men. Slater wrote of the "monotonous uniformity of the underlying personality. There were few who did not show to some degree a psychic asthenia, a feebleness of will and purpose, coupled with tendencies to worry, pessimism and moodiness or hysterical traits." Their sex lives were "impoverished" and "inadequate" rather than simply "inhibited" (Slater, 1943). These men were "as a rule useless as soldiers from the beginning"; thousands of neurotics had been recruited "who are not, never have been, and never will be, fit to be soldiers" (Hadfield, 1942, p. 283).

The psychiatrists' findings tended to reflect their different viewpoints. Thus, the prominent Kleinian, Ronald Fairbairn, concluded that "separation-anxiety" was "the greatest common measure of all forms of war neurosis" (Fairbairn, 1943), while J. A. Hadfield (a Tavistock eclectic) and Eliot Slater (Maudsley-trained and biologically minded) tried to tease out the relationship between nature and nurture. Hadfield found that "of 326 cases there was a predisposition of a constitutional or acquired type in 82% and apparently no predisposition in 18%". Hadfield then asked:

> The next question is, "How far is this predisposition 'constitutional' and how far 'psychological'"? By "constitutional" we mean innate, endogenous, and dependent upon the physiological

and biochemical make-up of the individual; by "psychological" we mean acquired and due to environmental conditions, especially in early childhood—such as bad training, infantile fears, an unhappy home, or other experiences affecting his psychological disposition, with the formation of morbid complexes. (1942, p. 284)

The two factors often interacted, said Hadfield, but it was important to differentiate them on account of treatment; for "we can give only palliative treatment for the constitutionally predisposed, but can radically cure the psychoneurotic and acquired type since it is in the nature of a conditioned reflex". His investigations had shown that the amount of predisposition in these patients "was found to be about equal: of 289 cases 49.4% were predominantly constitutional and 50.6% predominantly psychological" (Hadfield, 1942).

Eliot Slater's (1943) study of the "the neurotic constitution" in 2,000 soldiers concluded that "it seems fairly clear that processes resembling conditioning occur in man as well as in experimental animals, and that neurotic states have their own dynamics".

Our experience suggests that in the predisposed individual such reactive dispositions can be established with great rapidity. A man's association with dive-bombing did not have to be very prolonged for the association in his mind of certain types of noise and a fear-producing situation to become firmly fixed; and for a long time after similar sounds, though recognized as harmless, would continue to produce the physiological and mental changes typical of fear. The disposition once established was difficult to break up, and even when it had apparently passed off was easily re-established. If this effect can occur so easily in the adult, there is plausibility in the view that the plastic mind of the child is even more susceptible. (Slater, 1943, pp. 14–15)

Slater's hypothesis was that

neurosis represents a special case of a generalized type of behaviour and signifies a failure of adaptation. The two primary reagents are the individual constitution and the environmental setup of the moment. The individual constitution is in greater part determined by hereditary factors, to a lesser degree by environmental circumstances of the past producing their effects by organic lesion and psychological and physiological conditioning. (Slater, 1943, pp. 15–16)

The neurotic constitution, Slater concluded, was a useful hypothesis,

and one which ranks with inadequate intelligence in accounting for social insufficiency, breakdown and impairment of efficiency for military duties. It is interesting to compare these two biological handicaps one with the other. We know that intelligence is practically solely determined by genetic factors; our evidence suggests that the same may be true of the neurotic constitution. (Slater, 1943, pp. 15–16)

SELECTION IN THE US

Entering World War II on 7 December 1941, the United States once again had the chance to profit from the mistakes of the British. But there were also strong domestic reasons why a policy of selecting men for the armed forces would find favour in Washington in the early 1940s—both the reluctance of public opinion to get involved in another European war and the much quoted cost of psychiatric pensions from the last war made politicians receptive to bold schemes. "The one we have to look out for is the boy that just cannot face it," New York Mayor Fiorello La Guardia told a Congressional Committee in 1940.

That is the type. It is pathetic, but some types just cannot face fire. They go to pieces. Now medical science can easily discover those types, which we could not during the last war, as we did not know much about these things . . . But with the progress in medical science today you can discover those things . . . We can save those boys from horror. (Greene, 1977, p. 97)

Many experienced doctors doubted whether you could predict a man's behaviour in battle. Abram Kardiner, for example, hesitated to "offer any criteria that can be used to predict that a given candidate will have a traumatic neurosis", and simply suggested eliminating men with a history of fits, stammering, and other nervous disorders. But Harry Stack Sullivan and others who believed that you could make such predictions carried the day and the United States made an ambitious attempt to eliminate the predisposed. Recruits were tested, not simply for intelligence, but for their vulnerability to psycho-neurosis (Shephard, 2001).

The American policy was a disaster—or certainly is always presented as one (Ginzberg, Anderson, Ginzberg, & Herma, 1959; Glass, 1966; Greene, 1977; Jones et al., 2003). Large numbers of inductees were excluded from the armed forces—a process which led to much anguished public debate over "the state of the nation's young manhood" ("Youth in Crisis", 1943). Struggling to account for the hopeless immaturity of a third of America's young men, psychiatrists and commentators agreed that their domineering and over-possessive mothers were to blame. A popular literature on "Mom-ism" appeared (Wylie, 1942) and prominent psychiatrists like Edward Strecker lectured the mothers of America on how to let their sons alone (Strecker, 1945). Yet this radical policy of exclusion seemed to have no effect at all on levels of psychiatric "wastage". Not only did immense numbers of men break down while still in the continental United States—in September 1943 the Army lost 112,500 enlisted men and inducted 118,600 (Artiss, 1963, p. 1011), when US forces went into action in late 1942 in Tunisia and Guadalcanal, there were very high psychiatric casualties. Small wonder that in December 1943 the Army Chief of Staff, the great and good General George C. Marshall, should brush aside the psychiatrists and lay down new and tougher guidelines (Shephard, 2001).

Why was the American attempt to find the predisposed such a failure? Part of the explanation was practical—there simply weren't the resources (for example, in psychiatrically competent doctors) to do the job properly. But some of the underlying assumptions on which the plan was based were also flawed; there was much truth in William Menninger's later observation that

the psychiatrist in the observation centre had no possible way of evaluating the four most important factors of influence upon the adjustment of the soldier: the nature of the leadership that would be provided for him; the degree of motivation that he had to do the job or that could be instilled into him; the type of job to which he might be assigned; and the degree of stress which might confront him. (1948, p. 289)

And it was probably also true that, by importing psychiatry into the induction process, the Army was encouraging the population to develop psychiatric symptoms.

The failure of the World War II screening programme dealt the project of psychological selection a blow from which, in the United States, it never really recovered. In the short term, Marshall's explosion produced a 180° change in the direction of published papers; so that if, before the General's intervention, the consensus was often that only the best-equipped man could make a soldier, the decade after it saw a torrent of publications which combined professional breast beating—"as psychiatrists we may not have fully assisted in the utilization of all our serviceable manpower"—with evidence that men of "questionable soldier material" had in fact proved courageous and serviceable soldiers (Klein, 1951). For example, one paper showed that, of 395 mild psycho-neurotics salvaged during training, only 44 had failed to get through the Battle of the Bulge (Sharp, 1950). It was even suggested that neurotics might perhaps be better equipped to survive in battle than the "ordinary" person (Klein, 1951). Then, in the early 1950s, when the Armed Forces were much smaller, there was a backlash: military doctors pointed out that, whatever deeds of valour neurotics might be capable of in moments of wartime emergency, they were a heavy drain on resources and best excluded in peacetime soldiering (Hunt, Wittson, & Hunt, 1952).

WORLD WAR II: PREDISPOSITION IN BATTLE

Alongside the literature on "psychoneurotics in combat", World War II generated numerous studies of the behaviour of men in battle, in which individual predisposition was treated as just one of several variables, including leadership, group morale, and military circumstance. This literature tended to be shaped by where and when in the war the psychiatrist served (and the kind of patients he treated), and by the dominant social and political mood of the hour, whether it be post-Dunkirk idealism and pro-Soviet feeling in Britain or New Deal common man rhetoric in the United States.

Thus, examining the first 200 cases admitted to a US hospital in the South Pacific in 1943, two psychiatrists found "a disturbance in the family background" to be "strikingly constant in nearly every case" and "a certain pattern" to be apparent when that home background was studied:

> The mother was found to stand out. She was usually a "nervous" woman and had often had a nervous breakdown but was rarely hospitalized for it . . . About half the fathers drank to excess . . . The mother is an immature person who feels herself insecure and identifies strongly with her children . . . Often her letters [to her son who is in combat] are anxiety ridden and disturb him accordingly . . . It is a fact, vouchsafed by many, that when he went into combat he was more worried about the situation at home—as it had been relayed to him by his mother—than he was about himself. (Henderson & Moore, 1944, p. 276)

"The man who had developed a so-called 'war neurosis'," Henderson and Moore declared, "was predetermined before he entered the service. It might even be said that war neuroses are 'made in America' and only come to light or are labelled in combat." Yet, at the same time, they recorded that about 35% of their patients had "previously experienced a psychic trauma of a sudden and overwhelming nature comparable to that of the combat situation".

As the war went on, however, and the psychiatrists saw more patients and became more "embedded" in the military, the emphasis in their papers shifted. It began to be argued that the main cause of combat fatigue was not a soldier's pre-service personality but the intensity of battle itself. According to a later study, "the majority of psychiatric admissions in 1942–43 of US servicemen had pre-existing emotional disorders, but by 1944–45, combat had become the dominant factor and 50% of admissions for psychoneurosis were soldiers who had been assessed as clinically normal at entry" (Jones et al., 2003, p. 44).

The British had discerned a roughly similar pattern in World War I, but seldom saw the intensity of combat as the only important factor; for them, leadership was also a vital ingredient. In France in 1917, William Brown, the psychiatrist to Fourth Army, noted that a very high proportion of the men he treated came from the same units. "The better the discipline in any division," he told the 1922 Shell-shock Committee, "the less shell-shock there was in that division"(War Office, 1922, p. 5). Equally, British Army psychiatrists in Normandy in 1944 reckoned they could tell by a man's behaviour in the Exhaustion Centre which unit he came from. "The general morale seen from cases from 43rd Division was low. Very few indeed . . . showed any desire to return to their units," a psychiatrist recorded (Crew, 1962, p. 207; Copp & McAndrew, 1990, p. 131).

Harold Palmer was a tough, rebarbative man who treated some 12,000 cases between 1940 and 1945, mainly in the Western Desert and Italy, and was generally regarded as the most effective British psychiatrist of the war. He agreed that "the incidence of psychiatric casualties roughly corresponds to the extent to which a unit is engaged", but divided those casualties between the 65% of "low morale" patients who were predisposed to break down and the 35% ("high morale") who were not. Most of the "low morale" cases, he argued,

> have a hereditary constitutional predisposition to breakdown, with a history of previous neurotic traits and of emotional trauma in early life; hence they may be classified as insecure persons who have always been dependent on their families. The precipitating cause often seems to have reactivated the pre-existing pattern associated in their subconscious minds with the previous nervous breakdown. The most common precipitating cause is the real or imagined "near miss;" the most common contributing factor is the death of close comrade or platoon officer. (Palmer, 1945, p. 456)

By contrast, Palmer's 35% of high morale cases was made up of people with no previous history who had been subjected to "anguish reactions", usually as a result of being exposed to terrible situations (about 5% overall) or were simply worn out after being in the line for too long (Palmer, 1945; see also Condé, 1997).

Palmer's basic distinction might seem simplistic. But it is certainly confirmed by film of British soldiers arriving at a Corps Exhaustion Centre after "three hellish days" of fighting near Monte Cassino, in Italy, in early 1944. One can see immediately that many of the cases are young men with well-groomed hair, clean battledresses, and cheerful expressions, who have simply run away or not gone into battle—the low morale cases; while others are mature men, with the rock-like presence of professional soldiers, their faces etched with exhaustion, guilt, and self-reproach after years of hard fighting (Imperial War Museum, 1944). Similar observations led many front-line psychiatrists in World War II to distinguish between "false" and "true" battle exhaustion cases (Copp & McAndrew, 1990, p. 113).

Looking at these two groups, one's first thought is that the young men, scarcely touched by the flame of war, will be fine, and that it is the older men, who have gone through so much, who will have problems later on. But, as we have seen, experience between the wars tended to show that the opposite was the case: that the man who had fought long and hard before breaking down usually recovered more quickly (Culpin, 1921, p. 319). Was this also the case after World War II? Unfortunately, that question cannot be directly answered, because the 1940s' post-war literature does not really pose it; it has other preoccupations. First, several studies of the "personality of the successful soldier" were conducted, usually with boringly common-sense results. The Canadian Boyd McNeel concluded that your behaviour in battle depended "on how you are brought up" (McNeel

& Dancey, 1945). More ambitiously, Albert Glass and his US Army colleagues in Italy interviewed some 200 soldiers as they were about to go into action, attempting to assess family history for neuroticism and disharmony, childhood neurotic traits, medical history, adult neurotic manifestations, and, finally, the degree of insecurity—a tall order in 10–15 minutes and reliant, of course, on the soldier's own testimony. Glass acknowledged that the "degree of insecurity" was the most difficult trait to "evaluate in any objective manner". The examiner, he said, "followed the classification of [Karen] Horney and attempted to evaluate the character constellation which served to protect the individual from hostile external forces. The over-aggressive, over-careful individuals were rated as mild, moderate or severe, according to the impression made upon the examiner at the time of the interview." Having described these elaborate procedures, however, Glass himself simply concluded that "previous civilian performance of the individual is the most effective prognostic indicator of his combat effectiveness" (Glass, 1949).

Second, there were some comparative studies of predisposition in chronic cases. Roy R. Grinker and his colleagues at the Don Cesar Hospital in Florida compared aircrew who had broken down with those who had not and concluded, in line with the then prevailing wind, that men who developed operational fatigue were characterized by

> parental discord, broken homes and unhappy childhood, difficulty in sibling relations; parental alcoholism, parental inconsistency and insincerity in instilling ego ideals; earlier age of independent work, frequent changing of jobs; less interest in sports and disinclination for group sports; later participation in social and sexual intercourse; greater dependence on home, especially mother who was in turn dependent on the son; greater frequency of overt neuroses and neurotic trends such as sleep disturbances, enuresis, nail-biting, stammering and frequent accidents; greater reaction to disturbing situations such as deaths, divorces, girl trouble etc.

On the other hand, "those who survived the rigors of combat were, prior to army life and combat, more aggressive, alert, slightly faster learners, more independent, came from more stable homes, were more capable of group identifications, and displayed less predispositional neurotic trends" (Grinker, Willerman, Bradley, & Fastovsky, 1946, p. 214).

Third, there were several American follow-up studies of veterans with psychological problems which paid little attention to men's pre-war or service records, but looked more at the factors helping their post-war rehabilitation. They mostly concluded that a job and a girl helped a veteran more than anything else, but seldom explained how changes in the social and cultural background had helped to promote this: the full employment and steady economic growth enjoyed by the United States after 1945, compared with the troubles of the 1920s; the army of experts and communicators telling America's women to give their returning menfolk "lavish and undemanding affection" while expecting "no immediate return"; and the well-organized and lavishly-funded rehabilitation programmes of the Veterans' Administration in the 1940s, instead of the shambles of the 1920s (Shephard, 2001, pp. 328–330).

Even this brief survey of the very diverse World War II literature shows that while the issue of predisposition is present, it is seldom dominant, and it usually takes a hybrid form, in which nature and nurture are intertwined (except for the Freudians). Of course the clinical writing, easily found in medical libraries today, needs also to be seen within the more elusive social and cultural context of the time (Fussell, 1989, shows how difficult it is to recover this). In Britain, there was constant tension between the old public-school idea that war is a test of "character" (an extension of the school playing field, and best met with stiff upper lip, to which the Royal Air Force and Navy still subscribed), versus "intelligence" (more modern, Freud-derived, psychological formulations which explained breakdown, rather than condemned it). The dominant theme in the United States seems to have been the more democratic "every man has his breaking point" (Huston, 1946; Kardiner & Spiegel, 1947, p. 33).

VIETNAM

I now want to fast-forward a couple of decades, to the 1960s. In the Vietnam era, predisposition did not simply return; it became the fault-line across which American psychiatry split. Indeed, for over two decades the issue of vulnerability became "controversial" in psychiatry. To understand why this was, we need to examine the way selection worked in this period.

The fundamental instrument of selection in the Vietnam era was not intelligence, or aptitude, or "character"; it was social class. That is a contentious statement, which will have to be justified before we can proceed further, because over the last two decades a "bitter and slippery methodological dispute" has raged over the issue of class and ethnicity in Vietnam and much energy has been devoted to rebutting the old journalistic (or antiwar) "Nam" stereotypes of an ill-disciplined, drug-infested, atrocity-committing, conscript Army, in which black Americans bore an unfair share of the burden of combat (Burkett & Whitley, 1998; Dean, 1997). We are now told that in fact 88.4% of those who served in Vietnam were "Caucasians", that only 25% were draftees, and that African Americans suffered 12.5% of the deaths at a time when "blacks of military age" made up 13.5% of the population (Vietnam Warriors: A Statistical Profile). Statistics are the ultimate truth of our age, but in their way they too can lie. These figures cover the whole theatre of war and the 11-year time-span of the "Vietnam era"; they do not necessarily describe reality on the ground at a particular moment. Also, according to some historians, "the fact that three quarters of Vietnam veterans were volunteers, though technically true, may be misleading since many volunteered only when they expected to be drafted" (De Groot, 2000, p. 273). But the big point here is generally accepted: that "76% of the men sent to Vietnam were from lower/middle working class backgrounds" (Vietnam Warriors) and that, in the words of James Webb, "the privileged avoided their responsibilities"; or, in Baskir and Strauss's more elegant formula, "the draft worked as an instrument of Darwinian social policy. The 'fittest'—those with background, wit or money—managed to escape. Through an elaborate structure of deferments, exemptions, legal technicalities and non-combatant military alternatives, the draft manipulated the system to their advantage" (Baskir & Strauss, 1978, p. 7). Certainly that is how it was seen at the time. Whatever historians and veterans' groups may now argue, it was generally thought in the 1960s that a process of social selection was at work and that Vietnam was, to quote Leslie Fiedler, "a war fought for us by our servants" (Dean, 1997, p. 184). This sense that Vietnam was "not an equal opportunity war" raises two different issues, which we have to try to keep apart. First, what impact did this kind of social selection have on psychiatric casualties in Vietnam? Second—and perhaps more pertinently for our purposes—how far did the perception that the war was socially unfair influence the psychiatry of it?

The thrust of the first question is clear. If it was generally found in World War II that the "successful soldier" came from a good home, had been well "brought up", and was functioning effectively in civilian life before entering the military, what significance should be attached to the fact that a substantial percentage (though not a majority) of those sent to Vietnam did *not* have such a background? Certainly, an Australian psychiatrist in Vietnam believes that the "violent and often self-destructive behaviour of many of the American veterans of the war" was directly related to the "recruitment policy" in that era (Spragg, 2003, pp. 228–229). Unfortunately, no authoritative historical study of that policy has been done and we therefore have to rely on isolated and often contradictory statements. Initially the military tested recruits for intelligence, as they had successfully done in the Korean War, using the Armed Forces Qualifying Test, which "correlates quite highly with standard IQ tests and thus taps cognitive ability quite well" (McNally, personal communication). However, as the need for manpower grew, "the ease with which those at the top of society escaped service forced the government to relax standards pertaining to those at the bottom, namely the mentally deficient" (De Groot, 2000, p. 315). Under "Project 100,000", presented as giving opportunity to the disadvantaged, some 350,000 men, some with an IQ of 62, were recruited. According to one authority, "forty per cent of the Project 100,000 recruits were trained for combat, compared to just 25% in the services generally. Four out of ten were black" (De Groot, 2000, p. 315). The phrase "cannon fodder" springs to mind.

At the same time no real attempt was made to screen for psychological vulnerability. A 1970 account explains:

> As a result of the painful and expensive lessons learned during World War II, routine psychiatric screening of all inductees was abandoned, and psychiatric criteria for rejection of inductees were revised to the extent that only persons with gross psychiatric disability are rejected.
>
> Doubtful cases are resolved by observing the individuals during basic training, where their psychiatric fitness for active duty can be assessed under actual military conditions. Marginally adjusted individuals can then be transferred to less stressful assignments where environmental supports are more readily available. This more liberal and flexible policy proved effective during the Korean conflict, where only two per cent of examined inductees were rejected on psychiatric grounds compared to five per cent during World War II, while psychiatric disability discharge rates dropped significantly from an average of 1.2% per year during World War II to 0.4 per cent during the Korean conflict. (Frank & Hoedemaker, 1970, p. 501)

The authors then explain that current policy is to reject those with psychosis, severe and debilitating psycho-neurotic reactions, and personality disorders like homosexuality and alcoholism, but, they add, *"men with character and behavior disorders are usually acceptable since these individuals frequently do well in the highly structured military environment"* (Frank & Hoedemaker, 1970, p. 501, emphasis added). The Vietnam War was putting that proposition to the test.

The Pentagon's "liberal and flexible" approach to recruiting, coupled with the sense of social inequality of the war, brought issues of "predisposition" to the fore, yet also made them politically sensitive. The result was a sharp split in the psychiatric profession, to which the political divisions of the war and the generational conflicts of the 1960s also contributed. On one side were the doctors of the World War II vintage, still seeking to apply the assumptions, classifications, and treatment methods of the 1940s; on the other,

baby-boomers who passionately identified with the grunts in Vietnam and wanted psychiatry to help them. This division could be seen both in South-East Asia and back in the
United States. In Vietnam, some older psychiatrists tried to maintain the World War II distinction between "true" and "false" war neurosis. Dr Robert Strange, for example, divided
his patients into three groups: the "men with a past history of maladaptation to society
[who were] more likely to experience a break down of functions" were classified as
"pseudo-combat fatigue"; those for whom combat aggravated a long-standing neurotic
problem ("combat neurosis"); and the 15% of patients for whom the term "combat fatigue"
was reserved, who "had a good pre-morbid adjustment and who cracked under extreme
stress" (Strange, 1969, quoted in Cavenar & Nash, 1976).

Against that, some younger doctors argued that these World War II distinctions no
longer meant much in Vietnam, especially after 1970; and that an epidemic of behavioural disorders was produced there not just by the soldiers' pre-war personalities but
by the circumstances of the war (Renner, 1973). It is noticeable that this second view
has now been officially endorsed. Franklin D. Jones writes in the *Textbook of Military
Medicine*:

> A major failing in the psychiatric management of casualties in the Vietnam conflict was in not
> recognizing early enough that psychiatric casualties were taking new forms: alcohol and drug
> abuse, and venereal disease and malaria from failure to take prophylactic measures. Armed with
> a stereotypical model of combat fatigue and a recipe for its treatment, psychiatrists were slow to
> recognize that escape from battle ("evacuation syndrome") had taken a new form. Even when the
> recognition occurred, the ability to adapt "forward treatment" to these casualties was hampered
> by moralizing and punitive regulations and by stereotyping casualties as drug addicts, alcoholics,
> cowards, and waverers. (Jones, 1995, p. 70)

This is certainly not what Jones was saying in earlier decades (e.g., Jones & Johnson,
1975; Spragg, 2003, pp. 194–197).

The divisions in Vietnam, however, were as nothing compared to the sound and fury
which the issue of "predisposition" generated back in the United States. Veterans' advocates such as Sarah Haley have recalled the impotent rage they felt when they were told
by their superiors in the VA that their patients' problems had nothing to do with Vietnam
and everything to do with their pre-morbid personalities (Scott, 1993). In 1985, one of the
intellectual leaders of the younger generation, Arthur S. Blank, Jr, a Yale-trained psychiatrist who served in Vietnam and was for many years the National Director of the
Veterans Outreach programme, included "irrational insistence on the primacy of predisposition" among the "irrational reactions to Post-Traumatic Stress Disorder".

> The predisposition theory of war stress reaction is the view that pretrauma personality charac-
> teristics—defects, flaws, and weaknesses—are the primary or most influential variable in the
> production of the condition. This view has its roots in the early writings of European analysts,
> who observed traumatized soldiers during and after World War I and interpreted their findings in
> terms of the early theories of psycho-analysis (Blank, 1985, p. 81).

Here, Blank was referring to the volume on *War Neurosis* published in 1919, to which
Freud, Ferenczi, Abraham, Jones, and Simmel contributed. "This work," Blank went on,

> emphasized quite naturally, in light of what was being discovered by psycho-analysis at the time—
> reverberations of war trauma with early childhood memories and conflicts. In part because of a

resulting *post hoc, ergo propter hoc* fallacy, this led to significant enthusiasm, among American psychiatrists at the time of World War II, for predicting which soldiers would break down in combat on the basis of psychiatric history and examination. (1985, pp. 81–82)

Blank then rehearsed the story of the failure of the World War II screening programme and of the subsequent post-mortems which had concluded that predisposition was not "the major factor in the production of war neurosis". Rather, he said, it had come to be seen that the acute stress reaction to combat is influenced by many factors and "a similar multicausal view with respect to chronic PTSD has been supported by the bulk of research during the post-Vietnam war period". Two recent studies, he said, had "failed to find any preservice predictors of post-war stress-related symptoms". And so, Blank concluded, the predisposition theory "has no standing at all among expert clinicians who treat significant numbers of war veterans, nor does it have a standing among those treating stress disorders in rape victims or survivors of civilian disasters". This view of the primacy of predisposition, he went on, "involves a failure on the part of both clinicians and researchers to evaluate premilitary, military, and postmilitary variables and influences carefully and without bias. At this time the predisposition theory is an instance of blaming the victim" (Blank, 1985, p. 83).

Blank clearly believed that he was administering the last rites to predisposition, driving the final stake through its heart, hammering down the coffin lid, and locking the monster in its tomb. Yet, only ten years later, it had escaped and was once more terrorizing the psychiatric community. How had this happened?

THE RETURN OF PREDISPOSITION 2

Historians hesitate when they approach the modern era—knowing that the perspective is flatter, the sources less reliable, and the judgements less certain. But, for all that, let's try and take this story up to date.

Even as psychiatrists like Blank were dismissing predisposition, they were signing up to another proposition—that trauma in soldiers was essentially the same thing as trauma in civilian disaster victims, raped women, tortured prisoners, and so on—that there is a "single common post-traumatic syndrome that is the final common pathway reached through a wide variety of relatively severe stressors". This was because, in order to strengthen their case, the advocates of treatment for Vietnam veterans linked "post-Vietnam syndrome" to other kinds of "trauma" and made common cause with other social groups, most notably, with the women's movement. And so PTSD, as defined in DSM-III in 1980, yoked together a number of different experiences of trauma which had hitherto been kept apart and gave them a common label (Scott, 1993; Young, 1995).

Inevitably, in the process, the specific social and environmental variables (of which leadership in war and social support after it were most important to the soldier) tended to get sacrificed to the common model, leaving the primary emphasis on the "stressor" and the "stressed". That process was strengthened when, in order to provide some theoretical cover for their nakedness, the creators of PTSD took on board elements of Hans Selye's stress-adaptation paradigm, producing a model which "largely followed the quantitative conception of stressors, in which events are viewed abstractly, as independent of the subjective experience of individuals" (Breslau & Davis, 1987, p. 260). The logic of this position was that the magnitude of the stressor determined the response and that PTSD was a *normal* response to an *abnormal* stressor.

This unitary model of trauma soon came under intellectual strain. For a start, there were problems in drawing the dividing line between normal and abnormal stress. More seriously, detailed empirical studies of war veterans and other kinds of trauma victims showed that the magnitude of the stressor was not the main determining factor. As Breslau and Davis put it, the literature

> does not support the view that extreme stressors form a discrete class of stressors in terms of the *probability* of psychiatric sequelae or the *distinctive nature* of subsequent psychopathology. Extraordinary stressors are like more ordinary stressful events with respect to the complex differential effects upon individuals. *Personal characteristics* [emphasis added] and nature of the social environment modify the likelihood and form of the response of individuals to all types of stressors. (Breslau & Davis, 1987, p. 255)

Breslau and Davis's magisterial article "tacitly reiterate[d] the relevance of the *vulnerability factor* for stress-induced syndromes", i.e. brought predisposition back into the picture (Escobar, 1987). It provoked strong counter-argument. Critics claimed that they had ignored evidence showing "the quantity of stress to be one of the best predictors of breakdown" (Ursano, 1987) or warned that such criticism might slow "forward momentum in the field" and cause "the systematic study of survivors of catastrophe once more to be ignored" (Lindy, Green, & Grace, 1987).

Breslau and Davis's arguments were developed by McFarlane in 1990 and then served up with some aplomb in a celebrated article by Yehuda and McFarlane in the *American Journal of Psychiatry* in 1995. Seven years on, they could be more relaxed about the social arguments, and acknowledge the role of political advocacy in the genesis of PTSD. The authors state up front as accepted fact that, in the case of PTSD, the cart went before the horse; that the order of things was, first, social and political; second, theoretical; and only third, empirical. Thus, a diagnosis was first constructed which would serve the political purpose of getting treatment for veterans; then a theoretical model for it assembled, using hypotheses borrowed from other fields (such as Selye's stress theory); and only then was the phenomenon *studied*. The whole edifice, they repeatedly emphasize, was built on the assumption that PTSD represents a normal response to an abnormal stressor and that, consequently, the magnitude of the stressor determines the level of symptoms. There is a simple quantitative effect (Yehuda & McFarlane, 1995).

Yehuda and McFarlane then draw on numerous empirical studies to show that extraordinary stressors do *not* usually produce trauma and the incidence of PTSD varies considerably between different groups and different situations. They thus destroy the whole logical basis of PTSD, as created in the DSM-III. Far from being a *normal* response to an abnormal stressor, it is clearly an *abnormal* response, found in some people and not in others. An individual's response to a stressor is therefore determined not simply by the stressor but by the interaction between the stressor and the victim's own premorbid vulnerability.

Then, having demolished the whole logical basis of PTSD and restored the notion of predisposition, Yehuda and MacFarlane boldly offer their own conception of how that predisposition works. But, where Breslau and Davis had tried to restore the role of social and environmental factors, the 1995 authors instead emphasize biological vulnerability. It is as if a conjuror, having made a white rabbit disappear, suddenly replaces it with a black one.

It says something for the immense socio-political investment made in PTSD that the psychiatric profession not only could hold its head up high after this devastating blow, but could embrace the new faith now being offered, with the same fervour as the old. Nor did the unitary concept of trauma fragment, as, logically, it should have done. Yehuda and McFarlane had rescued PTSD—that was the main thing. Never mind that they had completely transformed it.

So, psychiatry's dominant model of trauma at the end of the twentieth century was much the same as at the beginning—biological fragility. How similar is today's model of biological predisposition to Frederick Mott's "neuropath", with his inherited and acquired weakness of the nervous system? The current hypothesis is:

> The development of PTSD is facilitated by a failure to contain the biologic stress response at the time of the trauma, resulting in a cascade of alterations that lead to intrusive recollections of the event, avoidance of reminders of the event, and symptoms of hyperarousal. This failure may represent an alternative trajectory to the normal process of adaptation and recovery after a traumatic event. Prospective studies have shown that patients in whom PTSD or symptoms of PTSD develop have attenuated increases in cortisol levels in the immediate aftermath of a traumatic event, which may be related to prior exposure to a traumatic event or other risk factors. They also have higher heart rates in the emergency room and one week later than persons in whom PTSD does not develop. These findings suggest that patients with PTSD have a greater degree of activation of the sympathetic nervous system. (Yehuda, 2002, pp. 111–112)

The definition of the nervous system has expanded somewhat and the tools for measuring it are, of course, vastly superior, but I suspect Mott would recognize the underlying argument.

INTELLIGENCE RETURNS

It is worth mentioning one other aspect of the cycle, the return of the issue of intelligence. During the first half of the twentieth century, intelligence played an important part in discussions of "war neurosis", albeit in different ways. First, it was thought that intelligence was a protective factor, enabling a man to function better in the military and to avoid trouble when in action (Ahrenfeldt, 1958; Hendin & Haas, 1984; Hendin, Haas, Singer, Gold, & Trigos, 1983), though there were also those who argued that, in getting through war, it helped not to be too imaginative (Moran, 1945). Second, intelligence was found to be an important factor in a man's rehabilitation after war. Those with low intelligence were less likely to find jobs, have good social support networks, and, most probably, understand their symptoms (Lee, Vaillant, Torrey, & Elder, 1995; Shephard, 1996).

Yet, for almost a decade, the issue of intelligence hardly featured in the Vietnam veterans' literature. Rather, it was the level of exposure to atrocities, life threats and grotesque death, and the quality of social support which were felt to be the chief predictors of subsequent PTSD. However, in the late 1980s the large-scale National Veterans Readjustment Study (Kulka et al., 1990) did find that "veterans with low levels of premilitary educational achievement were at greater risk for developing PTSD than were other veterans",

and a year later a team at West Haven, VA, found that "low scores on a premilitary arithmetic aptitude test were associated with chronic PTSD". Then, in 1995, McNally and Shin
completed a study of 105 Vietnam combat veterans, concluding that "cognitive variables
may affect the ability to cope with trauma, thereby affecting whether a person develops
PTSD" (p. 936). More recently, it has been argued that "people with lower intelligence
are more likely to develop PTSD than are those with higher intelligence" (Macklin et al.,
1998).

    As always, the social context should be borne in mind. The 1970s were a time of agi-
tation and advocacy on behalf of Vietnam veterans, culminating in the "invention" of
PTSD in 1979 and the creation of outreach centres (Scott, 1993). There then followed a
decade of therapeutic optimism, sympathy towards veterans, and generous funding for
"trauma" research. However, by the early 1990s a reaction was setting in. A new mood of
therapeutic burnout and doubt about the value of veterans' treatment programmes had
arrived, which would culminate in Shalev asking what "twenty years of passionate rhetoric about trauma and the treatment of trauma" had actually produced (Shalev, 1997), Young
and Scott giving critical accounts of the genesis of PTSD (Scott, 1993; Young, 1995), and
Burkett and Whitley (1998) accusing psychiatrists of naïveté and worse in their book
Stolen Valor. The failure of veterans to get better, despite the treatment programmes provided for them, was once again changing the agenda, causing researchers to ask "Why
aren't they recovering?" instead of "Why were they traumatized?" The question of intelligence, politically unaskable for the previous decade, and still very sensitive, had now
become inescapable.

MODERN MILITARY SELECTION

Where, finally, do the military now stand on selection? Pretty much where they have in
the past. The predictive value of testing is not rated very highly; yet those who do break
down are often found to have predisposing weaknesses (Jones et al., 2003). And the gulf
between the ideal and real worlds is greater than ever; the current recruitment policy being
designed more to fill vacancies than prevent PTSD. Two examples must suffice. The
United States now recruits a much larger number of women into its armed forces, and
sends more of them nearer to combat, than ever before (Goldstein, 2001; van Creveld,
2001); yet most studies suggest that women are more susceptible to PTSD than men
(O'Brien, 1998). Equally, the British Army has had considerable recruiting problems in
recent years—there have been headlines about "scouring the prisons". Anecdotal
evidence suggests that something like 50% of the current intake comes from one-parent
families, usually without a father (author's conversations with British Army officers,
2001). Probably, in an ideal world, the Army would reject some of these men, but in
the real world it cannot afford to.

CONCLUSION

Traumatic events have profound long-term psycho-physiological consequences—for some
people. Most people, however, are extraordinarily resilient. In understanding and treating
this phenomenon—in knowing what balance to strike between the tough and the tender—

clinical experience matters more than theoretical brilliance or good intentions; living in a robust, self-confident culture also helps. In this branch of psychiatry, the getting of wisdom is a hard business; again and again, inexperienced doctors have got it wrong. Only with front-line experience, for example, did American World War II psychiatrists learn to distinguish the normal reaction to battle from the pathological (Ranson, 1949); only with experience is the danger of iatrogenic suggestion understood. This is why a book like T. A. Ross's *Lectures on the War Neuroses* (1940), which distils four decades of successful clinical work in war and peace into limpid humane prose, may have as much to tell us, however dated some of it may seem, as the latest biological research.

Of course, psychiatrists and psychologists cannot be like medieval schoolmen, relying for a thousand years on the works of Aristotle; they must reinterpret old truths for a new age, by exploiting modern neuroscience, for example. And, whatever their claims to the contrary, mental health professionals usually reflect the social values, intellectual fashions, and prejudices of their era. Modern "biological" models of PTSD perfectly reflect the atomized, de-socialized, individualistic, consumerist ethos of the twenty-first-century United States, the biochemical sense of self which now pervades popular culture, and the power of the pharmaceutical industry in modern medicine.

But simply to ignore and reject hard-won past experience is perverse. The PTSD generation of doctors carried this process to extraordinary lengths—thanks to a combination of arrogance, ignorance, and a wilful baby-boomer Oedipal reaction against conventional wisdom; and has, consequently, spent many dollars and destroyed many Canadian forests reaching conclusions which its predecessors took in with their mothers' milk. In 2000, delegates to a conference entitled "Trapped by Trauma" paid large sums to hear a prominent psychiatrist tell them (in a dazzling PowerPoint presentation) that they should "respect the patient's coping strategy", i.e., leave him alone and not debrief him. A year later, a leading researcher lamely conceded that "the approach suggested by studies of fear in rats is not dramatic and may appear to be simply one of 'common sense'" (Ledoux & Gorman, 2001). The suggestibility of patients is no longer a taboo subject, and now, with rich irony, trauma programmes seek to reinvent themselves by teaching the new buzz word—"resiliency". At the same time, the tragic events of 11 September 2001 may perhaps have given American professionals in particular a clearer sense of proportion.

This chapter has found a considerable amount of continuity on the question of predisposition. Experience in the twentieth century showed that, when exposed to the sustained strains of service life and combat, vulnerable individuals succumbed first but in the end "everyone has his breaking point". It also showed, time and again, that most people will recover spontaneously. The central question now confronting modern psychiatry is not how to fiddle with the DSM-IV; it is how to restore that resiliency.

Will psychiatrists have the sense to realize that by medicalizing the human response to stressful situations, they have created a culture of trauma and thus undermined the general capacity to resist trauma? They could make a start by dismantling the unitary concept of trauma, an idea that has long outlived its purpose. Any unit of classification that simultaneously encompasses the experience of surviving Auschwitz and that of being told rude jokes at work must, by any reasonable lay standard, be a nonsense, a patent absurdity.

If "trauma" could now be broken up into its constituent parts, it would return to its social contexts and be de-medicalized. But for that to happen, psychiatry would have to surrender ground, and history teaches us that such acts of professional self-denial are indeed rare. Besides, it is now too late. Trauma has been vectored into the wider society by the law and the media; armies of half-trained counsellors now live off it. In the past, when psychiatry took a wrong turning, it often took the intervention of a major lay figure like General Marshall to restore sanity. How the present confusion will be brought to an end is hard to predict.

REFERENCES

Ahrenfeldt, R. H. (1958). *Psychiatry in the British Army in the Second World War*. London: Routledge.

Armstrong-Jones, R. (1917). The psychopathy of the barbed wire. *Nature, 100*, 1–3.

Artiss, K. L. (1963). Human behaviour under stress: From combat psychiatry to social psychiatry. *Military Medicine, 128*, 1011–1015.

Bailey, P., Williams, F. E., Komora, P. O., Salmon, T. W., & Fenton, N. (1929). *The Medical Department of the United States Army in the World War*, Vol. X, *Neuropsychiatry*. Washington, DC: US Government Printing Office.

Baskir, L. M., & Strauss, W. A. (1978). *Chance and circumstance*. New York: Knopf.

Benton, G. H. (1921). War neuroses and allied conditions in ex-servicemen. *Journal of the American Medical Association, 77*, 360–365.

Blank, A. S. (1985). Irrational reactions to Post-Traumatic Stress Disorder and Viet Nam veterans. In S. Sonnenberg et al. (eds), *The trauma of war: Stress and recovery in Viet Nam veterans*. Washington, DC: American Psychiatric Press.

Blank, A. S. (1993). The longitudinal course of posttraumatic stress disorder. In J. R. T. Davidson & E. B. Foa (eds), *Posttraumatic stress disorder: DSM IV and beyond*. Washington, DC: American Psychiatric Press.

Breslau, N., & Davis, G. C. (1987). Posttraumatic stress disorder: The stressor criterion. *Journal of Nervous and Mental Disease, 175*, 255–264.

Brill, N. Q., & Beebe, G. W. (1951). Follow-up study of psychoneuroses. *American Journal of Psychiatry, 108*, 417–425.

Burkett, B. G., & Whitley, G. (1998). *Stolen valor: How the Vietnam generation was robbed of its heroes and its history*. Dallas, TX: Verity.

Carson, J. (1993). Army alpha, army brass, and the search for army intelligence. *Isis, 84*, 278–309.

Cavenar, J. O., & Nash, J. L. (1976). The effects of combat on the normal personality: War neurosis in Vietnam returnees. *Comprehensive Psychiatry, 17*, 647–653.

Condé, A.-M. (1997). "The ordeal of adjustment": Australian psychiatric casualties in the Second World War. *War and Society, 15*, 61–74.

Copp, T., & McAndrew, B. (1990). *Battle exhaustion: Soldiers and psychiatrists in the Canadian Army, 1939–1945*. Montreal: McGill-Queen's University Press.

Cox, C. (2001). Invisible wounds: The American Legion, shell-shocked veterans and American society, 1919–1924. In M. S. Micale & P. Lerner (eds), *Traumatic pasts: History, psychiatry and trauma in the modern age, 1870–1930*. Cambridge: Cambridge University Press.

Crew, F. A. E. (1962). *The Army Medical Services: Campaigns*, Vol. IV, *North-West Europe*. London: Her Majesty's Stationery Office.

Culpin, M. (1921). The problem of the neurasthenic pensioner. *British Journal of Medical Psychology, 10*, 316–328.

Culpin, M. (1931). *Recent advances in the study of the psycho-neuroses*. London: Churchill.

Dean, E. T. (1997). *Shook over Hell: Post-traumatic stress, Vietnam and the Civil War*. Cambridge, MA: Harvard University Press.

De Groot, G. J. (2000). *A noble cause? America and the Vietnam War*. Harlow: Longman.

Escobar, J. I. (1987). Posttraumatic stress disorder and the perennial stress-diathesis controversy. *Journal of Nervous and Mental Disease, 175*, 265–266.

Fairbairn, W. R. D. (1943). The war neuroses: Their nature and significance. *British Medical Journal, i*, 183–186.

Frank, I. M., & Hoedemaker, F. S. (1970). The civilian psychiatrist and the draft. *American Journal of Psychiatry, 127*, 497–502.

Fussell, P. (1989). *Wartime: Understanding and behaviour in the Second World War*. New York: Oxford University Press.

Ginzberg, E., Anderson, J. K., Ginzberg, S. W., & Herma, J. L. (1959). *The ineffective soldier*. New York: Columbia University Press.

Glass, A. J. (1949). An attempt to predict probable combat effectiveness by brief psychiatric examination. *American Journal of Psychiatry, 106*, 81–90.

Glass, A. J. (ed.) (1966). *Neuropsychiatry in World War II*, Vol. 1. Washington, DC: Office of the Surgeon General.

Goldstein, J. S. (2001). *War and gender: How gender shapes the war system and vice versa*. Cambridge: Cambridge University Press.

Gould, S. J. (1981). *The mismeasure of man*. New York: Norton.

Greene, R. S. (1977). The role of the psychiatrist in World War II. PhD thesis, Columbia University.

Grinker, R., Willerman, B., Bradley, A. D., & Fastovsky, A. (1946). A study of psychological predisposition to the development of operational fatigue. *American Journal of Orthopsychiatry, 16*, 191–214.

Hadfield, J. A. (1942). War neurosis: A year in a neuropathic hospital. *British Medical Journal, i*, 281–285, 320–323.

Henderson, J. L., & Moore, M. (1944). The psychoneuroses of war. *New England Journal of Medicine, 230*, 273–278.

Hendin, H., & Haas, A. P. (1984). Combat adaptations of Vietnam veterans without posttraumatic stress disorders. *American Journal of Psychiatry, 141*, 956–960.

Hendin, H., Haas, A. P., Singer, P., Gold F., & Trigos, G. G. (1983). The influence of precombat personality on posttraumatic stress disorder. *Comprehensive Psychiatry, 24*, 530–534.

Hunt, W. A., Wittson, C. L., & Hunt, E. B. (1952). Military performance of a group of marginal neuropsychiatric cases. *American Journal of Psychiatry, 109*, 168–171.

Huston, J. (1946). *Let There Be Light*, directed by John Huston, US War Department.

Imperial War Museum (1944). Corps Exhaustion Centre, Department of Film.

Jones, E., Hodgins-Vermaas, R., McCartney, H., Beech, C., Palmer, I., Hyams, K. et al. (2003). Flashbacks and post-traumatic stress disorder: The genesis of a 20th-century diagnosis. *British Journal of Psychiatry, 182*, 158–163.

Jones, E., Hyams, K. C., & Wessely, S. (2003). Screening for vulnerability to psychological disorders in the military: An historical survey. *Journal of Medical Screening, 10*, 40–46.

Jones, E., & Wessely, S. (2001). Psychiatric battle casualties: An intra- and interwar comparison. *British Journal of Psychiatry, 178*, 242–247.

Jones, F. D. (1995). Disorders of frustration and loneliness. In F. D. Jones, L. R. Sparacino, V. L. Wilcox, J. M. Rothberg, & J. W. Stokes (eds), *Textbook of military medicine: War psychiatry*. Falls Church, VA: Office of the Surgeon General.

Jones, F. D., & Johnson, A. W. (1975). Medical and psychiatric treatment policy and practice in Vietnam. *Journal of Social Issues, 31*, 49–65.

Kardiner, A., & Spiegel, H. (1947). *War stress and neurotic illness*. New York: Hoeber.

Kevles, D. (1968). Testing the Army's intelligence: Psychology and the military in World War I. *Journal of American History, 55*, 565–581.

Klein, J. J. (1951). A study of unstable personalities after combat. *Journal of Nervous and Medical Disorder, 113*, 437–448.

Kulka, R. A., Schlenger, W. E., Fairbank, J. A., Hough, R. L., Jordan, B. K., Marmar, C. R. et al., (1990). *Trauma and the Vietnam generation.* New York: Brunner Mazel.

Ledoux, J. E., & Gorman, J. M. (2001). A call to action: Overcoming anxiety through active coping. *American Journal of Psychiatry, 158*, 1953–1955.

Lee, K. A., Vaillant, G. E., Torrey, W. C., & Elder, G. H. (1995). A 50-year prospective study of the psychological sequelae of World War II combat. *American Journal of Psychiatry, 152*, 516–522.

Lindy, J., Green, B. L., & Grace, M. C. (1987). Commentary: The stressor criterion and posttraumatic stress disorder. *Journal of Nervous and Mental Disease, 175*, 269–272.

Macklin, M. L., Metzger, L. J., Litz, B. T., McNally, R. J., Lasko, N. B., Orr, S. P. et al., (1998). Lower precombat intelligence is a risk factor for posttraumatic stress disorder. *Journal of Consulting and Clinical Psychology, 66*, 323–326.

McFarlane, A. C. (1990). Vulnerability to posttraumatic stress disorder. In M. E. Wolf & A. D. Mosnaim (eds), *Posttraumatic stress disorder: Etiology, phenomenology, and treatment* (pp. 2–21). Washington, DC: American Psychiatric Press.

McNally, R. J., & Shin, L. M. (1995). Association of intelligence with severity of posttraumatic stress disorder symptoms in Vietnam combat veterans. *American Journal of Psychiatry, 152*, 936–938.

McNeel, B. H., & Dancey, T. E. (1945). The personality of the successful soldier. *American Journal of Psychiatry, 102*, 337–342.

Menninger, W. C. (1948). *Psychiatry in a troubled world.* New York: Macmillan.

Moran, C. (1945). *The anatomy of courage.* London: Constable.

Mott, F. W. (1913). The neuropathic inheritance. *Journal of Mental Science, 59*, 222–261.

Mott, F. W. (1919). *War neuroses and shell shock.* Oxford: Oxford University Press.

O'Brien, L. S. (1998). *Traumatic events and mental health.* Cambridge: Cambridge University Press.

Palmer, H. (1945). Military psychiatric casualties: Experience with 12,000 cases. *Lancet, ii*, 454–457, 492–494.

Plesset, M. R. (1946). Psychoneurotics in combat. *American Journal of Psychiatry, 103*, 87–90.

Ranson, S. W. (1949). The normal battle reaction: Its relation to the pathologic battle reaction. *Bulletin of the US Army Medical Department, 9, Supplement*, 3–11.

Reed, J. (1987). Robert M. Yerkes and the mental testing movement. In M. Sokal (ed.), *Psychological testing and American society, 1890–1930.* Brunswick, NJ: Rutgers University Press.

Renner, J. A. (1973). The changing patterns of psychiatric problems in Vietnam. *Comprehensive Psychiatry, 14*, 169–180.

Ross, T. A. (1940). *Lectures on the war neuroses.* Oxford: Oxford University Press.

Samelson, F. (1977). World War I intelligence testing and the development of psychology. *Journal of the History of the Behavioural Sciences, 13*, 272–282.

Scott, W. (1993). *The politics of readjustment: Vietnam veterans since the war.* New York: Aldine de Gruyter.

Shalev, A. (1997). Discussion: Treatment of prolonged posttraumatic stress disorder. *Journal of Traumatic Stress, 10*, 415–423.

Sharp, W. L. (1950). Fate of 395 mild psychoneurotic cases salvaged from training period and taken into combat. *American Journal of Psychiatry, 106*, 801–807.

Shephard, B. (1996). "The early treatment of Mental Disorders": R. G. Rows and Maghull, 1914–1918. In H. Freeman & G. E. Berrios (eds), *150 years of British psychiatry,* Vol. II: *The aftermath.* London: Gaskell.

Shephard, B. (1999a). "Pitiless Psychology": The role of prevention in British military psychiatry in the Second World War. *History of Psychiatry, 10*, 491–524.

Shephard, B. (1999b). Shell-shock. In H. Freeman (ed.), *A century of psychiatry* (pp. 33–40). London: Mosby-Wolfe.

Shephard, B. (2001). *A war of nerves: Soldiers and psychiatrists in the twentieth century.* Cambridge, MA: Harvard University Press.

Shephard, B. (2002). The rise of the trauma culture. In J. E. Hovens & G. J. Van der Ploeg (eds), *De historie van de psychiatrie als basis voor de toekomst.* Rotterdam: Delta Psychiatrisch Ziekenhuis.

Slater, E. (1943). The neurotic constitution: A statistical study of two thousand neurotic soldiers. *Journal of Neurology and Psychiatry, 6*, 1–16.

Smith, G. E., & Pear, T. (1917). *Shell-shock and its lessons.* Manchester: Manchester University Press.

Spragg, G. (2003). *When good men do nothing.* Loftus, New South Wales: Australian Military History Publications.

Strange, R. E. (1969). Effects of combat stress on hospital ship psychiatric evacuees. In P. G. Bourne (ed.), *Psychology and physiology of stress* (pp. 75–83). New York: Academic Press.

Strecker, E. A. (1945). *Their mothers' sons: The psychiatrist examines an American problem.* Philadelphia, PA: Lippincott.

Thom, T. (1923). The patient and his attitude toward his neurosis. *Mental Hygiene, 8*, 234–247.

Ursano, R. J. (1987). Commentary: Posttraumatic stress disorder: The stressor criterion. *Journal of Nervous and Mental Disease, 175*, 273–275.

Van Creveld, M. (2001). *Men, women and war: Do women belong in the front line?* London: Cassell.

Vietnam Warriors: A statistical profile in uniform and in country. Reprinted from 1997 VFW magazine. www.namvets.com

War Office (1922). *Report of the War Office Committee of Enquiry into "Shell-Shock".* London: His Majesty's Stationery Office.

Wolfsohn, J. (1918). The pre-disposing factors of war psycho-neurosis. *The Lancet, i*, 177–180.

Wylie, P. (1942). *Generation of vipers.* New York: Farrar and Rinehardt.

Yehuda, R. (2002). Post-traumatic stress disorder. *New England Journal of Medicine, 346*, 108–114.

Yehuda, R., & McFarlane, A. C. (1995). Conflict between current knowledge about posttraumatic stress disorder and its original conceptual basis. *American Journal of Psychiatry, 152*, 1705–1713.

Young, A. (1995). *The harmony of illusions. Inventing post-traumatic stress disorder.* Princeton, NJ: Princeton University Press.

Young, A. (2001). Our traumatic neurosis and its brain. *Science in Context, 14*, 661–683.

"Youth in Crisis" (1943). *March of Time* newsreel.

4 Unresolved Issues in the Assessment of Trauma Exposure and Posttraumatic Reactions

B. CHRISTOPHER FRUEH

Department of Psychiatry and Behavioral Sciences, Medical University of South Carolina, USA

JON D. ELHAI

Disaster Mental Health Institute, University of South Dakota, USA

DANNY G. KALOUPEK

Department of Psychiatry and Behavioral Neuroscience, Boston University School of Medicine, USA

At the heart of current knowledge of traumatic events and posttraumatic reactions is our ability to assess these phenomena. Through these efforts we have data indicating that the lifetime prevalence of reported trauma exposure in the United States ranges between 40 and 70% (Breslau, Davis, Andreski, & Peterson, 1991; Kessler, Sonnega, Bromet, Hughes, & Nelson, 1995; Norris, 1992; Resnick, Kilpatrick, Dansky, Saunders, & Best, 1993), and lifetime prevalence of posttraumatic stress disorder (PTSD) ranges between 8 and 14% (Breslau, 2002; Kaplan, Sadock, & Grebb, 1994; Kessler et al., 1995). Furthermore, trauma and PTSD have been associated with a wide range of psychiatric comorbidity (Keane & Kaloupek, 1997; Keane & Wolfe, 1990; Kilpatrick et al., 2000, 2003), impaired functioning across the full spectrum of daily life (Jordan et al., 1992), decreased medical health status (Schnurr, Spiro, & Paris, 2000), increased medical care utilization (Calhoun, Bosworth, Grambow, Dudley, & Beckham, 2002; Deykin et al., 2001; Walker et al., 1999, 2003), and general societal costs (Kessler, 2000; Solomon & Davidson, 1997). This evidence characterizes the syndrome of PTSD as a prevalent, complex, and severe psychiatric disorder that adversely impacts the public health in diverse and costly ways.

Our knowledge and conceptual base of PTSD have grown dramatically since the disorder was first established in 1980. Nevertheless, a growing body of new evidence, and critical reconsideration of previous data, remind us that we are only beginning to understand the complexity of posttrauma reactions. Many fundamental issues, including several related to assessment, need clarification (Kroll, 2003; McNally, 2003a). A better understanding of those issues that impact our ability to accurately and reliably evaluate the psy-

Posttraumatic Stress Disorder: Issues and Controversies. Edited by G. M. Rosen.
© 2004 John Wiley & Sons, Ltd. ISBN 0-470-86284-X/0-470-86285-8.

chological consequences of trauma requires discussion of the phenomenology of PTSD, socio-cultural concerns, critical issues in the assessment of traumatic experiences and PTSD symptoms, the status of current assessment instruments, future research directions, and implications for clinical practice.

PHENOMENOLOGY OF PTSD

For all domains in mental health there is a reciprocal relationship between the instruments we use to evaluate the construct and our understanding of the nature (e.g., characteristics, epidemiology) of that construct. In other words, the manner in which we characterize psychiatric domains helps shape the content of associated assessment instruments, while application of the assessment instruments influences how we characterize and refine psychiatric domains. This iterative process generally involves the incremental incorporation of new scientific findings on a constant, ongoing basis. There are several phenomenological issues that limit our ability to most effectively conduct assessments of trauma exposure and PTSD. At the same time, there are important conceptual issues that studies using various assessment strategies may help resolve.

ASSESSING TRAUMATIC EVENTS

PTSD is nearly unique among psychiatric disorders in that the diagnostic criteria specify an etiological event (Criterion A). In the current *Diagnostic and Statistical Manual of Mental Disorders* (DSM-IV; APA, 1994) Criterion A for PTSD is represented as follows: (A1) that the event involved actual or threatened death or serious injury to self or others, and (A2) that the person's response involved intense fear, helplessness, or horror (APA, 1994). In the years since 1980 when PTSD was first recognized by the DSM, boundaries for Criterion A1 (i.e., defining a potentially traumatic event) have broadened to include not only events that an individual may have experienced, but also events that have been witnessed. These extensions of Criterion A are less obviously "traumatic" than the classic A1 experiences of a violent rape or military combat. The implication of this expansion of the criteria is to effectively shift emphasis away from A1 toward the subjective reactions outlined by A2. Individuals are now considered to have experienced trauma simply by being horrified by events they merely learn about, or by events that common sense and basic human experience identify as distressing or upsetting (e.g., death of a loved one, overhearing inappropriate jokes in the workplace). For example, several reports in the wake of the terrorist attacks on September 11, 2001, imply that watching news broadcasts depicting violent and horrific events constitutes a trauma (Schuster et al., 2001; Silver, Holman, McIntosh, Poulin, & Gil-Rivas, 2002). McNally (2003a) has termed this broadening of the stressor criterion, "conceptual bracket creep."

The expanded definition of "trauma" reflected a deliberate effort to eliminate the phrase "outside the range of normal human experience" (DSM-III-R) because evidence had indicated that potentially traumatic experiences were widespread and relatively common (e.g., Kessler et al., 1995). Findings also demonstrated that an expansion of Criterion A increased the range and number of events that could support a PTSD diagnosis (Breslau & Kessler, 2001), without drastically affecting PTSD prevalence rates. This means that many more people can now be considered "trauma victims," and efforts to evaluate the impact of traumas such as sexual assault or combat may be substantially diluted. The broadening of Criterion A also has important implications for litigation and disability claims, as will be discussed later.

Adding to difficulties with the current definition of the stressor criterion is the possibility that the subjective reactions contained in the A2 criterion of trauma (i.e., fear, helplessness, or horror) may not be very meaningful. Recent evidence suggests that A2 may not contribute much incremental validity to the definition of trauma or add clinically useful information (Brewin, Andrews, & Rose, 2000), because most people who meet A1 also meet A2 (Breslau & Kessler, 2001; Creamer, McFarlane, & Burgess, 2003). There also are conceptual problems with A2, including the retrospective nature of such reports, and the potential for current symptoms to influence memories of trauma reactions. Questions can be raised about how to interpret the reactions of trauma survivors who report that they dissociated and do not remember their peritraumatic emotions (reactions that occurred during the event). Finally, the suggestion has been made that A2 may be defined too narrowly, and should be broadened to include other intense emotions, such as anger or shame (Brewin et al., 2000).

ASSESSING THE SYMPTOM CRITERIA

According to the current DSM (DSM-IV; APA, 1994) the symptoms of PTSD are listed in three categories (i.e., clusters B–D), that include reexperiencing (cluster B), avoidance and emotional numbing (cluster C), and symptoms of hyperarousal (cluster D). There is only limited support for this three-factor model of the syndrome, a finding that calls into question our very definition of the construct. Recent studies using factor analyses have found best fit models ranging from 2 to 5 factors (Buckley, Blanchard, & Hickling, 1998; Cordova, Studts, Hann, Jacobsen, & Andrykowski, 2000; King, Leskin, King, & Weathers, 1998; Simms, Watson, & Doebbeling, 2002; Taylor, Kuch, Koch, Crockett, & Passey, 1998). The issue of the structure of PTSD remains unsettled, in part because no two studies have used the same methods with the same population. Therefore, we cannot know whether structural differences represented across studies are related to use of different measures, different analytic approaches, different populations, or error variance. What is clear is that the structure represented in DSM is open to question.

A related issue concerns a lack of clarity regarding PTSD subtypes. A number of recent cluster analytic studies have shown that there is significant heterogeneity in the manifestation of posttrauma responses among trauma survivors, including different patterns of symptom manifestation and severity (Elhai, Frueh, Davis, Jacobs, & Hamner, 2003b; Elhai, Klotz-Flitter, Gold, & Sellers, 2001; Follette, Naugle, & Follette, 1997), mediated perhaps by personality style (Miller, Greif, & Smith, 2003). At this point, no subtypes have been consistently recognized, again partly due to limited research and lack of uniformity with respect to measures, samples, and statistical approaches. Heterogeneity in PTSD presentations is potentially important for both classification and intervention purposes. In particular, it will be interesting to determine whether certain clusters or subtypes of PTSD are more responsive to specific treatment components (e.g., exposure therapy, social skills training, psychiatric medication), with the goal of developing treatment matching strategies.

Another issue related to lack of clarity in the factor structure of PTSD is that many of the defining symptoms overlap with other Axis I psychiatric disorders, most notably depression, specific phobia, and other anxiety disorders. Sleep disturbance, impaired concentration, social isolation, loss of interest in activities, restricted affect, anger and irritability all may represent symptoms of depression, while cued reactivity to salient environmental cues and avoidance may represent symptoms of other anxiety disorders. The extent to which evaluating these symptoms adds clarity to a differential diagnosis of PTSD is unclear at this point. A recent factor analysis of PTSD symptoms among Gulf War veterans illustrates the issue (Simms et al., 2002). In this study, a four-factor solution provided the best fit. One of the identified factors was a broad "dysphoria" that included several symptoms of numbing/hyperarousal and was highly correlated with depressive symptoms. Convergent and discriminant validity correlations further suggested that reexperiencing symptoms were relatively specific to PTSD (Simms et al., 2002). These findings supported earlier work that suggested reexperiencing, along with physiological and emotional reactivity, best distinguished PTSD from other affective or anxiety disorders (Foa & Riggs, 1995; Orr et al., 1990). However, these findings are not replicated, and it is not clear exactly which symptoms should be evaluated, or how they should be weighted to establish a diagnosis of PTSD. This means that the sensitivity and specificity of PTSD measures, along with our ability to make differential diagnoses and accurately recognize comorbid psychiatric disorders, are reduced.

Yet another issue of relevance to the factor structure of PTSD is that it is not clear whether the latent structure of the disorder is categorical (taxonic) or continuous (dimensional). Just as recent research has suggested that depression is dimensional in nature (Franklin, Strong, & Greene, 2002; A. M. Ruscio & J. Ruscio, 2002; J. Ruscio & A. M. Ruscio, 2000), at least one study has demonstrated that the latent structure of PTSD also is dimensional (A. M. Ruscio, J. Ruscio, & Keane, 2002). This suggests that what is often recognized as "PTSD" is not a discrete clinical syndrome, but rather the high end of an acute stress response continuum. Such findings argue against the use of instrument cutpoints to classify individuals as having, or not having, a diagnosis of PTSD. A dimensional view of PTSD also has implications for matching an assessment approach to the latent structure of the construct, perhaps incorporating dimensional scaling models such as item response theory (see J. Ruscio & A. M. Ruscio, 2002, for a comprehensive discussion of this issue). Otherwise, there is a potential mismatch between a categorical diagnostic system (DSM) and the continuum that better fits the latent structure of posttrauma reactions.

In summary, although we have made great progress since 1980 in refining the construct of PTSD, at this point there remains disagreement about the most suitable definition of "trauma," and uncertainty about the factor structure and latent structure of this disorder. There also remains a limited understanding regarding symptom overlap with other psychiatric disorders and limited progress toward identifying subtypes within the PTSD domain. Thus, we cannot say that we understand the syndrome of PTSD as well as we need, in order to evaluate and diagnose as accurately and reliably as one might wish. This statement has several implications. Most importantly, our understanding of the phenomenological characteristics of PTSD, as with virtually all psychiatric disorders, must be considered tentative; our current acceptance of PTSD prevalence rates must be considered preliminary; and our reliance on PTSD assessment instruments must be tempered with cautious skepticism and awareness that these measures are inherently developmental in nature.

SOCIO-CULTURAL ISSUES

The formal recognition of PTSD as a syndrome in DSM had its genesis in the aftermath of the wars of the twentieth century (for historical reviews see Burkett & Whitley, 1998; Shephard, 2001), particularly the Vietnam War when returning US soldiers were exhibiting a range of troublesome behaviors and symptoms. Since 1980, the socio-cultural role of trauma reactions and PTSD has evolved, as a large number of diverse groups—such as clinicians, investigators, politicians, victim advocates, human rights activists, and lawyers, to name but a few—have contributed and competed to shape what it means to be a trauma survivor. Perhaps more than any other psychiatric disorder, PTSD has a personal and political valence that influences how mental health professionals and society view the construct and respond to those who carry the diagnosis.

Recent years have seen an expansion of trauma-related disability-seeking and litigation. Because defining criteria include an etiological component (i.e., trauma exposure), PTSD is particularly well suited as a basis for seeking disability compensation or pursuing litigation. Although there are many possible instances of this growing trend throughout the United States, there are two recent examples that illustrate the point well. With regard to disability-seeking, evidence from the Veterans Affairs (VA) system indicates that PTSD disability claims among veterans reporting combat exposure has risen dramatically since 1985 (Murdoch, Nelson, & Fortier, 2003), reporting the largest number of claims for any psychiatric condition (Oboler, 2000). Furthermore, 69–94% of veterans seeking treatment within VA specialty PTSD mental health clinics apply for psychiatric disability (Fontana & Rosenheck, 1998; Frueh, Smith, & Barker, 1996; Frueh et al., 2003a). With regard to litigation, a multitude of lawsuits has been brought against Catholic churches in the United States (McNally, 2003b). Starting with a number of alleged childhood sexual abuse cases against members of the Boston archdiocese, a strategic effort by a relatively small number of tort lawyers sought out new claimants at the national level. It is expected now that hundreds of millions of dollars will be paid out over the next decade in legal settlements. The lesson has quickly been picked up by tort lawyers for other victim segments across the country, including those who claim to have been psychologically harmed by asbestos exposure, the fast food industry, harassment in the workplace, etc. Financial incentives for those who demonstrate they have been unfairly harmed, and have suffered deleterious post-traumatic reactions (i.e., PTSD), likely have important implications for our ability to assess PTSD symptoms in the individual case. These same considerations also could impact the scientific literature, possibly inflating PTSD prevalence rates in some studies. Accordingly, there has been a recent call for journal editors to require investigators to document and report the disability-seeking and litigation status of their subjects when studies pertain to trauma and PTSD (Rosen, 2004).

It may not be a coincidence that much of the expanding definition of trauma involves events or situations that have significant socio-cultural, legal, or political dimensions (e.g., sexual harassment, exposure to hazardous materials, coping with AIDS/HIV, vicarious trauma among care providers, and slavery reparations). This is not to say that these experiences cannot be traumatic (indeed, many clearly have the potential to meet DSM Criterion A for PTSD). At the same time, when non-scientific consider-ations weigh more heavily than research evidence, there is a risk to the integrity of the field.

TRENDS TOWARD PATHOLOGIZING NORMAL REACTIONS TO STRESS, ADVERSITY, AND TRAUMA

There appears to be a growing socio-cultural expectation that individuals who have expe-rienced extreme stress, adversity, or trauma will suffer significant psychological reactions. Nowhere was this more poignantly illustrated than in New York in the aftermath of the September 11, 2001, terrorist attacks. Several large survey studies conducted soon after the attacks reported high rates of PTSD (DeLisi et al., 2003; Galea et al., 2002; Schlenger et al., 2002). "Project Liberty" was initiated as a part of New York State's response to the attacks, funded by the Federal Emergency Management Agency. Evidently, initial expec-tations and concerns were exaggerated. Several subsequent studies showed that initial spikes in PTSD symptoms among New Yorkers were soon followed by a sharp drop in post-incident reactions (Silver et al., 2002), and the dramatic need for counseling services anticipated via Project Liberty never materialized (Boscarino, Galea, Ahern, Resnick, & Vlahov, 2002; Satel, in press). Such findings raise the concern that we should not rush to apply psychiatric labels to what may be relatively brief and normal human reactions in the face of tragic events. Put another way: most humans appear to be far less fragile than many mental health professionals anticipate (see Satel, in press, for a discussion of this issue).

ISSUES IN THE ASSESSMENT OF TRAUMA EXPOSURE AND PTSD SYMPTOMS

Given that the first element in providing a diagnosis of PTSD is a history of exposure to traumatic events (Criterion A), it seems clear that assessment of this etiological event is of critical importance. There are several unresolved issues that suggest this assessment may be problematic. First, as noted earlier, there are concerns regarding the broadened definition of "trauma," as well as inherent ambiguities in the definition. These issues make it difficult for clinicians and investigators to determine what "counts" as a traumatic event. For example, does a military veteran meet Criterion A for PTSD if his only experience in the field was to hear the sounds of combat from a distance, accompanied by the fear that the battle could move closer? How does this compare to the experience of a veteran involved directly in combat and wounded under fire? What about the trauma potential for a Midwestern American watching the evening news on September 11, 2001, as compared to the New York City resident who directly survived the terrorist attacks of that day?

A second unresolved issue in the assessment of trauma exposure concerns the fallibil-ity of memory (King et al., 2000; Krinsley, Gallagher, Weathers, Kutter, & Kaloupek, 2003; Roemer, Litz, Orsillo, Ehlich, & Friedman, 1998; Southwick, Morgan, Nicolaou, & Charney, 1997). Interviewers are usually reliant on the retrospective reports of trauma sur-vivors as the basis for identifying and quantifying the intensity of a traumatic stressor. Yet, there is evidence that individuals have difficulty providing accurate and reliable accounts of potentially traumatic experiences, especially when subjected to a heightened state of psychological distress (Loftus, 2003; McNally, 2003a, 2003b). For example, in a study of Gulf War veterans, close to 90% of the participants recounted aspects of their combat experiences differently over two points in time (Southwick et al., 1997). Two years after their initial evaluation, 70% described a traumatic combat event that they had not previously reported, while 46% failed to include a traumatic combat event that had been reported initially. Furthermore, PTSD severity at the time of the second evaluation was correlated with the number of newly reported traumatic events. The issue that human memory for traumatic events is fallible and influenced by current clinical status lies at the heart of controversies surrounding repressed and recovered memories of childhood sexual abuse (Brown, Scheflin, & Whitfield, 1999; Loftus, 2003; McNally, 2003a, 2003b; McNally, Clancy, Schacter, & Pitman, 2000; Pope, Hudson, Bodkin, & Oliva, 1998).

Inaccuracies in an individual's recall of past events highlights a need to objectively corroborate verbal reports. Unfortunately, this is not always possible. Individuals seen in clinical settings and PTSD research studies frequently report trauma histories that occurred in the distant past. Often, the reported events are so personal and private that they cannot be verified via historical records. As a consequence, it can be extremely difficult to detect not only benign memory distortion, but also intentional efforts to exaggerate or fake traumatic reports. A specific example of this problem is the contention that there are bogus combat veterans who have defrauded the VA system and distorted published research findings on PTSD (Burkett & Whitley, 1998). Frueh and colleagues demonstrated that such concerns are warranted (Frueh et al., 2003b). A request was filed under the Freedom of Information Act to obtain military records from the National Military Personnel Records on 100 consecutive veterans who reported Vietnam combat during their evaluations at a VA PTSD specialty clinic. Results from this preliminary study showed that 93% of the sample had clear documentation of having military service in Vietnam, but only 40% of the sample had clear evidence of combat exposure. Because military personnel records are an imperfect historical record, it is not possible to make definitive statements regarding the percentage of veterans who exaggerated or were untruthful about their combat experiences. Nevertheless, these findings speak to the challenge of validating verbal reports when exposure to traumatic events can weigh so heavily in decisions about mental health and disability compensation.

CONTEXT AND THE ASSESSMENT OF PTSD SYMPTOMS

As with the stressor criterion, assessment of PTSD symptoms can be compromised by context, with forensic settings being one of the most common and important contextual factors. As noted earlier, PTSD commonly serves as cause for disability compensation-seeking in both civilian and military domains. Further, there is evidence that financial incentive may influence the presentation of posttrauma symptomatology (Frueh et al., 2003a; Rosen, 1995), with civilian personal injury litigants demonstrating symptom over-reporting (Fox, Gerson, & Lees-Haley, 1995; Rothke et al., 1994), potential malingering (Lees-Haley, 1997), and bias in self-reported trauma exposure history (Lees-Haley, Williams, & English, 1996).

Data from studies conducted within the VA system also strongly suggest that the

availability of disability benefits influences the way in which veterans present their difficulties with symptoms and functioning. First, studies conducted within the VA consistently
demonstrate that veterans evaluated for combat-related PTSD exhibit extreme and diffuse
levels of psychopathology across domains of mental illness, along with elevations on the
validity scales of the Minnesota Multiphasic Personality Inventory (MMPI) in a "fake-
bad" direction (Fairbank, Keane, & Malloy, 1983; Frueh, Hamner, Cahill, Gold, & Hamlin,
2000). Next, several studies attempting to clarify this issue have found that compensation-
seeking veterans, as compared to veterans not seeking compensation, produce significantly
more pathological scores on clinical measures, while also obtaining higher elevations
on validity scales associated with malingering (Frueh, Smith, & Barker, 1996; Frueh et
al., 2003a). Differences on most indices exceeded effect sizes of 1.0, even when controlling for the effects of income, global functioning, and clinician-rated severity of PTSD. It
also is the case that extreme overreporters on the MMPI-2 ($F-K \geq 22$; $Fp \geq 7$) are over-
represented among compensation-seeking veterans (Frueh et al., 2003a; Gold & Frueh,
1999).

Treatment outcome studies provide additional evidence that contextual factors are of
great relevance to any discussion of assessment. Evaluation of treatment effects depends,
of course, upon the accurate and reliable assessment of psychiatric symptoms and associated functioning. Assessment of treatment outcome can be influenced by many of the unresolved issues discussed earlier, particularly in samples where disability compensation and
litigation are involved (Kimbrell & Freeman, 2003). Consider, for example, the general
lack of successful treatment efficacy data for combat-related PTSD, and the finding that
PTSD treatment effect sizes have been smaller for samples of veterans, as compared to
non-veterans (Hidalgo et al., 1999). This pattern of findings raises the possibility that evidence for treatment efficacy is skewed by a symptom-reporting pattern that reflects reluctance on the part of some veterans to acknowledge therapeutic gains due to concern about
losing disability payments.

Several studies have presented results that add to current concerns. In one investigation, veterans classified on the MMPI as "symptom overreporters" were less likely to
manifest improvement after six weeks of partial hospitalization, even though clinicians
did not view them as more dysfunctional at pre-treatment (Perconte & Griger, 1991). Other
treatment outcome studies have found prominent disparities between veterans' extreme
self-reported symptom patterns and data collected via clinician ratings, psychophysiological measures, and daily symptom frequency counts (Frueh, Turner, Beidel, Mirabella, &
Jones, 1996; Pitman et al., 1996; Reist et al., 1989). Data from a study of veterans treated
for PTSD within the VA system found compensation-seeking status associated with treatment effectiveness for inpatient veterans, but not for outpatients (Fontana & Rosenheck,
1998). Finally, there is evidence to suggest that motor vehicle accident victims with PTSD
show less improvement in treatment when they are involved in litigation (Blanchard et al.,
1998).

Apart from forensic contexts, primary medical care and public mental health systems
are two clinical settings in which assessment of trauma and posttraumatic reactions is
extremely important. For example, research suggests that 12–20% of patients in VA
primary care clinics meet PTSD diagnostic criteria (Hankin, Spiro, Miller, & Kazis, 1999;
Magruder et al., in press). At the same time, the disorder is not assessed routinely in most
VA primary care settings so that a large percentage of patients go undiagnosed, and there-

fore untreated (Magruder et al., in press; Spiro, Miller, Lee, & Kazis, 2001). Similar findings have been obtained in public mental health clinics, which serve populations at high
risk for trauma exposure. One multi-site study conducted within community mental health
centers across four states (Mueser et al., 1998) found that 42% of the sample met diagnostic criteria for PTSD, while only 2% of the sample were assigned the diagnosis in their
clinic record. Survey results from another study indicated that virtually no community
mental health centers in a state system routinely administered reliable and valid measures
of general trauma exposure or PTSD symptoms during intake interviews with new patients
(Frueh et al., 2002). These findings are particularly unfortunate because a growing body
of data supports the reliability of posttrauma assessment methods among persons with
severe mental illness (Mueser et al., 2001). Routine administration of appropriate measures in these settings could identify those individuals most severely affected by trauma,
thereby increasing the likelihood that treatment would be offered.

TRAUMA AND PTSD ASSESSMENT INSTRUMENTS

A variety of self-report instruments and structured clinical interviews have been developed to assess a history of exposure to traumatic events and PTSD symptoms. These measures can be classified within the following categories:

(1) trauma exposure measures, such as the Traumatic Life Events Questionnaire and
    Traumatic Stress Schedule, which assess trauma exposure only;
(2) symptom-referenced PTSD measures, such as the PTSD Symptom Scale and PTSD
    Checklist, which assess the symptoms of PTSD but not trauma history;
(3) PTSD diagnostic measures based on standard interview formats, such as the
    Structured Clinical Interview for DSM-IV (SCID) PTSD Module, and the Clinician-
    Administered PTSD Scale (CAPS), that assess the formal PTSD criteria, including
    symptoms and trauma exposure;
(4) psychometrically derived PTSD measures, such as the Mississippi Combat PTSD
    Scale and the Minnesota Multiphasic Personality Inventory-2 (MMPI-2), which do
    not necessarily assess symptoms of PTSD, but do discriminate between those with
    and without the diagnosis.

TRAUMA EXPOSURE MEASURES

Most measures that assess exposure to traumatic events have significant limitations. First,
their items often are not behaviorally specific when asking about traumatic events. For
example, a recently published study (Fricker, Smith, Davis, & Hanson, 2003) found that
asking a general question about sexual abuse exposure ("Before the age of 18, were you
ever sexually abused?") yielded lower (and presumably less accurate) sexual abuse prevalence rates than asking several behaviorally-specific questions (e.g., "Before the age of 18,
did anyone, male or female, ever make you touch their genitals or (for women) breasts
when you didn't want them to?"). A second problem with most methods for assessing
trauma exposure is their failure to include preparatory statements that demonstrate acceptance and normalization of a respondent's potentially traumatic experiences. Such prepa-

ration is needed to establish a context and willingness to report accurately (Resnick, Falsetti, Kilpatrick, & Freedy, 1996).

Many trauma history measures are limited by their narrow focus: addressing only a particular type of experience (childhood sexual assault); failing to cover the full range of experiences that meet DSM-IV Criterion A1 (indirect exposure, witnessing events); serving essentially as event checklists that do not inquire about other potentially important characteristics (age at onset, duration, number of episodes); or attempting to document the traumatic event without reference to PTSD's Criterion A2 (the individual's emotional response of fear, helplessness, or horror). These common instrument limitations reflect the ambiguity and complexity of the trauma construct itself.

Trauma exposure methods are limited further by their failure to require respondents to identify an index traumatic event. This omission makes it impossible to link a reported symptom to a specific event, or even to determine when the symptom appeared temporally in relation to the event. Some measures, including the Trauma Assessment for Adults (TAA), and the Traumatic Events Questionnaire (TEQ), now require respondents to nominate a "worst," or "most recent," traumatic event. But these instruments are the exception.

In addition to the above concerns, there is the more general issue that the psychometric validity of trauma exposure measures has not been formally established, again due, in part, to the ambiguous and complex nature of the trauma construct.

PTSD SELF-REPORT INVENTORIES

Objective psychometric inventories have a number of general strengths. They:

(1) are usually easy to administer;
(2) do not require a great deal of time to score or interpret;
(3) allow for standardized assessment procedures across multiple patients and sites;
(4) allow for comparison of individual patients or clinical populations;
(5) offer known, and usually adequate, reliability and validity coefficients; and
(6) allow patients to complete testing procedures and represent their affective experience at their own pace, without influence from examiners.

There also are several drawbacks to self-report inventories. Many PTSD self-report measures have limited psychometric validation, as they may have only been studied with one type of trauma population (e.g., combat veterans) and generalizability to other trauma populations is unknown. Other widely used PTSD measures lack sufficient criterion validity in that they yield poor sensitivity and specificity (e.g., Impact of Event Scale; see review by Newman, Kaloupek, & Keane, 1996). An additional psychometric limitation of self-report measures is that the consolidation of items into one scale means that equivalent scores by different respondents may be achieved for very different reasons. Scale scores on self-report inventories may call attention to a general domain, but more specific assessment of actual behaviors, antecedent situations, and the function of the behavior may be more relevant, particularly when developing treatment plans aimed at targeting specific areas of concern. This points to the importance of examining "critical items" to refine interpretation of general scale scores.

Validity of symptom reporting also is an important issue with self-report measures. Many trauma survivors evaluated for PTSD exhibit extreme and diffuse levels of psychopathology across instruments measuring different domains of mental illness. These individuals also can obtain extreme elevations on the validity scales of the MMPI in a "fake-bad" direction (Frueh et al., 2000). The occurrence of disability compensation-seeking and litigation highlights the importance of strategies for the detection of malingered PTSD (Hickling, Blanchard, Mundy, & Galovski, 2002; Resnick, 1998). The vast majority of PTSD-specific measures do not include validity scales to assess test-taking attitude, even though face-valid instruments have been shown to be extremely vulnerable to intentional feigning efforts (Lyons, Caddell, Pittman, Rawls, & Perrin, 1994). The one stand-alone PTSD measure that does contain validity scales, the Trauma Symptom Inventory (TSI), and its related measure, the Trauma Symptom Checklist for Children, have not had their validity scales empirically validated. Recent research on the TSI suggests that the proposed validity cut-points for malingering do not perform well (Rosen et al., 2004).

PTSD-STRUCTURED INTERVIEWS

The structured interview is the most frequently used assessment strategy for evaluating trauma survivors for PTSD. Interviews such as the Clinician Administered PTSD Scale (CAPS; Blake et al., 1990), and the PTSD module of the Structured Clinical Interview for DSM (SCID; First, Spitzer, Gibbon, & Williams, 1994), provide a strategy for assessing a range of relevant experiences and symptoms. These standardized interview formats allow the clinician to query the patient, and sometimes collateral sources, about functioning across a number of relevant areas. Clinical ratings can be made based not only on patient report, but also on behavioral observations. These interviews also help discipline clinicians by requiring them to obtain information on all symptom clusters. A systematic review of all symptom criteria decreases the likelihood that a clinician will improperly diagnose PTSD when a more focused problem, such as specific phobia, is presenting. By allowing for standardized assessment, structured interviews generally offer known reliability and validity coefficients.

Structured interviews also have important limitations. First, they may be vulnerable both to a negative reporting bias and to symptom overreporting or malingering. Second, there exist several problems with coding and scoring. Many interview-based PTSD diagnostic measures are scored dichotomously, in Yes/No fashion, instead of on a continuum. A dichotomous approach to posttrauma reactions portrays symptoms and diagnoses simplistically and fails to provide severity ratings that can track change over time. Some measures address this issue by querying on a continuous scale the frequency of symptoms (e.g., PTSD Symptom Scale), or by asking directly about the intensity of symptoms (e.g., CAPS). While these efforts are conceptually appealing, the relative importance of separating symptom frequency and intensity in relation to either the diagnosis or severity of PTSD has not been established.

PSYCHOMETRICALLY DERIVED PTSD MEASURES

In recent years, several studies have used more general clinical personality assessment instruments to discriminate between PTSD patients and individuals instructed to feign the disorder. Most of these studies have used the MMPI-2 (Bury & Bagby, 2002; Elhai, Gold, Sellers, & Dorfman, 2001; Lees-Haley, 1992; Wetter & Deitsch, 1996). A note of caution related to limitations in the MMPI validity scales is warranted. Several studies have demonstrated that although symptom overreporting is indeed high in compensation seeking, as well as general samples of trauma victims, such elevations do not rule out the presence of genuine trauma-related symptoms (Franklin, Repasky, Thompson, Shelton, & Uddo, 2002, 2003; Klotz-Flitter, Elhai, & Gold, 2003). Even with the otherwise robust-performing F and Fp MMPI-2 fake-bad scales, sensitivity and specificity rates in detecting malingered PTSD have not been impressive. In fact, a recent malingering meta-analysis demonstrated that studies examining differences on the MMPI validity scales between PTSD patients and PTSD simulators yielded lower effect sizes than studies assessing other types of malingered psychopathology (Rogers, Sewell, Martin, & Vitacco, 2003).

Because of problems with MMPI-2 fake-bad scales in detecting malingered PTSD, a new scale was recently constructed, the Infrequency-PTSD scale (*Fptsd*). *Fptsd* is based on MMPI-2 items that were infrequently endorsed by nearly 1,000 PTSD-diagnosed combat veterans (Elhai et al., 2002). In a preliminary study, *Fptsd* demonstrated superior performance to previously established malingering scales (F and Fp) in discriminating PTSD simulators from PTSD patients. Although these results are promising, research in this area is under-developed, and major questions remain on how to detect malingering with current self-report instruments. A key unresolved question is the base-rate for malingering, a necessary benchmark for evaluating psychometric detection strategies.

Evidence from civilian sexual trauma research (Carlin & Ward, 1992; Elhai et al., 2001; Follette et al., 1997), and combat trauma research (Elhai et al., 2003b; Forbes et al., 2003), suggests that trauma survivors do not constitute a homogeneous group. For example, previous work with cluster analysis (Elhai et al., 2003b) demonstrated that PTSD-diagnosed combat veterans could be statistically classified into four clusters/groups based on their MMPI-2 profiles, with groups described as nonpathological, extremely disturbed, and two moderately symptomatic groups. Further, studies on the MMPI and the MMPI-2 have demonstrated that there is significant heterogeneity of PTSD symptom profiles. For example, US veterans of the Vietnam and Gulf Wars diagnosed with PTSD have produced significantly different MMPI profiles (Glenn et al., 2002), while profiles for US and Australian Vietnam veterans are not meaningfully different (Elhai, Forbes, Creamer, McHugh, & Frueh, 2003a). Other studies have suggested that veterans exposed to combat often demonstrate high elevations on MMPI scales 2 and 8 (see Wise, 1996, for a review), while the majority of MMPI/MMPI-2 investigations of sexual assault and abuse survivors indicate primary elevations on scales 8 and 4. These findings on the absence of a consistent MMPI "trauma profile," and findings on the heterogeneity of trauma responses, reflect the complexity of the PTSD construct and the socio-cultural contexts within which it is evaluated.

One problem with personality assessment in trauma survivors and PTSD patients is that resulting test scores often inaccurately identify psychosis (Briere, 1997; Briere & Elliott, 1997). For example, results from one recent study indicate that genuine trauma-related difficulties of PTSD, depression, and dissociation accounted for a relatively large amount of variance in MMPI-2 scale 8 scores among a sample of adult survivors of child sexual abuse (Elhai, Gold, Mateus, & Astaphan, 2001). These findings caution the clinician against assuming that a trauma survivor, or PTSD patient, is experiencing a psychotic disorder based solely on personality inventory scores.

ADDITIONAL STRATEGIES FOR ASSESSING PTSD

A range of other measurement strategies offer promise for assessment of posttrauma reactions. Among these is psychophysiological challenge testing, a procedure based on the finding that cues associated with traumatic experiences can trigger autonomic (sympathetic) activation. In essence, physiological response to trauma reminders is compared with physiological response to affectively neutral cues in order to determine whether the former are differentially greater.

There is a substantial body of evidence demonstrating the utility of psychophysiological measures (e.g., heart rate, blood pressure) in the assessment of PTSD (e.g., Blanchard, Kolb, & Prins, 1991; Orr, Pitman, Lasko, & Herz, 1993; Pitman, Orr, Forgue, de Jong, & Claiborn, 1987). The prominence of autonomic symptoms and heightened reactivity in persons with PTSD has been consistently documented in studies of psychophysiological responding (Keane et al., 1998; Orr et al., 1990; Pitman et al., 1987). In these studies, persons with PTSD have significantly larger blood pressure and heart rate responses during traumatic cue exposure than do those without PTSD, with sensitivity and specificity ranging from .70–.90 and .80–1.00, respectively. There also is preliminary evidence suggesting that reduced physiological reactivity is associated with improvements in both PTSD symptoms and areas of social adjustment (Boudewyns & Hyer, 1990). Another strength of psychophysiological measures is that they may provide relatively good discrimination even when individuals attempt to exaggerate or disguise their responses (Gerardi, Blanchard, & Kolb, 1989; Orr & Pitman, 1993). At the same time, this assessment modality is limited by a large number of non-responders, thereby raising questions as to how the PTSD construct should be defined (Orr, McNally, Rosen, & Shalev, 2004).

Obtaining daily patient ratings of relevant social behaviors, activities, and problems is a data-collection strategy that is linked to specific and quantifiable behaviors and events. Although such reports can be feigned and there is no pre-trauma baseline data, this assessment approach has advantages over most alternative self-report methods because it is not retrospective, and the obtained data spans a specified period of time rather than providing only cross-sectional information. Patient ratings also can be developed for just about any behavior, tailored to an individual's needs, and expanded to include relevant antecedents, cognitions, and consequences, so as to provide more information about symptoms and social functioning. The approach, therefore, is not limited to targets that are represented by nomothetically derived instruments. One limitation of patient ratings, however, is that they require time (albeit only 2–5 minutes a day) and patient compliance with the procedure.

Very little research has been conducted to date on the use of patient ratings with trauma survivors. Frueh et al. (1996) used daily ratings as an outcome measure in evaluating the efficacy of a multicomponent behavioral treatment package. Veterans were asked to keep a daily log of relevant symptoms (e.g., nightmares, flashbacks) and social activities, for one-week periods, at three separate assessment points (pre-, mid-, and post-treatment). Results showed that patients reported significant symptom reductions, such as fewer nightmares, and increased social activities, despite the fact that no such changes were noted on more global self-report inventories administered at the same assessment points (e.g., Beck Depression Inventory, Mississippi Scale). Similar results were found in another study (Pitman et al., 1996) in which 20 Vietnam veterans with chronic PTSD reported decreased intrusive thoughts, even though the sample reported no symptom improvement on measures such as the Impact of Events Scale, SCL-90, or the CAPS. When these patients counted and recorded the number of intrusive combat memories for carefully timed intervals, they showed a 26% symptom reduction at posttreatment. However, these same veterans reported a 14% *increase* in symptoms at posttreatment interviews. This evidence suggests that daily patient ratings of specific symptoms provide very different information than more global, retrospective measures.

Finally, a number of other strategies including neuroimaging, neuropsychiatric assessment, stroop test paradigms (e.g., Buckley, Galovski, Blanchard, & Hickling, 2003), monitoring of visual eye-tracking and acoustic startle response, and even blood tests, may hold promise for improving our ability to evaluate posttraumatic reactions among trauma survivors (Frueh et al., 2000). A great deal of additional research is needed to understand how and when these strategies may prove useful, especially in discriminating genuine PTSD from feigned presentations of the disorder. Applied research in this area is scant, and there have been only limited attempts to apply standard malingering measures used in other fields. Rosen and Powel (2003) provide an example of how a Symptom Validity Test may be used in the forensic assessment of PTSD, and preliminary research with the Structured Interview of Reported Symptoms (SIRS) is under way (e.g., Kimbrell & Freeman, 2003).

RESEARCH DIRECTIONS AND IMPLICATIONS FOR CLINICAL PRACTICE

Although progress has been made in the assessment of trauma exposure and posttraumatic reactions, a number of important issues remain unresolved. Further research is needed in each of the four broad areas discussed in this chapter. With regard to the phenomenology of PTSD, the field needs to address unresolved questions related to the definition of "trauma;" whether PTSD is a continuous or categorical construct; the factor structure of the clinical syndrome; overlap with other psychiatric disorders (especially major depression and other anxiety disorders); subtypes of the disorder; and varied prevalence estimates as a function of defining features. Socio-cultural influences remain important topics of concern as related to the changing definitions of trauma, interpretation of reactions to major disasters and societal trauma, and the expanding number of trauma-related disability and litigation cases.

As regards general issues in the assessment of trauma exposure and PTSD symptoms, research is needed to improve our ability to evaluate trauma and PTSD in a variety of contexts, including forensic and medical care settings, as well as in treatment outcome research. Questions concerning the fallibility of memory and the impact of these concerns on measurement instruments require further study. Research also is needed to assist with translation and dissemination, so that appropriate state-of-the-art assessment strategies are implemented across a range of settings, including primary care and community mental health centers, thereby ensuring that treatment reaches genuine PTSD cases.

Finally, there remain a host of unresolved issues with available assessment instruments and the manner in which they are commonly used. These critical issues include: (1) developing and psychometrically validating trauma exposure indices that capture the complexity of traumatic experiences; (2) addressing a range of psychometric limitations of specific measures; (3) improving our ability to detect symptom overreporting and malingering across a range of contexts; (4) improving the sensitivity and specificity of measures as our conceptualization of the disorder evolves; and (5) better incorporating structured interviews and self-report instruments with data from alternative assessment strategies, such as psychophysiological assessment and neuroimaging.

Clinicians working with trauma survivors can be alert to a host of unresolved issues related to the phenomenology of the PTSD syndrome. These issues include concerns about the definition of trauma, factor structure of PTSD, overlap with other Axis I disorders, and whether the syndrome is continuous or categorical in nature. Clinicians also can pay careful attention to the context within which evaluations are conducted, including disability or litigation status of patients.

Because the syndrome of PTSD comprises a complex set of multidimensional domains, it seems improbable that any single measure will be sufficient to provide a comprehensive evaluation of posttrauma reactions. Clinicians should consider the benefits of not relying solely on self-report or structured interview measures. Instead, clinicians might consider relying on the "funnel" metaphor of assessment (see Hawkins, 1979). Within this metaphor, the global assessment provided by structured interviews and self-report inventories can identify general domains of reported psychopathology and interpersonal maladjustment. More specific behavioral assessments and patient ratings then can be used to identify specific behaviors and their antecedents and functions, after which a treatment plan can be formulated. Objective efforts to verify trauma exposure (e.g., police reports, military personnel records) and assess cued reactivity (e.g., psychophysiological assessment) may be indicated when disability compensation or litigation applies to the case, particularly when psychological tests (e.g., MMPI-2) demonstrate overreporting, or other findings question the validity of symptom reports.

REFERENCES

American Psychiatric Association (1994). *Diagnostic and statistical manual of mental disorders* (4th edn). Washington, DC: Author.

Blake, D. D., Weathers, F. W., Nagy, L. N., Kaloupek, D. G., Klauminser, G., Charney, D. S. et al. (1990). A clinician rating scale for assessing current and lifetime PTSD: The CAPS-1. *The Behavior Therapist*, *18*, 187–188.

Blanchard, E. B., Hickling, E. J., Taylor, A. E., Buckley, T. C., Loos, W. R., & Walsh, J. (1998). Effects of litigation settlements on posttraumatic stress symptoms in motor vehicle accident victims. *Journal of Traumatic Stress*, *11*, 337–354.

Blanchard, E. B., Kolb, L. C., & Prins, A. (1991). Psychophysiological responses in the diagnosis of posttraumatic stress disorder in Vietnam veterans. *Journal of Nervous and Mental Disease*, *179*, 99–103.

Boudewyns, P. A., & Hyer, L. (1990). Physiological response to combat memories and preliminary treatment outcome in Vietnam veteran PTSD patients treated with direct therapeutic exposure. *Behavior Therapy, 21*, 63–87.

Boscarino, J. A., Galea, S., Ahern, J., Resnick, H., & Vlahov, D. (2002). Utilization of mental health services following the September 11th terrorist attacks in Manhattan, New York City. *International Journal of Emergency Mental Health, 4*, 143–155.

Breslau, N. (2002). Epidemiologic studies of trauma, posttraumatic stress disorder, and other psychiatric disorders. *Canadian Journal of Psychiatry, 47*, 923–929.

Breslau, N., Davis, G. C., Andreski, P., & Peterson, E. (1991). Traumatic events and posttraumatic stress disorder in an urban population of young adults. *Archives of General Psychiatry, 48*, 216–222.

Breslau, N., & Kessler, R. C. (2001). The stressor criterion in DSM-IV posttraumatic stress disorder: An empirical investigation. *Biological Psychiatry, 50*, 699–704.

Brewin, C. R., Andrews, B., & Rose, S. (2000). Fear, helplessness, and horror in posttraumatic stress disorder: Investigating DSM-IV criterion A2 in victims of violent crime. *Journal of Traumatic Stress, 13*, 499–509.

Briere, J. (1997). *Psychological assessment of adult posttraumatic states.* Washington, DC: American Psychological Association.

Briere, J., & Elliott, D. M. (1997). Psychological assessment of interpersonal victimization effects in adults and children. *Psychotherapy, 34*, 353–364.

Brown, D., Scheflin, A. W., & Whitfield, C. L. (1999). Recovered memories: The current weight of the evidence in science and in the courts. *Journal of Psychiatry and Law, 27*, 5–156.

Buckley, T. C., Blanchard, E. B., & Hickling, E. J. (1998). A confirmatory factor analysis of posttraumatic stress symptoms. *Behavior Research and Therapy, 36*, 1091–1099.

Buckley, T. C., Galovski, T., Blanchard, E. B., & Hickling, E. J. (2003). Is the emotional Stroop paradigm sensitive to malingering? A between-groups study with professional actors and actual trauma survivors. *Journal of Traumatic Stress, 16*, 59–66.

Burkett, B. G., & Whitley, G. (1998). *Stolen valor: How the Vietnam generation was robbed of its heroes and its history.* Dallas, TX: Verity.

Bury, A. S., & Bagby, R. M. (2002). The detection of feigned uncoached and coached posttraumatic stress disorder with the MMPI-2 in a sample of workplace accident victims. *Psychological Assessment, 14*, 472–484.

Calhoun, P. S., Bosworth, H. B., Grambow, S. C., Dudley, T. K., & Beckham, J. C. (2002). Medical service utilization by veterans seeking help for posttraumatic stress disorder. *American Journal of Psychiatry, 159*, 2081–2086.

Carlin, A. S., & Ward, N. G. (1992). Subtypes of psychiatric inpatient women who have been sexually abused. *Journal of Nervous and Mental Disease, 180*, 392–397.

Cordova, M. J., Studts, J. L., Hann, D. M., Jacobsen, P. B., & Andrykowski, M. A. (2000). Symptom structure of PTSD following breast cancer. *Journal of Traumatic Stress, 13*, 301–319.

Creamer, M., McFarlane, A. C., & Burgess, P. (2003). Psychopathology following trauma: The role of subjective experience. Unpublished manuscript, Australian Centre for Posttraumatic Mental Health, University of Melbourne.

Crowson, J. J., Frueh, B. C., Beidel, D. C., & Turner, S. M. (1998). Self-reported symptoms of social anxiety in a sample of combat veterans with posttraumatic stress disorder. *Journal of Anxiety Disorders, 12*, 605–612.

DeLisi, L. E., Maurizio, A., Yost, M., Papparozzi, C. F., Fulchino, C., Katz, C. L. et al. (2003). A survey of New Yorkers after the Sept. 11, 2001, terrorist attacks. *American Journal of Psychiatry, 160*, 780–783.

Deykin, E. Y., Keane, T. M., Kaloupek, D., Fincke, G., Rothendler, J., Siegfried, M. et al. (2001). Posttraumatic stress disorder and the use of health services. *Psychosomatic Medicine, 63*, 835–841.

Elhai, J. D., Forbes, D., Creamer, M., McHugh, T. F., & Frueh, B. C. (2003a). Clinical symptomatology of posttraumatic stress disorder-diagnosed Australian and United States Vietnam
combat veterans: An MMPI-2 comparison. *Journal of Nervous and Mental Disease, 191*, 458–
464.

Elhai, J. D., Frueh, B. C., Davis, J. L., Jacobs, G. A., & Hamner, M. B. (2003b). Clinical presentations in combat veterans diagnosed with posttraumatic stress disorder. *Journal of Clinical
Psychology, 59*, 385–397.

Elhai, J. D., Gold, S. N., Mateus, L. F., & Astaphan, T. A. (2001). Scale 8 elevations on the
MMPI-2 among women survivors of childhood sexual abuse: Evaluating posttraumatic stress,
depression, and dissociation as predictors. *Journal of Family Violence, 16*, 47–57.

Elhai, J. D., Gold, S. N., Sellers, A. H., & Dorfman, W. I. (2001). The detection of malingered
posttraumatic stress disorder with MMPI-2 fake bad indices. *Assessment, 8*, 221–236.

Elhai, J. D., Klotz-Flitter, J. M., Gold, S. N., & Sellers, A. H. (2001). Identifying subtypes of women
survivors of childhood sexual abuse: An MMPI-2 cluster analysis. *Journal of Traumatic Stress,
14*, 157–175.

Elhai, J. D., Ruggiero, K. J., Frueh, B. C., Beckham, J. C., Gold, P. B., & Feldman, M. E. (2002).
The Infrequency-Posttraumatic Stress Disorder scale (Fptsd) for the MMPI-2: Development
and initial validation with veterans presenting with combat-related PTSD. *Journal of Personality Assessment, 79*, 531–549.

Fairbank, J. A., Keane, T. M., & Malloy, P. F. (1983). Some preliminary data on the psychological
characteristics of Vietnam veterans with posttraumatic stress disorder. *Journal of Consulting
and Clinical Psychology, 51*, 912–919.

First, M. B., Spitzer, R. L., Gibbon, M., & Williams, J. B. (1994). *Structured Clinical Interview for
Axis I DSM-IV Disorders—Patient Edition*. New York: Biometrics Research Department.

Foa, E. B., & Riggs, D. S. (1995). Posttraumatic Stress Disorder following assault: Theoretical
considerations and empirical findings. *Current Directions in Psychological Science, 4*, 61–65.

Follette, W. C., Naugle, A. E., & Follette, V. M. (1997). MMPI-2 profiles of adult women with child
sexual abuse histories: Cluster-analytic findings. *Journal of Consulting and Clinical Psychology, 65*, 858–866.

Fontana, A., & Rosenheck, R. (1998). Effects of compensation seeking on treatment outcomes
among veterans with posttraumatic stress disorder. *Journal of Nervous and Mental Disease,
186*, 223–230.

Forbes, D., Creamer, M., Allen, N., Elliott, P., McHugh, T., Debenham, P. et al. (2003). MMPI-2
based subgroups of veterans with combat-related PTSD: Differential patterns of symptom
change following treatment. *Journal of Nervous and Mental Disease, 191*, 531–537.

Fox, D. D., Gerson, A., & Lees-Haley, P. R. (1995). Interrelationship of MMPI-2 validity scales in
personal injury claims. *Journal of Clinical Psychology, 51*, 42–47.

Franklin, C. L., Repasky, S. A., Thompson, K. E., Shelton, S. A., & Uddo, M. (2002). Differentiat-
ing overreporting and extreme distress: MMPI-2 use with compensation-seeking veterans with
PTSD. *Journal of Personality Assessment, 79*, 274–285.

Franklin, C. L., Repasky, S. A., Thompson, K. E., Shelton, S. A., & Uddo, M. (2003). Assessment
of response style in combat veterans seeking compensation for posttraumatic stress disorder.
Journal of Traumatic Stress, 16, 251–255.

Franklin, C. L., Strong, D. R., & Greene, R. L. (2002). A taxometric analyses of the MMPI-2
Depression scales. *Journal of Personality Assessment, 79*, 110–121.

Fricker, A. E., Smith, D. W., Davis, J. L., & Hanson, R. F. (2003). Effects of context and question
type on endorsement of childhood sexual abuse. *Journal of Traumatic Stress, 16*, 265–268.

Frueh, B. C., Cousins, V. C., Hiers, T. G., Cavanaugh, S. D., Cusack, K. J., & Santos, A. B. (2002).
The need for trauma assessment and related clinical services in a state public mental health
system. *Community Mental Health Journal, 38*, 351–356.

Frueh, B. C., Elhai, J. D., Gold, P. B., Monnier, J., Magruder, K. M., Keane, T. M. et al. (2003a). Disability compensation seeking among veterans evaluated for posttraumatic stress disorder. *Psychiatric Services, 54,* 84–91.

Frueh, B. C., Elhai, J. D., Monnier, J., Sauvageot, J. A., Grubaugh, A. L., & Burkett, B. G. (2003b). Military records of veterans seeking treatment for combat-related PTSD. Poster presented at the Nineteenth Annual Meeting of the International Society for Traumatic Stress Studies, November, Chicago, IL.

Frueh, B. C., Hamner, M. B., Cahill, S. P., Gold, P. B., & Hamlin, K. (2000). Apparent symptom overreporting among combat veterans evaluated for PTSD. *Clinical Psychology Review, 20,* 853–885.

Frueh, B. C., Smith, D. W., & Barker, S. E. (1996). Compensation seeking status and psychometric assessment of combat veterans seeking treatment for PTSD. *Journal of Traumatic Stress, 9,* 427–439.

Frueh, B. C., Turner, S. M., Beidel, D. C., Mirabella, R. F., & Jones, W. J. (1996). Trauma Management Therapy: A preliminary evaluation of a multicomponent behavioral treatment for chronic combat-related PTSD. *Behaviour Research and Therapy, 34,* 533–543.

Galea, S., Ahern, J., Resnick, H., Kilpatrick, D., Bucuvalas, M., Gold, J. et al. (2002). Psychological sequelae of the September 11 terrorist attacks in New York City. *New England Journal of Medicine, 346,* 982–987.

Gerardi, R. J., Blanchard, E. B., & Kolb, L. C. (1989). Ability of Vietnam veterans to dissimulate a psychophysiological assessment for post-traumatic stress disorder. *Behavior Therapy, 20,* 229–243.

Glenn, D. M., Beckham, J. C., Sampson, W. S., Feldman, M. E., Hertzberg, M. A., & Moore, S. D. (2002). MMPI-2 profiles of Gulf and Vietnam combat veterans with chronic posttraumatic stress disorder. *Journal of Clinical Psychology, 58,* 371–381.

Gold, P. B., & Frueh, B. C. (1999). Compensation-seeking and extreme exaggeration of psychopathology among combat veterans evaluated for PTSD. *Journal of Nervous and Mental Disease, 187,* 680–684.

Hankin, C. S., Spiro, A., Miller, D. R., & Kazis, L. (1999). Mental disorders and mental health treatment among US Department of Veterans Affairs outpatients: The Veterans Health Study. *American Journal of Psychiatry, 156,* 1924–1930.

Hawkins, R. P. (1979). The functions of assessment: Implications for selection and development of devices for assessing repertoires in clinical, educational, and other settings. *Journal of Applied Behavior Analysis, 12,* 501–516.

Hickling, E. J., Blanchard, E. B., Mundy, E., & Galovski, T. E. (2002). Detection of malingered MVA related posttraumatic stress disorder: An investigation of the ability to detect professional actors by experienced clinicians, psychological tests, and psychophysiological assessment. *Journal of Forensic Psychology Practice, 2,* 33–54.

Hidalgo, R., Hertzberg, M. A., Mellman, T., Petty, F., Tucker, P., Weisler, R. et al. (1999). Nefazadone in post-traumatic stress disorder: Results from six open-label trials. *International Clinical Psychopharmacology, 14,* 61–68.

Hyer, L., & Stanger, E. (1997). Interaction of posttraumatic stress disorder and major depressive disorder among older combat veterans. *Psychological Reports, 80,* 785–786.

Jordan, B. K., Marmar, C. R., Fairbank, J. A., Schlenger, W. E., Kulka, R. A., Hough, R. L. et al. (1992). Problems in families of male Vietnam veterans with posttraumatic stress disorder. *Journal of Consulting and Clinical Psychology, 60,* 916–926.

Kaplan, H. I., Sadock, B. J., & Grebb, J. A. (1994). *Synopsis of psychiatry: Behavioral sciences, clinical psychiatry* (7th edn). Baltimore, MD: Williams & Watkins.

Keane, T. M., & Kaloupek, D. G. (1997). Comorbid psychiatric disorders in PTSD: Implications for research. *Annual New York Academy of Sciences, 21,* 24–34.

Keane, T. M., Kolb, L. C., Kaloupek, D. G., Orr, S. P., Blanchard, E. B., Thomas, R. G. et al. (1998). Utility of psychophysiological measurement in the diagnosis of posttraumatic stress disorder: Results from a Department of Veterans Affairs Cooperative Study. *Journal of Consulting and Clinical Psychology*, 66, 914–923.

Keane, T. M., & Wolfe, J. (1990). Comorbidity in Post-Traumatic Stress Disorder: An analysis of community and clinical studies. *Journal of Applied Social Psychology*, 20, 1776–1788.

Kessler, R. C. (2000). Posttraumatic stress disorder: The burden to the individual and to society. *Journal of Clinical Psychiatry*, 61 (*supplement 5*), 4–12.

Kessler, R. C., Sonnega, A., Bromet, E., Hughes, M., & Nelson, C. B. (1995). Posttraumatic stress disorder in the National Comorbidity Study. *Archives of General Psychiatry*, 52, 1048–1060.

Kilpatrick, D. G., Acierno, R., Saunders, B., Resnick, H. S., Best, C. L., & Schnurr, P. P. (2000). Risk factors for adolescent substance abuse and dependence: Data from a national sample. *Journal of Consulting and Clinical Psychology*, 68, 19–30.

Kilpatrick, D. G., Ruggiero, K. J., Acierno, R., Saunders, B., Resnick, H. S., & Best, C. L. (2003). Violence and risk of PTSD, major depression, substance abuse/dependence, and comorbidity: Results from the National Survey of Adolescents. *Journal of Consulting and Clinical Psychology*, 71, 692–700.

Kimbrell, T. A., & Freeman, T. W. (2003). Clinical care of veterans seeking compensation. *Psychiatric Services*, 54, 910–911.

King, D. W., King, L. A., Erickson, D. J., Huang, M. T., Sharkansky, E. J., & Wolfe, J. (2000). Posttraumatic stress disorder and retrospectively reported stressor exposure: A longitudinal prediction model. *Journal of Abnormal Psychology*, 109, 624–633.

King, D. W., Leskin, G. A., King, L. A., & Weathers, F. W. (1998). Confirmatory factor analysis of the Clinician-Administered PTSD Scale: Evidence for the dimensionality of posttraumatic stress disorder. *Psychological Assessment*, 10, 90–96.

Klotz-Flitter, J. M., Elhai, J. D., & Gold, S. N. (2003). MMPI-2 F scale elevations in adult victims of child sexual abuse. *Journal of Traumatic Stress*, 16, 269–274.

Krinsley, K. E., Gallagher, J. G., Weathers, F. W., Kutter, C. J., & Kaloupek, D. G. (2003). Consistency of retrospective reporting about exposure to traumatic events. *Journal of Traumatic Stress*, 16, 399–409.

Kroll, J. (2003). Posttraumatic symptoms and the complexity of responses to trauma. *Journal of the American Medical Association*, 290, 667–670.

Lees-Haley, P. R. (1992). Efficacy of MMPI-2 validity scales and MCMI-II modifier scales for detecting spurious PTSD claims: F, F-K, Fake Bad Scale, Ego Strength, Subtle-Obvious subscales, DIS, and DEB. *Journal of Clinical Psychology*, 48, 681–689.

Lees-Haley, P. R. (1997). MMPI-2 base rates for 492 personal injury plaintiffs: Implications and challenges for forensic assessment. *Journal of Clinical Psychology*, 53, 745–755.

Lees-Haley, P. R., Williams, C. W., & English, L. T. (1996). Response bias in self-reported history of plaintiffs compared with nonlitigating patients. *Psychological Reports*, 79, 811–818.

Loftus, E. (2003). Our changeable memories: Legal and practical implications. *Nature Reviews: Neuroscience*, 4, 231–234.

Lyons, J. A., Caddell, J. M., Pittman, R. L., Rawls, R., & Perrin, S. (1994). The potential for faking on the Mississippi Scale for combat-related PTSD. *Journal of Traumatic Stress*, 7, 441–445.

Magruder, K. M., Frueh, B. C., Knapp, R. G., Johnson, M. R., Vaughan, J. A., Carson, T. C. et al. (in press). PTSD symptoms, demographic characteristics, and functional status among veterans treated in VA primary care clinics. *Journal of Traumatic Stress*.

McNally, R. J. (2003a). Progress and controversy in the study of posttraumatic stress disorder. *Annual Review of Psychology*, 54, 229–252.

McNally, R. J. (2003b). *Remembering trauma*. Cambridge, MA: Harvard University Press.

McNally, R. J., Clancy, S. A., Schacter, D. L., & Pitman, R. K. (2000). Personality profiles, dissociation, and absorption in women reporting repressed, recovered, or continuous memories of childhood sexual abuse. *Journal of Consulting and Clinical Psychology, 68,* 1033–1037.

Miller, M. W., Greif, J. L., & Smith, A. A. (2003). Multidimensional Personality Questionnaire profiles of veterans with traumatic combat exposure: Externalizing and internalizing subtypes. *Psychological Assessment, 15,* 205–215.

Mueser, K. T., Goodman, L. B., Trumbetta, S. L., Rosenberg, S. D., Osher, F. C., Vidaver, R. et al. (1998). Trauma and posttraumatic stress disorder in severe mental illness. *Journal of Consulting and Clinical Psychology, 66,* 493–499.

Mueser, K. T., Salyers, M. P., Rosenberg, S. D., Ford, J. D., Fox, L., & Carty, P. (2001). Psychometric evaluation of trauma and posttraumatic stress disorder assessments in persons with severe mental illness. *Psychological Assessment, 13,* 110–117.

Murdoch, M., Nelson, D. B., & Fortier, L. (2003). Time, gender, and regional trends in the application for service-related post-traumatic stress disorder disability benefits, 1980–1998. *Military Medicine, 168,* 662–670.

Newman, E., Kaloupek, D. G., & Keane, T. M. (1996). Assessment of posttraumatic stress disorder in clinical and research settings. In B. A. van der Kolk, A. C. McFarlane, & L. Weisaeth (eds), *Traumatic stress: The effects of overwhelming experience on mind, body, and society* (pp. 242–275). New York: Guilford Press.

Norris, F. H. (1992). Epidemiology of trauma: Frequency and impact of different potentially traumatic events on different demographic groups. *Journal of Consulting and Clinical Psychology, 60,* 409–418.

Oboler, S. (2000). Disability evaluations under the Department of Veterans Affairs. In R. D. Rondinelli & R. T. Katz (eds), *Impairment rating and disability evaluation* (pp. 187–217). Philadelphia, PA: Saunders Company.

Orr, S. P., Claiborn, J. M., Altman, B., Forgue, D. F., de Jong, J. B., Pitman, R. K. et al. (1990). Psychometric profile of posttraumatic stress disorder, anxious, and healthy Vietnam veterans: Correlations with psychophysiologic responses. *Journal of Consulting and Clinical Psychology, 58,* 329–335.

Orr, S. P., McNally, R. J., Rosen, G. M., & Shalev, A. Y. (2004). Psychophysiological reactivity: Implications for conceptualizing PTSD. In G. M. Rosen (ed.), *Posttraumatic stress disorder: Issues and controversies* (pp. 101–126). Chichester: John Wiley & Sons.

Orr, S. P., & Pitman, R. K. (1993). Psychophysiologic assessment of attempts to simulate posttraumatic stress disorder. *Biological Psychiatry, 33,* 127–129.

Orr, S. P., Pitman, R. K., Lasko, N. B., & Herz, L. R. (1993). Psychophysiological assessment of posttraumatic stress disorder imagery in World War II and Korean combat veterans. *Journal of Abnormal Psychology, 102,* 152–159.

Perconte, S. T., & Griger, M. L. (1991). Comparison of successful, unsuccessful, and relapsed Vietnam veterans treated for posttraumatic stress disorder. *Journal of Nervous and Mental Disease, 179,* 558–562.

Pitman, R. K., Orr, S. P., Altman, B., Longpre, R. E., Poire, R. E., Macklin, M. L. et al. (1996). Emotional processing and outcome of imaginal flooding therapy in Vietnam veterans with chronic posttraumatic stress disorder. *Comprehensive Psychiatry, 37,* 409–418.

Pitman, R. K., Orr, S. P., Forgue, D. F., de Jong, J. B., & Claiborn, J. M. (1987). Psychophysiologic assessment of posttraumatic stress disorder imagery in Vietnam combat veterans. *Archives of General Psychiatry, 44,* 970–975.

Pope, H. G., Hudson, J. I., Bodkin, J. A., & Oliva, P. (1998). Questionable validity of "dissociative amnesia" in trauma victims. *British Journal of Psychiatry, 172,* 210–215.

Reist, C., Kauffman, C. D., Haier, R. J., Sangdahl, C., DeMet, E. M., Chicz-DeMet, A. et al. (1989). A controlled trial of desipramine in 18 men with posttraumatic stress disorder. *American Journal of Psychiatry*, *146*, 513–516.

Resnick, H. S., Falsetti, S. A., Kilpatrick, D. G., & Freedy, J. R. (1996). Assessment of rape and other civilian trauma-related PTSD: Emphasis on assessment of potentially traumatic events. In T. W. Miller (ed.), *Theory and assessment of stressful life events* (2nd edn, pp. 235–271). Madison, CT: International Universities Press.

Resnick, H. S., Kilpatrick, D. G., Dansky, B. S., Saunders, B. E., & Best, C. L. (1993). Prevalence of civilian trauma and posttraumatic stress disorder in a representative national sample of women. *Journal of Consulting and Clinical Psychology*, *61*, 984–991.

Resnick, P. J. (1998). Malingering of posttraumatic psychiatric disorders. *Journal of Practical Psychiatry and Behavioral Health*, *4*, 329–339.

Roemer, L., Litz, B. T., Orsillo, S. M., Ehlich, P. J., & Friedman, M. J. (1998). Increases in retrospective accounts of war-zone exposure over time: The role of PTSD symptom severity. *Journal of Traumatic Stress*, *11*, 597–605.

Rogers, R., Sewell, K. W., Martin, M. A., & Vitacco, M. J. (2003). Detection of feigned mental disorders: A meta-analysis of the MMPI-2 and malingering. *Assessment*, *10*, 160–177.

Rosen, G. M. (1995). The *Aleutian Enterprise* sinking and posttraumatic stress disorder: Misdiagnosis in clinical and forensic settings. *Professional Psychology: Research and Practice*, *26*, 82–87.

Rosen, G. M. (2004). Litigation and reported rates of posttraumatic stress disorder. *Personality and Individual Differences*, *36*, 1291–1294.

Rosen, G. M., & Powel, J. H. (2003). Use of a symptom validity test in the forensic assessment of posttraumatic stress disorder. *Journal of Anxiety Disorders*, *17*, 361–367.

Rosen, G. M., Sawchuk, C., Atkins, D. C., Brown, M., Price, J. R., & Lees-Haley, P. R. (2004). The risk of false-positives when using ATR cut-scores to detect malingered posttraumatic reactions on the Trauma Symptom Inventory (TSI). Manuscript submitted for publication.

Rothke, S. E., Friedman, A. F., Dahlstrom, W. G., Greene, R. L., Arredondo, R., & Mann, A. W. (1994). MMPI normative data for the F-K index: Implications for clinical, neuropsychological, and forensic practice. *Assessment*, *1*, 1–15.

Ruscio, A. M., & Ruscio, J. (2002). The latent structure of analogue depression: Should the Beck Depression Inventory be used to classify groups? *Psychological Assessment*, *14*, 135–145.

Ruscio, A. M., Ruscio, J., & Keane, T. M. (2002). The latent structure of posttraumatic stress disorder: A taxometric investigation of reactions to extreme stress. *Journal of Abnormal Psychology*, *111*, 290–301.

Ruscio, J., & Ruscio, A. M. (2000). Informing the continuity controversy: A taxometric analysis of depression. *Journal of Abnormal Psychology*, *109*, 473–487.

Ruscio, J., & Ruscio, A. M. (2002). A structure-based approach to psychological assessment: Matching measurement models to latent structure. *Assessment*, *9*, 4–16.

Satel, S. (in press). September 11. In C. H. Sommers & S. Satel (eds), *One nation under therapy*. New York: St Martin's Press.

Schlenger, W. E., Caddell, J. M., Ebert, L., Jordan, B. K., Rourke, K. M., Wilson, D. et al. (2002). Psychological reactions to terrorist attacks: Findings from the National Study of Americans' Reactions to September 11. *Journal of the American Medical Association*, *288*, 581–588.

Schnurr, P. P., Spiro, A., & Paris, A. H. (2000). Physician-diagnosed medical disorders in relation to PTSD symptoms in older male military veterans. *Health Psychology*, *19*, 91–97.

Schuster, M. A., Stein, B. D., Jaycox, L. H., Collins, R. L., Marshall, G. N., Elliott, M. N. et al. (2001). A national survey of stress reactions after the September 11, 2001, terrorist attacks. *New England Journal of Medicine*, *345*, 1507–1512.

Shephard, B. (2001). *A war of nerves: Soldiers and psychiatrists in the twentieth century.* Cambridge, MA: Harvard University Press.

Silver, R. C., Holman, E. A., McIntosh, D. N., Poulin, M., & Gil-Rivas, V. (2002). Nationwide longitudinal study of psychological responses to September 11. *Journal of the American Medical Association, 288,* 1235–1244.

Simms, L. J., Watson, D., & Doebbeling, B. N. (2002). Confirmatory factor analyses of posttraumatic stress symptoms in deployed and nondeployed veterans of the Gulf War. *Journal of Abnormal Psychology, 111,* 637–647.

Solomon, S. D., & Davidson, J. R. T. (1997). Trauma: Prevalence, impairment, service use, and cost. *Journal of Clinical Psychiatry, 58,* 5–11.

Southwick, S. M., Morgan, C. A., III, Nicolaou, A. L., & Charney, D. S. (1997). Consistency of memory for combat-related traumatic events in veterans of Operation Desert Storm. *American Journal of Psychiatry, 154,* 173–177.

Spiro, A., III, Miller, D. R., Lee, A., & Kazis, L. (2001). *Mental disorders in the Veterans Health Administration: The 1999 Health Survey of Veterans.* Abstract from VA HSR&D Service 19th Annual Meeting, February, Washington, DC.

Taylor, S., Kuch, K., Koch, W. J., Crockett, D. J., & Passey, G. (1998). The structure of posttraumatic stress symptoms. *Journal of Abnormal Psychology, 107,* 154–160.

Walker, E. A., Katon, W., Russo, J., Ciechanowski, P., Newman, E., & Wagner, A. W. (2003). Health care costs associated with posttraumatic stress disorder symptoms in women. *Archives of General Psychiatry, 60,* 369–374.

Walker, E. A., Unutzer, J., Rutter, C., Gelfand, A., Saunders, K., von Korff, M. et al. (1999). Costs of health care use by women HMO members with a history of childhood abuse and neglect. *Archives of General Psychiatry, 56,* 609–613.

Wetter, M. W., & Deitsch, S. E. (1996). Faking specific disorders and temporal response consistency on the MMPI-2. *Psychological Assessment, 8,* 39–47.

Wise, E. A. (1996). Diagnosing posttraumatic stress disorder with the MMPI clinical scales: A review of the literature. *Journal of Psychopathology and Behavioral Assessment, 18,* 71–82.

5   Malingering and the PTSD Data Base

GERALD M. ROSEN

Department of Psychology, University of Washington, Seattle, USA

A historical perspective is useful when considering the dictum provided in DSM-IV's (APA, 1994) discussion on posttraumatic stress disorder (PTSD), that "Malingering should be ruled out in those situations in which financial remuneration, benefit eligibility, and forensic determinations play a role" (p. 467). This perspective demonstrates that concerns regarding feigned presentations of posttrauma reactions are not novel to current disability policies or contemporary developments in litigation and the courts.

In the late nineteenth century, compensation claims were brought against railway insurance companies, and distinguishing between real and feigned injuries was a central concern. For example, John Erichsen (1882) cautioned physicians that their first task was to determine if claimants really had been injured. Herbert Page (1891) devoted an entire chapter to "Malingering," and observed:

> It is extraordinary how persons in the humbler walks of life possess a knowledge of the kinds of injury, which are popularly deemed inevitable in a collision. Provincial journals are to some extent responsible for this, for in them are often to be found in considerable detail the history and symptoms of those who, by litigation or otherwise, have received compensation from railway or tramway companies. And if a man has in this way learned that large compensation was awarded for injuries apparently like his own, it is a great temptation to him to adopt courses which seem to him potential of future gain. (p. 113)

In the same time frame, Allan Hamilton and Lawrence Godkin edited two volumes entitled "A System of Legal Medicine," with contributions by Dana (1894) on "The Traumatic Neuroses," and by Knapp (1894) on "Feigned Diseases of the Mind and Nervous System." Hamilton (1904) then wrote his own text, *Railway and Other Accidents with Relation to Injury and Disease of the Nervous System: A Book for Court Use.*

Like Hamilton, Page, and Erichsen, modern commentators have recognized the problem of malingered posttrauma reactions. With regard to contemporary definitions of PTSD, Slovenko (1994) observed:

> In tort litigation, PTSD is a favored diagnosis in cases of emotional distress because it is incident specific. It tends to rule out other factors important to the determination of causation. Thus plaintiffs can argue that all of their psychological problems issue from the alleged traumatic event and not from myriad other sources encountered in life. A diagnosis of depression, in contrast, opens the issue of causation to many factors other than the stated cause of action. (p. 441)

Posttraumatic Stress Disorder: Issues and Controversies. Edited by G. M. Rosen.
© 2004 John Wiley & Sons, Ltd.   ISBN 0-470-86284-X/0-470-86285-8.

Sparr and Atkinson (1986) cautioned that the diagnosis of PTSD was difficult because the "symptoms are mostly subjective, often non-specific, usually well publicized, and therefore, relatively easy to imitate" (p. 608). Trimble (1985) noted how PTSD, "sanctioned so neatly by the DSM-III, clearly has both conceptual and medico-legal implications . . . [it] will give a great deal of leverage to those seeking compensation and the counting off of symptoms in checklist fashion will become routine practice in many a lawyer's office" (pp. 12–13). Lees-Haley (1986) appreciated the lure of PTSD for claimants and their counsel when he commented, "If mental disorders were listed on the New York exchange, PTSD would be a growth stock to watch" (p. 17).

In the context of past and contemporary concerns, it should have come as no surprise when the DSM-IV introduced its cautionary statement to rule out malingering. If any surprises were to be had, it was earlier, when DSM-III introduced PTSD without a cautionary statement (APA, 1980), and DSM-III-R similarly failed to address the issue seven years later (APA, 1987).

FALSIFYING EVENTS

The first report to document false claims of PTSD was provided by Sparr and Pankratz (1983). These authors identified individuals who claimed disability from combat in Vietnam when the claimants had never been to that country. Sparr and Pankratz referred to these cases as "factitious," because the feigned symptoms were thought to be motivated by the patient role rather than conscious malingering (APA, 2000; Phillips, 2001). A few years later, Lynn and Belza (1984) reported additional cases of factitious PTSD; J. D. Hamilton (1985) discussed "Pseudo-posttraumatic stress disorder;" and Lacoursiere (1993) analyzed the diverse motives that contributed to such presentations. The task of documenting falsified claims of combat-related PTSD then remained largely ignored until the publication of *Stolen Valor* (Burkett & Whitley, 1998). In this text, Burkett and Whitley exposed how widespread was the problem of malingering among veterans, with many cases falsifying entire combat histories that never had occurred. More recent research further documents these concerns (Frueh et al., 2003).

Findings on individuals who falsely claimed combat-related PTSD illustrate how the stressor criterion can be misreported. Other published cases of individuals falsifying the occurrence of an event are rare. There is one case report of a young boy who lied about sexual abuse to divert attention from his own misbehavior (Trankell, 1958), and an autobiographical account of similar behavior on the part of an adult woman who falsely alleged rape (Webb & Chapian, 1985). Insurance sting operations have exposed individuals who claim exposure to trauma while remaining totally free of harm's way. For example, New Jersey's State Insurance Department staged bus accidents, after which people were videotaped scrambling onto the vehicles before police arrived (Kerr, 1993). In addition to falsely reporting the occurrence of events, individuals can misreport the cause of an incident. Over a century ago, Lewis and Bombaugh (1896) discussed cases of self-mutilation for the purpose of obtaining accident insurance. These authors documented how the frequency of non-dominant versus dominant amputated hands and feet varied according to the size and availability of insurance policies. By implication, individuals were shooting themselves when sufficiently motivated by large financial rewards.

Since the inception of PTSD, there has been pressure to expand the range of events that can be considered traumatic (Criterion A). As noted by Davidson and Foa (1991), this pressure comes, in part, from forensic considerations and the desire to include the full range of trauma victims. Pressure also comes from unresolved debates on the validity of Criterion A (Breslau & Davis, 1987; Lindy, Green, & Grace, 1987), and ambiguities in the construct's defining boundaries (Breslau, 1990; Young, 1995). Over time, and through repeated revisions of the DSM, the class of events subsumed under Criterion A has been expanded, leading to a type of conceptual bracket creep (McNally, 2003).

This expansion of Criterion A can have negative consequences that go to the core of the PTSD construct. As observed by the co-chairs of DSM-IV's committee on PTSD (Davidson & Foa, 1991): "A broadened criterion A risks trivializing PTSD as a disorder and may have serious forensic consequences" (p. 260). The reality of such concerns was demonstrated recently when Avina and O'Donohue (2002) proposed that ambiguous instances of sexual harassment (e.g., repeated sexual jokes, or other inappropriate comments in the workplace) could be traumatic because

> The victim may be legitimately worried [that] whatever is occurring now will increase in severity. Victims can worry that if a perpetrator is capable of the norm violation of, for example, comments about breasts, then he might also be capable of touching her inappropriately. (p. 73)

In effect, Avina and O'Donohue extended the range of events subsumed under Criterion A to the realm of expectations, creating the conceptual equivalent of "pretraumatic stress disorder." Within the logic of this newest demonstration of criterion creep, an otherwise non-traumatic event could meet criterion threshold because it created the fear of worse things to come.

A review of the history of PTSD suggests that numerous political interests and social forces have contributed to the definition of this disorder (Scott, 1990; Young, 1995). In light of this historical analysis, which observes that changes in the definition of PTSD criteria occur in social contexts, it becomes relevant to ask why Avina and O'Donohue proposed that non-traumatic harassing events should be subsumed under Criterion A, particularly when the potential consequences of hostile environments already are appreciated (Charney & Russell, 1994). As it turns out, Avina and O'Donohue provided an answer to this question when they plainly stated in their article:

> If the direct link of sexual harassment as a viable event that results in PTSD is widely supported, this can be reflected in judicial decisions regarding the appropriate monetary compensations for victims of sexual harassment. Victims can be seen as legitimately suffering from a serious mental disorder and be compensated appropriately for this. (p. 74)

These comments call to mind the warnings of multiple commentators who cautioned that forensic interests could trivialize the construct of PTSD (Davidson & Foa, 1991; Lees-Haley, 1986; Slovenko, 1994; Trimble, 1985).

The proposal advanced by Avina and O'Donohue raises new issues regarding the false reporting of traumatic events. After all, if individuals can falsify the details of actual events (e.g., rape, war, and accidents), imagine how easily they can misreport subjective fantasies of events yet to be. This concern, however important, is not the only problem with the proposal by Avina and O'Donohue. If the construct of PTSD is to have any meaning, then there must remain reasonable boundaries to its defining criteria. Without a clear basis for delineating traumatic events, and without brakes on the social forces that press for expansion, PTSD runs the risk of becoming a cultural narrative for significant human suffering after any unpleasant incident. If this happens, the study of PTSD will have turned on itself, engulfing the broader study of human stress responses from which it emerged.

FEIGNING SYMPTOMS

In addition to falsifying the occurrence and circumstances of traumatic events, people can feign the subjective symptoms of PTSD (Eldridge, 1991; Sparr & Atkinson, 1986). Individuals can present symptoms they never really had; symptoms experienced at one point in time that are no longer present; and/or existing problems whose severity is misreported (Collie, 1912; Pankratz, 1998). The most notable demonstration of this problem occurred among the survivors of a maritime disaster, the sinking of the *Aleutian Enterprise* (Rosen, 1995). The *Aleutian Enterprise* was a fish-processing vessel with a crew of 31 that sank in the Bering Sea in March 1990. Nine crew were lost at sea, two survivors returned to their former employment, and the remaining 20 retained counsel and filed personal injury lawsuits. Nineteen of the litigating survivors then presented to treating psychiatrists and/or psychologists the hallmark symptoms of PTSD. Further, none of the 19 plaintiffs reported significant improvement, leading all of them to carry the diagnosis of PTSD, chronic.

The diagnosis of chronic PTSD among 19 plaintiffs led to an 86% incidence rate of the disorder, an incident rate in stark contrast to what is known about the epidemiology of PTSD. For example, in an epidemiological survey of an inner-city sample from Detroit (Breslau, Davis, Andreski, & Peterson, 1991), nearly 40% of residents had experienced a traumatic event, but only 23.6% of these individuals met criteria for PTSD. Rates of PTSD after trauma were even lower when survey methods randomly chose the indexed event rather than having respondents report on the "worst" trauma ever experienced (Breslau et al., 1998). In the National Comorbidity Survey, over 50% of the sample reported a traumatic event, while 8.2% of males and 20.4% of females received a PTSD diagnosis (Kessler, Sonnega, Bromet, Hughes, & Nelson, 1995). Additional epidemiologic studies further document that most individuals who experience life-threatening traumatic accidents do not develop PTSD (e.g., Davidson, Hughes, Blazer, & George, 1991; Helzer, Robins, & McEvoy, 1987; Norris, 1992; Stein, Walker, Hazen, & Forde, 1997). Further, among those who do meet PTSD criteria, half to two-thirds recover within three months (APA, 2000; Rothbaum, Foa, Riggs, Murdock, & Walsh, 1992). These findings led Yehuda and McFarlane (1995) to observe, "the available epidemiological data show that PTSD, and certainly chronic PTSD, is more unusual than usual following exposure to a variety of traumatic events" (p. 1708).

It also can be observed that among patients diagnosed with PTSD, there is variability in symptom presentation. Foa, Riggs, and Gershuny (1995) found that among a group of assault victims all diagnosed with PTSD, 60% reported sleep disturbance, 38% reported nightmares, and 45% reported flashbacks. In contrast to the symptom variability of nonlitigating PTSD-diagnosed assault victims, 100% of the litigating plaintiffs from the *Aleutian Enterprise* endorsed chronic problems with insomnia, nightmares, and flashbacks.

As it turned out, the extraordinary findings among plaintiffs from the *Aleutian Enterprise* were explained by attorney coaching and symptom sharing, revealed during interviews by an independent examiner (IE) retained by defense. While it can be argued that defense-funded assessments are biased (Otto, 1989), certain findings in the present case were indisputable: six plaintiffs provided unambiguous reports that some form of attorney advice had occurred with regard to PTSD symptoms, the merits of seeing a doctor, and/or not going back to work. One case, in particular, illustrated these issues:

> [The crew member] explained that he did not know why he went to see a psychologist except that his attorney wanted him to be evaluated. He said he wanted to go back to fishing but his attorney told him it would look better if he did not work. After several months, he badly needed income and returned to fishing in Alaska. He intended this to be kept secret but his mother mistakenly told his attorney during a telephone call. If it had not been for that leak of information, he would have continued reporting fear of boats, nightmares, and other posttrauma reactions. When the IE specifically asked if he would have "scammed" during the interview, if not for his mother's disclosure, he answered, "I'm sure that's what the others are doing." (cited in Rosen, 1995, p. 84)

Findings from the *Aleutian Enterprise* reinforce concerns expressed a century ago (Erichsen, 1882; Page, 1891), and call attention to more recent cautions that individuals can simulate the subjective symptoms of PTSD (Eldridge, 1991; Sparr & Atkinson, 1986; Trimble, 1985).

Although there are no other demonstrations of malingering comparable to the *Aleutian Enterprise* incident, additional findings on trauma reactions provide cause for concern. For example, Edward Blanchard and Edward Hickling have reviewed their extensive research efforts in the Albany MVA (motor vehicle accident) Project (Blanchard & Hickling, 1997). This project studied 158 MVA "survivors" and found rates of PTSD and subsyndromal PTSD (significant reports of symptomatology that fall short of DSM criteria) of 39.2% and 28.5% respectively, one month post-incident. At four-month follow-up, eight survivors who presented with initial subsyndromal PTSD had gone on to develop full PTSD, resulting in a 44.3% rate for diagnosing the disorder. Blanchard and Hickling observed that rates of PTSD obtained in their sample were higher than other studies on MVA victims. They provided various interpretations for their findings and then explained:

> We made no effort to check on the veracity of our research participants' reports, either details of the accident or reports of their psychological symptoms at any point in the follow-up. The interviewers were all experienced clinicians and probed when answers were inconsistent or when the nonverbal behavior was inconsistent with verbal content. We had no instances in which we felt we had been misled. (p. 186)

Blanchard and Hickling's reliance on clinician skills and the belief clients are truthful are remarkable, when separate research from their center demonstrated that involvement in litigation was one of four variables predicting PTSD status (Blanchard et al., 1996). This relationship between litigation and receiving a diagnosis of PTSD has been found by others (Mayou, Ehlers, & Bryant, 2002). Further, in a study conducted at the Albany MVA Project several years later, six actors feigned PTSD while undergoing a full assessment procedure.

All six actors went undetected and received a PTSD diagnosis (Hickling, Blanchard, Mundy, & Galovski, 2002).

THE DIFFICULT TASK OF DETECTING MALINGERING

Although the DSM tells clinicians and researchers to rule out malingering, the text does not provide guidelines on how this task should be accomplished. Although writers in the field have recommended a multi-method approach to assessment, encouraging clinicians to use a variety of interview formats and test instruments (Eldridge, 1991; Fairbank, McCaffrey, & Keane, 1985; Keane, 1991; Lyons, 1991), there is no preferred method to detect malingering among PTSD claimants (Guriel & Fremouw, 2003). Further, clinicians are unlikely to use tests in their regular practice, relying instead on the apparent sincerity of clients in the context of a developing therapeutic alliance (Greenberg & Shuman, 1997; Strasburger, Gutheil, & Brodsky, 1997). This point was illustrated when one of the therapists who saw multiple plaintiffs in the *Aleutian Enterprise* case observed:

> At this time I have not used psychological testing because the facts of the sinking are undisputed, and the symptoms expressed by each of the men that I assessed were so clear and severe . . . given that the symptoms were almost writing themselves out of the book, it didn't seem as if I had a difficult diagnostic picture in front of me. (cited in Rosen, 1995, p. 84)

The touch of unintended irony in this psychologist's statement will not be lost on the reader.

Many clinicians believe that clinical assessment interviews and additional treatment contacts provide a sufficient basis to detect malingering. Evidence is strongly against this. In a classic paper on catching liars, Ekman and O'Sullivan (1991) found that mental health professionals performed no better than chance when viewing videotapes of individuals who told the truth or misreported. Ekman, O'Sullivan, and Frank (1999) later claimed that specialized training in a workshop setting improved lie detection for some. However, Ekman used videotapes preselected for facial expressions that participants had been taught to identify, thereby limiting the external validity of his study. Further, improved detection rates (70%) obtained by some still left room for error, and a substantial number of participants continued to perform at, or below, chance. Ekman et al. (1999) concluded, "It is unlikely that judging deception from demeanor will ever be sufficiently accurate to be admissible in the courtroom" (p. 265). A recent review supports this conclusion (Vrij & Mann, 2003).

An argument might be made that contact with a real patient is different from the analogue situation used in Ekman's work. However, evidence in real-life settings is no more encouraging. In the field of medicine there are multiple studies using "simulated patients"—individuals who act the part of an illness to assess physician performance in practice settings (Rosen & Phillips, in press). Across these studies, physicians are notoriously poor at identifying actors who present with depression (Carney et al., 1999; Owen & Winkler, 1974) and a variety of other complaints (e.g., Gordon, Sanson-Fisher, & Saunders, 1988; Kopelow et al., 1992). Of greatest concern to the question of a clinician's ability to detect malingered PTSD is the previously cited study by Hickling et al. (2002), in which six actors went undetected when simulating the symptoms of PTSD at a clinic specializing in the disorder (Albany MVA Project). Repeated demonstrations that clinicians are unable to detect malingering are consistent with Slovenko's (2002) observation: "A sharp poker player probably knows better than a psychiatrist whether a person is lying . . . A psychiatrist is a doctor, not a lie-detector" (p. 122).

It sometimes is argued that therapists can detect malingering because of their extended contact with a patient over multiple therapy sessions. This position has no empirical support and rests on the weak assumption that a person who misreports nightmares during an intake session will not just as easily misreport the same phenomenon weeks later. Wetter and Deitsch (1996) have cast further doubt on the consistency of reporting argument by demonstrating temporal response consistency on the MMPI-2.

Structured interviews such as the Clinician-Administered PTSD Scale (CAPS) and Structure Clinical Interview for DSM (SCID) have been recommended to improve the reliability and validity of diagnosing PTSD (Keane, 1991; Weiss, 1997). In research settings, where subjects are assumed to report accurately, and in clinic settings where most patients are similarly motivated, a formal structured interview does assure that symptom criteria will be covered systematically. However, in disability and forensic settings, where motivation to report cannot be assumed, structured interviews have no incremental validity over less structured interactions. In fact, under such circumstances, an unstructured interview may be preferred. When a clinician asks, "What kinds of problems are you having?," this open-ended question requires a respondent to report problems known from experience, or feigned problems committed to memory. A structured interview, on the other hand, eliminates the rigor of memory, and allows a respondent to simply endorse items as the clinician systematically lists each symptom. For these same reasons, symptom checklists are of little assistance when ruling out malingering, since people can fake with ease the subjective symptoms of PTSD and depression (Lees-Haley, 1989, 1990). Symptom checklists that contain validity scales, such as the Trauma Symptom Inventory, offer no demonstrated benefit over simpler instruments because their validity scales are inadequately developed and proposed cut-off scores obtain unacceptable levels of specificity and sensitivity (Rosen et al., 2004).

Other assessment strategies can be useful, although each has its limitations. The MMPI-2 contains validity scales to identify individuals motivated to malinger (Elhai, Gold, Frueh, & Gold, 2000; Wetter, Baer, Berry, Robison, & Sumpter, 1993), but coaching on these scales reduces their effectiveness (Bury & Bagby, 2002; Storm & Graham, 2000; Walters & Clopton, 2000). Findings on survivors of the *Aleutian Enterprise* demonstrated that attorney coaching does occur, as did a case report by Youngjohn (1995). The threat that attorney coaching poses to the validity of psychological evaluations has been discussed by Lees-Haley (1997). Further, a survey by Wetter and Corrigan (1995) demonstrates that most attorneys consider it an ethical responsibility to instruct clients on what is known about psychological tests. Because attorney–client communications are privileged, there is no practical way to assess this significant issue, until such time as exceptions to the privilege are established (Aronson, Rosenwald, & Rosen, 2001).

It has been recommended that physiological assessment of reactions to trauma-relevant stimuli can further the assessment of PTSD (Orr & Kaloupek, 1997; Orr & Pitman, 1993; Shalev, Orr, & Pitman, 1993), and the DSM-IV suggests this approach (APA, 2000, p.

465). However, upwards of 40% of PTSD-diagnosed patients do not demonstrate physio-logical reactivity (Orr, McNally, Rosen, & Shalev, 2004). Further, there are no current decision rules for physiological data that allow a determination of PTSD caseness with established levels of specificity and sensitivity. The absence of clear empirically derived decision rules also is a concern with alternative approaches to assessment (see, for example, Buckley, Galovski, Blanchard, & Hickling, 2003, who employed the emotional Stroop paradigm; also, Rosen & Powel, 2003, who employed a Symptom Validity Test).

WHAT CAN RESEARCHERS AND CLINICIANS DO?

At the present time there are no clear methodologies that allow researchers and clinicians to fulfill DSM-IV's cautionary guideline to "rule out" malingering. In appreciation of this situation, M. Miller (personal communication, June, 2003) observed that the DSM should have provided a more realistic statement, cautioning that, "Although necessary, it is often impossible to rule out malingering."

Despite limitations in current assessment tools, researchers and clinicians should use these instruments and not rely solely on an individual's report of subjective symptoms (Stone et al., 2000; Williams, Lees-Haley, & Djanogly, 1999). To rely solely on self-report is to abdicate totally the challenge provided in DSM-IV's cautionary guideline.

A recent study illustrates the problem. Daly and Johnston (2002) reported on 150 patrons of a tavern in Northern Ireland who were held hostage for three hours. Daly and Johnston described how some customers had guns pointed to their heads and were threatened in a "very abusive manner." After three hours, all hostages were released without serious injury. Six months after the incident, 68 of the survivors were referred to Daly by attorneys for medico-legal assessments, thereby providing an opportunity to assess "the nature and severity of the psychological effects" of the "Derryhirk Inn Incident." A semi-structured interview, General Health Questionnaire, and the Clinician-Administered PTSD Scale (all self-report measures) were used to determine the presence of posttrauma symptomatology. Applying criteria from DSM-IV (APA, 1994), Daly and Johnston found that 67% of subjects fulfilled criteria for the diagnosis of chronic PTSD.

Daly and Johnston noted in their (2002) paper that inferences drawn from the study might be limited because all participants were litigants seeking compensation. At the same time, Daly and Johnston provided these observations:

> . . . the victims involved in this incident appear to have been genuine, honest people. Despite the majority having previously been involved in traumatic incidents, only a minority had ever previously pursued litigation. They were largely a law-abiding group who had previously shown respect for, and trust in, authority. (p. 463)

The stance adopted by Daly and Johnston, with regard to the Derryhirk Inn Incident, is essentially the same as that expressed by Blanchard and Hickling in their Albany MVA Project. This belief in the integrity of generally law-abiding citizens provides no basis on which to rule out malingering. As has been shown, health professionals have not demonstrated ability to detect when subjective symptoms are falsely reported. Further, one would expect Daly and Johnston to have been more skeptical of a 67% rate for chronic PTSD, when, for example, 47% of women who have been raped (Rothbaum et al., 1992), and less than 5% of tortured POWs (Nice, Garland, Hilton, Baggett, & Mitchell, 1996), developed the disorder.

Despite limitations with the MMPI-2, Daly and Johnston could have administered this instrument to provide some measure of response set. With appropriate equipment, it also would have been possible to monitor heart rate responses to neutral and trauma-relevant stimuli, thereby providing an opportunity for some litigants to demonstrate a convincing physiological response. At the very least, physicians' records should have been reviewed in an attempt to corroborate reports of sleep disturbance or other health complaints. These efforts provide some basis to rule out malingering beyond reliance on fallible self-reports. Further, these methods are feasible for most practicing clinicians who find themselves involved in the assessment of PTSD claimants.

Since Daly and Johnston were dealing with a group of litigants, they could have conducted further analyses that are not available in the individual case. For example, the presenting problems of PTSD claimants could have been analyzed for the presence of symptom variability. If variability in symptom reporting was absent among the multiple claimants, then the occurrence of outside coaching and/or symptom sharing could be suspected.

When the cautionary guideline from the DSM-IV is taken seriously, one becomes skeptical of other reported incident rates in the PTSD literature. A sampling of publications on maritime disasters provides a basis for additional concern. William Yule and his associates have published extensively on a 1988 maritime incident, the sinking of the cruise ship *Jupiter* (Yule et al., 2000; Bolton, O'Ryan, Udwin, Boyle, & Yule, 2000; Udwin, Boyle, Yule, Bolton, & O'Ryan, 2000). Yule et al. (2000) found that 51.7% of 217 adolescent survivors developed PTSD, and reported, "Most of the survivors were screened about 5 months after the accident, as part of their legal action against the shipping company, using a number of self-report measures" (p. 504). Udwin et al. (2000) provided a similar statement: "Given the large number of survivors, and the authors' involvement in screening and assessing many of them subsequently as part of their legal action against the shipping company, this disaster provided a unique opportunity to investigate key questions" (p. 970). No mention was made by either Yule or Udwin of efforts to rule out malingering or to assess possible biasing effects of litigation.

Yule and his associates, like Daly and Johnston who reported on the Derryhirk incident, are to be credited for disclosing the litigant status of their subjects, even though no attempts were made to rule out malingering. Such disclosure of ongoing litigation is not always provided. Raphael and Meldrum (1993), for example, discussed PTSD incident rates occurring after various trauma in Australia. They had this to say about survivors of a maritime incident involving the *HMAS Voyager*:

Eighty-two persons were lost when *HMAS Voyager* was cut in half by the *HMAS Melbourne* on February 10, 1964 . . . Burges Watson (1986) examined 22 of the 236 survivors of the *HMAS Voyager* between August 1985 and September, 1986, 21–22 years later . . . It was determined that 86% could be diagnosed as suffering from chronic PTSD (pp. 80–81).

Burges Watson (personal communication, October 2, 2002) clarified that all 22 of the assessed survivors were part of a large litigation effort that eventually led to significant compensation payouts, a fact not established in the Raphael and Meldrum paper. The failure of Raphael and Meldrum to clarify this point could lead a reader to think that 86% was a reasonable estimate for chronic PTSD after a maritime disaster. In fact, this error has been made (see Eid, Johnsen, & Thayer, 2001).

DSM'S CAUTIONARY STATEMENT CAN PROTECT THE PTSD DATA BASE

Clinicians, researchers, and journal editors have not taken to heart the cautionary guideline from the DSM-IV. There may be many reasons for this, including the belief that ruling out malingering is a good idea in the abstract, but difficult to accomplish in reality. There also may be strong emotional prohibitions against questioning the psychological suffering of an individual who reports trauma. Against such resistance, clinicians, researchers, and journal editors must consider the consequences of ignoring concerns that PTSD can be feigned. In the individual case, the consequences of malingering are limited to a claimant receiving compensation that may not be warranted. However, when malingering influences research findings, the consequences extend beyond the individual case and implications are far-reaching. Summerfield (1999) noted that tainted findings "are liable to publication in medical journals as hard evidence" (p. 1450). Richard McNally (2003) cautioned, "the integrity of the PTSD data base is at issue here" (p. 236).

Clinicians can take seriously DSM-IV's cautionary statement on malingering by following a number of guidelines: (1) acknowledge an inability to detect lying on the basis of interview alone; (2) do not rely solely on self-report; (3) employ what few assessment strategies are available while recognizing their limitations; and (4) remain mindful that false presentations of subjective posttrauma symptoms can go undetected. Further, clinicians want to be cautious when called upon to testify on the clinical status of a PTSD claimant. When a clinician testifies that an individual suffers from nightmares, his or her "findings" may be interpreted as independent verification of the individual's presenting complaints, when in fact the professional has only repeated or "parroted" what he or she has been told. This phenomenon creates an "echo attribution" (Rosen & Davison, 2001), wherein a false sense of validity is gained by attributing to a prestige source what is nothing more than an echo from the original communicator. When testifying on the actual occurrence of subjective complaints, or the truthfulness of an individual's report, clinicians should explain the limits of their findings.

Researchers who take seriously the cautionary guideline in DSM-IV should engage in the same activities recommended to clinicians, and they certainly should disclose in published reports the status of their subjects. There is no excuse for not assessing and reporting on this issue. Even when conducting general epidemiologic surveys, it is possible to include a single question on the occurrence of disability claims or personal injury lawsuits. In this context, journal editors are encouraged to adopt editorial policies that require clear disclosures concerning the status of subjects, as well as a discussion of steps, if any, that were taken to assess situational sources of bias (Rosen, 2004). Until such time that these editorial policies are adopted and enforced, the PTSD data base remains at risk.

REFERENCES

American Psychiatric Association (1980). *Diagnostic and statistical manual of mental disorders* (3rd edn). Washington, DC: Author.

American Psychiatric Association (1987). *Diagnostic and statistical manual of mental disorders* (3rd edn, revised). Washington, DC: Author.

American Psychiatric Association (1994). *Diagnostic and statistical manual of mental disorders* (4th edn). Washington, DC: Author.

American Psychiatric Association (2000). *Diagnostic and statistical manual of mental disorders* (4th edn, text revision). Washington, DC: Author.

Aronson, R. H., Rosenwald, L., & Rosen, G. M. (2001). Attorney–client confidentiality and the assessment of claimants who allege posttraumatic stress disorder. *Washington Law Review, 76,* 313–347.

Avina, C., & O'Donohue, W. (2002). Sexual harassment and PTSD: Is sexual harassment diagnosable trauma? *Journal of Traumatic Stress, 15,* 69–75.

Blanchard, E. B., & Hickling, E. J. (1997). *After the crash: Assessment and treatment of motor vehicle accident survivors.* Washington, DC: American Psychological Association.

Blanchard, E. B., Hickling, E. J., Taylor, A. E., Loos, W. R., Forneris, C. A., & Jaccaard, J. (1996). Who develops PTSD from motor vehicle accidents? *Behaviour Research and Therapy, 34,* 1–10.

Bolton, D., O'Ryan, D., Udwin, O., Boyle, S., & Yule, W. (2000). The long-term psychological effects of a disaster experienced in adolescence: II: General psychopathology. *Journal of Child Psychology and Psychiatry, 41,* 513–523.

Breslau, N. (1990). Stressors: Continuous and discontinuous. *Journal of Applied Social Psychology, 20,* 1666–1673.

Breslau, N., & Davis, G. C. (1987). Posttraumatic stress disorder: The stressor criterion. *The Journal of Nervous and Mental Disease, 175,* 255–264.

Breslau, N., Davis, G. C., Andreski, P., & Peterson, E. (1991). Traumatic events and posttraumatic stress disorder in an urban population of young adults. *Archives of General Psychiatry, 48,* 216–222.

Breslau, N., Kessler, R. C., Chilcoat, H. D., Schultz, L. R., Davis, G. C., & Andreski, P. (1998). Trauma and posttraumatic stress disorder in the community: The 1996 Detroit area survey of trauma. *Archives of General Psychiatry, 55,* 626–632.

Buckley, T. C., Galovski, T., Blanchard, E. B., & Hickling, E. J. (2003). Is the Emotional Stroop paradigm sensitive to malingering? A between-groups study with professional actors and actual trauma survivors. *Journal of Traumatic Stress, 16,* 59–66.

Burkett, B. G., & Whitley, G. (1998). *Stolen valor: How the Vietnam generation was robbed of its heroes and its history.* Dallas, TX: Verity.

Bury, A. S., & Bagby, R. M. (2002). The detection of feigned uncoached and coached posttraumatic stress disorder with the MMPI-2 in a sample of workplace accident victims. *Psychological Assessment, 14,* 474–484.

Carney, P. A., Eliassen, S., Wolford, G. L., Owen, M., Badger, L. W., & Dietrich, A. J. (1999). How physician communication influences recognition of depression in primary care. *Journal of Family Practice, 48,* 958–964.

Charney, D. A., & Russell, R. C. (1994). An overview of sexual harassment. *American Journal of Psychiatry, 151,* 10–17.

Collie, J. (1912). *Malingering and feigned sickness.* London: Edward Arnold.

Daly, O. E., & Johnston, T. G. (2002). The Derryhirk Inn Incident: The psychological sequelae. *Journal of Traumatic Stress, 15,* 461–464.

Dana, C. L. (1894). The traumatic neuroses: Being a description of the chronic nervous disorders that follow shock and injury. In A. M. Hamilton & L. Godkin (eds), *A system of legal medicine,* Vol. II. New York: E. B. Treat.

Davidson, J. R. T., & Foa, E. B. (1991). Refining criteria for posttraumatic stress disorder. *Hospital and Community Psychiatry, 42,* 259–261.

Davidson, J. R. T., Hughes, D., Blazer, D. G., & George, L. K. (1991). Post-traumatic stress disorder in the community: An epidemiological study. *Psychological Medicine, 21,* 713–722.

Eid, J., Johnsen, B. H., & Thayer, J. F. (2001). Post-traumatic stress symptoms following shipwreck of a Norwegian Navy frigate: An early follow-up. *Personality and Individual Differences, 30,* 1283–1295.

Ekman, P., & O'Sullivan, M. (1991). Who can catch a liar? *American Psychologist, 46,* 913–920.

Ekman, P., O'Sullivan, M., & Frank, M. G. (1999). A few can catch a liar. *Psychological Science, 10,* 263–266.

Eldridge, G. (1991). Contextual issues in the assessment of posttraumatic stress disorder. *Journal of Traumatic Stress, 4,* 7–23.

Elhai, J. D., Gold, P. B., Frueh, B. C., & Gold, S. N. (2000). Cross-validation of the MMPI-2 in detecting malingered posttraumatic stress disorder. *Journal of Personality Assessment, 75,* 449–463.

Erichsen, J. E. (1882). *On concussion of the spine, nervous shock, and other obscure injuries of the nervous system, in their clinical and medico-legal aspects.* New York: Bermingham & Co.

Fairbank, J. A., McCaffrey, R. J., & Keane, T. N. (1985). Psychometric detection of fabricated symptoms of post-traumatic stress disorder. *American Journal of Psychiatry, 142,* 501–503.

Foa, E. B., Riggs, D. S., & Gershuny, B. S. (1995). Arousal, numbing, and intrusion: Symptom structure of PTSD following assault. *American Journal of Psychiatry, 152,* 116–120.

Frueh, B. C., Elhai, J. D., Monnier, J., Sauvageot, J. A., Grubaugh, A. L., & Burkett, B. G. (2003). Military records of veterans seeking treatment for combat-related PTSD. Poster presented at the Nineteenth Annual Meeting of the International Society for Traumatic Stress Studies, November, Chicago, IL.

Gordon, J., Sanson-Fisher, R., & Saunders, N. A. (1988). Identification of simulated patients by interns in a casualty setting. *Medical Education, 22,* 533–538.

Greenberg, S. A., & Shuman, D. W. (1997). Irreconcilable conflict between therapeutic and forensic roles. *Professional Psychology: Research and Practice, 28,* 50–57.

Guriel, J., & Fremouw, W. (2003). Assessing malingered posttraumatic stress disorder: A critical review. *Clinical Psychology Review, 23,* 881–904.

Hamilton, A. M. (1904). *Railway and other accidents with relation to injury and disease of the nervous system: A book for court use.* New York: William Wood & Co.

Hamilton, J. D. (1985). Pseudo-posttraumatic stress disorder. *Military Medicine, 150,* 353–356.

Helzer, J. E., Robins, L. N., & McEvoy, L. (1987). Post-traumatic stress disorder in the general population: Findings of the epidemiologic catchment area survey. *The New England Journal of Medicine, 317,* 1630–1634.

Hickling, E. J., Blanchard, E. B., Mundy, E., & Galovski, T. E. (2002). Detection of malingered MVA related posttraumatic stress disorder: An investigation of the ability to detect professional actors by experienced clinicians, psychological tests and psychophysiological assessment. *Journal of Forensic Psychology Practice, 2,* 33–54.

Keane, T. M. (1991). Guidelines for the forensic psychological assessment of posttraumatic stress disorder claimants. In R. I. Simon (ed.), *Posttraumatic stress disorder in litigation*. Washington, DC: American Psychiatric Press.

Kerr, P. (1993). "Ghost Riders" are target of an insurance sting. *New York Times*, August, p. 18.

Kessler, R. C., Sonnega, A., Bromet, E., Hughes, M., & Nelson, C. B. (1995). Posttraumatic stress disorder in the National Comorbidity Survey. *Archives of General Psychiatry*, *52*, 1048–1060.

Knapp, P. C. (1894). Feigned diseases of the mind and nervous system. In A. M. Hamilton & L. Godkin (eds), *A system of legal medicine*, Vol. II. New York: E. B. Treat.

Kopelow, M. L., Schnabl, G. K., Hassard, T. H., Tamblyn, R. M., Klass, D. J., Beazley, G. et al. (1992). Assessment of performance in the office setting with standardized patients: Assessing practicing physicians in two settings using standardized patients. *Academic Medicine*, *67(suppl)*, S19–S21.

Lacoursiere, R. B. (1993). Diverse motives for fictitious post-traumatic stress disorder. *Journal of Traumatic Stress*, *6*, 141–149.

Lees-Haley, P. R. (1986). Pseudo post-traumatic stress disorder. *Trial Diplomacy Journal*, *9*, 17–20.

Lees-Haley, P. R. (1989). Malingering traumatic mental disorder on the Beck Depression Inventory: Cancer phobia and toxic exposure. *Psychological Reports*, *65*, 623–626.

Lees-Haley, P. R. (1990). Malingering mental disorder on the Impact of Events Scale (IES): Toxic exposure and cancer phobia. *Journal of Traumatic Stress*, *3*, 315–321.

Lees-Haley, P. R. (1997). Attorneys influence expert evidence in forensic psychological and neuropsychological cases. *Assessment*, *4*, 321–324.

Lewis, J. B., & Bombaugh, C. C. (1896) (2nd edn). *Stratagems and conspiracies to defraud life insurance companies: An authentic record of remarkable cases*. Baltimore, MD: James H. McClellan.

Lindy, J. D., Green, B. G., & Grace, M. B. (1987). Posttraumatic stress disorder: The stressor criterion (commentary). *The Journal of Nervous and Mental Disease*, *175*, 269–272.

Lynn, E. J., & Belza, N. (1984). Factitious post-traumatic stress disorder: The veteran who never got to Vietnam. *Hospital and Community Psychiatry*, *35*, 697–701.

Lyons, J. A. (1991). Strategies for assessing the potential for positive adjustment following trauma. *Journal of Traumatic Stress*, *4*, 93–111.

Mayou, R. A., Ehlers, A., & Bryant, B. (2002). Posttraumatic stress disorder after motor vehicle accidents: 3-year follow-up of a prospective longitudinal study. *Behaviour Research and Therapy*, *40*, 665–675.

McNally, R. J. (2003). Progress and controversy in the study of posttraumatic stress disorder. *Annual Review of Psychology*, *54*, 229–252.

Nice, D. S., Garland, C. F., Hilton, S. M., Baggett, J. C., & Mitchell, R. E. (1996). Long-term health outcomes and medical effects of torture among US Navy prisoners of war in Vietnam. *JAMA*, *276*, 375–381.

Norris, F. H. (1992). Epidemiology of trauma: Frequency and impact of different potentially traumatic events on different demographic groups. *Journal of Consulting and Clinical Psychology*, *60*, 409–418.

Orr, S. P., & Kaloupek, D. G. (1997). Psychophysiological assessment of posttraumatic stress disorder. In J. P. Wilson & T. M. Keane (eds), *Assessing psychological trauma and PTSD* (pp. 69–97). New York: Guilford Press.

Orr, S. P., McNally, R. J., Rosen, G. M., & Shaler, A. Y. (2004). Psychophysiological reactivity: Implications for conceptualizing PTSD. In G. M. Rosen (ed.), *Posttraumatic stress disorder: Issues and controversies* (pp. 101–126). Chichester: John Wiley & Sons.

Orr, S. P., & Pitman, R. K. (1993). Psychophysiological assessment of attempts to simulate posttraumatic stress disorder. *Biological Psychiatry*, *33*, 127–129.

Otto, R. K. (1989). Bias and expert testimony of mental health professionals in adversarial pro-
    ceedings: A preliminary investigation. *Behavioral Sciences and the Law, 7,* 267–273.

Owen, A., & Winkler, R. (1974). General practitioners and psychosocial problems: An evaluation
    using pseudopatients. *Medical Journal of Australia, 2,* 393.

Page, H. W. (1891). *Railway injuries: With special reference to those of the back and nervous system,
    in their medico-legal and clinical aspects.* London: Charles Griffin & Co.

Pankratz, L. (1998). *Patients who deceive: Assessment and management of risk in providing health
    care and financial benefits.* Springfield, IL: Charles C. Thomas.

Phillips, K. A. (ed.) (2001). *Somatoform and factitious disorders.* Washington, DC: American
    Psychiatric Publishing.

Raphael, B., & Meldrum, L. (1993). The evolution of mental health responses and research in
    Australian disasters. *Journal of Traumatic Stress, 6,* 65–89.

Rosen, G. M. (1995). The *Aleutian Enterprise* sinking and posttraumatic stress disorder: Misdiag-
    nosis in clinical and forensic settings. *Professional Psychology: Research and Practice, 26,*
    82–87.

Rosen, G. M. (2004). Litigation and reported rates of posttraumatic stress disorder. *Personality and
    Individual Differences, 36,* 1291–1294.

Rosen, G. M., & Davison, G. C. (2001). "Echo attributions" and other risks when publishing on
    novel therapies without peer review. *Journal of Clinical Psychology, 57,* 1245–1250.

Rosen, G. M., & Phillips, W. R. (in press). A cautionary lesson from simulated patients. *Journal of
    the American Academy of Psychiatry and the Law.*

Rosen, G. M., & Powel, J. H. (2003). Use of a symptom validity test in the forensic assessment of
    posttraumatic stress disorder. *Journal of Anxiety Disorders, 17,* 361–367.

Rosen, G. M., Sawchuk, C., Atkins, D. C., Brown, M., Price, J. R., & Lees-Haley, P. R. (2004). The
    risk of false-positives when using ATR cut-scores to detect malingered posttraumatic reactions
    on the Trauma Symptom Inventory (TSI). Manuscript submitted for publication.

Rothbaum, B. O., Foa, E. B., Riggs, D. S., Murdock, T., & Walsh, W. (1992). A prospective exami-
    nation of post-traumatic stress disorder in rape victims. *Journal of Traumatic Stress, 3,* 455–475.

Scott, W. (1990). PTSD in DSM-III: A case in the politics of diagnosis and disease. *Social
    Problems, 37,* 294–310.

Shalev, A. Y., Orr, S. P., & Pitman, R. K. (1993). Psychophysiologic assessment of traumatic imagery
    in Israeli civilian patients with posttraumatic stress disorder. *American Journal of Psychiatry,
    150,* 620–624.

Slovenko, R. (1994). Legal aspects of post-traumatic stress disorder. In D. A. Tomb (ed.), *The
    Psychiatric Clinics of North America: Post-traumatic Stress Disorder, 17,* 439–446.

Slovenko, R. (2002). *Psychiatry in law/law in psychiatry.* New York: Brunner Routledge.

Sparr, L. F., & Atkinson, R. M. (1986). Post-traumatic stress disorder as an insanity defense:
    Medico-legal quicksand. *American Journal of Psychiatry, 143,* 608–613.

Sparr, L. F., & Pankratz, L. (1983). Factitious post-traumatic stress disorder. *American Journal of
    Psychiatry, 140,* 1016–1019.

Stein, M. B., Walker, J. R., Hazen, A. L., & Forde, D. R. (1997). Full and partial posttraumatic stress
    disorder: Findings from a community survey. *American Journal of Psychiatry, 154,* 1114–1119.

Stone, A. A., Turkkan, J. S., Bachrach, C. A., Jobe, J. B., Kurtzman, H. S., & Cain, V. S. (eds) (2000).
    The science of self-report: Implications for research and practice. Mahwah, NJ: Lawrence
    Erlbaum Associates.

Storm, J., & Graham, J. R. (2000). Detection of coached general malingering on the MMPI-2.
    Psychological Assessment, 12, 158–165.

Strasburger, L. H. G., Gutheil, T. G., & Brodsky, A. (1997). On wearing two hats: Role conflict
    in serving as both psychotherapist and expert witness. *American Journal of Psychiatry, 154,*
    448–456.

Summerfield, D. (1999). A critique of seven assumptions behind psychological trauma programmes in war-affected areas. *Social Science and Medicine, 48*, 1449–1462.

Trankell, A. (1958). Was Lars sexually assaulted? A study in the reliability of witnesses and of experts. *Journal of Abnormal and Social Psychology, 56*, 385–395.

Trimble, M. (1985). Post-traumatic stress disorder: History of a concept. In C. Figley (ed.), *Trauma and its wake* (pp. 5–14). New York: Brunner/Mazel.

Udwin, O., Boyle, S., Yule, W., Bolton, D., & O'Ryan, D. (2000). Risk factors for long-term psychological effects of a disaster experienced in adolescence: Predictors of post-traumatic stress disorder. *Journal of Child Psychology and Psychiatry, 41*, 969–979.

Vrij, A., & Mann, S. (2003). Deceptive responses and detecting deceit. In P. W. Halligan, C. Bass, & D. A. Oakley (eds), *Malingering and illness deception*. Oxford: Oxford University Press.

Walters, G. L., & Clopton, J. R. (2000). Effect of symptom information and validity scale information on the malingering of depression on the MMPI-2. *Journal of Personality Assessment, 75*, 183–199.

Webb, C. C., & Chapian, M. (1985). *Forgive me*. Old Tappan, NJ: Fleming H. Revell Co.

Weiss, D. S. (1997). Structured clinical interview techniques. In J. P. Wilson & T. M. Keane (eds), *Assessing psychological trauma and PTSD*. New York: Guilford Press.

Wetter, M. W., Baer, R. A., Berry, D. T. R., Robison, L. H., & Sumpter, J. (1993). MMPI-2 profiles of motivated fakers given specific symptom information: A comparison to matched patients. *Psychological Assessment, 5*, 317–323.

Wetter, M. W., & Corrigan, S. K. (1995). Providing information to clients about psychological tests: A survey of attorneys' and law students' attitudes. *Professional Psychology: Research and Practice, 26*, 474–477.

Wetter, M. W., & Deitsch, S. E. (1996). Faking specific disorders and temporal response consistency on the MMPI-2. *Psychological Assessment, 8*, 39–47.

Williams, C. W., Lees-Haley, P. R., & Djanogly, S. E. (1999). Clinical scrutiny of litigants' self-reports. *Professional Psychology: Research and Practice, 30*, 361–367.

Yehuda, R., & McFarlane, A. C. (1995). Conflict between current knowledge about posttraumatic stress disorder and its original conceptual basis. *American Journal of Psychiatry, 152*, 1705–1713.

Young, A. (1995). *The harmony of illusions: Inventing post-traumatic stress disorder*. Princeton, NJ: Princeton University Press.

Youngjohn, J. R. (1995). Confirmed attorney coaching prior to neuropsychological evaluation. *Assessment, 2*, 279–283.

Yule, W., Bolton, D., Udwin, O., Boyle, S., O'Ryan, D., & Nurrish, J. (2000). The long-term psychological effects of a disaster experienced in adolescence: I: The incidence and course of PTSD. *Journal of Child Psychology and Psychiatry, 41*, 503–511.

6 Psychophysiologic Reactivity: Implications for Conceptualizing PTSD

SCOTT P. ORR
Department of Psychiatry, Harvard Medical School, and Veterans Healthcare Administration, USA

RICHARD J. McNALLY
Department of Psychology, Harvard University, USA

GERALD M. ROSEN
Department of Psychology, University of Washington, Seattle, USA

ARIEH Y. SHALEV
Department of Psychiatry, Hadassah University Hospital, Jerusalem, Israel

Posttraumatic stress disorder (PTSD) is characterized by symptoms that reflect some form of persistent *reexperiencing* of the original traumatic event. The presence of at least one reexperiencing symptom (PTSD Category B), from among a group of five, is required by the *Diagnostic and Statistical Manual of Mental Disorders* (DSM-IV-TR; APA, 2000) to confer the PTSD diagnosis. Possible symptoms of reexperiencing include: recurrent and intrusive distressing recollections of the event (B1); recurrent distressing dreams of the event (B2); acting or feeling as if the event was recurring (B3); intense psychological distress at exposure to cues (internal or external) that resemble an aspect of the traumatic event (B4); and physiological reactivity on exposure to cues (internal or external) that resemble an aspect of the traumatic event (B5). Each of these symptoms, with the possible exception of B4, implies the presence of an emotional response related to the traumatic event.

Evidence for the presence and severity of one or more of the reexperiencing symptoms is currently based on what an individual reports, as is the case for most psychiatric symptoms. Consequently, diagnostic accuracy, as well as the integrity of the diagnostic category itself, rests upon the accuracy of self-reported phenomenology. Some highly reliable psychophysiologic findings in PTSD pose an important challenge and raise the possibility that reliance on self-reports leads to an overdiagnosis of the disorder.

Results from more than 20 studies conducted over the past 20 years have provided clear and consistent evidence of heightened psychophysiologic reactivity to cues reminiscent of a traumatic event in individuals with, compared to without, a diagnosis of current PTSD (for review see Orr, Metzger, Miller, & Kaloupek, in press). In other words, the majority

Posttraumatic Stress Disorder: Issues and Controversies. Edited by G. M. Rosen.
© 2004 John Wiley & Sons, Ltd. ISBN 0-470-86284-X/0-470-86285-8.

of individuals with PTSD when exposed to stimuli related to their prior trauma, such as sounds or descriptions of the event, show measurably larger sweat (skin conductance), heart rate, blood pressure, or facial electromyogram responses when compared to individuals who have had similar traumatic experiences, but did not develop PTSD. Heightened reactivity has been demonstrated with standardized, fixed stimuli such as light flashes, combat sounds, or pictures of combat situations (e.g., Blanchard, Kolb, Gerardi, Ryan, & Pallmeyer, 1986; Dobbs & Wilson, 1960; Malloy, Fairbank, & Keane, 1983; McFall, Murburg, Ko, & Veith, 1990), and individually tailored imagery scripts (e.g., Blanchard et al., 1996; Carson et al., 2000; Orr et al., 1998a; Orr, Pitman, Lasko, & Herz, 1993; Pitman et al., 1990; Pitman, Orr, Forgue, de Jong, & Claiborn, 1987).

Most studies suggest that heightened reactivity observed in individuals with PTSD does not result from generalized reactivity to all emotional stimuli; rather, it is specific to emotional stimuli related to the traumatic event. For example, Orr and Roth (2000) combined the data from five studies (yielding 72 PTSD and 65 non-PTSD subjects) that used the same script-driven imagery procedure, and compared individuals' reactivity to recollections of personalized trauma-related events with responses to personalized stressful events unrelated to the trauma. Results from this analysis indicated that individuals with PTSD were significantly more reactive to trauma-related scripts than to scripts describing other personally stressful events. Additional evidence for the relative specificity of emotional reactivity comes from findings demonstrating that individuals with PTSD show comparable or somewhat smaller autonomic responses during performance of mental arithmetic, as compared to individuals without PTSD (Blanchard et al., 1986; Keane et al., 1998; McDonagh-Coyle et al., 2001; Orr, Meyerhoff, Edwards, & Pitman, 1998b). A purely physical stressor, orthostatic challenge, also produces comparable increases in heart rate and blood pressure among PTSD and non-PTSD groups (Orr et al., 1998b).

In contrast to the above findings, Kinzie et al. (1998) found a more generalized increase in reactivity across a range of stressful stimuli. In this study, male and female Cambodian refugees with PTSD from prolonged and intense trauma demonstrated elevated HR responses to videotaped scenes of an auto accident, domestic violence, the Vietnam War, and a hurricane, as well as to scenes of a Cambodian refugee camp. It is possible that the pervasiveness and severity of traumatic events experienced by the refugees became associated with a wide range of stimuli that subsequently became capable of producing emotional responses. It also is possible that cultural factors played a role in the mediation or moderation of the Cambodian refugees' physiologic responses. For example, catastrophic interpretations of the dizziness experienced during orthostasis can precipitate panic attacks and trauma-related flashbacks in Cambodian refugee psychiatric patients (e.g., Hinton Pollack, Pitman, & Orr, 2004). In this way, exposure to any stressful stimulus capable of producing a perceptible physiologic response in a Cambodian patient may have the potential to precipitate catastrophic interpretations, intrusive recollections, and/or panic, which in turn could amplify physiologic responses.

There also is evidence suggesting that individuals with PTSD are more reactive to particular types or classes of stimuli not directly related to the index traumatic event. For example, individuals with PTSD are more physiologically reactive to aversive stimuli such as loud sounds or mild electric shock than are those without PTSD (e.g., Casada, Amdur,

Larsen, & Liberzon, 1998; Orr, Lasko, Shalev, & Pitman, 1995). Beckham and colleagues (2002) reported that Vietnam combat veterans produced larger blood pressure responses (and a trend toward larger increases in HR) during recollection of a past experience of anger, compared to veterans without PTSD. This finding accords well with previous evidence of increased anger and hostility in some individuals with PTSD (e.g., Beckham, Moore, & Reynolds, 2000).

The finding that individuals with PTSD produce significantly larger psychophysiologic responses upon exposure to trauma-related cues, compared to individuals without the disorder, led to the inclusion of "physiologic reactivity" as a formal symptom criterion. This symptom was originally included in the category of arousal symptoms (Criterion D6) in the DSM-III-R. However, in the subsequent revision of the diagnostic manual (DSM-IV), this symptom was moved to the category of reexperiencing symptoms (Criterion B5). Reclassification of the physiological reactivity symptom reflected an important reconceptualization: from the view that this symptom is simply an indication of generally heightened arousal, to the recognition that it measures the degree to which an event is emotionally reexperienced.

The pathogenesis of heightened physiologic reactivity can be explained within a classical conditioning framework as the manifestation of a conditioned emotional response. In this framework, the original traumatic event serves as an unconditioned stimulus, and the accompanying fear, helplessness, or horror is the unconditioned response (e.g., Keane, Fairbank, Caddell, Zimering, & Bender, 1985; Kolb & Multalipassi, 1982; Pitman, 1988). Subsequent exposures to reminders of the original traumatic event then serve to elicit the conditioned emotional responses that define Criterion B5. However, a simple conditioning model of PTSD is limited by its inability to explain why the emotional responses persist over time (i.e., are resistant to extinction). Lang's (1985) bioinformational theory of emotion offers an alternative framework for conceptualizing the heightened and persistent physiologic reactivity associated with PTSD (e.g., Orr et al., 1993; Pitman et al., 1987). Within this framework, PTSD is comprised of one or more pathological emotion networks that can produce physiologic reactivity and other reexperiencing symptoms when activated. An important feature of these emotion networks is the ability to maintain their integrity over long periods of time, as suggested by findings that demonstrate heightened physiologic reactivity occurring 40–50 years after an event (Orr et al., 1993).

As PTSD is currently defined, the presence of heightened physiologic reactivity to cues that resemble an aspect of the trauma is neither necessary nor sufficient for conferring the diagnosis. It is only necessary for an individual to endorse any one or more of the five Category B reexperiencing symptoms. Thus, an individual's failure to demonstrate a heightened physiologic response to trauma-related reminders does not preclude his or her receiving the PTSD diagnosis, provided that one of the other reexperiencing symptoms is present. At the same time, studies have examined whether Criterion B5 alone can be used to identify those with the disorder versus those without (e.g., Blanchard, Kolb, & Prins, 1991; Malloy et al., 1983; Orr et al., 1998a; Pitman et al., 1987; Shalev, Orr, & Pitman, 1993). In these studies, the presence or absence of heightened physiologic reactivity is used as the basis to infer the presence or absence of full PTSD. Results from this work have demonstrated that psychophysiologic reactivity alone can accurately classify approximately 55–90% of individuals who are diagnosed on the basis of clinical interview with current PTSD (sensitivity), and 80–100% of individuals who are identified as never having met criteria for the disorder (specificity).

Based on the above work, it is clearly evident that the majority of individuals diagnosed with PTSD demonstrate, under controlled laboratory conditions, heightened physiologic reactivity upon exposure to cues related to their traumatic events. Even so, there is a substantial minority of individuals who meet DSM criteria for PTSD (on the basis of self-reported symptoms during clinical interview), yet do not demonstrate heightened psychophysiologic reactivity when exposed to cues related to their traumatic event. Explanations for the failure of some individuals with PTSD to show heightened psychophysiologic reactivity, and implications for conceptualizing this disorder, have been given only limited attention (e.g., Orr et al., in press). Yet, the finding that roughly 40% of individuals who meet full DSM-IV criteria for PTSD also show little or no physiologic reactivity raises significant issues. One important question is whether PTSD-diagnosed individuals who fail to demonstrate heightened physiologic reactivity during exposure to trauma-related stimuli also report diminished subjective experiences of emotional arousal to such stimuli. The results of comparisons between physiologic responder and non-responders in Keane et al.'s (1998) study produced a non-significant trend toward lower SUDS (subjective units of distress) in the non-responder group. The question of whether physiologic non-responders report correspondingly lower subjective emotions bears on issues central to the field of trauma studies.

NEW DATA ON A CENTRAL QUESTION

A discriminant function analysis was performed for the purposes of this chapter, to clarify some of the issues that may underlie the finding that a substantial minority of PTSD-diagnosed individuals are not physiologically reactive to trauma-relevant stimuli presented in research studies. This analysis combined psychophysiologic data from the script-driven, trauma-related imagery studies of Vietnam combat veterans (Pitman et al., 1987, 1990), World War II and Korean veterans (Orr et al., 1993), Israeli civilian trauma (Shalev et al., 1993), childhood sexual abuse (Orr et al., 1998a), and female Vietnam veteran nurses (Carson et al., 2000). These studies provided combined samples of 91 individuals diagnosed with current PTSD, and 84 individuals who never had PTSD, based on DSM-III-R or DSM-IV criteria. The discriminant function was derived from the skin conductance, heart rate, and lateral frontalis electromyogram responses during personalized trauma-related imagery (average of two scripts), and produced a sensitivity of 57% (51/91 with PTSD) and a specificity of 89% (75/84 without PTSD). In other words, 57% of individuals with a PTSD diagnosis demonstrated heightened psychophysiologic reactivity when recalling prior trauma events, whereas 89% of individuals without PTSD did not demonstrate this response. It is evident from this analysis and our prior review of the literature that a majority of PTSD-diagnosed individuals demonstrate, under controlled laboratory conditions, heightened physiologic reactivity upon exposure to trauma-relevant cues. At the same time, a substantial minority of individuals who meet criteria for PTSD (on the basis of self-reported symptoms during clinical interview) do not demonstrate heightened psychophysiologic reactivity.

Table 6.1. Physiologic and self-reported emotional responses to trauma-related scripts in psychophysiologic responders and non-responders meeting DSM (III-R, IV) criteria for current PTSD

Variable	Psychophysiologic Responders (n = 44)		Psychophysiologic Non-Responders (n = 35)		t (77)	p
	M	SD	M	SD		
Physiologic Responses						
Heart rate (bpm)	12.4	12.3	3.4	3.6	4.2	<.001
Skin conductance (μS)	1.6	1.2	0.2	0.4	6.6	<.001
LF-EMG (μV)	4.2	4.8	1.0	1.2	3.8	<.001
Self-report Responses						
Vividness	10.6	2.1	10.7	2.2	−0.2	.85
Emotion Dimension						
Arousal	9.9	2.4	10.0	2.8	−0.1	.95
Valence-Pleasantness	0.8	1.5	0.4	0.8	1.3	.20
Dominance-Control	2.3	2.7	2.4	3.0	−0.2	.88
Discrete Emotions						
Happiness	0.4	1.3	0.1	0.4	−1.2	.25
Sadness	9.9	2.7	8.6	3.4	1.9	.06
Fear	9.1	2.9	9.8	3.0	−1.0	.34
Surprise	7.8	3.9	8.1	3.7	−0.3	.77
Anger	9.9	3.0	9.6	3.3	0.4	.70
Disgust	9.0	4.0	9.6	2.7	0.8	.44
Guilt[1]	7.2	3.9	7.4	3.8	−0.2	.85

[1] Guilt self-reports were not obtained in the earliest script-driven imagery studies. Consequently, the sample sizes for the responder (n = 34) and non-responder (n = 23) groups are somewhat smaller than for the other self-report measures.

The discriminant function was used to classify individuals diagnosed with PTSD into physiologic "Responder" and "Non-responder" subgroups. On the basis of physiologic responses during trauma-related imagery, individuals with a discriminant function posterior probability score >.50 were classified as responders and those with a posterior probability score ≤.50 were classified as non-responders. Comparisons of mean physiologic responses and self-reported subjective experiences during trauma-related imagery for these subgroups are presented in Table 6.1. All self-reports were obtained using 0–12 point Likert-type scales following the imagining of each script. Scores represent the averaged response for two trauma-related scripts. Self-report data were only available for 79/91 PTSD subjects because self-reports were not obtained in the Shalev et al. (1993) study.

As can be seen, the physiologic responder and non-responder subgroups reported strikingly similar levels of imagery vividness, arousal, and negative emotional experiences while recalling traumatic events. Although there was a tendency for responders to provide higher ratings for sadness ($p = .06$), this finding seems insufficient to explain the substantive group differences in physiologic reactivity.

Findings from the current analysis indicate that the failure of PTSD-diagnosed individuals to demonstrate physiologic reactivity in the presence of trauma-related stimuli is not explained by diminished subjective emotional experiences or perceived vividness of scripted imagery. In the remainder of this chapter we consider alternative hypotheses, and implications of these findings for our understanding of the PTSD construct.

EXPLAINING THE LACK OF PSYCHOPHYSIOLOGIC REACTIVITY

Numerous competing hypotheses can be postulated to account for the finding that a substantial minority of individuals diagnosed with PTSD are not physiologically reactive to trauma-relevant cues when assessed in a laboratory setting. Broadly speaking, these hypotheses fall into several general areas: (1) a psychological process or mechanism is operating that acts to block or diminish physiologic activity; (2) the measures and/or methods used in the laboratory setting do not provide an adequate assessment of individuals who are otherwise reactive; (3) there exist problems inherent to self-reports of emotional reactivity; (4) PTSD is not a categorical construct; and/or (5) individuals can meet the criteria of PTSD without having an anxiety disorder and associated psychophysiologic reactivity.

PSYCHOLOGICAL PROCESSES MAY BLOCK OR DIMINISH REACTIVITY

Several psychological processes (e.g., dissociation, cognitive avoidance) can be advanced to explain the diminished physiologic reactivity of some individuals diagnosed with PTSD. In each case, the essential assumption is that some individuals guard against the arousal of trauma-relevant cues by psychologically disengaging from the stimulus. These explanatory frameworks would predict that non-responders on physiologic measures should also demonstrate diminished subjective reports of emotional distress as a consequence of their detachment, purposeful avoidance, or other psychological process.

ANXIETY SENSITIVITY AND COGNITIVE AVOIDANCE

Elevated *anxiety sensitivity* in people with PTSD may explain why some PTSD patients fail to respond physiologically to personalized trauma scripts in script-driven imagery studies. Anxiety sensitivity refers to fears of anxiety-related sensations (Reiss & McNally, 1985). Just as people vary in their proneness to experience episodes of anxiety (i.e., trait anxiety), so do they vary in their fear of anxiety-related sensations (i.e., anxiety sensitivity). Individuals with elevated anxiety sensitivity often hold beliefs about the harmfulness of these sensations. For example, such individuals may regard heart palpitations as signifying an impending heart attack, whereas other individuals would regard such sensations as simply annoying. Accordingly, episodes of fear or anxiety are much more aversive for people with high anxiety sensitivity. Considerable research has established the Anxiety Sensitivity Index (ASI; Peterson & Reiss, 1992; Reiss, Peterson, Gursky, & McNally, 1986) as a reliable and valid measure of this construct (for reviews, see McNally, 2002; Taylor, 1999). Further, individuals with PTSD tend to score high on the ASI (McNally et al., 1987) and in the same range as panic disorder patients, many of whom have agoraphobia (Taylor, Koch, & McNally, 1992). This suggests that many individuals suffering from PTSD are likely to dread the experience of anxiety symptoms themselves.

It is possible that individuals scoring high on the ASI may be disinclined to process distressing scenarios during script-driven imagery. A fear of bodily sensations associated with anxiety-linked arousal may render some individuals reluctant to produce the imagery prompted by the script. Such individuals may engage in cognitive avoidance, and thereby attenuate their physiologic response. Indeed, patients with panic disorder and agoraphobia fail to exhibit the expected heightened physiologic response to scenarios of their phobic or panic-related fears in script-driven imagery studies (Cook, Melamed, Cuthbert, McNeil, & Lang, 1988; Zander & McNally, 1988). Given that the ASI scores of PTSD patients are nearly as high as those with panic disorder, elevated anxiety sensitivity may foster cognitive avoidance in some PTSD patients, thereby abolishing their physiologic response during imagery of trauma. Moreover, in one study, PTSD subjects who had scored high on a questionnaire tapping ability to control one's imagery were physiologically non-reactive to traumatic scripts (Laor et al., 1998). Perhaps individuals who are both motivated to avoid disturbing imagery (those high on anxiety sensitivity) and capable of controlling such imagery might be those most likely to be non-responders in the laboratory.

The self-report findings presented in Table 6.1, however, seem inconsistent with the argument that control of one's imagery provides an explanation for why some individuals with PTSD are physiologically non-reactive. As can be seen in Table 6.1, self-reported experiences of dominance or feeling "in control" were comparably low in the two subgroups. Feelings of being in control would seemingly be higher in the non-responder subgroup if this variable was responsible for reduced physiologic reactivity. In other words, having greater control over one's imagery ability ought to be reflected in an individual's report of how "in control" they felt while recalling their traumatic event. Perhaps it could be argued that individuals with high anxiety sensitivity perceived a lack of control because of their inability to handle an image they were instructed to hold. Even if this proposal had merit, however, it would not account for non-responders and responders providing equivalent ratings for image vividness and emotional arousal.

IMAGERY ABILITY AND ABSORPTION

People vary in their ability to generate vivid imagery, and psychologists have devised different questionnaire measures to capture these individual differences. Relative difficulty in generating imagery may attenuate physiologic responses in paradigms such as that of script-driven imagery. Lang (1979) studied anxiety reactions of phobic individuals and observed that, "not all scripts will evoke vivid images, even in responsive subjects" (p. 499). Lang attributed the limitations of script-driven procedures to several factors, including an individual's ability to vividly imagine scenes. In several studies, training in visualization, with additional scripted instructions, increased physiologic responses (Lang,

1977; Lang, Levin, Miller, & Kozak, 1983). Is it possible that relatively poor imagery ability accounts for physiologic non-responders among PTSD patients?

Certainly individuals characterized by powerful imagery abilities are especially responsive during script-driving imagery. For example, two of us (McNally and Orr) conducted a study of 10 persons whose traumatic event allegedly was having been abducted by space aliens (McNally et al., in press). Each person had experienced at least one episode of apparent sleep paralysis accompanied by hypnopompic (upon awakening) hallucinations. During these episodes, the sleeper begins to awaken from rapid eye movement (REM) sleep—the stage of sleep marked by vivid dreams and full body paralysis—but the cognitive/perceptual and motoric aspects of REM become temporarily desynchronized. The sleeper awakens to discover that he or she is paralyzed, and often becomes very frightened. Dream mentation may intrude into emerging wakefulness congruent with the emotion of intense anxiety. This mentation takes the form of hallucinated figures in the bedroom, which our subjects interpreted as space aliens. Eight of our "abductees" underwent hypnotic regression sessions in which they recovered "memories" of having been taken aboard spaceships and subjected to intrusive "medical" and sexual probing.

Relative to control subjects who heard the personalized neutral, positive, stressful, and traumatic abduction scripts of the abductees, the abductees were markedly more responsive on heart rate, skin conductance, and electromyogram measures. Indeed, the magnitude of responding to abduction scripts resembles that of the responses of PTSD patients to scripts of their traumatic experiences. The mean heart rate, skin conductance, and lateral frontalis electromyogram (LF-EMG) responses of the abductees during recollection of their abduction scripts were 7.8 bpm, 1.8 µS, and 1.8 µV (respectively), whereas the corresponding mean values for 72 PTSD subjects during recollection of their trauma scripts were 7.9 bpm, 1.0 µS, and 2.6 µV (Orr & Roth, 2000). However, unlike most PTSD patients, the abductees also showed heightened physiologic reactivity to their other stressful scripts unrelated to alien abduction.

Findings from the abductee study indicated that presumably false traumatic memories are capable of producing physiologic reactivity of similar magnitude to that produced by verifiable traumatic events. This study also revealed the potential importance of absorption (Tellegen & Atkinson, 1974), a personality trait related to fantasy proneness and capability. People scoring high on the absorption scale have rich imagery capabilities, and the abductees scored much higher than control subjects on Tellegen and Atkinson's absorption scale (21.6 versus 9.6). Taken together, these data suggest that people high on imagery ability or absorption are especially likely to exhibit marked psychophysiologic reactivity to negative emotional scripts during script-driven imagery experiments. Conversely, people who fail to respond physiologically may score relatively low on measures of imagery ability or absorption.

Although individuals characterized by powerful imagery abilities are especially responsive during script-driving imagery, the self-report findings for physiologic responder and non-responder subgroups presented in Table 6.1 suggest that reduced imagery ability is not a likely explanation for why some individuals with PTSD are non-reactive. As can be seen in Table 6.1, self-reported imagery vividness during recollection of the traumatic events was comparably high in the physiologic responder and non-responder subgroups. This comparability is consistent with findings from early script-driven imagery studies

(Orr et al., 1993; Pitman et al., 1987, 1990) of no differences in imagery ability assessed with the Questionnaire on Mental Imagery (Sheehan, 1967) between PTSD and non-PTSD groups. In addition, the similarities of self-reported emotion intensities in the responder and non-responder subgroups are inconsistent with putative differences in imagery ability. Reduced imagery ability ought to be associated with less intense emotional experiences across all channels; there is no reason to expect that it would only influence physiologic responses.

EMOTIONAL NUMBING

Numbing of general responsiveness is a core feature of PTSD represented within Category C symptoms of PTSD. Litz et al. (1997) have proposed that emotional numbing is a consequence of chronically heightened arousal, noting a strong correlation between self-reported emotional numbing symptoms and symptoms of hyperarousal. A study that re-examined data from the large psychophysiologic study of Keane et al. (1998) also found self-reported hyperarousal symptoms (DSM-IV, PTSD Category D) to be strongly correlated with a composite measure of emotional numbing (Flack, Litz, Hsieh, Kaloupek, & Keane, 2000). Of particular relevance to the present discussion, data from the Keane et al. study provided an opportunity to examine the relationship between physiologic reactivity and emotional numbing. If increased emotional numbing is responsible for decreased physiologic reactivity to trauma-related stimuli, a significant negative correlation would be expected between these two variables. Contrary to this expectation, Flack et al. observed a small *positive* correlation between their measure of heart rate reactivity to the challenge procedure (trauma—neutral) and the composite measure of emotional numbing.

It is also worth noting that the comparison between physiologic responders and non-responders performed in the Keane et al. (1998) study revealed only a single difference for the Category C symptoms. This difference reflected increased endorsement by physiologic responders of the symptom related to "sense of foreshortened future." Thus, non-responders were not more likely to endorse emotional numbing symptoms, as would be expected if emotional numbing were responsible for the reduced physiologic reactivity to trauma-related stimuli. The present comparison of physiologic responders and non-responders also fails to support the emotional-numbing explanation by demonstrating that non-responders and responders report the same level of subjective emotional engagement during imagery of their traumatic event.

DISSOCIATION

The concept of dissociation and its potential role in the development and maintenance of PTSD has received increased interest and emphasis in recent years. Considerable attention has been given to assessing whether peritraumatic dissociation is useful for predicting risk for PTSD (see McNally, Bryant, & Ehlers, 2003). Diagnostically, symptoms of dissociation are a requisite feature of acute stress disorder, so that the presence of at least three dissociative symptoms is needed to confer the diagnosis (DSM-IV). The dissociation symptom requirement in acute stress disorder, which otherwise is symptomatically similar to PTSD, has generated considerable debate (e.g., Brewin, Andrews, Rose, & Kirk,

1999; Bryant & Harvey, 2000; Harvey & Bryant, 1999). For example, in a prospective study of acute trauma victims, Shalev, Peri, Canetti, and Schreiber (1996) found that dissociative symptoms experienced during the traumatic event, and measured within one week, predicted PTSD status at six months. On the other hand, measures that assess dissociation as a trait-like phenomenon (e.g., Dissociative Experiences Scale; Bernstein & Putnam, 1986) do not appear to be good predictors of PTSD risk (e.g., Dancu, Riggs, Hearst-Ikeda, Shoyer, & Foa, 1996; Feeny, Zoellner, Fitzgibbons, & Foa, 2000).

The relationship between dissociative tendencies and the failure to show heightened physiologic reactivity when confronted with trauma-related reminders has received some consideration. For example, Cuthbert et al. (2003) raised the possibility that suppression or dissociation might explain the failure of their predominantly female PTSD sample to show heightened physiologic responses while imagining trauma-related scenes. Gender alone is an unlikely explanation for this reduced reactivity, given that several studies have demonstrated heightened physiologic reactivity in female PTSD samples (e.g., Carson et al., 2000; Orr et al., 1998a; Pitman et al., 2001).

Griffin, Resick, and Mechanic (1997) studied women who had been sexually assaulted, and assessed physiological reactivity while they described their past experiences. Women who had developed PTSD following the sexual assault and who retrospectively reported greater peritraumatic dissociation (depersonalization) at the time of the rape were less physiologically reactive, compared to women who reported less dissociation. However, secondary analyses of the large Vietnam veteran data set obtained by Keane et al. (1998) failed to find the expected negative relationship between self-reported peritraumatic dissociation and psychophysiologic reactivity (Kaufman et al., 2002). The explanation for these discrepant findings is not clear, but could be attributable to sample differences in PTSD chronicity. The trauma sample studied by Griffin and colleagues had relatively acute PTSD, whereas the veterans studied by Keane and colleagues had PTSD of long-standing duration.

Results from a study of individuals who had previously suffered a serious cardiac event suggest that reactivity to some stimuli may be increased in individuals who report high peritraumatic dissociation (Ladwig et al., 2002). Individuals who retrospectively reported high dissociation were found to produce larger skin conductance and eyeblink electromyogram responses to startling tones, compared to individuals who reported little or no peritraumatic dissociation. Within the group that reported high peritraumatic dissociation, significantly larger electromyogram, but not skin conductance, responses to the loud tones were observed in the PTSD subgroup (individuals with full or partial PTSD) compared to those without PTSD. In contrast to the increased reactivity observed for peritraumatic dissociation, chronic depersonalization disorder has been found to be associated with smaller skin conductance reactivity to unpleasant pictures (Sierra et al., 2002).

The present analysis raises a significant challenge to the argument that dissociation accounts for physiologic non-reactivity in individuals with PTSD. Given that physiologic non-responders produced high scores on the arousal and emotion self-report measures, one would need to explain how and why a dissociative process selectively suppresses the physiologic component of the emotional experience while leaving the subjective experience intact. Although such a selective influence may be possible, it seems unlikely. Further, the existence of a selective influence would raise questions about the protective value of dissociation, given that only the physiologic component of emotion appears reduced. An argument might be made that the self-reports of the non-responder group were primarily driven by situational demands rather than emotional experience, and that the imputed dissociative process did in fact reduce the subjective, as well as physiologic, emotion component. However, this sort of explanation places the concept of dissociation on a slippery slope; it becomes essentially untestable if it can be invoked to explain any outcome. This latter argument would also indicate that self-reports are an unreliable index of subjective emotional experiences.

REPRESSION

The concept of repression would seem to provide a possible explanation for why some individuals are not physiologically reactive when exposed to trauma-related stimuli. In other words, unconscious defenses, such as repression, may be used to keep psychologically and emotionally distressing memories or information from reaching awareness, which would otherwise lead to an overwhelming level of distress. Explanations for reduced physiologic reactivity to trauma-related stimuli that presume the operation of an unconscious defense mechanism are problematic. First, as noted above in the discussion of dissociation, it is not clear how or why a process such as repression would selectively suppress the physiological component of the emotional experience while leaving the subjective, self-report-based experience intact. It would seem more likely that repression would lead to the diminution of both subjective reports of emotional arousal and physiologic reactivity. Second, if repression were capable of significantly reducing physiologic reactivity to trauma-related stimuli, it also seems likely that it would diminish other PTSD-reexperiencing symptoms. Consequently, an individual using the defense mechanism of repression would be less likely to meet full DSM criteria for PTSD and thereby would not be included in the non-reactive PTSD group. Third, there is some evidence suggesting that unexpressive individuals or those suppressing their emotions are actually more, rather than less, physiologically reactive (e.g., Buck, 1979; Notarius & Levenson, 1979).

INTELLECTUALIZATION, DISTRACTION, CONCEALING

One factor that may influence reactivity in the laboratory is whether subjects adopt an intellectualized cognitive set (e.g., "I am participating in a scientific experiment and none of this is really threatening"). Related to this hypothesis, Lazarus and colleagues demonstrated many years ago that intellectualized cognitive sets can reduce arousal to a variety of stimuli, including threatening films of work site injuries (e.g., Koriat, Melkman, Averill, & Lazarus, 1972) and primitive "subincision" rites (e.g., Speisman, Lazarus, Mordkoff, & Davison, 1964).

There also is evidence suggesting that the modification of overt expressive behavior can reduce physiologic reactivity. For example, Lanzetta, Cartwright-Smith, and Kleck (1976) instructed college undergraduates to either conceal (or exaggerate) their facial expressions when anticipating and receiving painful electric shocks. Skin conductance responses and subjective reports of arousal were reduced when individuals attempted to conceal their expressive behavior. A study that examined the effect of reducing facial expressive behavior by means of a social manipulation (i.e., being observed) also found correspondingly reduced skin conductance and self-reported pain responses to an electric shock (Kleck et al., 1976).

There is limited evidence suggesting that individuals with PTSD may intentionally attempt to withhold their emotional responses, both positive and negative. Combat veterans with PTSD have been found to report more frequent and intense attempts to conceal their emotional responses, compared to veterans without PTSD (Roemer, Litz, Orsillo, & Wagner, 2001). However, the results from a study that directly examined veterans' ability to hide (dissimulate) heightened physiologic reactivity found that individuals diagnosed with PTSD were not able to significantly reduce their physiologic responses to combat-related stimuli when explicitly instructed to do so (Gerardi, Blanchard, & Kolb, 1989). This suggests that the physiologic components of the emotional response associated with a traumatic event are sufficiently potent in reactive individuals with PTSD that they will manifest even when there is an "inhibiting" instructional set.

FAILURE OF MEASURES AND/OR METHODS

THE RELEVANT PHYSIOLOGIC CHANNEL(S) ARE NOT BEING MEASURED FOR ALL INDIVIDUALS

Research examining psychophysiologic reactivity to trauma-related stimuli has focused on a relatively specific set of measures including heart rate, electrodermal activity, blood pressure, and electromyogram (see Table 6.1, Orr et al., in press). In one or more studies, each of these measures alone and/or in combination has demonstrated relatively good sensitivity and specificity for discriminating between individuals with and without PTSD. Even so, the possibility exists that some individuals "fail" to demonstrate heightened physiologic reactivity to trauma-related stimuli in the laboratory because the physiologic channel that is most personally relevant is not being measured. It has long been known that individuals may be more reactive in one physiologic channel than another. For example, a study comparing cardiovascular and electrodermal responses to a mental arithmetic stressor observed that individuals who were not reactive in heart rate tended to be more reactive in skin conductance (Lawler, 1980). Thus, an assessment that relies solely on heart rate as its physiologic measure of emotional reactivity would risk missing or underestimating the reactivity of an individual who is more responsive through electrodermal activity.

Even though individuals may differ in the amount of activation they demonstrate in one physiologic channel or another, strong emotional experiences are likely to produce some amount of activation (Cacioppo et al., 1992), which presumably can be measured. The operational characteristics of the physiologic systems involved in emotional experience and expression may explain some individual differences in reactivity. More specifically, Cacioppo et al. (1992) suggested that individual differences in the *gains* (ratio of input to output) of somatic and sympathetic nervous systems may explain why some individuals show relatively greater or lesser expressive (somatic) and/or sympathetic reactions. A system with a higher, compared to lower, gain will produce a larger physiologic response to an emotional stimulus of a given intensity. Furthermore, it is possible that within the same individual one system will have a high gain whereas another system will have a low gain. Thus, an individual could show large skin conductance responses and relatively small facial electromyogram responses because the sympathetic nervous system has high gain whereas the somatic system has a low gain. Of greatest relevance to the present discussion, however, is the recognition that somatic and sympathetic activity will increase, even in channels with low gains, as emotional intensity increases. It is difficult to imagine that strong emotions, such as those captured by the PTSD-reexperiencing symptoms, would fail to produce some amount of measurable activity in at least one physiologic system.

The likelihood that physiologic reactivity will be "missed," especially in the presence of strong emotion, is substantially reduced when multiple physiologic channels are measured simultaneously. For example, the script-driven imagery studies of Orr and colleagues have classified physiologic reactivity to trauma-related stimuli using a discriminant function based on a combination of skin conductance, heart rate, and facial electromyogram responses, as done for Table 6.1 (see also Orr & Roth, 2000). Thus, classification as a physiologic "non-responder" represents relatively reduced reactivity across three distinct physiologic channels, i.e., sweat, cardiovascular, and somatic. Although someone classified as a "non-responder" might have shown a modest response in one physiologic channel or another, the response would have been of sufficiently small magnitude so as to result in classification as a non-responder.

INHERENT LIMITATIONS OF SELF-REPORT

DESYNCHRONY BETWEEN RESPONSE MODALITIES

Instances where an individual reports heightened physiologic reactivity to reminders of their trauma (B5), but fails to demonstrate such reactivity when actually measured under controlled conditions, raises the possibility that some individuals may be overreporting the presence and/or severity of PTSD symptoms. In fact, in the large-scale psychophysiologic study of PTSD in Vietnam combat veterans, 70% of 120 individuals with current PTSD who were physiologic non-responders endorsed the symptom of "physiologic reactivity upon exposure to events . . ." during a structured clinical interview (Keane et al., 1998). Thus, a substantial majority of individuals who were clearly non-reactive in the laboratory reported that they experienced physiologic reactivity in the presence of trauma-related events.

In a study that included an examination of heart rate responses to videotaped combat scenes, 13 of 16 (81%) Vietnam veterans diagnosed with PTSD reported that the scenes were highly disturbing, but only 2 (13%) individuals showed a substantive heart rate response to the scenes (Kinzie et al., 1998). The results presented in Table 6.1 also demonstrate a marked discrepancy between the self-reported subjective measures of emotional arousal and physiologic reactivity experienced during trauma-related imagery in the physiologic non-responder group. Taken together, the Keane et al. (1998) and Kinzie et al. (1998) findings, as well as those presented in Table 6.1, demonstrate the potential for substantial discrepancies between self-reported experiences and physiologic reactivity. There is no question that psychophysiologic measures and assessment procedures provide an imperfect index of an individual's emotional experiences. However, the magnitude of this discrepancy clearly raises concerns about the accuracy of diagnostic determinations based solely on self-reported behaviors and subjective experiences.

The lack of physiologic reactivity to trauma-relevant cues among some individuals who report PTSD symptoms calls to mind a discussion of similar issues in the 1960s, when behavior therapists first began to systematically measure different response modalities among phobic subjects (Lang, 1968). The observed "desynchrony" across various response modalities led to the "three system" model of anxiety and fear phenomenon (Lang, 1968, 1979). The relevance of this phenomenon to the question of whether a diagnosis of PTSD should be made in the absence of physiologic findings is an important matter that will be considered later in this chapter.

DISTORTIONS AND BIAS IN REPORTING

There may be several reasons why individuals can report high levels of distress while physiological markers of emotional distress are absent. Individuals who malinger the symptoms of PTSD would be expected to produce elevated self-reported distress while showing little or no physiological reactivity. The fact that PTSD is a compensable disorder may serve to motivate some individuals to feign or exaggerate symptoms. At the same time, psychiatric issues and motivations that lead to misreporting and simulation of clinical disorders are not limited to malingering, and can involve such diverse and complex issues as factitious disorders, or the desire to explain shortcomings and a dysfunctional life (Lacoursiere, 1993). It seems possible that such presentations of "Pseudo-posttraumatic stress disorder" (Hamilton, 1985) could include high levels of reported emotional distress and PTSD symptoms in the absence of elevated psychophysiologic reactivity to trauma-related stimuli.

People who are experiencing psychological distress from uncertain sources may attribute their difficulties to earlier adverse experiences that are now remembered as "traumatic." Even though the original experience did not qualify as a genuine traumatic conditioning event, distressed individuals may later remember it as having been more terrifying than it was at the time it occurred. Such retrospective reappraisal may not only lead individuals to attribute their difficulties to earlier events, but also to express their distress within the symptomatic language of PTSD. For example, although only 15% of men who served in the Vietnam War were actually assigned to combat units (Dean, 1997, p. 209), 30.9% of all military personnel subsequently qualified for PTSD (Kulka et al., 1990, p. 63). Perhaps some of these men, such as those meeting criteria for delayed-onset PTSD, had reappraised their military experiences as traumatic years later. Consistent with this possibility, Roemer, Litz, Orsillo, Ehlich, and Friedman (1998) observed an average increase in retrospective reports of war-zone trauma from post-deployment to follow-up assessments, which were conducted 1–3 years later. Current posttraumatic symptom severity was found to be positively related to the change in reported war-zone trauma. It is possible that PTSD resulting from reappraisal of a prior event is less likely to be associated with heightened psychophysiologic reactivity.

Particular personality traits also may be associated with exaggerated reporting of physical and psychological complaints. For example, the construct of "anxiety sensitivity" that was discussed earlier can lead an individual to over-emphasize the slightest indicant of emotional discomfort. Biased symptom reporting also has been found to be associated with neuroticism (or trait negative affectivity). Individuals with high neuroticism tend to view life and personal experiences with general dissatisfaction, and are likely to report greater dissatisfaction and distress even when there is little apparent stress (Watson & Clark,

1984). The increased health complaints of individuals high in neuroticism are typically not supported by objective measures of disease or dysfunction (see Watson & Pennebaker, 1989). For example, a study that assessed symptom reporting following exposure to a respiratory virus found that the increased complaints among individuals with high trait negative affectivity were relatively independent of objective illness (Cohen, Doyle, Skoner, Gwaltney, & Newson, 1995).

Bowman and Yehuda (2004) have noted that neuroticism appears to explain more of the variance in combat-related PTSD symptoms than do measures of combat exposure. This relationship may reflect the fact that individuals high in neuroticism are more sensitive to, or less able to manage, the emotional consequences of a traumatic event, and thereby more likely to develop PTSD. Lauterbach and Vrana (2001) observed that PTSD symptom severity was strongly correlated with trauma severity in a sample of college students high in neuroticism, but not in students low in neuroticism. These results suggest that neuroticism influences the severity of PTSD symptoms by moderating the emotional impact of the traumatic event. If this is correct, then one might expect to observe a positive relationship between neuroticism and physiologic reactivity to trauma-related stimuli. However, it is also possible that the link between PTSD and neuroticism may simply reflect biased symptom reporting, so that individuals high in neuroticism are more likely to overreport symptom severity and thereby increase the chances of meeting diagnostic criteria for PTSD. In this case, the relationship between neuroticism and physiologic reactivity to trauma-related stimuli would likely be negligible or even negative.

Reporting bias might also explain the pattern of findings obtained by Wagner, Roemer, Orsillo, and Litz (2003), in a study of women with and without PTSD related to sexual assault. This study examined facial expressive behavior (using the Facial Expression Coding System; see Kring, Smith, & Neale, 1994), and self-reported arousal to various positive, neutral, and negative emotional stimuli in women with PTSD related to sexual assault. Although the PTSD group reported higher levels of arousal to both positive and negative emotional stimuli, their facial expressive behavior was comparable to that of the non-PTSD group. Conclusions from this study are necessarily limited by small sample sizes. However, the findings are consistent with the possibility that some individuals with PTSD have an apparent discordance between measures of self-reported experiences and measures based on behavioral or psychophysiologic assessments.

PTSD MAY NOT BE CATEGORICAL

Research using taxometric methods has provided compelling support for a dimensional model of PTSD. Ruscio, Ruscio, and Keane (2002) examined the latent structure of self-reported PTSD symptoms from 1,230 combat veterans. They found that PTSD was best conceptualized as a disorder lying at the upper end of a continuum of responses to stress, rather than as a discrete syndrome. It is important to recognize that classifying individuals into dichotomous groups of physiologic responders and non-responders ignores the fact that such classification is based on a composite index score (posterior probability) that represents a continuous measure of physiologic reactivity. A somewhat arbitrary cut-off score is selected, either by statistical or other means, to serve as the criterion by which an individual is placed into the responder or non-responder group. Individuals with physiologic scores near the cut-off value will be assigned to one group or the other even though their scores are only somewhat above or below the cut-off value. In such instances it is difficult to argue that the "responder" versus "non-responder" classification represents a meaningful difference between the magnitudes of physiologic reactivity.

The issue of whether PTSD is categorical or dimensional interacts with the possibility that heightened psychophysiologic reactivity is primarily associated with relatively severe PTSD symptomatology, as suggested by evidence supporting a positive relationship between PTSD symptom severity and physiologic reactivity. In a study of PTSD related to childhood sexual abuse, Orr et al. (1998a) found that PTSD-diagnosed individuals identified as physiologic non-responders during trauma-related imagery had a mean Clinician-Administered PTSD Scale (CAPS) total score substantially below that of physiologic responders. Keane et al. (1998) also noted that Vietnam veterans diagnosed with combat-related PTSD who showed reduced physiologic responses to trauma-related cues had less severe PTSD symptoms than those who showed heightened physiologic responses. The failure of a sample of Gulf War veterans diagnosed with PTSD to show heightened physiologic reactivity during trauma-related imagery seems likely to have resulted from relatively low severity of their PTSD symptoms (Davis, Adams, Uddo, Vasterling, & Sutker, 1996).

Additional support for a relationship between heightened physiologic reactivity and severity of PTSD symptoms comes from a prospective study of acute trauma victims. Blanchard et al. (1996) measured HR and BP responses during trauma-related imagery in individuals who had experienced a recent motor vehicle accident within the previous 1–4 months, and then reassessed them one year later. Accident victims with acute PTSD showed greater HR reactivity during trauma-related imagery than those without PTSD when initially assessed. Most importantly, individuals with PTSD that did not remit within one year of the accident produced significantly larger HR responses to the initial trauma-related imagery assessment, compared to individuals with PTSD that did remit. Thus, heightened physiologic reactivity to trauma-related stimuli was related to development of more severe and debilitating PTSD. Other, non-physiologically based support for this relationship is provided by a large-scale study of young adults who experienced a traumatic event. Breslau and Davis (1992) found that those with chronic PTSD (i.e., lasting one year or longer) were more likely to self-report experiencing psychological and physiologic overreactivity to stimuli that symbolized the traumatic event, compared to individuals with PTSD that remitted within one year.

PTSD MAY NOT BE AN ANXIETY DISORDER

BEYOND THE CONDITIONED-FEAR MODEL OF PTSD

As noted above, classical fear conditioning has been proposed as a possible mechanism by which heightened physiologic responses to trauma-related stimuli are acquired (e.g., Keane et al., 1985; Kolb & Multalipassi, 1982; Pitman, 1988). Symptoms of avoidance and distress upon exposure to a feared stimulus or situation can be accommodated within a conditioned-fear framework. However, PTSD symptoms also include avoidance of mental representations and the recurrent and involuntary emergence of representations as intrusive recollections of the traumatic event. The latter are often spontaneous, such as in dreams or flashbacks, and are not readily explained as conditioned fear responses to external reminders of the traumatic event. Intrusive recollections typical of PTSD can include memories of dead, injured, or mutilated human bodies, which posed no direct threat to the observer, as well as emotional experiences unrelated to fear, such as revulsion, shame, guilt, or helplessness.

A fear-conditioning model of PTSD would require that there be a sufficiently strong unconditioned response produced by the traumatic event so as to support the development of a conditioned response. Physiologic arousal that is assessed very soon after a traumatic event presumably would reflect the strength of the unconditioned response. This has been examined in prospective studies of PTSD and some of this work has observed a stable but weak relationship between physiologic arousal at the time of the traumatic event (e.g., heart rate) and subsequent PTSD (Bryant, Harvey, Guthrie, & Moulds, 2000; Shalev et al., 1998), while other work has not (Blanchard, Hickling, Galovski, & Veazey, 2002). This relationship appears to explain only a relatively small proportion of the total variance in the development of PTSD symptoms.

Moreover, pharmacological reduction of the underlying adrenergic drive does not appear to prevent diagnosable PTSD, although it does significantly reduce physiologic responses during mental imagery of the traumatic event several weeks later (Pitman et al., 2002).

THE ROLE OF SHATTERED ASSUMPTIONS

Janoff-Bulman (1985, 1992) has proposed that posttraumatic stress results from the shattering of basic "assumptions" that individuals hold about themselves and their world. Within this conceptual framework, the central feature of PTSD is the phenomenon of "information shock," and although anxiety might be an expected response, it would not necessarily be required. Instead, some percentage of PTSD-diagnosed individuals might avoid reminders and thoughts of an incident, and demonstrate additional defining symptom criteria, because of their profound sadness, depression, and sense of loss. For example, in a recent *Newsweek* report from Iraq, an Army captain reports memories of having buried babies that were caught in cross-fire and of trying to resuscitate a fellow officer who died in the field (Nordland & Gegax, 2004). Remarkably, in both situations the captain did not report being in danger, rather, he witnessed unthinkable tragedies. Through processes of elaboration and assimilation such memories may become even stronger when rescue efforts are finished (Zatzick et al., 2002). One might escape from a torrential flood and be thankful to be alive, but when children's bodies are seen floating in the water, the experience of successful survival turns into feelings of horror (Stern, 1977).

Experiences that produce profound sadness, loss, or horror are probably more akin to traumatic bereavement (Jacob, 1999; Prigerson et al., 1997; Shear & Smith-Caroff, 2002), than they are to an underlying anxiety disorder. Consistent with this position, O'Donohue and Elliott (1992) analyzed the varied presentations of PTSD and recommended that it should not be listed within the anxiety disorders. Although neuroendocrine correlates of bereavement, immune system changes, and other physical correlates of bereavement have been studied (Hall & Irwin, 2001), there has not been a demonstration of heart rate increases or other physiologic indices of anxiety to emotional reminders of loss. For example, measures of psychophysiologic reactivity were not included in published studies of bereaved parents who met PTSD criteria (e.g., Murphy et al., 1999).

A study by Carson et al. (2000) challenges the hypothesis that PTSD-diagnosed patients may be physiologic non-responders to trauma-relevant stimuli because they are experiencing emotions other than anxiety. Carson et al. (2000) found strong physiological responses to reminders of traumatic exposure in military nurses with PTSD who had witnessed trauma to others. Physiologic reactivity discriminated nurses with and without PTSD with the same accuracy as it has in combat soldiers. The overall pattern of results for physiologic reactivity looked very much like previous results for PTSD related to combat, terrorist attacks, or road traffic accidents. Importantly, although the nurses were in a combat environment and occasionally subjected to life-threatening events such as rocket or mortar attacks, the majority reported that their most distressing experiences were witnessed traumas related to care giving. In fact, when analyses were confined to only those individuals who reported witnessed events as their most traumatic, the PTSD group continued to show a pattern of heightened physiologic reactivity compared to the non-PTSD group. It is also worth noting that sadness, rather than fear or anger, was the highest-rated emotion during nurses' imagery of their traumatic experiences.

Although the heightened physiologic reactivity observed to trauma-related stimuli in some individuals with PTSD may reflect conditioned fear, there is no reason to expect that this invariably will be the case. Findings from the Carson et al. (2000) study indicate that PTSD may result from strong emotional experiences other than fear, and that such experiences are capable of producing heightened physiological reactivity. Such findings support the hypothesis that PTSD may be too narrowly construed when it is subsumed under the anxiety disorders classification. At the same time, and importantly, the absence of heightened physiological reactivity to trauma-related cues should not be narrowly interpreted to simply mean that there is no conditioned fear. The absence of heightened physiologic reactivity more broadly suggests the absence of any strong negative emotional experience or the possibility that something is interfering with its manifestation.

CONCLUSION

The fact that a substantial percentage of individuals formally diagnosed with PTSD are not physiologically reactive when exposed to reminders of their traumatic event should not be trivialized or simply ignored. How can two individuals diagnosed with the same disorder produce markedly different patterns of physiologic reactivity, so that one individual shows a high degree of reactivity, whereas another individual shows little or none? Several possible explanations for such findings have been considered above. Some of the suggested explanations seem inadequate, whereas others are more plausible and may explain at least part of the phenomenon. No single explanation is likely to account for all instances of physiologic non-reactivity. Non-reactivity may be associated with symptom overreporting in some cases, excessively broad or non-specific PTSD criteria in other cases, and methodological failures in others.

This chapter does not resolve the puzzling questions raised by those PTSD-diagnosed individuals who do not respond physiologically to trauma-relevant stimuli in research

studies. Rather, this chapter points to the need for further discussion, and careful exploration of the reasons why individuals who formally meet diagnostic criteria for PTSD can
be physiologically non-reactive when exposed to reminders of their traumatic events. A
greater conceptual grasp of this contradiction is likely to lead to improved understanding
of the disorder. The comparison of physiologic responders and non-responders presented
in this chapter demonstrates some of the potential insights to be gained by this approach.

Of particular note is the similarity of physiologic responders' and non-responders'
self-reported experiences in the context of marked differences in physiologic reactivity.
The striking lack of concordance between self-reported subjective experiences and
physiologic reactivity among the non-responders clearly demonstrates that Psychophysiologic assessment provides information that cannot be obtained simply by asking individuals to report their emotional experiences. Yet, the diagnostic "gold standard" for
PTSD, as for most psychiatric disorders, has relied on self-reported phenomenology. In
light of current findings, a crucial question is whether it is reasonable to assume and profess
that self-reported experiences provide an adequate basis on which to establish the PTSD
diagnosis. Some might argue that all that really matters is an individual's "subjective"
experience, but it remains uncertain whether self-reporting provides a more accurate
window into one's inner experiences than physiologic measurements. Miller (1996) raised
two very provocative questions when he asked, "Why not turn first to psychophysiologic
data if your goal is to study subjective experience? Why start, and especially why stop,
with self-report?" (p. 623).

If one takes the perspective that heightened psychophysiologic reactivity is necessary,
but not sufficient, to confer the PTSD diagnosis, then the finding that approximately 40%
of diagnosed individuals are physiologically non-reactive when exposed to trauma-related
stimuli suggests that DSM-IV criteria are overly broad. Because overly broad criteria will
result in the identification of a heterogeneous group of individuals, it seems reasonable to
suggest that a scientific understanding of PTSD would be more likely to advance if a
narrower definition of the symptom criteria were adopted. One such definition would
place physiologic activation in a more central role, making it necessary, but not sufficient,
for conferring the diagnosis. Of course, such a proposal is likely to generate considerable controversy.

An alternative and very different position to account for current findings is that anxiety
in general, and physiological reactivity in particular, should not be considered as defining
criteria for PTSD. Within this framework, the failure of a substantial minority of individuals with PTSD to show heightened physiological reactivity to trauma-related stimuli
points to the possibility that anxiety is an important, but not essential, feature of the disorder. O'Donohue and Elliott (1992) advanced this position and proposed that PTSD
should be removed from the subclassification of anxiety disorders entirely. These authors
observed, "Although we recognize that anxiety is a common correlate of PTSD,
removing it from the anxiety disorders would facilitate a recognition of the full range of
behavioral and affective responses which occur in addition to the experience of anxiety"
(p. 434).

In addition to questions concerning the role of anxiety in PTSD, contentious debate continues between those who want to define PTSD in a restrictive manner and those who
argue for as broad a definition as possible. On the one hand, a broad definition may assure
that clinical services will be made available to a wide range of individuals who experi-

ence significant distress after a traumatic event. On the other hand, a broad definition is likely to interfere with advancing our understanding of the core disorder that the construct of PTSD is intended to identify. These concerns have been reflected in numerous writings. In their discussion of the stressor criterion, the chairs of the DSM-IV Committee (Davidson & Foa, 1991) observed, "A broadened Criterion A risks trivializing PTSD as a disorder and may have serious forensic consequences. These considerations are balanced against concerns that a definition that is too restrictive may keep individuals who otherwise have PTSD from obtaining help" (p. 260). March (1990) expressed similar concerns with reference to Criterion A, "Thus, expanding the range of stressful events beyond those commonly associated with DSM-III-R PTSD runs the risk of trivializing the diagnosis by weakening the ability of the construct to discriminate between disorders" (p. 72). Similar concerns apply to the symptom criteria, where a more restrictive set of rules would exclude many individuals from receiving the diagnosis.

Some patients may seek, and diagnosticians confer, a diagnosis of PTSD in order to explain or validate an individual's distress and suffering. As observed by Sommers and Satel (in press), mental health professionals may feel pressure to provide a diagnosis of PTSD, "to signify the seriousness of the abuse inflicted on their clients. In other words, if one did not get PTSD from his ordeal, how bad could it have been?" While the desire to help victims of trauma is understandable, holding to an overly broad definition of PTSD could ultimately undermine the credibility of the PTSD diagnosis itself. Further, the exclusion of individuals from the PTSD diagnosis need not be a problem if one accepts that PTSD is only one possible outcome, from among many potential negative outcomes, that can result from severe trauma. As wryly stated by Sparr (1990), "PTSD should not be the only admission to the ballpark" (p. 259). There are many faces to human suffering and labeling all posttraumatic reactions as PTSD may not serve anyone very well.

REFERENCES

American Psychiatric Association (2000). *Diagnostic and statistical manual of mental disorders* (4th edn, rev.). Washington, DC: Author.

Beckham, J. C., Moore, S. D., & Reynolds, V. (2000). Interpersonal hostility and violence in Vietnam combat veterans with chronic posttraumatic stress disorder: A review of theoretical models and empirical evidence. *Aggression and Violent Behavior, 5,* 451–466.

Beckham, J. C., Vrana, S. R., Barefoot, J. C., Feldman, M. E., Fairbank, J., & Moore, S. D. (2002). Magnitude and duration of cardiovascular responses to anger in Vietnam veterans with and without posttraumatic stress disorder. *Journal of Consulting and Clinical Psychology, 70,* 228–234.

Bernstein, E. M., & Putnam, F. W. (1986). Development, reliability, and validity of a dissociation scale. *Journal of Nervous and Mental Disease, 174,* 727–735.

Blanchard, E. B., Hickling, E. J., Buckley, T. C., Taylor, A. E., Vollmer, A., & Loos, W. R. (1996). The psychophysiology of motor vehicle accident related posttraumatic stress disorder: Replication and extension. *Journal of Consulting and Clinical Psychology, 64,* 742–751.

Blanchard, E. B., Hickling, E. J., Galovski, T., & Veazey, C. (2002). Emergency room vital signs and PTSD in a treatment seeking sample of motor vehicle accident survivors. *Journal of Traumatic Stress, 15,* 199–204.

Blanchard, E. B., Kolb, L. C., Gerardi, R. J., Ryan, P., & Pallmeyer, T. P. (1986). Cardiac response to relevant stimuli as an adjunctive tool for diagnosing post-traumatic stress disorder in Vietnam veterans. *Behavior Therapy*, *17*, 592–606.

Blanchard, E. B., Kolb, L. C., & Prins, A. (1991). Psychophysiologic responses in the diagnosis of posttraumatic stress disorder in Vietnam veterans. *Journal of Nervous and Mental Disease*, *179*, 97–101.

Bowman, M. L., & Yehuda, R. (2004). Risk factors and the adversity-stress model. In G. M. Rosen (ed.), *Posttraumatic stress disorder: Issues and controversies* (pp. 15–38). Chichester: John Wiley & Sons.

Breslau, N., & Davis, G. C. (1992). Posttraumatic stress disorder in an urban population of young adults: Risk factors for chronicity. *American Journal of Psychiatry*, *149*, 671–675.

Brewin, C. R., Andrews, B., Rose, S., & Kirk, M. (1999). Acute stress disorder and posttraumatic stress disorder in victims of violent crime. *American Journal of Psychiatry*, *156*, 360–366.

Bryant, R. A., & Harvey, A. G. (2000). *Acute stress disorder: A handbook of theory, assessment, and treatment*. Washington, DC: American Psychological Association.

Bryant, A., Harvey, A. G., Guthrie, R. M., & Moulds, M. L. (2000). A prospective study of psychophysiologic arousal, acute stress disorder, and posttraumatic stress disorder. *Journal of Abnormal Psychology*, *109*, 341–344.

Buck, R. (1979). Individual differences in nonverbal sending accuracy and electrodermal responding: The externalizing–internalizing dimension. In R. Rosenthal (ed.), *Skill in nonverbal communication* (pp. 140–170). Cambridge, MA: Oelgeschlager, Gunn, & Hairn.

Cacioppo, J. T., Uchino, B. N., Crites, S. L., Syndersmith, M. A., Smith, G., Bernston, G. G. et al. (1992). Relationship between facial expressiveness and sympathetic activation in emotion: A critical review, with emphasis on modeling underlying mechanisms and individual differences. *Journal of Personality and Social Psychology*, *62*, 110–112.

Carson, M. A., Paulus, L. A., Lasko, N. B., Metzger, L. J., Wolfe, J., Orr, S. P. et al. (2000). Psychophysiologic assessment of posttraumatic stress disorder in Vietnam veterans who witnessed injury or death. *Journal of Consulting and Clinical Psychology*, *68*, 890–897.

Casada, J. H., Amdur, R., Larsen, R., & Liberzon, I. (1998). Psychophysiologic responsivity in posttraumatic stress disorder: Generalized hyperresponsiveness versus trauma specificity. *Biological Psychiatry*, *44*, 1037–1044.

Cohen, S., Doyle, W. J., Skoner, D. P., Gwaltney, J. M., & Newson, J. T. (1995). State and trait negative affect as predictors of objective and subjective symptoms of respiratory viral infections. *Journal of Personality and Social Psychology*, *68*, 159–169.

Cook, E. W., III, Melamed, B. G., Cuthbert, B. N., McNeil, D. W., & Lang, P. J. (1988). Emotional imagery and the differential diagnosis of anxiety. *Journal of Consulting and Clinical Psychology*, *56*, 734–740.

Cuthbert, B. N., Lang, P. J., Strauss, C., Drobes, D., Patrick, C. J., & Bradley, M. M. (2003). The psychophysiology of anxiety disorder: Fear memory imagery. *Psychophysiology*, *40*, 407–422.

Dancu, C. V., Riggs, D. S., Hearst-Ikeda, D., Shoyer, B. G., & Foa, E. B. (1996). Dissociative experiences and posttraumatic stress disorder among female victims of criminal assault and rape. *Journal of Traumatic Stress*, *9*, 253–267.

Davidson, J. R. T., & Foa, E. B. (1991). Refining criteria for posttraumatic stress disorder. *Hospital and Community Psychiatry*, *42*, 259–261.

Davis, J. M., Adams, H. E., Uddo, M., Vasterling, J. J., & Sutker, P. B. (1996). Physiological arousal and attention in veterans with posttraumatic stress disorder. *Journal of Psychopathology and Behavioral Assessment*, *18*, 1–20.

Dean, E. T., Jr (1997). *Shook over hell: Post-traumatic stress, Vietnam, and the Civil War*. Cambridge, MA: Harvard University Press.

Dobbs, D., & Wilson, W. P. (1960). Observations on the persistence of war neurosis. *Diseases of the Nervous System, 21*, 686–691.

Feeny, N. C., Zoellner, L. A., Fitzgibbons, L. A., & Foa, E. B. (2000). Exploring the roles of emotional numbing, depression, and dissociation in PTSD. *Journal of Traumatic Stress, 13*, 489–498.

Flack, W. F., Litz, B. T., Hsieh, F. Y., Kaloupek, D. G., & Keane, T. M. (2000). Predictors of emotional numbing, revisited: A replication and extension. *Journal of Traumatic Stress, 13*, 611–618.

Gerardi, R., Blanchard, E. B., & Kolb, L. C. (1989). Ability of Vietnam veterans to dissimulate a psychophysiologic assessment for post-traumatic stress disorder. *Behavior Therapy, 20*, 229–243.

Griffin, M. G., Resick, P. A., & Mechanic, M. B. (1997). Objective assessment of peritraumatic dissociation: Psychophysiologic indicators. *American Journal of Psychiatry, 154*, 1081–1088.

Hall, M., & Irwin, M. (2001). Physiological indices of functioning in bereavement. In M. S. Stroebe, R. O. Hansson, W. Stroebe, & H. Schut (eds), *Handbook of bereavement research: Consequences, coping, and care* (pp. 473–492). Washington, DC: American Psychological Association.

Hamilton, J. D. (1985). Pseudo-posttraumatic stress disorder. *Military Medicine, 150*, 353–356.

Harvey, A. G., & Bryant, R. A. (1999). The relationship between acute stress disorder and post-traumatic stress disorder: A 2-year prospective evaluation. *Journal of Consulting and Clinical Psychology, 67*, 985–988.

Hinton, D., So, V., Pollack, M., Pitman, R. K., & Orr, S. P. (2004). The psychophysiology of orthostatic panic in Cambodian refugees attending a psychiatric clinic. *Journal of Psychopathology and Behavioral Assessment, 26*, 1–14.

Jacob, S. (1999). *Traumatic grief: Diagnosis, treatment, and prevention.* Philadelphia, PA: Brunner/Mazel.

Janoff-Bulman, R. (1985). The aftermath of victimization: Rebuilding shattered assumptions. In C. R. Figley (ed.), *Trauma and its wake: The study and treatment of post-traumatic stress disorder* (pp. 15–35). New York: Brunner/Mazel.

Janoff-Bulman, R. (1992). *Shattered assumptions: Toward a new psychology of trauma.* New York: Free Press.

Kaufman, M. L., Kimble, M. O., Kaloupek, D. G., McTeague, L. M., Bachrach, P., Forti, A. M. et al. (2002). Peritraumatic dissociation and physiological response to trauma-relevant stimuli in Vietnam combat veterans with posttraumatic stress disorder. *Journal of Nervous and Mental Disease, 190*, 167–174.

Keane, T. M., Fairbank, J. A., Caddell, J. M., Zimering, R. T., & Bender, M. E. (1985). A behavioral approach to assessing and treating post-traumatic stress disorder. In C. R. Figley (ed.), *Trauma and its wake: The study and treatment of post-traumatic stress disorder* (pp. 257–294). New York: Brunner/Mazel.

Keane, T. M., Kolb, L. C., Kaloupek, D. G., Orr, S. P., Blanchard, E. B., Thomas, R. G. et al. (1998). Utility of psychophysiologic measurement in the diagnosis of post-traumatic stress disorder: Results from a Department of Veterans Affairs Cooperative Study. *Journal of Consulting and Clinical Psychology, 66*, 914–923.

Kinzie, J. D., Denney, D., Riley, C., Boehnlein, J., McFarland, B., & Leung, P. (1998). A cross-cultural study of reactivation of posttraumatic stress disorder symptoms: American and Cambodian psychophysiologic response to viewing traumatic video scenes. *Journal of Nervous and Mental Disease, 186*, 670–676.

Kleck, R. E., Vaughan, R. C., Cartwright-Smith, J., Vaughan, K. B., Colby, C. Z., & Lanzetta, J. T. (1976). Effects of being observed on expressive, subjective, and physiological responses to painful stimuli. *Journal of Personality and Social Psychology, 34*, 1211–1218.

Kolb, L. C., & Multalipassi, L. R. (1982). The conditioned emotional response: A sub-class of the chronic and delayed post-traumatic stress disorder. *Psychiatric Annals, 12*, 979–987.

Koriat, A., Melkman, R., Averill, J. R., & Lazarus, R. S. (1972). The self-control of emotional reactions to a stressful film. *Journal of Personality, 40*, 601–619.

Kring, A. M., Smith, D. A., & Neale, J. M. (1994). Individual differences in dispositional expressiveness: Development and validation of the Emotional Expressivity Scale. *Journal of Personality and Social Psychology, 66*, 934–949.

Kulka, R. A., Schlenger, W. E., Fairbank, J. A., Hough, R. L., Jordan, B. K., Marmar, C. R. et al. (1990). *Trauma and the Vietnam War generation: Report of findings from the National Vietnam Veterans Readjustment Study.* New York: Brunner/Mazel.

Lacoursiere, R. B. (1993). Diverse motives for fictitious post-traumatic stress disorder. *Journal of Traumatic Stress, 6*, 141–149.

Ladwig, K. H., Marten-Mittag, B., Deisenhofer, I., Hofmann, B., Schapperer, J., Weyerbrock, S. et al. (2002). Psychophysiologic correlates of peritraumatic dissociative responses in survivors of life-threatening cardiac events. *Psychopathology, 35*, 241–248.

Lang, P. J. (1968). Fear reduction and fear behavior: Problems in treating a construct. *Research in Psychotherapy, 3*, 90–102.

Lang, P. J. (1977). Imagery in therapy: An information processing analysis of fear. *Behavior Therapy, 8*, 862–886.

Lang, P. J. (1979). A bio-information theory of emotional imagery. *Psychophysiology, 16*, 495–512.

Lang, P. J. (1985). The cognitive psychophysiology of emotion: Fear and anxiety. In A. Tuma & J. Maser (eds), *Anxiety and the anxiety disorders* (pp. 131–170). Hillsdale, NJ: Erlbaum.

Lang, P. J., Levin, D. N., Miller, G. A., & Kozak, M. J. (1983). Fear behavior, fear imagery, and the psychophysiology of emotion: The problem of affective response integration. *Journal of Abnormal Psychology, 92*, 276–306.

Lanzetta, J. T., Cartwright-Smith, J., & Kleck, R. E. (1976). Effects of nonverbal dissimulation on emotional experience and autonomic arousal. *Journal of Personality and Social Psychology, 33*, 354–370.

Laor, N., Wolmer, L., Wiener, Z., Reiss, A., Muller, U., Weizman, R. et al. (1998). The function of image control in the psychophysiology of posttraumatic stress disorder. *Journal of Traumatic Stress, 11*, 679–695.

Lauterbach, D., & Vrana, S. (2001). The relationship among personality variables, exposure to traumatic events, and severity of posttraumatic stress symptoms. *Journal of Traumatic Stress, 14*, 29–45.

Lawler, K. A. (1980). Cardiovascular and electrodermal response patterns in heart rate reactive individuals during psychological stress. *Psychophysiology, 17*, 464–470.

Litz, B. T., Schlenger, W. E., Weathers, F. W., Caddell, J. M., Fairbank, J. A., & LaVange, L. M. (1997). Predictors of emotional numbing in posttraumatic stress disorder. *Journal of Traumatic Stress, 10*, 607–617.

Malloy, P. F., Fairbank, J. A., & Keane, T. M. (1983). Validation of a multimethod assessment of posttraumatic stress disorders in Vietnam veterans. *Journal of Consulting and Clinical Psychology, 51*, 488–494.

March, J. S. (1990). The nosology of posttraumatic stress disorder. *Journal of Anxiety Disorders, 4*, 61–82.

McDonagh-Coyle, A., McHugo, G. J., Friedman, M. J., Schnurr, P. P., Zayfert, C., & Descamps, M. (2001). Psychophysiologic reactivity in female sexual abuse survivors. *Journal of Traumatic Stress, 14*, 667–683.

McFall, M. E., Murburg, M. M., Ko, G. N., & Veith, R. C. (1990). Autonomic responses to stress in Vietnam combat veterans with posttraumatic stress disorder. *Biological Psychiatry, 27*, 1165–1175.

McNally, R. J. (2002). Anxiety sensitivity and panic disorder. *Biological Psychiatry, 52*, 938–946.

McNally, R. J., Bryant, R. A., & Ehlers, A. (2003). Does early psychological intervention promote recovery from posttraumatic stress? *Psychological Science in the Public Interest, 4*, 45–79.

McNally, R. J., Lasko, N. B., Clancy, S. A., Macklin, M. L., Pitman, R. K., & Orr, S. P. (in press). Psychophysiologic responding during script-driven imagery in people reporting abduction by space aliens. *Psychological Science.*

McNally, R. J., Luedke, D. L., Besyner, J. K., Peterson, R. A., Bohm, K., & Lips, O. J. (1987). Sensitivity to stress-relevant stimuli in posttraumatic stress disorder. *Journal of Anxiety Disorders, 1*, 105–116.

Miller, G. A. (1996). How we think about cognition, emotion, and biology in psychopathology. *Psychophysiology, 33*, 615–628.

Murphy, S. A., Braun, T., Tillery, L., Cain, K. C., Johnson, L. C., & Beaton, R. D. (1999). PTSD among bereaved parents following the violent deaths of their 12- to 28-year-old children: A longitudinal prospective analysis. *Journal of Traumatic Stress, 12*, 273–291.

Nordland, R., & Gegax, T. T. (2004). Stressed out at the Front. *Newsweek*, January 12, pp. 34–37.

Notarius, C. I., & Levenson, R. W. (1979). Expressive tendencies and physiological response to stress. *Journal of Personality and Social Psychology, 37*, 1204–1210.

O'Donohue, W., & Elliott, A. (1992). The current status of post-traumatic stress disorder as a diagnostic category: Problems and proposals. *Journal of Traumatic Stress, 5*, 421–439.

Orr, S. P., Lasko, N. B., Metzger, L. J., Berry, N. J., Ahern, C. E., & Pitman, R. K. (1998a). Psychophysiologic assessment of women with posttraumatic stress disorder resulting from childhood sexual abuse. *Journal of Consulting and Clinical Psychology, 66*, 906–913.

Orr, S. P., Lasko, N. B., Shalev, A. Y., & Pitman, R. K. (1995). Physiologic responses to loud tones in Vietnam veterans with posttraumatic stress disorder. *Journal of Abnormal Psychology, 104*, 75–82.

Orr, S. P., Metzger, L. J., Miller, M. W., & Kaloupek, D. G. (in press). Psychophysiologic assessment of PTSD. In J. P. Wilson & T. M. Keane (eds), *Assessing psychological trauma and PTSD: A handbook for practitioners* (2nd edn, pp. 473–542). New York: Guilford Press.

Orr, S. P., Meyerhoff, J. L., Edwards, J. V., & Pitman, R. K. (1998b). Heart rate and blood pressure resting levels and responses to generic stressors in Vietnam veterans with posttraumatic stress disorder. *Journal of Traumatic Stress, 11*, 155–164.

Orr, S. P., Pitman, R. K., Lasko, N. B., & Herz, L. R. (1993). Psychophysiologic assessment of posttraumatic stress disorder imagery in World War II and Korean combat veterans. *Journal of Abnormal Psychology, 102*, 152–159.

Orr, S. P., & Roth, W. T. (2000). Psychophysiologic assessment: Clinical applications for PTSD. *Journal of Affective Disorders, 61*, 225–240.

Peterson, R. A., & Reiss, S. (1992). *Anxiety sensitivity index manual* (2nd edn). Worthington, OH: International Diagnostic Systems.

Pitman, R. K. (1988). Post-traumatic stress disorder: Conditioning and network theory. *Psychiatric Annals, 18*, 182–189.

Pitman, R. K., Lanes, D. M., Williston, S. K., Guillaume, J. L., Metzger, L. J., Gehr, G. M. et al. (2001). Psychophysiologic assessment of posttraumatic stress disorder in breast cancer patients. *Psychosomatics, 42*, 133–140.

Pitman, R. K., Orr, S. P., Forgue, D. F., Altman, B., de Jong, J. B., & Herz, L. R. (1990). Psychophysiologic responses to combat imagery of Vietnam veterans with posttraumatic stress disorder versus other anxiety disorders. *Journal of Abnormal Psychology, 99*, 49–54.

Pitman, R. K., Orr, S. P., Forgue, D. F., de Jong, J. B., & Claiborn, J. M. (1987). Psychophysiologic assessment of posttraumatic stress disorder imagery in Vietnam combat veterans. *Archives of General Psychiatry, 44*, 970–975.

Pitman, R. K., Sanders, K. M., Zusman, R. M., Healy, A. R., Cheema, F., Lasko, N. B. et al. (2002). Pilot study of secondary prevention of posttraumatic stress disorder with propranolol. *Biological Psychiatry*, *51*, 189–192.

Prigerson, H. G., Shear, M. K., Frank, E., Beery, L. C., Silberman, R., Prigerson, J. et al. (1997). Traumatic grief: A case of loss-induced trauma. *American Journal of Psychiatry*, *154*, 1003–1009.

Reiss, S., & McNally, R. J. (1985). Expectancy model of fear. In S. Reiss & R. R. Bootzin (eds), *Theoretical issues in behavior therapy* (pp. 107–121). San Diego, CA: Academic Press.

Reiss, S., Peterson, R. A., Gursky, D. M., & McNally, R. J. (1986). Anxiety sensitivity, anxiety frequency and the prediction of fearfulness. *Behaviour Research and Therapy*, *24*, 1–8.

Roemer, L., Litz, B. T., Orsillo, S. M., Ehlich, P. J., & Friedman, M. J. (1998). Increases in retrospective accounts of war-zone exposure over time: The role of PTSD symptom severity. *Journal of Traumatic Stress*, *11*, 597–605.

Roemer, L., Litz, B. T., Orsillo, S. M., & Wagner, A. W. (2001). A preliminary investigation of the role of strategic withholding of emotion. *Journal of Traumatic Stress*, *14*, 149–156.

Ruscio, M. A., Ruscio, J., & Keane, T. M. (2002). The latent structure of posttraumatic stress disorder: A taxometric investigation of reactions to extreme stress. *Journal of Abnormal Psychology*, *111*, 290–301.

Shalev, A. Y., Orr, S. P., & Pitman, R. K. (1993). Psychophysiologic assessment of traumatic imagery in Israeli civilian patients with posttraumatic stress disorder. *American Journal of Psychiatry*, *150*, 620–624.

Shalev, A., Peri, T., Canetti, L., & Schreiber, S. (1996). Predictors of PTSD in injured trauma survivors: A prospective study. *American Journal of Psychiatry*, *153*, 219–225.

Shalev, A. Y., Sahar, T., Freedman, S. A., Peri, T., Glick, N., Brandes, D. et al. (1998). A prospective study of heart rate response following trauma and the subsequent development of posttraumatic stress disorder. *Archives of General Psychiatry*, *55*, 553–559.

Shear, M. K., & Smith-Caroff, K. (2002). Traumatic loss and the syndrome of complicated grief. *PTSD Research Quarterly*, *13*, 1–7.

Sheehan, P. Q. (1967). A shortened form of Bett's Questionnaire Upon Mental Imagery. *Journal of Consulting and Clinical Psychology*, *23*, 386–389.

Sierra, M., Senior, C., Dalton, J., McDonough, M., Bond, A., Phillips, M. L. et al. (2002). Autonomic response in depersonalization disorder. *Archives of General Psychiatry*, *59*, 833–838.

Sommers, C. H., & Satel, S. (in press). *One nation under therapy*. New York: St Martin's Press.

Sparr, L. F. (1990). Legal aspects of posttraumatic stress disorder: Uses and abuses. In M. E. Wolf & A. D. Mosnaim (eds), *Posttraumatic stress disorder: Etiology, phenomenology, and treatment* (pp. 238–264). Washington, DC: American Psychiatric Press.

Speisman, J. C., Lazarus, R. S., Mordkoff, A. M., & Davison, L. (1964). Experiential reduction of stress based on ego-defense theory. *Journal of Abnormal and Social Psychology*, *68*, 367–380.

Stern, G. M. (1977). *The Buffalo Creek disaster*. New York: Vintage Books.

Taylor, S. (ed.) (1999). *Anxiety sensitivity: Theory, research, and treatment of the fear of anxiety*. Mahwah, NJ: Erlbaum.

Taylor, S., Koch, W. J., & McNally, R. J. (1992). How does anxiety sensitivity vary across the anxiety disorders? *Journal of Anxiety Disorders*, *6*, 249–259.

Tellegen, A., & Atkinson, G. (1974). Openness to absorbing and self-altering experiences ("absorption"), a trait related to hypnotic susceptibility. *Journal of Abnormal Psychology*, *83*, 268–277.

Wagner, A. W., Roemer, L., Orsillo, S. M., & Litz, B. T. (2003). Emotional experiencing in women with posttraumatic stress disorder: Congruence between facial expressivity and self-report. *Journal of Traumatic Stress*, *16*, 67–75.

Watson, D., & Clark, A. L. (1984). Negative affectivity: The disposition to experience aversive emotional states. *Psychological Bulletin*, *96*, 465–490.

Watson, D., & Pennebaker, J. W. (1989). Health complaints, stress, and distress: Exploring the central role of negative affectivity. *Psychological Review*, *96*, 234–254.

Zander, J. R., & McNally, R. J. (1988). Bio-informational processing in agoraphobia. *Behaviour Research and Therapy*, *26*, 421–429.

Zatzick, D. F., Kang, S. M., Müller, H. G., Russo, J. E., Rivara, F. P., Katon, W. J. et al. (2002). Predicting posttraumatic distress in hospitalized trauma survivors with acute injuries. *American Journal of Psychiatry*, *159*, 941–946.

7   When Traumatic Memory Was a Problem: On the Historical Antecedents of PTSD

ALLAN YOUNG

Department of Social Studies of Medicine, McGill University, Montreal, Canada

The publication of DSM-III was a revolutionary event for American psychiatry. It established a national standard for classifying and diagnosing mental disorders based on an "atheoretical" approach. Nothing would be taken for granted regarding etiology and pathophysiological process. Diagnostic classifications would be valued for their clinical utility and as platforms for research: syndromes first, then etiologies. An exception would be made for a few disorders, notably "organic mental disorders," whose causes and mechanisms had been established by scientific evidence. Otherwise, definitions would be based on menus of "clinical features" (symptoms). The term "neurotic disorder" would henceforth be used only descriptively, as a paraphrase (as in "phobic neuroses") and "without any implication of a special etiological process" (American Psychiatric Association, 1980, pp. 5–10).

> The crucial issue [following the DSM-III revolution] is whether psychiatric syndromes are separated from one another, and from normality, by *zones of rarity* or whether they are merely arbitrary loci in a multidimensional space in which variation in both symptoms and etiology is more or less continuous. (Kendell & Jablensky, 2003, p. 7; my emphasis)

Because natural classes have fuzzy boundaries, we must expect to find *interforms*—cases sharing the features of two or more syndromes (classifications). A "zone of rarity" emerges when symptoms cluster neatly into syndromes and interforms are uncommon, although not altogether absent. Fuzzy boundaries and interforms are a special problem for PTSD, since the disorder's symptoms "are not diagnostically specific. Most of them characterize other mental disorders and are used in the definition of these disorders," notably depression and other anxiety disorders (Breslau, Chase, & Anthony, 2002, p. 575). A zone of rarity was created for PTSD in a different way: by connecting its symptoms to an etiology (traumatic experience) and pathogenic mechanism (traumatic memory). In this way, symptomatic "reexperiences" (PTSD's diagnostic Criterion B) are differentiated from "ruminations" common in depression; "avoidance behavior" (Criterion C: aimed at stimuli that trigger traumatic memory) is differentiated from fear-based symptoms associated with phobic disorders; and so on (Breslau & Davis, 1987; Brewin, 1998). By connecting PTSD's symptoms internally, as causes and effects, the classification achieves unique

Posttraumatic Stress Disorder: Issues and Controversies. Edited by G. M. Rosen.
© 2004 John Wiley & Sons, Ltd.   ISBN 0-470-86284-X/0-470-86285-8.

status but does not conform to the "atheoretical" approach and DSM-III's promise to take nothing for granted. This exception was made for PTSD nevertheless: its advocates won a concession based on the disorder's (supposed) historical legitimacy and on the clinical needs and pension rights of a deserving patient population, notably American veterans of the Vietnam War (Dean, 1997; Lembke, 1998; Scott, 1993; Shephard, 2000; Young, 1995).

PTSD's inner logic, emphasizing etiology and mechanisms, is now taken for granted and this presumption has undesirable consequences. For one thing, it forecloses the pursuit of alternative interpretations and research programs that such interpretations might justify. Less obviously, the taken-for-grantedness of traumatic memory merges two questions that ought to be regarded separately. Is PTSD a valid diagnosis? Can the PTSD classification, as represented in the DSMs and put into action in diagnostic practices, differentiate between cases that do and do not conform to PTSD's inner logic? If the answer to the validity question is *no*, then it is unnecessary to proceed to the second question, concerning the heterogeneity of cases routinely diagnosed as PTSD. On the other hand, if the answer to the validity question is *yes*, it is reasonable to ask the second question. In other words, there are two ways to criticize PTSD as we know it today. The first way is to *reject* the disorder's inner logic entirely. The second way is to *accept* PTSD's inner logic in principle, but to argue that, in practice, PTSD groups together heterogeneous cases (i.e., with and without the defining etiological mechanism). In this chapter, I advocate the second critique. A final point before moving on. Many psychiatric classifications group heterogeneous cases. For example, experts generally believe that clinical depression is the product of multiple etiological pathways. However, these other disorders are defined by distinctive symptom lists rather than an inner logic; the discovery of etiologies is in the future and currently irrelevant to differential diagnosis. This is what makes PTSD different.

THE FALLACY OF AN IMMUTABLE SYNDROME

I want to excavate PTSD's inner logic. Fortunately, good historical accounts of the posttraumatic disorders are now available (Bianchi, 2001; Brunner, 2001; Caplan, 2001; Crouthamel, 2002; Eghigian, 2001; Harrington, 2001; Jones et al., 2002a, 2003; Jones, Palmer, & Wessely, 2002b; Jones & Wessely, 2001; Kaufmann, 1999; Killen, 2003; Leese, 1989, 2001; Leys, 2000; Lerner, 2001; Raftery, 2003; Roudebush, 2001; Schäffner, 2001; Shephard, 2000; Young, 1999). These histories trace the rise and fall of clinical and experimental systems dedicated to trauma, from the late nineteenth century to the 1990s, and make it possible to compare the epistemologies of psychiatric cultures past and present.

A team of researchers at the Institute of Psychiatry in London has recently examined the pension files of 1,856 British war veterans, from the Boer War to the Gulf War (Jones et al., 2002a, 2002b, 2003; Jones & Wessely, 2001). Medical assessment procedures remained fairly constant throughout this period. Symptoms were recorded for the time spent in military service and following discharge. The examiners made detailed medical notes and included the servicemen's explanations for their symptoms. The researchers' analysis is focused on post-combat syndromes; organic disorders and psychoses are excluded. Their statistical analysis identifies three overlapping clusters of symptoms.

In the first cluster, chronic fatigue and feelings of weakness predominate. Shortness of breath is frequently mentioned and also anxiety. Psychological symptoms such as depression, memory impairment, irritability, and poor concentration are absent. The diagnostic exemplar is "Effort Syndrome."

Cluster two concentrates on the heart. Characteristic symptoms include rapid heartbeat, shortness of breath, and dizziness. Anxiety is often mentioned. The exemplar is "Disordered Action of the Heart."

Cluster three focuses on a neuropsychiatric syndrome and the associated somatic symptoms. Depression, anxiety, fatigue, and sleep problems are conspicuous. Rapid heartbeat, irritability, jumpiness, changes in personality, and localized chronic pain are "moderately represented". The exemplar is "Traumatic Neurasthenia."

Prevalence changes over time. The fatigue cluster was most common from the Boer War to World War I; the heart cluster during and following World War I; and the neuropsychiatric cluster predominates from World War II onward. (See Hyams, Wignall, & Roswell, 1996, for similar findings relating to US military forces.)

The variations are partly the product of advances in medical knowledge and diagnostic technology. Those developments moved the boundary between "organic disorders" and "functional syndromes," characterized by the absence of consensus among experts regarding a syndrome's etiology, pathogenesis, and intrinsic unity. Take the example of "irritable heart" (also called "DaCosta's syndrome" and "soldier's heart"), a cluster two classification used during World War I. Medical experts believed that it originated in various conditions, including hyperthyroidism, myocarditis, undetected valvular heart disease, and anomalies of the autonomic nervous system (Peabody, Wearn, & Tompkins, 1918, pp. 507–508). Onset usually occurred during training or garrison duty in the United States. The most frequently mentioned symptoms are self-reported: pain over the heart, dyspnea, shortness of breath, and weakness. A positive diagnosis usually meant permanent reassignment to physically undemanding duties and sometimes a medical discharge. When asked to trace the origins of their syndromes, patients identified a jumble of pre-military conditions, including croup, mumps, head injury, heredity, mother's perinatal health, overwork, worry, and nocturnal emissions (Wearn & Sturgis, 1919, pp. 7–11). On the other hand, soldiers who were diagnosed with irritable heart post-combat traced their condition to experiences in the trenches. Army doctors shared this view:

> The commonest etiologic factors seem to be infection, gassing, and nervous and physical strain of warfare. In many instances, patients in this category are analogous to those in whom the diagnosis of "shell-shock" is made . . . It seems to be purely a matter of chance as to whether they are sent to a cardiac ward or neurologic ward. (Peabody, 1918, p. 1485)

Research conducted on trainees and combat soldiers during the war suggested a shared set of pathogenic pathways, e.g., psychic trauma, gassing, or childhood infections might equally cause irritable heart by affecting the thyroid gland or the autonomic nervous system.

Improvements in diagnosis explain only part of the variations that occurred from one period to the next. Changes in medical culture would have been more significant—that is to say, changes in how soldiers and veterans choose to report their symptoms and how doctors interpret the symptoms. Clinical presentations and interpretations are shaped by the etiologies, pathophysiologies, and diagnostic classifications in circulation at the time, and by the cultural, economic, and institutional significance attributed to particular symptoms—for example, what qualified as a compensable disability (see Shorter, 1992, pp. 1–2, 307–314, on "symptom pool" and "disease template;" also Hyams et al., 1996, p. 402). It is unnecessary to hypothesize that this *may have been* the case. There is a wealth of historical evidence to support this conclusion, much of it originating in national debates in England and Germany during the inter-war years, over veterans' pensions and workers' compensation (Cox, 2001; Crouthamel, 2002; Eghigian, 2001; Kaufmann, 1999; Killen, 2003; Shephard, 2000).

We can see this process of cultural change taking place in our own times, in the medical claims made by veterans of the Gulf War (1991). The US Department of Veterans Affairs was prepared to offer disability compensation for the numerous cases of "Gulf War Syndrome" (GWS) involving symptoms commonly associated with PTSD, including depression, memory problems, sleeping difficulties, disturbing dreams, jumpiness, avoidance behavior, a sense of alienation, and outbursts of anger (Haley, Kurt, & Hom, 1997; Ismail et al., 1999). Gulf War veterans and their families in the United States and the United Kingdom have generally rejected a psychiatric etiology. They believe that GWS is a distinctive disorder, affecting the immune system and reproductive system and caused by chemical toxins (vaccines, nerve gas residues, depleted uranium) rather than mental stress or trauma. In support of this theory, they point to symptoms that are unequivocally physical (skin lesions, rheumatoid and respiratory complaints, tingling or numbness in fingers or toes) and can affect the veterans' wives (causing an intra-vaginal "burning" sensation during coitus) and offspring (causing fetal anomalies). But researchers in the United Kingdom reached a different conclusion, consistent with the findings reported by Jones and his collaborators: "[T]here is no convincing evidence of a new syndrome unique to Gulf veterans but there are more Gulf veterans who seem to be reporting neuropsychological or musculoskeletal symptoms and a much smaller group of Gulf veterans that span all body symptoms compared to non-Gulf veterans" (Everitt, Ismail, David, & Wessely, 2002, p. 1376).

The symptom clusters identified by Jones et al. are products of history, not facts of nature. Each cluster brackets an assortment of syndromes and a single syndrome may cross-cut clusters, as illustrated in Peabody's comment above. Syndromes are likewise shaped by clinical practices, technologies, metrics, expectations, explanatory models, etc., that determine rules of inclusion and exclusion, whether a given experience, attribution, or self-report will count as relevant (a "symptom," a "precipitant") or incidental. Where does the PTSD syndrome fit into this picture? If we define PTSD as a list of symptoms, then we find it dispersed over all three clusters. If we include its traumatic stressor in the definition, then this syndrome belongs in cluster three and coincides more or less with diagnoses like shell-shock and traumatic neurasthenia. If we include in the definition PTSD's characteristic inner logic and unique memory mechanism, then the syndrome becomes exceptional.

THE INNER LOGIC OF PTSD

Even doctors retrospectively famous for their memory work did not suppose that all post-traumatic cases are driven by memories. Perhaps the most famous of these doctors, W. H. R. Rivers, believed that traumatic neurasthenia was a product of nerve exhaustion caused by stressful events, unremitting demands, and difficult physical conditions. Traumatic memories figured into these cases mainly as symptoms, rather than mechanisms. The diagnosis of traumatic neurasthenia was restricted mainly to officers, the corresponding diagnosis for ordinary soldiers was traumatic hysteria. Rivers believed that the hysteria syndrome was driven by memory, but this memory was said to be phylogenetic (the experiences of our early ancestors) rather than personal, expressing itself in sensory and motor symptoms (paralysis, trembling, contractures, hyperasthenia, anasthenia, mutism, deafness, blindness, etc.) rather than declarative memory (Young, 1999).

Even psychoanalytically oriented army doctors such as Karl Abraham showed little interest in developing memory-based theories and therapies. If battlefield memories were a source of disturbing dreams and nightmares, they were of course significant. But they were essentially symptomatic and, like the patient's somatic symptoms, best understood in terms of the vicissitudes of ego and libido:

> In wartime, these men . . . must at all times be prepared to sacrifice themselves unconditionally for the general good. This involves the renunciation of all narcissistic privileges. Healthy individuals are able to suppress their narcissism entirely . . . [and] sacrifice their ego for the community. In this respect those predisposed to neurosis fall behind those who are healthy. . . . [They] show the traits of complete feminine passivity in the way in which they abandon themselves to their suffering. In their symptoms they relive over and over again the situation which caused the outbreak of their neurosis, and try to gain the sympathy of others. (Abraham, 1955, orig. 1918, pp. 61–62)

By and large, when army doctors in both world wars were interested in traumatic memory it was mainly in the context of therapy rather than pathogenesis. Men like William Brown (in World War I) and William Sargent (in World War II) believed they could cure patients by abreacting trauma-linked emotions.

> [T]he reinstatement of intense emotion acted physically in overcoming synaptic resistances in specific parts of the nervous system, and so put the nervous system in working order again. The effect is . . . selective and occurs only in just those parts of the system concerned with the productions of symptoms. (Brown, 1923, p. 385)

Traumatic memories, retrieved through hypnosis, suggestion, and narcotic drugs, were vehicles for dragging the emotions into consciousness where they might be abreacted. The content and veracity of these memories were irrelevant and uninteresting (Shephard, 2000, Chapter 15). In other words, what makes PTSD exceptional in historical perspective is precisely what is taken for granted about PTSD today, its inner logic.

Histories of PTSD describe Abram Kardiner's *Traumatic Neuroses of War* (1941) as the starting point for the DSM-III classification. The book is organized around case histories Kardiner collected while working as a psychiatrist in a Veterans Administration hospital in the 1920s. Kardiner believed that trauma initiates an abrupt change in the organism's adaptation to the world, and that the consequent neurosis was a new adaptation, characterized by a lower level of functioning and a constriction of the ego. He described four kinds of posttraumatic neuroses, including an epileptoid type to which he gives much attention. This interest in posttraumatic epilepsy (Kardiner, 1932) was shared by other psychoanalytic doctors in the inter-war period (Bladin, 2000; Leys, 2000, Chapters 4, 5; and see Micale, 1994, for an account of Charcot's efforts to link epilepsy with hysteria in the late nineteenth century).

In 1959, Kardiner published a short paper on the traumatic neuroses of war. The 1941 book mentioned Freud just in passing, as making "some extremely important observations." The paper, however, pushes Freud center stage, focusing on the analysis of traumatic neurosis in *Beyond the Pleasure Principle* (1920). Freud's account begins with the "stimulus barrier" (*Reizschutz*), a hypothetical neurological structure said to protect the brain from excessive inputs of energy that would overload the neural circuitry. Traumatic experience combines intense fear with complete surprise (*Schreck*, fright). The brain's defenses are caught off guard, the stimulus barrier is activated too late, pain and perturbation follow. The organism/mind is by nature compelled to achieve mastery over the past by anticipating the event, thus eliminating the element of surprise. To this end, the moment is repeated in traumatic dreams. The intense anxiety that accompanies the dreams signals the mind's effort to anticipate this moment. It is here, in Freud's traumatic neurosis, that one discovers the inner logic of the disorder's subsequent incarnation, PTSD. Kardiner's 1941 book included a symptom list: the patient is fixated on his trauma, has a distorted conception of self and the outer world, has characteristic dreams, and is irritable, with a tendency to explosive reactions. In Kardiner's 1959 paper, the list becomes a structure.

Freud's repetition compulsion, arriving via Kardiner, was the platform on which DSM-III's Committee on Reactive Disorders built the PTSD diagnostic classification. The committee introduced two important modifications. First, the mythical stimulus barrier was abandoned. PTSD was given a neurophysiological component (connecting Criterion D, arousal, to the disorder's inner logic), but rooted in the evolutionary biology of the autonomic nervous system (Young, 1998). Second, the committee wrote a new script for the repetition compulsion. Symptomatic reexperiencing continued to have a function, but it no longer aimed at anticipating traumatizing events. Rather, it signaled an engagement with the past aimed at transforming and assimilating the meaning of the trauma. Because remembering would be so painful, there would have to be some means of limiting these engagements, namely Criterion C (avoidance and numbing). The "bi-phasic processing model" reached the committee through its consultant, Mardi Horowitz, and his influential monograph, *Stress Response Syndromes* (1976).

Within a few years of publication, PTSD and its memory-centered theory had monopolized the field of psychological trauma in the United States. The American Psychiatric Association invested DSM-III with an unprecedented institutional authority. I am not arguing that the process of institutionalizing PTSD was misguided, only that there was nothing inevitable about its consequences. Things could have turned out differently and we might then have been equally happy to take the alternative ending for granted (for instance, River's neurasthenia-threshold option).

VARIETIES OF TRAUMATIC MEMORY

In developing and applying etiologic and diagnostic models of trauma, medical practitioners have been guided by their suspicions as much as by scientific reasoning. To a large extent . . . the history of the discourse on trauma is the history of such suspicions and the various . . . groups and individuals on which they have been cast. (Brunner, 2002, p. 179)

Two decades after the publication of DSM-III, suspicions about traumatic memory have become generally unpopular, and seen as symptomatic of hidden motives and interests (economic, political, ideological, etc.) victimizing needy and vulnerable people such as refugee claimants (Silove, Steel, & Watters, 2000, p. 605). This view toward dissenting opinion was not entirely lacking in the past. In a widely read monograph, Herbert Page (1883), surgeon-consultant to the London and North-West Railway, observed that precipitating events such as railway accidents are connected to patients' symptoms most often through auto-suggestion rather than veridical memory. A contemporary, the neurologist Philip Coombs Knapp, deplored Page's suspicions and described him as "a special pleader for the railway companies" (Caplan, 2001, p. 67). Freud was similarly critical of the attitudes of nerve doctors, such as Max Nonne and Fritz Kaufmann, during World War I (Brunner, 1991).

We must not rush to judgment. The fact of the matter is that the suspicions were often justified. These doctors were suspicious about two things. There was first the credibility of the idea of traumatic memory, the notion that mental representations of frightening events can cause the associated symptoms. And if one tacitly accepted the credibility of traumatic memory, there was a second concern, regarding the detection of false positives (people whose symptoms and self-reports consciously or unconsciously mimic cases of traumatic memory).

Doctors were aware of different kinds of trauma mimicry, but the kinds were not "marked" or named in the medical literature. Rather they were represented as clinical "cases" that either matched or contrasted with the current notion of traumatic memory— that is, an *iconic memory*. DSM-III codified an iconic traumatic memory that is our standard today; previous to this, clinicians employed a range of iconic memories, with overlapping features. These iconic memories, past and present, share a core feature, the idea that time flows in a single direction, from past (cause) to present (effect). A frightening event installs a memory, and the memory produces either characteristic symptoms or is itself part of the patient's symptomatology.

Trauma mimicry takes four forms: factitious, fictitious (malingering), attributed, and belated memories. To understand how they work, we begin with ordinary episodic memory. The retrieval of episodic memory is a reconstructive process, in which elements (information) distributed throughout the brain are activated and intersected and represented as declarative content. Process and content are affected by the individual's current mental and emotional states, information acquired between drafts, reflective processing (the "effort after meaning" described in Bartlett, 1932), his interaction with interlocutors, and his priorities and intentions. Information recalled in one draft may disappear in the next, but return embellished in a third, and be conflated with memories of other events in a fourth (Johnson & Raye, 2000). In other words, ordinary episodic memory is malleable, open to revision.

Some experiences are more memorable than others. Iconic traumatic memories are said to be exceptionally memorable, that is, characteristically vivid, emotionally charged, and unchanging. This claim is supported by abundant clinical (anecdotal) evidence. And experiments conducted by cognitive psychologists, in which participants watched highly disturbing films or photos, replicated the memory-conserving effect to the extent that recall of central details remained constant over time (McNally, 2003, p. 62). Recovery occurs when an iconic memory loses these characteristics, and becomes malleable ("metabolized" according to Mardi Horowitz) and ordinary. This was the goal of W. H. R. Rivers, whose technique, "autognosis," focused quite deliberately on a transformative "effort after meaning:"

> [This] takes the form of long talks between the physician and the patient, in which the latter is encouraged to describe as minutely as possible his exact feelings and thoughts at the time of the outbreak of his symptoms, and just before, and also his present mental condition, his hopes and fears for the future, and his regrets for the past. He is then led backwards to discuss the emotional memories of the past [including but not limited to war-time experiences, and] . . . encouraged to look at his wishes, longings, interests, ambitions, personal relations with others from all points of view. (Brown, 1923, p. 103)

On the other hand, Rivers' German counterparts were generally concerned with the reverse process, the ways in which malleable ordinary memories are transformed, whether consciously or unconsciously, into a simulacrum of iconic traumatic memory.

The boundary between ordinary episodic memory and *factitious memory* is porous. Factitious memories are based on imagined or borrowed autobiographical events. The individual believes that the memories are accurate representations of his own experiences; it is their origins that make them factitious.

In 1997, Southwick and colleagues published a study concerned with the malleability or factitiousness of traumatic memory (Southwick, Morgan, Nicolaou, & Charney, 1997). American veterans of the first Gulf War (1991) were interviewed one month after returning home, and two years later. On each occasion, veterans completed a questionnaire listing "potential traumatic stressors" that they might have experienced during the war. Some 70% of the veterans reported at least one event at two years that was unreported at six months. The most common, rediscovered events were "extreme threat to your personal safety," "bizarre disfigurement of bodies as a result of wounds," and "seeing others killed or wounded." Parallel findings have been reported for a second cohort of Gulf War veterans and men who served in military operations in Somalia (King et al., 2000; Roemer, Litz, Orsillo, Ehlich, & Friedman, 1998).

The findings can be explained in several ways. Memories were affected by media accounts of the war after returning home. Conversations with fellow veterans about their experiences would have similar effect. The other possibility is that there were "individuals who became increasingly symptomatic over time [and] unknowingly exaggerated their memory for traumatic events as a way to understand or explain their emerging psychopathology" (Southwick et al., 1997, p. 176). Or perhaps the redrafted memories were ways to validate "negative (or positive) feelings and evaluations of the self" (King et al., 2000, p. 631).

While these are the first longitudinal studies of factitious memory in relation to posttraumatic disorders (King et al., 2000, pp. 624–625), clinical interest in the subject began in the nineteenth century. The most famous example is Jean-Martin Charcot's account of a patient, "Le Log-," whose traumatic event occurred when he was knocked down by a horse-drawn van:

> [A]t this time he complained of a feeling of heaviness, of weight, almost a sensation of absence of his legs, and, moreover, the lower extremities were notably paretic. It is very probable that these phenomena with the presence of ecchymoses [black and blue marks], gave rise to the con-

viction in Le Log-'s mind that the wheels of the van [had] . . . "passed over his body," as he puts it. Nevertheless, this conviction, which has even appeared to him in his dreams, is absolutely erroneous [compared against] . . . the most accurate information furnished to us by eye witnesses." (Charcot, 1991, orig. 1889, p. 387)

Charcot's interest in Le Log-'s memory content is unusual. When his contemporaries refer to the effects of traumatic events on memory, they are nearly always referring to problems ("loss of memory") with semantic memory, such as spelling errors, inability to add figures, failure to recall significant dates, or the names of one's children (e.g., Erichsen, 1866, pp. 71, 98; Page, 1883, p. 165).

This situation changed during World War I. According to Charcot, Le Log-'s factitious memory was an attempt to reconcile his symptoms with his knowledge of the precipitating event. Le Log-'s memory was symptomatic of a constitutional diathesis, since normal people do not develop traumatic memories (autonomous, dissociated, a "mental parasite") following events of this sort. German Army doctors had a similar story, but organized around the concept of will power. If Le Log-'s factitious memory was the product of an effort after meaning, the factitious memories of the war neurotics had another origin, the effort to make a desire come true (*Begehrungsvorstellungen*), a psychological tendency first described by Adolph Strümpell in 1895 (Schäffner, 2001, p. 84). The war neurotic's desire was to avoid the unconditional sacrifice—death or mutilation—that healthy-minded patriotism and manliness might eventually demand. Factitious memory of the future was his way out.

In the eyes of the nerve doctors, the factitious memories were symptoms of a weak personality, of ego-ism or self-love, similar to the pathological narcissism that Karl Abraham discovered among his soldier patients. In their writing, the nerve doctors repeatedly call attention to the absence of war neurosis among wounded soldiers and prisoners-of-war, as evidence of Strümpell's pathological wish complex. According to Max Nonne and like-minded German doctors, a clinician could "cure" only by imposing his will on his patients. Nonne championed suggestion via hypnosis as the most effective medium for imposing self-control, and claimed a 95% cure rate. For Georg Simmel, who employed hypnosis for abreacting pathogenic emotion, Nonne's "battle of the wills" (*Willenskampf*) to get into his patient's mind was nothing less than the "rape of the psyche" (Lerner, 1998, pp. 84–87). Fritz Kaufmann took the battle a step further with a technique called the "attack" method, intended to "overwhelm" the patient through painful electric shock combined with suggestion. Kaufmann's aim was to get neurotic casualties back into the trenches, but some patients, already profoundly depressed on arrival, chose suicide instead (Eissler, 1986, pp. 302–305). French nerve doctors, notably Charcot's protegé, Joseph Babinski, likewise viewed treatment as an effort to overcome the patient's will and employed their own version of the attack method, the *torpillage* (Roudebush, 2001, pp. 261–269). Similar attitudes could be found among British doctors: "The persistence of symptoms often resolves itself into a *tour de force* in the struggle for ascendancy . . . [In order] for the physician to be able to throw his weight into the scale on behalf of the [patient], there must be no barriers of escape between the patient and himself" (War Office, 1922, p. 130, and p. 17, on the use of electricity).

A distinction was made between factitious and fictitious (malingering) memories. Both kinds of memories are strategic (goal-directed) and operate by reconstructing the past.

What distinguishes them from one another is self-awareness, since malingering involves conscious fabrication and the imagined past is externalized, a mere token. But in certain cases this is a distinction without a difference. To escape suspicion, successful malingerers must be more than liars. They must live their lies convincingly and expose themselves to a process that the doctors called "auto-suggestion," the self-induced state in which both factitious memory and somatic symptoms of traumatic hysteria are born:

> The ordinary malingering soldier is not difficult to expose. The really difficult cases are those in which the determination to remain unfit manifests itself only by the semi-conscious counterfeiting of nerve disease. The thin line which divides genuine functional nerve disease and shamming is exceedingly difficult to define. It is usual . . . to be slow in believing the worst of these cases. But every now and then a case makes one, as it were, stop and think. (Collie, 1917, p. 375; see also Jones & Llewellyn, 1917, p. 129; also War Office, 1922, p. 142)

The therapeutic counterpart of auto-suggestion was "hetero-suggestion" and consists of the doctor's verbal effort to alter his patient's perceptions, attitudes, and desires (Hurst, 1918, p. 21). The success of hetero-suggestion, alone or combined with hypnosis or the *torpillage*, would depend on a clinician's self-confidence, authority (as a military officer and a physician), steadfast determination, and expert knowledge (Babinsky & Froment, 1918; War Office, 1922, p. 130). On the other hand, a doctor deficient in these respects could produce the opposite effect, by colluding with his patient, to the extent perhaps of installing a traumatic neurosis. This possibility brings us to the third kind of mimicry, *attributed memory*.

Attributed memory is the mirror image of the iconic memory. The iconic version proceeds from an event to a memory and from this memory to a characteristic syndrome. Attributed memory runs in the opposite direction. The sequence begins with a psychiatric condition and proceeds to the selection of a real memory that qualifies, *post hoc*, as the origin of the condition:

> [W]hen the man began to have a number of disturbances, such as loss of sleep, etc. he either consciously or unconsciously looked for an explanation, and this tended to centre around some particular experience, in many cases a comparatively trivial experience. (W. H. R. Rivers, quoted in War Office, 1922, p. 56)

Belated memory follows this sequence, but with a further development: the patient infuses the recalled memory with intense emotion that it (and the event that it recalls) did not originally possess. The belated memory becomes meaningful in a new way (that is, it explains the onset of the syndrome), distressful in itself, and, in some instances, a source of additional symptoms, e.g., intrusive thoughts, phobic behavior. (This is different from memory associated with "delayed onset PTSD." In the latter case, an iconic memory is installed at the time of the event. During the asymptomatic period, the patient's subjective engagement with it is modulated by psychological mechanisms particular to the diagnostic Criterion C. The memory's pathogenic potential is there from the beginning, "waiting to be expressed.")

During World War I, only a small proportion of army doctors practiced "psychological medicine." These officers were often ridiculed for both their etiological beliefs and their inability to tell the difference between iconic memories (according to many critics, a dubious proposition) and imitations—that is, attributed and belated memories—constructed for the occasion by the doctor and his patient:

> This method of retrieving memories [was] . . . under general condemnation. . . . It was denied that memories were suppressed; that, if suppressed, they could be restored; and that, if restored, they had any relation to symptoms. Those who used the method were supposed to be peculiarly credulous people fooled by artful neurotics or malingerers. A study of the contemporary literature will give general confirmation of those statements. (Culpin, 1940, p. 35; see also Miller, 1919)

By World War II, psychological medicine was no longer an obscure and despised presence in British and American military psychiatry. The official diagnostic language now traced the post-combat syndromes to depleted nervous energy, variously "combat exhaustion" (US Army), "combat fatigue" (US Navy), and "operational fatigue" (US Army Air Force). In practice, these "euphemisms . . . fooled few people . . . [P]atients knew what the problem was, regardless of what it was called . . . [T]he fundamental difficulty was psychological" (Menninger, 1948, p. 262). By 1945, the psychiatric nosology had expanded to include "psychoneurotic disorders," such as "anxiety reaction" and "dissociative reaction" (War Department, 1946). Traumatic memory had no place in these diagnostic classifications and persisted mainly as a vehicle facilitating abreactive therapies. Consequently, traumatic memory was no longer an object of suspicion, since it was no longer an object of strategic consequence. Attributed and belated memories could now buy nothing, not even a pension, and they faded out of sight, until DSM-III.

A PUZZLE

In the century leading up to the DSM-III revolution, the iconic traumatic memory—and, therefore, the inner logic that defines PTSD—was a problem. For many doctors, the iconic traumatic memory was itself a problem: it was not a credible explanation for the somatic and behavioral symptoms associated with shell-shock, traumatic neurosis, anxiety neurosis, railway spine, combat exhaustion, etc. For doctors open to the possibility of an iconic traumatic memory, there was another problem. Once the iconic memory was incorporated into clinical practice, it would be readily imitated (either unconsciously or by intention) and it might be difficult, if not impossible, for doctors to separate the authentic article from imitations.

We arrive at the puzzle on which this chapter turns. Our situation is unlike the era before DSM-III in these respects. First, the iconic traumatic memory has moved from the periphery of psychiatric practice to the center. Its inner logic is now the standard way to understand the syndromes previously dispersed among multiple diagnoses and theories of pathogenesis. Second, most psychiatrists, psychologists, and educated people in general believe that remembering is a reconstructive process. Declarative memory is affected by our current mental and emotional states, the acquisition of new information, reflective processing, and the social circumstances in which recall is undertaken. The "malleability" of autobiographical memory is taken for granted, and it is easy to understand how multiple forms of traumatic memory—iconic, factitious, belated, etc.—might be internally connected.

Given these two developments, interest in the memory problem should be more acute than in the past. It is the iconic traumatic memory that creates the "zone of rarity" that justifies PTSD's place inside the official nosology and, by extension, its place in the courts, in reckoning pensions, and so on. An outsider might expect intense interest in the multiplicity of memory problems. But there is none.

RESOLVING THE MEMORY PROBLEM

The malleability of memory problem is easy to ignore when a patient's self-reported symptoms and precipitating experience match the DSM diagnostic criteria for PTSD and there is no competing classification (cf. a classification that qualifies as a comorbid disorder). For the end-users (clinicians, researchers), the standardized, pre-calibrated diagnostic instruments (protocols, scales) used for matching symptoms to diagnostic classifications function as black boxes. The malleability of memory is someone else's problem and, if it is a problem, it is certain to be a matter of refining technology rather than inquiring into epistemology (e.g., compare Franklin et al., 2003, and Joseph, 2000, with Foa, Keane, & Friedman, 2000).

There is nothing unusual about this arrangement. It is simply the way that we make certain kinds of knowledge at the beginning of the twenty-first century. "Traumatic memory" is a clinical object that incorporates heterogeneous flows of time and causality. It is the product of an *epistemic culture* that articulates technologies (diagnosis, assessment, treatment, research, etc.), raw materials (self-reports, psychophysiological responses, etc.), technical and moral vocabularies, institutional structures (clinical, forensic, research, etc.), and explicit and taken-for-granted knowledge. Before DSM-III, there were other epistemic cultures likewise organized around posttraumatic syndromes. Like the current system, the earlier ones were empirical, self-confirming, self-validating (setting their own standards of efficacy, proof, etc.), and able to explain unexpected outcomes (see Hacking, 1999, Chapters 1–4). Not all epistemic cultures are equal, and it is useful to consider differences among epistemic cultures in psychiatry, past and present.

The first difference concerns standardization, the emergence after 1980 of a universal nosology (DSM-III to DSM-IV) and a universal set of diagnostic technologies (SCID, DIS, Impact of Event Scale, etc.). This development has had two important effects: a near-absence of interest or debate concerning PTSD's inner logic and the accumulation of large amounts of commensurable statistical data. Compare this situation with the World War I and II periods, when rival theories were hotly debated and rival epistemologies bitterly contested (e.g., Lerner, 1998 and 2001, describing the contretemps between Nonne and Oppenheim).

The second difference concerns institutional imperatives. Nonne and Kaufmann made it clear that the war doctor's top priority must be the national interest rather than the patient's distress. The doctor's job was to make men fit to return to service, not to provide a way out. This attitude was shared by many physicians in other armies—British, French, and Italian. Things were different in 1980. PTSD was formed during a post-war situation. The institutional focus had shifted to individuals (mainly war veterans) suffering a chronic, comorbid form of posttraumatic disorder. As in the period between the world wars, the trauma doctors' social imperative focused on regulating access to pensions rather than conserving troop strength.

These two differences—standardization, the shift in institutional priorities—tell how the epistemic cultures past and present are unlike, but not why one system is intrinsically superior, getting its participants closer to the truth. But the third difference would seem to fit the bill: we know vastly more about the cognitive and biological dimensions of memory systems and memory processing than our predecessors did.

Take the example of the Lamarckian concept of "phylogenetic memory"—the idea that the experiences of our archaic ancestors are laid down within the nervous system, that access to these memories is inhibited by functions in the neo-cortex, and that when these functions are rendered inoperative by extreme fear, drugs, sleep, or disease, we not only regain these phylogenetic memories but may also reexperience them. Rivers and Freud and many of their contemporaries believed this theory and incorporated it into their own theories (Young, 1999). The idea strikes us as absurd because it cannot be reconciled with our knowledge of biological evolution and neuroscience (see Silove, 1998, for an interesting Darwinian account). But it is not enough to know that this new knowledge never penetrated the epistemic cultures of the past and that, consequently, we know more about memory than they did. One also needs to ask how the sciences of memory—cognitive and biological—are incorporated into the epistemic culture of PTSD.

Researchers have shown relatively little interest in investigating the cognitive processes underlying "traumatic memory" except in relation to special features of iconic memory, such as "flashbulb" memory and dissociation. There is an impressive clinical and experimental literature on memory distortion (Ceci, 1995; Loftus, Feldman, & Dashiell, 1995; McNally, 2003; Schacter, 1995), but its implications for understanding the formation of traumatic memory are not incorporated into the epistemic culture of PTSD. On the other hand, PTSD researchers have an intense interest in the *biological* correlates of memory, and it is here that one might expect to find a significant advantage over earlier efforts to understand traumatic memory.

Biological research on PTSD is currently concentrated in three areas: the hypothalamic–pituitary–adrenal axis (HPA axis); the hippocampus region of the brain; and the autonomic nervous system (ANS). The HPA marker for PTSD is "hypocorticalism," a statistically significant difference between the mean values (cortisol excretion) in PTSD groups and comparison groups. Researchers believe that the marker originates in a dysfunction in the HPA axis (Yehuda, 2002). Hippocampus researchers likewise compare mean values (the volumes of right and left hippocampi) between PTSD and comparison groups. Research involving monozygotic twins indicates that "smaller hippocampi in PTSD represent a pre-existing, familial vulnerability factor rather than the neurotoxic effect of trauma exposure *per se*" (Gilbertson et al., 2002, p. 1245), but this conclusion is disputed (Bremner, 2001). ANS research compares responses to experimental stimuli: heart rate, blood pressure, skin conductance, eye-blink startle response, event-related brain potentials (electrical changes recorded on the surface of the scalp). Resting heart rates are also compared (Orr et al., 1998).

To learn whether this research advances our understanding of traumatic memory, we must consider three questions. (1) Is the putative association between the biological marker and PTSD valid? (2) Is the marker visible only when comparing groups, or can it also diagnose individuals? (3) Is the research limited to "traumatic memory" in the inclusive sense, or can it be used to compare different forms of traumatic memory, iconic and otherwise?

Biological research is focused on establishing the validity of markers and speculating on mechanisms and directionality—for example, whether smaller hippocampal volume is an effect or facilitator of traumatic experiences and reexperiences. These markers are generally visible as properties of groups and only inferentially as non-diagnosable tendencies within the bodies of individuals. When researchers rely on standard protocols and scales for sorting individuals into experimental groups, findings are nearly always limited to "traumatic memory" in the inclusive sense. There are exceptions, however. Consider the following research.

Bryant and Harvey (1998) compared three groups. Group one was composed of medical outpatients, previously hospitalized following motor vehicle accidents and currently diagnosed with PTSD. Group two ("controls") was composed of people who had been in motor vehicle accidents but who never developed PTSD. Group three ("simulators") were psychology students told to imagine that they had developed PTSD following a motor vehicle accident. Simulators (comparable to "malingerers") were given no specific information about the nature of PTSD or trauma responses. All participants were asked to listen to an audiotape that included the sound of "a motor vehicle accelerating, then screeching its brakes, and finally crashing." Then they described their immediate subjective experiences, including mental imagery. The experiences were rated for vividness, intrusiveness, emotion, and other features relevant to traumatic memory.

The responses provided by the PTSD group and the simulators were similar, with ratings much higher than the controls' responses. According to Bryant and Harvey, this is evidence that "the nature of traumatic intrusive imagery is readily simulated." They traced the simulators' success to a cultural awareness of trauma reactions. (The research included a fourth group, whose members were unconscious during their accidents, suffered brain injuries, and had "pseudomemories" (confabulation?) of the events, i.e., recollections inconsistent with police reports. Although their responses and ratings were similar to the PTSD and simulator groups, the results cannot be generalized to other populations (notably people with factitious traumatic memories), because closed head injury is involved.

Recent research, by Buckley, Galovski, Blanchard and Hickling (2003; see also Hickling, Blanchard, Mundy, & Galovski, 2002), takes the simulation thesis one step further. Three groups were compared: PTSD patients who had been in motor vehicle accidents, controls (no accident, no anxiety disorder), and simulators (professional actors). A motor vehicle accident scenario was constructed for each simulator and a method-acting coach helped them to portray accident victims. They were told the PTSD symptom criteria in DSM-IV, and "instructed to stay in role and respond as they thought necessary to present as if they were suffering from PTSD."

The simulators were covertly enrolled as volunteers in the pre-treatment phase of an outcome study, and assessed via self-report psychometric instruments (Posttraumatic Checklist, Beck Depression Inventory), a standardized clinical interview (Clinician-Administered PTSD Scale), and open interviews. The assessors believed that the simulators were real accident victims. In the Stroop task segment of the research, the three groups were asked to respond to two categories of stimuli: neutral words and threat words specific to PTSD. Each word appeared four times, once in each of four colors in a randomized format. Participants were told to vocalize each word as it appeared on a computer screen; reaction times were compared between groups. Experts believe that these "vocal response latencies" are beyond volitional control of the patient and extremely difficult to fake.

In the first part of the experiment, psychometric assessments of the PTSD and simulator groups were nearly identical regarding symptomatic responses. In the Stroop task, simulator responses resembled the PTSD group across the board, but they did not modulate latencies between stimulus categories. Reaction time to threat words remained constant; in the PTSD group it increased. However, "results might have been appreciably different if the actors had been coached on how to take the Stroop task" (Buckley et al., 2003, pp. 64–65).

These experiments give us a glimpse of what happens when "traumatic memory" moves from telling a lie (the simplest kind of malingering) to living the lie (as a method actor in this case). The transition is the experimental counterpart of Ian Hacking's notion of "looping," the idea that patients respond to the classifications into which they are placed, these responses affect the perceptions, expectations, and behavior of the medical experts with whom they interact. A loop is created, in which knowledge, practice, and subjectivity are both confirmed and modified over time (Hacking, 1998, 1999, Chapter 4). (The transformation of the PTSD stressor criterion from DSM-III to DSM-IV is an example of a modification through looping.) Hacking further suggests that effects may occasionally include biological changes, "bio-looping," either exogenous (via drugs) or possibly endogenous. Perhaps this is what we see in the simulators' response to the procedure described in the Buckley experiment—an effect not entirely cognitive and volitional, but involving the process that Rivers called "auto-suggestion."

Now we come to the final experiment (Clancy, McNally, Schacter, Lenzenweger, & Pitman, 2002; McNally, 2003; McNally et al., in press). This research moves us to belated and factitious kinds of traumatic memory. The research concerns a group of people who believed they were abducted and physically violated by space aliens. They reported the same sequence of events, beginning with a brief episode, at the moment of awakening, in which they experienced full body paralysis and meaningless hallucinations—tingling sensations, buzzing sounds, flashing lights, and vague, hovering figures. Some individuals had multiple episodes. The experiences were frightening but neurologically normal. No one in the group had diagnosable psychopathology, including PTSD.

Following the episode, the individuals sought explanations. All were familiar with alien abduction stories and suspected that they too had been abducted. Several consulted clinicians who hypnotized them in order to recover "repressed" memories. A subgroup "recovered" these memories; others recovered "no explicit autobiographical memories of the suspected events . . . but cited a variety of signs and symptoms that they believed indicated an abduction history" (Clancy et al., 2002, pp. 456–457).

In this experiment (Clancy et al., 2002; McNally et al., in press), researchers measured psychophysiological responses. Individualized scripts were prepared, based on the abduction event and other autobiographical events (stressful, positive, neutral). While the participants listened to audiotapes of their scripts, ANS responses were monitored. A control group (no abduction, no anxiety disorder) followed a parallel procedure. These are the results: abductees' heart rate and skin conductance responses to their abduction scripts were comparable to the responses of PTSD veterans and sexual abuse survivors to their traumatic event scripts (Orr et al., 1998; Pitman, Orr, de Jong, & Claiborn, 1987), and significantly higher than the responses of the controls.

CONCLUSION

We can assume that most people diagnosed with PTSD are in distress. In cases of iconic memory, distress follows after the formation of traumatic memory and its precipitating events. With attributed and belated memories, the distress precedes the formation of traumatic memory. It would be a mistake to think that the distress in the latter instance is necessarily less real than the distress associated with iconic memory. Cases of malingering and factitious memory are different in this regard. Is it useful for clinicians to know that there are several kinds of traumatic memory, but that they are generally indistinguishable? We must ask the practitioners who already have this knowledge or suspicion.

On the other hand, the implications of the memory problem for PTSD science are unambiguous. The inner logic that defines PTSD (the iconic memory) accounts for only a portion of the people who are diagnosed with PTSD. The proportion of iconic cases is not constant across populations diagnosed with PTSD. If we use "symptom over-reporting" as one indicator of the memory problem, then it is safe to conclude that certain patient populations are especially heterogeneous, notably where PTSD is chronic and accompanied by major depression, acute levels of global distress, delayed onset, and compensation seeking (Frueh, Hamner, Cahill, Gold, & Hamlin, 2000). And these populations, notably veterans of the Vietnam War, are historically the richest source of raw materials for the epistemic culture of PTSD.

This is the bottom line. All epistemic cultures are self-confirming (providing empirical evidence consistent with their premises), self-validating (establishing their own standards of proof, efficacy, etc.), and self-vindicating (accommodating and appropriating unexpected results). But not all epistemic cultures are equal, in getting closer to the truth. Because of advances in biological science and, more specifically, in the psychophysiology of the ANS, we have an advantage over the past regarding the processes underlying "traumatic memory," defined in its most inclusive sense. Although relatively little research has focused on the memory problem, the findings suggest that many of our predecessors were nevertheless on the right track. The epistemic culture of PTSD is vastly more humane than the epistemic culture of traumatic neurosis and shell-shock, but perhaps less wise.

REFERENCES

Abraham, K. (1955; orig. 1918). Psycho-analysis and the war neuroses. In *Clinical papers and essays on psycho-analysis* (pp. 59–67). London: Hogarth Press.

American Psychiatric Association (1980). *Diagnostic and statistical manual of mental disorders* (3rd edn). Washington, DC: Author.

Babinsky, J., & Froment, J. (1918). *Hysteria, or pthiatism, and reflex nervous disorders in the neurology of war.* London: University of London Press.

Bartlett, F. (1932). *Remembering: A study in experimental and social psychology.* Cambridge: Cambridge University Press.

Bianchi, B. (2001). Psychiatrists, soldiers, and officers in Italy during the Great War. In M. Micale & P. Lerner (eds), *Traumatic pasts: History, psychiatry, and trauma in the modern age, 1870–1930* (pp. 222–252). Cambridge: Cambridge University Press.

Bladin, P. F. (2000). "The epileptic constitution": The psychoanalytic concept of epilepsy. *Journal of the History of the Neurosciences, 9,* 94–109.

Bremner, J. D. (2001). Hypotheses and controversies related to effects of stress on the hippocampus: An argument for stress-induced damage to the hippocampus in patients with posttraumatic stress disorder. *Hippocampus, 11,* 75–81.

Breslau, N., Chase, G. A., & Anthony, J. C. (2002). The uniqueness of the DSM definition of post-traumatic stress disorder: Implications for research. *Psychological Medicine, 32,* 573–576.

Breslau, N., & Davis, G. (1987). Post-traumatic stress disorder: The stressor criterion. *Journal of Nervous and Mental Disease, 175,* 255–264.

Brewin, C. P. (1998). Intrusive autobiographical memories in depression and post-traumatic stress disorder. *Applied Cognitive Psychology, 12,* 359–370.

Brown, W. (1923). *Psychology and psychotherapy.* London: Edward Arnold.

Brunner, J. (1991). Psychiatry, psychoanalysis, and politics during the First World War. *Journal of the History of the Behavioral Sciences, 27,* 352–365.

Brunner, J. (2001). Will, desire and experience: Etiology and ideology in the German and Austrian medical discourse on war neuroses, 1914–1922. *Transcultural Psychiatry, 37,* 295–320.

Brunner, J. (2002). Identifications, suspicions, and the history of traumatic disorders. *Harvard Review of Psychiatry, 10,* 179–184.

Bryant, R. A., & Harvey, A. G. (1998). Traumatic memories and pseudomemories in posttraumatic stress disorder. *Applied Cognitive Psychology, 12,* 81–88.

Buckley, T. C., Galovski, T., Blanchard, E. B., & Hickling, E. J. (2003). Is the Emotional Stroop paradigm sensitive to malingering? A between-groups study with professional actors and actual trauma survivors. *Journal of Traumatic Stress, 16,* 59–66.

Caplan, E. (2001). Trains and trauma in the American Gilded Age. In M. Micale & P. Lerner (eds), *Traumatic pasts: History, psychiatry, and trauma in the modern age, 1870–1930* (pp. 57–77). Cambridge: Cambridge University Press.

Ceci, S. J. (1995). False beliefs: Some developmental and clinical considerations. In D. L. Schacter (ed.), *Memory distortion: How minds, brains, and societies reconstruct the past* (pp. 91–125). Cambridge, MA: Harvard University Press.

Charcot, J. (1991; orig. 1889). *Clinical lectures on diseases of the nervous system, delivered at the Infirmary of la Salpetrière.* Trans. Ruth Harris. London: Tavistock.

Clancy, S. A., McNally, R. J., Schacter, D. L., Lenzenweger, M. F., & Pitman, R. K. (2002). Memory distortion in people reporting abduction by aliens. *Journal of Abnormal Psychology, 111,* 455–461.

Collie, J. (1917). *Malingering.* London: Edward Arnold.

Cox, C. (2001). Invisible wounds: The American Legion, shell-shocked veterans, and American society, 1919–1924. In M. Micale & P. Lerner (eds), *Traumatic pasts: History, psychiatry, and trauma in the modern age, 1870–1930* (pp. 280–305). Cambridge: Cambridge University Press.

Crouthamel, J. (2002). War neurosis versus savings psychosis: Working-class politics and psychological trauma in Weimar Germany. *Journal of Contemporary History, 37,* 163–182.

Culpin, M. (1940). Mode of onset of the neuroses in war. In E. Miller (ed.), *The neuroses of war* (pp. 33–54). New York: Macmillan.

Dean, E. (1997). *Shook over hell: Post-traumatic stress, Vietnam, and the Civil War.* Cambridge, MA: Harvard University Press.

Eghigian, G. A. (2001). The German welfare state as a discourse of trauma. In M. Micale & P. Lerner (eds), *Traumatic pasts: History, psychiatry, and trauma in the modern age, 1870–1930* (pp. 92–112). Cambridge: Cambridge University Press.

Eissler, K. R. (1986). *Freud as an expert witness: The discussion of war neuroses between Freud and Wagner-Jauregg.* Madison, CT: International Universities Presses.

Erichsen, J. E. (1866). *On railway and other injuries of the nervous system*. London: Walton and Maberly.

Everitt, B., Ismail, K., David, A. S., & Wessely, S. (2002). Searching for a Gulf War syndrome using cluster analysis. *Psychological Medicine, 32*, 1371–1378.

Foa, E. B., Keane, T. M., & Friedman, M. J. (2000). Guidelines for treatment of PTSD. *Journal of Traumatic Stress, 13*, 539–588.

Franklin, C. L., Rapasky, S. A., Thompson, K. E., Shelton, S. A., & Uddo, M. (2003). Assessment response style in combat veterans seeking compensation for posttraumatic stress disorder. *Journal of Traumatic Stress, 16*, 251–255.

Frueh, B. C., Hamner, M. B., Cahill, S. P., Gold, P. B., & Hamlin, K. L. (2000). Apparent symptom overreporting in combat veterans evaluated for PTSD. *Clinical Psychological Review, 20*, 853–885.

Gilbertson, M. W., Shenton, M. E., Ciszewski, A., Kasai, K, Lasko, N. B., Orr, S. P. et al. (2002). Smaller hippocampal volume predicts pathological vulnerability to psychological trauma. *Nature Neuroscience, 5*, 1242–1247.

Hacking, I. (1998). *Mad travelers: Reflections on the reality of transient mental illnesses*. Charlottesburg, VA: University of Virginia Press.

Hacking, I. (1999). *The social construction of what?* Cambridge, MA: Harvard University Press.

Haley, R. W., Kurt, T. L., & Hom, J. (1997). Is there a Gulf War syndrome? Searching for syndromes by factor analysis of symptoms. *JAMA, 277*, 215–222.

Harrington, R. (2001). The railway accident: Trains, trauma, and technological crisis in nineteenth-century Britain. In M. Micale & P. Lerner (eds), *Traumatic pasts: History, psychiatry, and trauma in the modern age, 1870–1930* (pp. 31–56). Cambridge: Cambridge University Press.

Hickling, E. J., Blanchard, E. B., Mundy, E., & Galovski, T. E. (2002). Detection of malingered MVA related posttraumatic stress disorder: An investigation of the ability to detect professional actors by experienced clinicians, psychological tests and psychophysiological assessment. *Journal of Forensic Psychology Practice, 2*, 33–54.

Horowitz, M. (1976). *Stress response syndromes*. New York: Aronson.

Hurst, A. F. (1918). *Medical diseases of the war* (2nd edn). London: Edward Arnold.

Hyams, K. C., Wignall, F. S., & Roswell, R. (1996). War syndromes and their evaluation: From the US Civil War to the Persian Gulf War. *Annals of Internal Medicine, 125*, 398–405.

Ismail, K., Everitt, B., Blatchley, N., Hull, L., Unwin, C., David, A. et al. (1999). Is there a Gulf War syndrome? *Lancet, 353*, 179–182.

Johnson, M. K., & Raye, C. L. (2000). Cognitive and brain mechanisms of false memories and beliefs. In D. L. Schacter & E. Scarry (eds), *Memory, brain, and belief* (pp. 35–86). Cambridge, MA: Harvard University Press.

Jones, A. B., & Llewellyn, L. J. (1917). *Malingering or the simulation of disease*. London: Heinemann.

Jones, E., Hodgins-Vermaas, R., Everitt, B., Beech, C., Poynter, D., Palmer, I. et al. (2002a). Post-combat syndromes from the Boer War to the Gulf War: A cluster analysis of their nature and attribution. *British Medical Journal, 324*, 1–7.

Jones, E., Hodgins-Vermaas, R., McCartney, H., Beech, C., Palmer, I., Hyams, K. et al. (2003). Flashbacks and post-traumatic stress disorder: The genesis of a 20th-century diagnosis. *British Journal of Psychiatry, 182*, 158–163.

Jones, E., Palmer, I., & Wessely, S. (2002b). War pensions (1900–1945): Changing models of psychological understanding. *British Journal of Psychiatry, 180*, 374–379.

Jones, E., & Wessely, S. (2001). Psychiatric battle casualties: An intra- and interwar comparison. *British Journal of Psychiatry, 178*, 242–247.

Joseph, S. (2000). Psychometric evaluation of Horowitz's Impact of Event Scale: A review. *Journal of Traumatic Stress, 13*, 101–113.

Kardiner, A. (1932). The bio-analysis of epileptic reaction. *Psychoanalytic Quarterly*, *1*, 375–483.

Kardiner, A. (1941). *The traumatic neuroses of war*. Washington, DC: National Research Council.

Kardiner, A. (1959). Traumatic neuroses of war. In S. Arieti (ed.), *American handbook of psychiatry* (pp. 245–257). New York: Basic Books.

Kaufmann, D. (1999). Science as cultural practice: Psychiatry in the First World War and Weimar Germany. *Journal of Contemporary History*, *34*, 125–144.

Kendell, R., & Jablensky, A. (2003). Distinguishing between the validity and utility of psychiatric diagnoses. *American Journal of Psychiatry*, *160*, 4–12.

Killen, A. (2003). From shock to *Schreck*: Psychiatrists, telephone operators and traumatic neurosis in Germany, 1900–26. *Journal of Contemporary History*, *38*, 201–220.

King, D. W., King, L. A., Erickson, D. J., Huang, M. T., Sharkansky, E. J., & Wolfe, J. (2000). Posttraumatic stress disorder and retrospectively reported stressor exposure: A longitudinal prediction model. *Journal of Abnormal Psychology*, *109*, 624–633.

Leese, P. (1989). A social and cultural history of shellshock, with particular reference to the experience of British soldiers during the Great War. PhD dissertation, The Open University, Milton Keynes.

Leese, P. (2001). "Why are they not cured?" British shell shock treatment during the Great War. In M. Micale & P. Lerner (eds), *Traumatic pasts: History, psychiatry, and trauma in the modern age, 1870–1930* (pp. 205–221). Cambridge: Cambridge University Press.

Lembke, J. (1998). *The spitting image: Myth, memory, and the legacy of Vietnam*. New York: New York University.

Lerner, P. (1998). Hysterical cures: Hypnosis, gender and performance in World War I and Weimar Germany. *History Workshop Journal*, *45*, 79–101.

Lerner, P. (2001). From traumatic neurosis to male hysteria: The decline and fall of Hermann Oppenheim, 1889–1919. In M. Micale & P. Lerner (eds), *Traumatic pasts: History, psychiatry, and trauma in the modern age, 1870–1930* (pp. 140–171). Cambridge: Cambridge University Press.

Leys, R. (2000). *Trauma: A genealogy*. Chicago: University of Chicago Press.

Loftus, E. F., Feldman, J., & Dashiell, R. (1995). The reality of illusory memories. In D. L. Schacter (ed.), *Memory distortion: How minds, brains, and societies reconstruct the past* (pp. 47–68). Cambridge, MA: Harvard University Press.

McNally, R. J. (2003). *Remembering trauma*. Cambridge, MA: Harvard University Press,

McNally, R. J., Lasko, N. B., Clancy, S. A., Macklin, M. L., Pitman, R. K., & Orr, S. P. (in press). Psychophysiologic responding during script-driven imagery in people reporting abduction by space aliens. *Psychological Science*.

Menninger, W. (1948). *Psychiatry in a troubled world: Yesterday's war and today's challenge*. New York: Macmillan.

Micale, M. (1994). Charcot and *Les Névroses Traumatiques*: Historical and scientific reflections. *Revue Neurologique*, *150*, 498–505.

Miller, H. C. (1919). War neuroses: The discussion at the special clinical meeting of the British Medical Association (letter). *Lancet*, *3 (May)*, 766.

Orr, S. P., Lasko, N. B., Metzger, L. J., Barry, N. J., Ahern, C. E., & Pitman, R. K. (1998). Psychophysiologic assessment of women with posttraumatic stress disorder resulting from childhood sexual abuse. *Journal of Consulting and Clinical Psychology*, *66*, 906–913.

Orr, S. P., Metzger, L. J., & Pitman, R. K. (2002). Psychophysiology of post-traumatic stress disorder. *Psychiatric Clinics of North America*, *25*, 271–293.

Page, H. W. (1883). *Injuries of the spine and spinal cord without apparent mechanical lesion and nervous shock, in their surgical and medico-legal aspect*. London: J. & A. Churchill.

Peabody, F. W. (1918). Some lessons of the war in the field of cardiac disease. *Medical Clinics of North America*, *2*, 1469–1488.

Peabody, F. W., Wearn, J. T., & Tompkins, E. H. (1918). The basal metabolism in cases of the "irritable heart of soldiers." *Medical Clinics of North America, 2,* 507–515.

Pitman, R. K., Orr, S. P., de Jong, J. B., & Claiborn, J. M. (1987). Psychophysiologic assessment of posttraumatic stress disorder imagery in Vietnam combat veterans. *Archives of General Psychiatry, 44,* 970–975.

Raftery, J. (2003). *Marks of war: War neurosis and the legacy of Kokoda.* Adelaide, Australia: Lythrum Press.

Roemer, L., Litz, B. T., Orsillo, S. M., Ehlich, P. J., & Friedman, M. J. (1998). Increases in retrospective accounts of war-zone exposure over time: The role of PTSD symptom severity. *Journal of Traumatic Stress, 11,* 597–605.

Roudebush, M. (2001). A battle of nerves: Hysteria and its treatment in France during World War I. In M. Micale & P. Lerner (eds), *Traumatic pasts: History, psychiatry, and trauma in the modern age, 1870–1930* (pp. 253–279). Cambridge: Cambridge University Press.

Schacter, D. L. (1995). Memory distortion: History and current status. In D. L. Schacter (ed.), *Memory distortion: How minds, brains, and societies reconstruct the past* (pp. 1–43). Cambridge, MA: Harvard University Press.

Schäffner, W. (2001). Event, series, trauma: The probabilistic revolution of the mind in the late nineteenth and early twentieth centuries. In M. Micale & P. Lerner (eds), *Traumatic pasts: History, psychiatry, and trauma in the modern age, 1870–1930* (pp. 81–91). Cambridge: Cambridge University Press.

Scott, W. (1993). *The politics of readjustment: Vietnam veterans since the war.* New York: Aldine de Gruyter.

Shephard, B. (2000). *A war of nerves: Soldiers and psychiatrists 1914–1994.* Cambridge, MA: Harvard University Press.

Shorter, E. (1992). *From paralysis to fatigue: A history of psychosomatic illness in the modern era.* New York: Free Press.

Silove, D. (1998). Is posttraumatic stress disorder an overlearned survival response? An evolutionary-learning hypothesis. *Psychiatry, 61,* 181–190.

Silove, D., Steel, Z., & Watters, C. (2000). Policies of deterrence and the mental health of asylum seekers. *JAMA, 384,* 604–611.

Southwick, S. M., Morgan, C. A., III, Nicolaou, A. L., & Charney, D. S. (1997). Consistency of memory for combat-related traumatic events in veterans of Operation Desert Storm. *American Journal of Psychiatry, 154,* 173–177.

War Department (1946; orig. 1945). Psychiatric nomenclature. *Journal of Nervous and Mental Disease, 104,* 180–199.

War Office (1922). *Report of the War Office Committee of Enquiry into "Shell-Shock."* London: His Majesty's Stationery Office.

Wearn, J. T., & Sturgis, C. C. (1919). Effects of the injection of epinephrine in soldiers with "irritable heart." *Archives of Internal Medicine, 24,* 247–268.

Yehuda, R. (2002). Current status of cortisol findings in post-traumatic stress disorder. *Psychiatric Clinics of North America, 25,* 341–368.

Young, A. (1995). *The harmony of illusions: Inventing posttraumatic stress disorder.* Princeton, NJ: Princeton University Press.

Young, A. (1998). Walter Cannon and the psychophysiology of fear. In C. Lawrence & G. Weisz (eds), *Greater than the parts: Holism in biomedicine, 1920–1950* (pp. 234–256). New York: Oxford University Press.

Young, A. (1999). W. H. R. Rivers and the war neuroses. *Journal of the History of the Behavioral Sciences, 35,* 359–378.

8 On the Uniqueness of Trauma Memories in PTSD

LORI A. ZOELLNER AND JOYCE N. BITTENGER

Department of Psychology, University of Washington, Seattle, USA

. . . What should I tell him? What's he going to do? Should I say something? Should I say something? Should I not say something? Should I keep my mouth shut? Oh God, oh God, I'm so embarrassed. Oh, I feel like I'm leaving parts out. I mean, uh, yeah, um, um, he's um, um, oh God, what happened? Um, okay, yeah, yeah, so, um, it seems like there's, I don't know. I don't know. Maybe nothing.

Often when trauma victims recount a traumatic memory for the first time during therapy that recounting is characterized by a multitude of repetitions, speech fillers, and confusion regarding the sequence of events. This clinical phenomenon is termed "fragmentation."

CLINICAL AND HISTORICAL CONTEXT

In the field of traumatic stress studies, it is considered almost common knowledge that the traumatic memory for an individual with posttraumatic stress disorder (PTSD) is fragmented and requires integration for the resolution of PTSD symptoms. Not surprisingly, the nineteenth annual conference of one of the leading organizations for clinicians and researchers who study and treat traumatic stress, the International Society for Traumatic Stress Studies, focused on the theme of "Fragmentation and Integration in the Wake of Psychological Trauma." This title reflects the strong consensus in both clinical observation and historical analysis that traumatic memories are unique, particularly due to their fragmentary qualities. Clinically, these fragmentary qualities are often experienced by trauma victims as intense sensory components such as vivid visual images, sounds, feelings, or sensations associated with the traumatic event. Further, individuals with chronic PTSD often have difficulty generating a coherent verbal narrative of the traumatic event; instead, the narrative is characterized by frequent repetitions, speech fillers, and temporal sequencing problems. Over time, through either natural or therapeutic recovery, the experience of the traumatic memory as fragmented (both in terms of its sensory components and verbal narratives) dissipates.

Historically, clinical observations of memory fragmentation have their roots in the psychodynamic tradition, with clear references to fragmentation seen in the works of both Pierre Janet and Sigmund Freud. Janet wrote that traumatic memory fragments were remembered with particular vividness, but resisted integration into existing mental structures, leaving the traumatized patient "incapable of making the necessary narrative which we call memory regarding the event" (Janet, 1919/1925, p. 663; as cited in Hopper & van der Kolk, 2001). Similarly, Breuer and Freud observed, over one hundred years ago:

> We found, to our great surprise at first, that each individual symptom immediately and permanently disappeared when we had succeeded in bringing clearly to light the memory of the event by which it was provoked and in arousing its accompanying affects, and when the patient had described that event in the greatest possible detail and had put the affect into words. Recollection without affect almost invariably produces no result. The psychical process which originally took place must be repeated as vividly as possible; it must be brought back to its *status nascendi* and then given verbal utterance. (Breuer & Freud, 1893–1895/1955, p. 6, as cited in Nemiah, 1998)

The "fragmentation hypothesis" is at the heart of the debate over whether trauma memories are unique from other types of distressing, emotional memories. That is, are traumatic memories *qualitatively* different (i.e., processed and stored differently) from other types of memories, thereby involving distinct mechanisms apart from those associated with general memory functioning? Or, are they simply *quantitatively* different (i.e., at the extreme end of a continuum of memory processing and storage)? This chapter will consider current theories on the pivotal role fragmentation is thought to play in the development of, maintenance of, and recovery from PTSD. Current problems with the conceptualization and operationalization of fragmentation will be highlighted. Finally, within and across these topics, the qualitative versus quantitative nature of fragmented memories for individuals with chronic PTSD will be discussed.

THEORIES OF FRAGMENTATION AND PTSD

Only a minority of traumatized individuals develop chronic PTSD (e.g., Kessler, Sonnega, Bromet, Hughes, & Nelson, 1995; Resnick, Kilpatrick, Dansky, Saunders, & Best, 1993; Rothbaum, Foa, Murdock, Riggs, & Walsh, 1992). Theorists of various schools have posited that the successful processing of traumatic experience requires special efforts and that failure to adequately process traumatic memories leads to chronic psychopathology, most notably PTSD (e.g., Foa & Rothbaum, 1998; Horowitz, 1997; van der Kolk, 1987). Many of the current theories draw initially on classic cognitive network models of memory. These theories suggest that the memory system is made up of networks or schemas of related information, and that activation of one aspect of the network facilitates the retrieval of associated memories and inhibits the retrieval of others. Within these network models, emotions and sensations are believed to serve as critical cues for retrieval of information along associative pathways, stimulating activation of particular cognitive schemas. In the following section, three prominent network-based models will be discussed, associated with the writings of van der Kolk (1987, 1994, 1996, 1997), Brewin (1996, 2001), and Ehlers and Clark (2000). Rather than representing these theories fully, those aspects that highlight the fragmentation hypothesis will be detailed. The reader is encouraged to examine these primary sources for a more complete understanding of additional mechanisms proposed by the authors.

Van der Kolk's theory of the psychobiology of traumatic memory (1987, 1994, 1996, 1997) suggests that memory is split off from the individual's general associative and schematic network. He puts forward that this dissociation is due in part to the trauma's highly emotional qualities, lack of attention to aspects of the experience during encoding, and lack of higher cortical processing both during and after the trauma. These factors are thought to affect the biological processing of the traumatic material, routing the memory through a qualitatively distinct series of biochemical pathways in the brain, thereby prohibiting the traumatic material from interacting with memories of normal events and the normal associative network. This distinctly different processing keeps material in a non-elaborated or disconnected form that results in a lack of temporal organization and likely lack of meaning. The resulting failure to organize the memory into a narrative then leads to certain elements of the trauma memory intruding into consciousness, being experienced as a terrifying reliving of the traumatic event, etc.

The lack of integration of the traumatic memory is thought to be the pathogenic agent leading to the development of further complex biobehavioral changes (e.g., PTSD). As van der Kolk states:

> Traumatic memories come back as emotional and sensory states with little verbal representation. This failure to process information on a symbolic level, which is essential for proper categorization and integration with other experience, is at the very core of the pathology of PTSD. (1996, p. 296)

Van der Kolk also suggests that traumatic stress is qualitatively different from more ordinary stressors, resulting in unique variants in the way information is stored and retrieved. In particular, he argues that with traumatic stress the sensory perceptions reported in PTSD may reflect actual imprints of sensations recorded at the time of the trauma (possibly etched into the mind), where they remain unaltered by both subsequent experience and the passage of time. Thus, as proposed in van der Kolk's theory, traumatic events are well preserved in implicit memory as vivid sensations, images, and feeling, but not stored in explicit memory, as verbalized narratives.

Brewin (1996, 2001) also utilizes a dual representational model to elucidate mechanisms underlying the development of chronic PTSD, positing separate memory systems that underlie vivid reexperiencing and ordinary autobiographic memories of the trauma. In his dual representation theory, Brewin proposes two different representational formats: (1) consciously controlled memories (verbally accessible memory; VAM); and (2) unconscious or situationally controlled memories (situationally accessible memory; SAM). VAM representations are easily verbalized, autobiographical memories that can be purposely accessed with full awareness of past, present, and future, as well as full recognition of the emotions felt during and after an event. VAM memories can be consciously edited and can interact with the rest of the autobiographical memory base. Alternatively, SAM representations are a unique set of representations, difficult to verbalize deliberately, easily triggered when sufficient retrieval cues are present, and poorly inhibited by higher-level cortical representations. Because the SAM system does not use a verbal code, these memories may be difficult to communicate and do not necessarily interact with other autobiographical knowledge. In Brewin's model, a non-pathological trauma response is related to the creation of detailed VAM representations that are fully integrated with pre-existing knowledge structures. In contrast, a pathological trauma response is related to a failure to create VAM representations, allowing for a considerable amount of trauma information to reside solely in the SAM system. Global organization of the traumatic memory, while still desirable, is not critical to Brewin's model: rather, therapy assists in the construction or transfer of detailed consciously accessible memories (VAM) that were previously represented only in the SAM system. That is, it may not be necessary for patients to achieve coherent, streamlined verbal narratives for symptom relief; rather, the incorporation of critical elements of SAM into VAM becomes the essential therapeutic goal.

Ehlers and Clark (2000) have proposed a cognitive processing model of PTSD. They suggest that PTSD becomes persistent when individuals process the trauma in a way that leads to a sense of serious current threat. These appraisals of the trauma and its sequelae, as well as the nature of the trauma memory itself, are hypothesized to be factors critical in how an individual reacts to trauma. Similar to other models, storage of autobiographical events is thought to occur through associations with thematically- and temporally-related experiences within the autobiographical memory base. In contrast to other models, a dual representation in memory is not proposed. Rather, Ehlers and Clark propose that elaboration of a memory will increase the number of associations, facilitate the intentional retrieval of memories through higher-order search strategies, and simultaneously inhibit direct, lower-level retrieval through matching sensory cues. Memory that is poorly elaborated within an autobiographical memory base will be more vulnerable to unintentional triggering by matching sensory cues, and intentional retrieval of these memories will be impaired. Thus, the way a trauma memory is encoded depends, in part, on the amount of "adaptive conceptual processing" (i.e., processing the meaning of an event in an organized way, appropriate to context) versus "data-driven processing" (i.e., processing of sensory impressions). In addition, Ehlers and Clark suggest that unorganized memories seen in persistent PTSD may result from an inability to establish a self-referential perspective during the trauma, thereby preventing the integration of traumatic memories into the autobiographical memory base.

Across all three theories, individuals diagnosed with PTSD are thought to have developed memories that are either poorly elaborated or largely non-verbal in nature. Further, the lack of severe or persistent posttrauma problems is thought to involve some form of cognitive processing whereby the overall memory record is more elaborated or verbal in nature. Some clear and consistent predictions come out of these models. Specifically, cognitive processing during the trauma should be related to the disorganization of the overall trauma memory record; and this processing and subsequent disorganization of trauma memories should also be related to subsequent PTSD symptoms.

THE ROLE OF DISSOCIATION

One factor that is present in all of the above theories is the role of dissociation in both the encoding of the traumatic event and in the subsequent retrieval from memory. Trauma victims often report that they experienced alterations of perception during the traumatic event, such as time slowing or rapidly accelerating, out-of-body experiences, profound unreality about the occurrence of the event, and altered pain perception (Spiegel, 1993). These experiences have been labeled "peritraumatic dissociation," that is, dissociation that occurs either during or immediately after the event (Marmar, Weiss, & Metzler, 1997).

There is growing evidence to suggest a potentially causal relationship between peritraumatic dissociation and the development of PTSD (Holen, 1991; Koopman, Classen, & Spiegel, 1994; Marmar et al., 1999; Shalev, Peri, Canetti, & Schreiber, 1996; Tichenor, Marmar, Weiss, Metzler, & Ronfeldt, 1996). While some studies have not documented this association (e.g., Freedman, Brandes, Peri, & Shalev, 1999), the bulk of the literature suggests that peritraumatic dissociation may be related to later PTSD.

One of the critical mechanisms underlying the relationship between peritraumatic dissociation and PTSD may involve impaired encoding of the traumatic event in memory. Reflecting alterations of processing during the traumatic event, Krystal and colleagues have suggested that peritraumatic dissociation may result in weird or distorted traumatic memories (Krystal, Southwick, & Charney, 1995). Other theorists have posited a "dissociative encoding style," in which individuals disengage attention from threatening stimuli and direct it elsewhere (Gelinas, 1983; Terr, 1991). Further, as described above, van der Kolk and colleagues have suggested that dissociation helps to explain the fragmentation seen in traumatic memories (van der Kolk & Fisler, 1995). Likewise, Foa and colleagues (Foa & Kozak, 1986; Foa & Riggs, 1993) have proposed that persistent emotional disturbances result from inadequate processing of the trauma memory. Thus, peritraumatic dissociation may generate disorganized and fragmented memories that are resistant to streamlining and organization.

THE EMPIRICAL LITERATURE: QUALITATIVE OR QUANTITATIVE?

William of Occham (1285–1347) proposed his now famous principle, "Pluralitas non est ponenda sine neccesitate" which translates as "entities should not be multiplied unnecessarily." In other words, when one is confronted with two competing theories, the simplest explanation of an entity is preferred.

Occham's Razor can be applied to the current debate on the nature of traumatic memory. As discussed previously, the qualitative versus quantitative debate poses the question of whether trauma memories seen in PTSD are unique from other types of distressing, emotional memories. Van der Kolk and Brewin's dual representation theories of PTSD imply that the fragmentary nature of traumatic memories is qualitatively unique (i.e., different mechanisms underlie traumatic versus normal memories). The alternative view is that traumatic and non-traumatic memories are of the same kind, but differ in degree. Following Occham's Razor, when two competing theories yield different predictions, one does experiments that require sensitivity to see which theory is the most accurate.

When exploring the quantitative versus qualitative nature of traumatic memories seen in chronic PTSD, clear predictions are possible. The quantitative theory suggests that traumatic memories seen in PTSD should behave like other memories, albeit on the extreme end of a spectrum. Alternatively, the qualitative theory suggests that traumatic memories seen in PTSD should behave differently from traumatic memories that do not result in PTSD, differently from memories of other distressing events, and differently from memories of events associated with the onset of psychopathology other than PTSD. These predictions can be tested.

When evaluating the empirical literature, it is proposed that a minimum of three criteria, although not necessarily exclusive, should be met to reject the quantitative view and postulate unique memory mechanisms in the development of PTSD. When examining memory fragmentation for events associated with the development of PTSD, the following controls are needed.

Criterion 1: Controlling for PTSD

PTSD and non-PTSD states should differ in fragmentation. Traumatic memory fragmentation must be greater in trauma-exposed individuals with PTSD than trauma-exposed individuals without PTSD. Similarly, within multiple traumatized individuals, fragmentation must be greater for traumatic memories resulting in PTSD than traumatic memories that do not. Finally, fragmentation must decrease as the result of either natural or therapeutic recovery.

Criterion 2: Controlling for type of event

Traumatic memories associated with PTSD should differ in fragmentation from other distressing, but non-traumatic, memories. Thus, memory fragmentation must be greater following trauma exposure resulting in PTSD than following exposure to other distressing, emotional events such as the death of a loved one, the end of a significant relationship, divorce, the loss of a job, etc.

Criterion 3: Controlling for psychopathology other than PTSD

Traumatic memories seen in PTSD and memories from other events that are associated with the onset of other forms of psychopathology should differ in fragmentation. For example, this should be the case for memories of events associated with fear conditioning seen in other anxiety disorders (e.g., panic, obsessive-compulsive, social anxiety, specific phobia). Similarly, memories from extreme life stressors (e.g., divorce, bankruptcy) that are associated with the onset of psychopathology other than PTSD (e.g., major depression) must also differ in fragmentation.

While these criteria are not all-inclusive, nor definitive in establishing the qualitative nature of memory in PTSD, they do provide a strong initial template to test the fragmentation hypothesis. Specifically, the rejection of any one of these criteria would suggest the need to alter the qualitative view of fragmentation of traumatic memories seen in PTSD. If Criterion 1 is rejected, then fragmentation is not unique to PTSD and the qualitative view must encompass traumatic memories for both PTSD and non-PTSD states. If Criterion 2 is rejected, then the qualitative view must be expanded to include other types of distressing memories. If Criterion 3 is rejected, then fragmentation is not unique to trauma exposure or PTSD and the qualitative view must broaden its realm to include other forms of classically conditioned fear or other stressful life events that are associated with psychopathology. Unless all three of these criteria are passed, it becomes difficult to sustain the view that, in PTSD, fragmentary memory processes are qualitatively distinct from those of normal memory processes.

When evaluating the empirical literature, it should be noted that the exploration of the fragmentation hypothesis is limited by a number of factors. Quite obviously, memory for potentially traumatic events associated with the development of PTSD is difficult to study under controlled conditions. As van der Kolk, Hopper, and Osterman (2001) and others point out, there are clear ethical reasons for not evoking the extreme fear and helplessness associated with DSM-IV Criterion A trauma exposure (APA, 1994) in the laboratory. Therefore, controlled laboratory studies may lack the perception of life threat and thus differ from real-world traumatic events. This does not mean that laboratory research cannot contribute to developing knowledge of the nature of traumatic memories and PTSD; rather, laboratory results must be understood within their limited contexts.

Research on traumatic memories also has investigated those memories after the natural occurrence of traumatic events. Yet, even this approach has limitations. When moving away from controlled laboratory conditions, a number of third variables may influence results. These variables include lack of knowledge regarding pre-trauma cognitive functioning, lack of information regarding the attentional focus of the trauma victim during the traumatic event, elapsed time between the traumatic event and subsequent study, and the nature and amount of previous retrieval for the trauma memory. Thus, both the experimental and applied literatures have inherent limitations which are difficult to surmount. Nevertheless, if fragmentation of memory plays a unique role in the development of PTSD, then both lines of research (laboratory and real-world trauma) should converge and show a consistent pattern of results.

Finally, while studies of traumatic events experienced in childhood are germane to this debate, inclusion of these types of traumatic events confound the issues of infant/childhood amnesia, developmental memory processes, and fragmentation of traumatic memories. Therefore, the current review of empirical studies will focus on findings with adults.

OPERATIONALIZING THE CONSTRUCT OF FRAGMENTATION

One of the most difficult issues in addressing whether fragmentation makes traumatic memories unique is pinning down what various theorists mean by fragmentation and how to operationalize the concept. Generally speaking, theorists have assumed that fragmentation refers to the underlying organization of the traumatic event in memory and its integration into the overall autobiographical memory network. Yet, the exact nature of this fragmentation is often not specified and the operationalization of the concept varies greatly. The two most common methods of operationalizing fragmentation focus on narrative or metamemory analyses. Narrative analysis asks the question: Does fragmentation mean that the traumatic memory is verbally expressed or verbally accessible in a different manner from other types of memories? Metamemory analysis asks the question: Does fragmentation mean that the traumatic memory is judged by trauma victims as more fragmented than other types of memories? Each of these methods for operationalizing fragmentation in individuals with PTSD will be evaluated below, using the previously specified criteria.

NARRATIVE STUDIES

To assess the verbal expression or accessibility of traumatic memories, the most common method utilized to explore the relationship between fragmentation and PTSD has been narrative analysis. The cohesiveness and semantic structure of narratives are evaluated through a coding system, either via computer program or trained raters. Fragmentation here is often operationalized as the presence of repetitions, unfinished thoughts and speech fillers, as an overall coherence of the narrative, or as the grade level/reading ease of the narrative.

A number of narrative studies have explored our first criterion by investigating PTSD and non-PTSD states in fragmentation (Amir, Stafford, Freshman, & Foa, 1998; Gray & Lombardo, 2001; Halligan, Michael, Clark, & Ehlers, 2003; Harvey & Bryant, 1999; Murray, Ehlers, & Mayou, 2002; van Minnen, Wessel, Dijkstra, & Roelofs, 2002). In prospective studies that have utilized a variety of methods, narrative fragmentation has been associated with the development of chronic PTSD (Amir et al., 1998; Halligan et al., 2003; Murray et al., 2002). However, the picture becomes more complicated when response to treatment is assessed. While Foa, Molnar, and Cashman (1995) found that trauma narratives increased in organization from the first to last treatment session, and this increase was associated with reductions in anxiety and depression, fragmentation itself did not change with treatment. Furthermore, van Minnen and colleagues (2002) used a similar protocol and failed to find a relationship between treatment response and change in level of fragmentation. Interestingly, all patients in this study, independent of therapeutic improvement, showed a decrease in disorganized thoughts. Thus, changes in trauma narrative fragmentation may simply be an artifact, resulting from the repeated recounting of an incident during exposure therapy.

When directly comparing trauma narratives from traumatized individuals with and without PTSD, the lack of qualitative differences becomes even clearer. Harvey and Bryant (1999) compared narratives of individuals with and without acute stress disorder and found only a trend toward group differences. Two other studies failed to find group differences in narrative fragmentation. Halligan et al. (2003) found that while the PTSD group differed from victims with recovered PTSD on all measures of psychopathology, they did not differ on either experimenter's subjective ratings of narrative disorganization or coded narrative disorganization. Similarly, Gray and Lombardo (2001) replicated Amir and colleagues' general findings (1998) but found that fragmentation disappeared after controlling for verbal ability and writing skill. Specifically, Gray and Lombardo were neither able to discriminate between PTSD and non-PTSD states, nor were they able to discriminate between trauma, unpleasant, and pleasant narratives. These findings raise important concerns about the lack of control for crucial third variables in narrative studies.

To summarize the narrative fragmentation literature, it has been shown that while fragmentation was associated with the development of PTSD, fragmentation was not consistently associated with therapeutic recovery nor did it consistently discriminate between traumatized individuals with and without PTSD. These findings raise serious concerns about narrative fragmentation as a key indicator of qualitative differences. Further, only one narrative study (Gray & Lombardo, 2001) compared trauma narratives to other distressing memories, again finding no differences. Finally, no narrative studies with PTSD-diagnosed individuals have explored the third qualitative criterion. Thus, current data simply are not consistent with narrative fragmentation and the hypothesis that traumatic memories in PTSD are unique.

If the narrative literature does not strongly support fragmentation of traumatic memories in PTSD, what then accounts for the widely reported clinical phenomenon of fragmentation? The role of third variables, raised in the Gray and Lombardo (2001) study, may provide an explanation. For example, clinical issues such as avoidance and fear may play a role in the recounting of the trauma narrative in individuals with chronic PTSD. In these individuals, the discussion of the trauma memory, particularly its most distressing aspects, is likely to be avoided. When asked for a detailed description of the traumatic event, individuals may experience a heightened state of anxiety and extreme fear that directly interferes with the coherence of the verbal recounting. Similarly, anecdotal reports of increasing narrative coherence, over the course of therapy, may reflect increased familiarity with the material and the reduction of this anxiety and fear.

A second possible explanation for the clinical phenomenon of fragmentation may be the role of cognitive impairments seen in chronic PTSD. Cognitive ability and education level undoubtedly impact the content and structure of narrative recounting. A variety of cognitive difficulties such as lower intelligence and memory impairment have been linked to PTSD (Macklin et al., 1998; McNally & Shin, 1995; Silva et al., 2000; Vasterling et al., 2002). Furthermore, greater intellectual resources, particularly verbal skills, may buffer against the development of psychopathology following trauma exposure (Vasterling, Brailey, Constans, Borges, & Sutker, 1997). Thus, pre-existing cognitive impairments, as well as cognitive impairments seen as a result of PTSD, may account for any fragmentation seen in narrative recounting.

In summary, the explanation for the clinical phenomenon of fragmented narratives may be quite simple. Narrative fragmentation may be an epiphenomenon: reflecting anxiety or fear experienced during recounting, or reflecting general cognitive or articulation difficulties typically seen in individuals with PTSD.

METAMEMORY STUDIES

The study of metamemory, in contrast to that of narrative analysis, explores the knowledge individuals possess about memory in general, particularly the state of their own memory and their subjective experiences during remembering or not remembering (Schwartz, Benjamin, & Bjork, 1997). These judgments, called metamemory appraisals, require global introspective judgments about the nature of the memory of the traumatic event. Thus, an alternative way of operationalizing fragmentation has been to suggest that, in their metamemory appraisals, individuals with PTSD perceive the memory of the traumatic event as disorganized and fragmented.

One of the largest metamemory studies was conducted by Koss and colleagues (published under both Koss, Figueredo, Bell, Tharan, & Tromp, 1996, and Tromp, Koss, Figueredo, & Tharan, 1995). This study lacks assessment of Criterion A (the traumatic event) and PTSD diagnostic status (the symptom criteria) and, thus, is of limited value in exploring the fragmentation hypothesis in PTSD. Yet, their findings merit brief comment both for the pioneering nature of the work and for the large-scale nature of the study. The main finding of import here was that rape had a direct negative impact on perceived memory characteristics. Specifically, rape memories, as compared to other unpleasant memories, were characterized by such qualities as temporal disorganization, lack of vividness, and poorer overall memory. These are provocative findings that suggest possible fragmentation of traumatic memories, at least among victims of rape.

Two metamemory studies by van der Kolk and colleagues also suggest that victims of adult trauma report an initial experience of the trauma memory as comprised of predominantly somatosensory components or emotional flashback experiences, initially lacking a verbal narrative that only emerges over time (van der Kolk, Burbridge, & Suzuki, 1997; van der Kolk & Fisler, 1995). However, the initial experience of the metamemory in the form of somatosensory experiences has not been consistently replicated (van der Kolk et al., 2001).

Although metamemory research suggests the emergence of a coherent verbal narrative over time, the picture becomes more complicated when examining PTSD and non-PTSD states (Halligan et al., 2003; Hopper & van der Kolk, 2001; Murray et al., 2002). Murray and colleagues (2002) found, in an outpatient sample, that initial metamemory of fragmentation, and the persistence of metamemory fragmentation, were associated with later PTSD symptom severity. However, in a smaller inpatient sample, metamemory of fragmentation or persistence of fragmentation were not strongly associated with later PTSD severity. Similarly, Halligan and colleagues (2003) found that metamemory disorganization was associated with later PTSD severity; however, initial metamemory disorganization by itself did not contribute uniquely to the prediction of later PTSD, nor did changes in metamemory disorganization relate to changes in PTSD severity. A similar, mixed pattern emerges in the sole metamemory study that has compared pre- to post-treatment states. Hopper and van der Kolk (2001) reported a reduction in visual and affective metamemory components with successful PTSD treatment, but only in two out of three patients.

When directly comparing traumatized individuals with PTSD to those without PTSD, the pattern of results is also mixed. Van der Kolk and colleagues (2001) reported an increase over time in participants' perceived ability to communicate a memory in narrative form, with this pattern more pronounced in the PTSD group. However, contrary to these findings, Halligan and colleagues (2003) reported that metamemory disorganization discriminated between individuals with PTSD and those who never had PTSD, but not from individuals recovered from PTSD. Furthermore, in a non-clinical sample, Berntsen, Willert, and Ruben (2003) found that while trauma victims with PTSD symptoms reported more vivid recollections of emotional and sensory impressions than trauma victims without PTSD symptoms, there was no difference between groups in metamemory fragmentation.

Few studies have compared traumatic memories in individuals with PTSD to other distressing or unpleasant memories (Berntsen et al., 2003; Byrne, Hyman, & Scott, 2001; Halligan et al., 2003; Porter & Birt, 2001; van der Kolk & Fisler, 1995). Initial investigations of metamemory fragmentation reported differences across memory types. For example, van der Kolk and Fisler (1995) reported that all participants recalled that their initial memory of a target trauma was in the form of a somatosensory or emotional flashback experience. None reported the initial memory as narrative in nature. In contrast, non-traumatic but distressing memories were absent from these somatosensory and flashback characteristics. Similarly, Halligan and colleagues (2003) found that, relative to non-traumatic, unpleasant memories, assault memories were rated as more disorganized. Furthermore, this higher rating of trauma disorganization was largely reported by individuals who developed PTSD. Thus, both of these metamemory studies reported fragmentation differences across memory types.

Yet, when non-clinical samples with tighter experimental controls are included, the pattern of results changes dramatically. Two studies, to date, directly question the qualitatively different nature of fragmentation and PTSD (Byrne et al., 2001; Porter & Birt, 2001). Byrne and colleagues (2001) reported that, while pre-event metamemory was worse in both potentially traumatic and negative events than in positive ones, there were no differences across memory types with regard to the main event sequence. Furthermore, no clear pattern emerged between metamemory characteristics and current psychological functioning. This finding is significant because PTSD symptoms occur at measurable levels even in non-clinical samples. Similarly, Porter and Birt (2001) reported that potentially traumatic memories were associated with more details and emotional information than positive memories; however, they did not reliably differ from other types of memory in terms of overall quality, clarity, or coherence. Furthermore, memory quality was not associated with self-reported PTSD symptoms. Thus, in two non-clinical studies, metamemory quality was not associated with PTSD symptomatology and did not discriminate between other unpleasant memories, findings that argue against the fragmentation hypothesis.

One of the implicit assumptions with metamemory studies is that they accurately assess the nature of the overall autobiographical traumatic memory record. This assumption comes from the perspective that metamemory taps into data-driven processes. This "direct-access" approach suggests that metamemory judgments are based on a sensitivity to the actual memory traces, so they should never be systematically inaccurate (Schwartz et al. 1997). Contrary to these assumptions, a growing body of literature supports an inferential, rather than a direct-access view of metamemory (e.g., Nelson, Gerler, & Narens, 1984; Schwartz, 1994; Schwartz et al. 1997). This "inferential approach" suggests that metamemory judgments are not based on direct access to memory traces; rather, metamemory judgments are based on a variety of sources of information, including "related information that is retrieved to a cue, the fluency with which an item has been recalled, or the familiarity of a cue to which the to be retrieved information is associated" (Schwartz et al., 1997, p. 133).

This inferential view of metamemory suggests that various factors may affect memory and metamemory differently. Kindt and van den Hout (2003) recently published a study addressing this question. In an analogue design, they examined the role of state dissociation and fragmentary memory in response to an adverse film. Besides completing a cued recall and recognition task to assess memory content, actual fragmentation was assessed via a sequential memory task and metamemory for fragmentation was assessed via a visual analogue scale. Interestingly, participants who reported state dissociation during the film reported their metamemory for the film as more fragmentary than those who did not; yet, sequential memory for the film was comparable between groups. Based on these findings, Kindt and van den Hout suggested that the impact of dissociation on memory appears to be localized in metamemory judgments. They further observed: "It is tempting to speculate that dissociative subjects think they cannot make head or tails of traumatic experiences, but in fact they can" (2003, p. 176).

Overall, measures of metamemory fragmentation have not consistently discriminated between traumatized individuals with and without PTSD (Berntsen et al., 2003; Halligan et al., 2003; Murray et al., 2002). Further, two studies found differences in metamemory fragmentation between PTSD-related memories and other unpleasant memories (Halligan et al., 2003; van der Kolk & Fisler, 1995) but better controlled studies (albeit non-clinical) failed to show this effect (Byrne et al., 2001; Porter & Birt 2001). Finally, no metamemory studies with traumatized individuals with PTSD have examined the third qualitative criterion. Perhaps, most importantly, metamemory fragmentation judgments may not reflect the underlying traumatic memory structure but may instead reflect a multitude of other factors. Thus, metamemory judgments do not provide solid empirical evidence for the uniqueness of underlying traumatic memories.

AN APPRAISAL OF THE FRAGMENTATION HYPOTHESIS

Clinical observation, historical records, and extant theories provide the underpinnings upon which the traumatology community holds to the importance of memory fragmentation in determining posttrauma morbidity. What is missing to support these widely held notions on traumatic memory is strong empirical evidence. One of the biggest problems in this literature is the operationalization of fragmentation itself. A second and no less important problem is the lack of studies that are sensitive to test divergent hypotheses. Few studies employ comparisons with non-PTSD states, other distressing memories, or other memories associated with the onset of psychopathology. When these comparisons are integrated in study designs, negative findings emerge and fragmentation typically does not discriminate well either within or between subjects. Current findings simply do not robustly pass the three proposed criteria for identifying if qualitative differences apply to PTSD traumatic memories.

One might be tempted to interpret the presence of negative findings as an indication of a continuous distribution, wherein traumatic memories seen in PTSD are quantitatively similar to other memories and not qualitatively unique. Yet, this conclusion would be a mistake. Negative results do not provide strong support for the continuity of memory in PTSD. Just as a statistically significant difference between members of two groups does not prove their distinction is valid (Kendall, 1989), so is the lack of a difference insufficient to prove that their distinction is invalid. Specifically, it is possible to have overlapping distributions and still have two qualitatively different groups emerging from separate or distinct distributions (Beauchaine, 2003). Therefore, memory fragmentation in PTSD may substantially overlap with non-PTSD states, other distressing memories, and memories from other events associated with the onset of psychopathology, and still be qualitatively unique. For this reason, traditional statistical methods are of limited value in the detection of an underlying "type" or "taxa" that would reflect a difference in kind rather than just a difference in degree (Meehl, 1992). To accomplish this task, formal taxometric procedures are required (Beauchaine, 2003; Meehl, 1994). Accordingly, in order to resolve the debate regarding the uniqueness of trauma memories seen in PTSD, one of the next steps would be the use of formal taxometric procedures that employ a variety of indicators of memory fragmentation. The use of these procedures requires the development of valid indicators of the latent construct, indicators from multiple levels of analysis (not solely rating scales or clinical judgments), and large representative sampling (Beauchaine, 2003), all of which are largely absent from the current literature.

Ultimately, as suggested by Ockham's Razor, when faced with a lack of compelling evidence, parsimony should prevail, the simpler explanation is preferred, and the simpler explanation should be the more vigorously explored. The proposition that PTSD involves dual memory processes uniquely associated with the fragmentation of traumatic memories is unduly cumbersome. In comparison, a quantitative theory, which necessitates no separate memory processes, is clearly the simpler explanation. Without stronger evidence to the contrary, the simpler, quantitative explanation of traumatic memories in PTSD remains preferred.

CLINICAL IMPLICATIONS

Fragmentation theorists suggest that the advancement of new and more effective therapies for the prevention and treatment of chronic PTSD should focus on the elaboration, organization, and integration of fragmented, non-verbal aspects of the trauma memory so that a verbal, integrated form of the trauma narrative can be achieved. Within this framework, clinicians are encouraged to focus on particularly fragmented aspects of the trauma memory and push for verbal integration of those aspects.

The view of fragmentation theorists is in the spirit of Kendall's observation:

> Modern clinical science is largely focused on the elucidation of underlying mechanism because experience has taught us that this is almost always the most effective way of predicting outcome, of acquiring new and more effective therapies, and—most important of all—of preventing the disorder developing in the first place. (1989, p. 46)

This clinical emphasis on identifying narrative fragmentation and subsequent integration may be misguided, not because these approaches are ineffective, but because they may focus on the wrong mechanism, thereby diverting attention from the key mechanisms that are at play. For example, taking a more quantitative view of memory and PTSD, and shifting the focus of clinicians to the *meaning* of trauma and its sequelae, leads to an analysis of proposed mechanisms more consistent with views on other anxiety disorders (e.g., Bouton, 1988; Ehlers & Clark, 2000; Foa & Kozak, 1986). Within this analytic framework, clinicians ought to focus on accessing underlying fear structures, promoting fear reduction, and modifying dysfunctional cognitions. For the clinician and the patient, this distinction between competing perspectives is not immaterial.

REFERENCES

American Psychiatric Association (1994). *Diagnostic and statistical manual of mental disorders* (4th edn). Washington, DC: Author.

Amir, N., Stafford, J., Freshman, M. S., & Foa, E. B. (1998). Relationship between trauma narratives and trauma pathology. *Journal of Traumatic Stress, 11*, 385–392.

Beauchaine, T. P. (2003). Taxometrics and developmental psychopathology. *Development and Psychopathology, 15*, 501–527.

Berntsen, D., Willert, M., & Rubin, D. (2003). Splintered memories or vivid landmarks? Qualities and organization of traumatic memories with and without PTSD. *Applied Cognitive Psychology, 17*, 675–693.

Bouton, M. E. (1988). Context and ambiguity in the extinction of emotional learning: Implications for exposure therapy. *Behaviour Research and Therapy, 26*, 137–149.

Brewin, C. R. (1996). Cognitive processing of adverse experiences. *International Review of Psychiatry*, *8*, 333–339.

Brewin, C. R. (2001). A cognitive neuroscience account of posttraumatic stress disorder and its treatment. *Behaviour Research and Therapy*, *39*, 373–393.

Byrne, C. A., Hyman, I. E., & Scott, K. L. (2001). Comparison of memories for traumatic events and other experiences. *Applied Cognitive Psychology*, *15*, S119–S133.

Ehlers, A., & Clark, D. M. (2000). A cognitive model of posttraumatic stress disorder. *Behaviour Research and Therapy*, *38*, 219–345.

Foa, E. B., & Kozak, M. J. (1986). Emotional processing of fear: Exposure to corrective information. *Psychological Bulletin*, *99*, 20–35.

Foa, E. B., Molnar, C., & Cashman, L. (1995). Change in rape narratives during exposure therapy for posttraumatic stress disorder. *Journal of Traumatic Stress*, *8*, 675–690.

Foa, E. B., & Riggs, D. S. (1993). Posttraumatic stress disorder in rape victims. In J. Oldham, M. B. Riba, & A. Tasman (eds), *American psychiatric press review of psychiatry*, Vol. 12 (pp. 273–303). Washington, DC: American Psychiatric Press.

Foa, E. B., & Rothbaum, B. O. (1998). *Treating the trauma of rape*. New York: Guilford Press.

Freedman, S. A., Brandes, D., Peri, T., & Shalev, A. (1999). Predictors of chronic posttraumatic stress disorder: A prospective study. *British Journal of Psychiatry*, *174*, 353–359.

Gelinas, D. J. (1983). The persisting negative effects of incest. *Psychiatry*, *46*, 312–332.

Gray, M. J., & Lombardo, T. W. (2001). Complexity of trauma narratives as an index of fragmented memory in PTSD: A critical analysis. *Applied Cognitive Psychology*, *15*, S171–S186.

Halligan, S. A., Michael, T., Clark, D. M., & Ehlers, A. (2003). Posttraumatic stress disorder following assault: The role of cognitive processing, trauma memory, and appraisals. *Journal of Consulting and Clinical Psychology*, *71*, 419–431.

Harvey, A. G., & Bryant, R. A. (1999). A qualitative investigation of the organization of traumatic memories. *British Journal of Clinical Psychology*, *38*, 401–405.

Holen, A. (1991). A longitudinal study of the occurrence and persistence of post-traumatic health problems in disaster survivors. *Stress Medicine*, *7*, 11–17.

Hopper, J. W., & van der Kolk, B. A. (2001). Retrieving, assessing, and classifying traumatic memories: A preliminary report on three case studies of a new standardized method. *Journal of Aggression, Maltreatment, and Trauma*, *4*, 33–71.

Horowitz, M. J. (1997). *Stress response syndromes: PTSD, grief, and adjustment disorders* (3rd edn). New Jersey: Aronson.

Kendall, R. E. (1989). Clinical validity. *Psychological Medicine*, *19*, 44–55.

Kessler, R. C., Sonnega, A., Bromet, E., Hughes, M., & Nelson, C. B. (1995). Posttraumatic stress disorder in the National Comorbidity Survey. *Archives of General Psychiatry*, *52*, 1048–1060.

Kindt, M., & van den Hout, M. (2003). Dissociation and memory fragmentation: Experimental effects on metamemory but not on actual memory performance. *Behaviour Research and Therapy*, *41*, 167–178.

Koopman, C., Classen, C., & Spiegel, D. (1994). Predictors of posttraumatic stress symptoms among survivors of the Oakland/Berkeley, California, Firestorm. *American Journal of Psychiatry*, *151*, 888–894.

Koss, M. P., Figueredo, A. J., Bell, I., Tharan, M., & Tromp, S. (1996). Traumatic memory characteristics: A cross-validated mediation model of response to rape among employed women. *Journal of Abnormal Psychology*, *105*, 421–432.

Krystal, J. H., Southwick, S. M., & Charney, D. S. (1995). Posttraumatic stress disorder: Psychobiological mechanisms of traumatic remembrance. In D. L. Schacter (ed.), *Memory distortions: How minds, brains, and societies reconstruct the past*. Cambridge, MA: Harvard University Press.

Macklin, M. L., Metzger, I. J., Litz, B. T., McNally, R. J., & Lasko, N. B., et al. (1998). Lower pre-combat intelligence is a risk factor for posttraumatic stress disorder. *Journal of Consulting and Clinical Psychology*, 66, 323–326.

Marmar, C. R., Weiss, D. S., & Metzler, T. J. (1997). The peritraumatic dissociative experiences questionnaire. In J. P. Wilson & T. M. Keane (eds), *Assessing psychological trauma and PTSD*. New York and London: Guilford Press.

Marmar, C. R., Weiss, D. S., Metzler, T. J., Delucchi, K. L., Best, S. R., & Wentworth, K. A. (1999). Longitudinal course and predictors of continuing distress following critical incident exposure in emergency services personnel. *Journal of Nervous and Mental Disease*, 187, 15–22.

McNally, R. J., & Shin, L. M. (1995). Association of intelligence with severity of posttraumatic stress disorder symptoms in Vietnam combat veterans. *American Journal of Psychiatry*, 152, 936–938.

Meehl, P. E. (1992). Factors and taxa, traits and types, differences of degree and differences in kind. *Journal of Personality*, 60, 117–174.

Meehl, P. E. (1994). Bootstraps taxometrics: Solving the classification problem in psychopathology. *American Psychologist*, 50, 266–275.

Murray, J., Ehlers, A., & Mayou, R. A. (2002). Dissociation and post-traumatic stress disorder: Two prospective studies of road traffic accident survivors. *British Journal of Psychiatry*, 180, 363–368.

Nelson, T. O., Gerler, D., & Narens, L. (1984). Accuracy of feeling-of-knowing judgments for predicting perceptual identification and relearning. *Journal of Experimental Psychology: General*, 113, 282–300.

Nemiah, J. C. (1998). Early concepts of trauma, dissociation, and the unconscious: Their history and current implications. In J. D. Bremner & C. R. Marmar (eds), *Trauma, memory, and dissociation* (pp. 1–26). Washington, DC: American Psychiatric Press.

Porter, S., & Birt, A. R. (2001). Is traumatic memory special? A comparison of traumatic memory characteristics with memory for other emotional life experiences. *Applied Cognitive Psychology*, 15, S101–S117.

Resnick, H. S., Kilpatrick, D. G., Dansky, B. S., Saunders, B. E., & Best, C. L. (1993). Prevalence of civilian trauma and posttraumatic stress disorder in a representative national sample of women. *Journal of Consulting and Clinical Psychology*, 61, 984–991.

Rothbaum, B., Foa, E. B., Murdock, T., Riggs, D. S., & Walsh, W. (1992). A prospective examination of post-traumatic stress disorder in rape victims. *Journal of Traumatic Stress*, 5, 455–475.

Schwartz, B. L. (1994). Sources of information in metamemory: Judgments of learning and feelings of knowing. *Psychometric Bulletin and Review*, 1, 357–375.

Schwartz, B. L., Benjamin, A., & Bjork, R. (1997). The inferential and experiential bases of metamemory. *Current Directions in Psychological Science*, 6, 132–137.

Shalev, A. Y., Peri, T., Canetti, L., & Schreiber, S. (1996). Predictors of PTSD in injured trauma survivors: A prospective study. *American Journal of Psychiatry*, 153, 219–225.

Silva, R. R., Alpert, M., Munoz, D. M., Singh, S., Matzner, F., & Dummitt, S. (2000). Stress and vulnerability to posttraumatic stress disorder in children and adolescents. *American Journal of Psychiatry*, 157, 1229–1235.

Spiegel, D. (1993). Dissociation and trauma. In D. Spiegel (ed.), *Dissociative disorders: A clinical review*. Lutherville, MD: Sidran Press.

Terr, L. C. (1991). Childhood traumas: An outline and overview. *American Journal of Psychiatry*, 148, 10–20.

Tichenor, V., Marmar, C. R., Weiss, D. S., Metzler, T. J., & Ronfeldt, H. M. (1996). The relationship of peritraumatic dissociation and posttraumatic stress: Findings in female Vietnam theater veterans. *Journal of Consulting and Clinical Psychology*, 64, 1054–1059.

Tromp, S., Koss, M. P., Figueredo, A. J., & Tharan, M. (1995). Are rape memories different? A comparison of rape, other unpleasant, and pleasant memories among employed women. *Journal of Traumatic Stress, 8,* 607–627.

van der Kolk, B. A. (1987). *Psychological trauma.* Washington, DC: American Psychiatric Press.

van der Kolk, B. A. (1994). The body keeps score: Memory and the evolving psychobiology of posttraumatic stress. *Harvard Review of Psychiatry, 1,* 253–265.

van der Kolk, B. A. (1996). Trauma and memory. In B. A. van der Kolk, A. C. McFarlane, & L. Weisaeth (eds), *Traumatic stress: The effects of overwhelming experience on mind, body and society* (pp. 279–302). New York: Guilford Press.

van der Kolk, B. A. (1997). The psychobiology of posttraumatic stress disorder. *Journal of Clinical Psychiatry, 58,* 16–24.

van der Kolk, B. A., Burbridge, J., & Suzuki, J. (1997). The psychobiology of traumatic memory: Clinical implications of neuroimaging studies. In R. Yehuda & A. McFarlane (eds), *Psychobiology of posttraumatic stress disorder* (pp. 99–113). New York: Annals of the New York Academy of Sciences.

van der Kolk, B. A., & Fisler, R. (1995). Dissociation and the fragmentary nature of traumatic memories: Overview and exploratory study. *Journal of Traumatic Stress, 8,* 505–525.

van der Kolk, B. A., Hopper, J. W., & Osterman, J. E. (2001). Exploring the nature of traumatic memory: Combining clinical knowledge with laboratory methods. *Journal of Aggression, Maltreatment, and Trauma, 4,* 9–31.

van Minnen, A., Wessel, I., Dijkstra, T., & Roelofs, K. (2002). Changes in PTSD patients' narratives during prolonged exposure therapy: A replication and extension. *Journal of Traumatic Stress, 15,* 255–258.

Vasterling, J. J., Brailey, K., Constans, J. I., Borges, A., & Sutker, P. B. (1997). Assessment of intellectual resources in Gulf War veterans: Relationship to PTSD. *Assessment, 1,* 51–59.

Vasterling, J. J., Duke, L. M., Brailey, K., Constans, J. I., Allain, A. N., Fr, & Sutker, P. B. (2002). Attention, learning, and memory performances and intellectual resources in Vietnam veterans: PTSD and no disorder comparisons. *Neuropsychology, 16,* 5–14.

9   Memory, Trauma, and Dissociation

STEVEN J. LYNN
Department of Psychology, Binghamton University, NY, USA

JOSHUA A. KNOX
Department of Psychology, Binghamton University, NY, USA

OLIVER FASSLER
Department of Psychology, Binghamton University, NY, USA

SCOTT O. LILIENFELD
Department of Psychology, Emory University, Atlanta, USA

ELIZABETH F. LOFTUS
Department of Psychology and Social Behavior, University of California, Irvine, USA

Some time ago, one of the authors (SJL) was consulted by a college-educated, 42-year-old woman, "Ms. M.," who stated she was a "multiple personality" and wanted help to fully integrate herself and her memories. She had moved recently from a large city and had been in treatment for three years with another therapist. She received the diagnosis of dissociative identity disorder (DID), formerly known as multiple personality disorder, after her therapist had referred her to a specialty hospital clinic for DID. After a two-week stay at this clinic, she stated that she "recovered" many memories of sexual abuse by her mother, father, and several clergy persons, all of whom she claimed participated in a satanic cult that was involved in the ritual murder and cannibalism of children in her neighborhood. She was convinced that the abuse began as early as the age of 8 months.

Prior to her hospitalization, Ms. M. was seriously depressed following the death of her father, her mother's developing Alzheimer's disease, her son's paralysis in a skiing accident, and her divorce, all within a 14-month period. At the height of her depression, she began to experience morbid dreams that included people she loved hurting her. She also suffered from sleep paralysis, and experienced malevolent "presences" near her bed. Her therapist told her that her dreams and sleep-related fears indicated probable abuse. She was instructed to keep a dream journal to draw associations between what she dreamt and her current and past life. These ideas and techniques were reinforced during her treatment at the inpatient facility for DID. At one point, her therapist uncovered 13 personalities, including personalities of the opposite gender. Now, Ms. M. reported that she was "mostly integrated, but still depressed."

Posttraumatic Stress Disorder: Issues and Controversies. Edited by G. M. Rosen.
© 2004 John Wiley & Sons, Ltd.   ISBN 0-470-86284-X/0-470-86285-8.

This brief vignette raises fascinating questions about the veracity of recovered memories of trauma. Can people banish traumatic memories to the nether-regions of the unconscious where they are preserved intact until they are later recovered? Can traumatic memories breathe life into a dissociated personality that exerts influence on a hapless host personality? Or are such recovered memories mere chimeras, the product of inadvertent suggestions and the very procedures used to unearth the recollections? These and other questions related to the delayed recall of traumatic memories have proved controversial since the days of Freud and Janet. There is little debate about memories that are continuously remembered, nor is there much dispute that people are capable of remembering events they have not thought about for some time, even years after their occurrence. What is at issue is: (1) whether special mechanisms of repression or dissociation account for the forgetting of traumatic material; and (2) whether it is necessary or perhaps harmful to use procedures like hypnosis or guided imagery to recover purportedly repressed or dissociated memories.

We will argue that accounts of delayed recall and recovered memories based on repression and dissociation are inadequate. We will further contend that suggestive influences inherent in many memory recovery procedures, in combination with problems in distinguishing fantasy and reality, account for many, if not all, instances of "recovered memories."

REPRESSION AND DISSOCIATION

Many psychotherapists readily accept the idea of massive repression of early traumatic memories (Bruhn, 1990). Such statements in popular books as "half of all incest survivors do not remember that the abuse occurred" (Blume, 1990, p. 81) or "millions of people have blocked out frightening episodes of abuse, years of their life, or their entire childhood" (Frederickson, 1992, p. 15), exemplify beliefs that can be traced to Freud's views of the origin of obsessional neuroses and hysteria. Freud, along with Breuer, contended that these disorders were the byproduct of repressed experiences of sexual molestation. In this context, Freud described repression as occurring when the "ego was confronted by an experience, an idea, a feeling, arousing an affect so painful that the person resolved to forget it, since he had no confidence in his power to resolve the incompatibility between the unbearable idea and his ego by the processes of thought" (Freud, 1894, pp. 61–62). As McNally (2003) observed, despite the fact that Freud used the term "resolved to forget," Freud and others conceptualized repression as the unconscious motivated forgetting of unpleasant material (Holmes, 1990; McNally, 2003).

Freud's explanation for the cause of childhood hysteria was not warmly embraced by his colleagues for reasons that anticipate current concerns about recovered memories. That is, the techniques (e.g., hypnosis) that Freud used to unearth purportedly repressed memories were viewed as highly suggestive (Cioffi, 1974; Powell & Boer, 1994, 1995). Moreover, it was not evident that the abreaction of repressed memories played a role in the successful treatment of hysteria (Israels & Schatzman, 1993; McNally, 2003). Freud ultimately abandoned the seduction theory in favor of the idea that clients repress *fantasies* of sexual seduction. However, the notion that repressed traumatic memories must be revealed has endured as a cornerstone of both contemporary psychoanalysis (Galatzer-Levy, 1997) and modern memory recovery therapists (Crews, 1998).

The idea that the memory of events can be forever isolated, yet exert a profound influence on the rest of mental life, is also integral to the concept of dissociation. Early writings on dissociation provided the foundation for the modern "posttraumatic model" of severe dissociative disorders, particularly DID, diagnosed by the presence of two or more distinct personalities (i.e., alters) or "personality states." Proponents of the posttraumatic model (e.g., Gleaves, 1996; Gleaves, May, & Cardena, 2001; Ross, 1997) posit that DID arises primarily from a history of severe physical abuse, sexual abuse, or both in childhood. Individuals who undergo horrific trauma in early life are thought to compartmentalize their personalities into discrete alters as a means of coping with intense emotional pain.

This modern view closely resembles the historical concept of dissociation first introduced by the French neurologist Pierre Janet around the time that Freud and Breuer introduced the concept of repression. Janet regarded dissociation (which he termed "desaggregation") as horizontal splitting within different parts of the unconscious, as opposed to the concept of repression which involved the vertical splitting between the conscious and unconscious. For Janet, this splitting resulted in "double consciousness," which is similar in many ways to the modern-day concept of DID. Freud and his followers countered Janet's views and contended that most, if not all, cases of multiple personality resulted from the suggestive influence of therapists upon patients, an argument allied to the contentions of modern critics of the posttraumatic model of DID.

CLASSICAL DISSOCIATION AND NEODISSOCIATION THEORIES

Interest in dissociation has waxed and waned since Janet's (1889) landmark writings. The decline of the concept was fueled by the eclipse of dissociation theory by psychoanalysis, with its emphasis on repression, and by the rise of behaviorism, with its rejection of mentalist constructs. A third reason why classical dissociation theory fell out of favor was the lack of empirical support for the phenomenon of non-interference. According to this principle, two tasks performed simultaneously, like two "personalities," theoretically could function independently. More specifically, simultaneous task performance should result in less interference when one task is performed subconsciously, as compared to when multiple tasks are performed consciously.

To test the hypothesis of non-interference, hypnotic techniques have been used to experimentally manipulate conscious and subconscious task performance. In an early investigation, Prince (1929) examined the ability of highly hypnotizable subjects to perform two or more tasks simultaneously (e.g., adding numbers while copying literature) following posthypnotic suggestions for subconscious performance of one of the tasks. Prince found that performance on one task degraded performance on the other. Subsequent experiments (Hull, 1933; Messerschmidt, 1927–1928; Mitchell, 1932) with hypnotizable subjects similarly showed that, following posthypnotic suggestions, concurrent tasks interfered with one another. These findings failed to support one of the central predictions resulting from classical dissociation theory.

Hilgard (1977, 1986, 1994) attempted to bridge the divide between dissociation theory and research by advancing a "neodissociation" theory that allowed for the possibility that all dissociations are not necessarily complete. Hilgard's model is based on three tenets: (1) the existence of interacting subordinate cognitive systems, with relative unity and functional autonomy; (2) the existence of some sort of hierarchical control of the interaction among these systems; and (3) the existence of an "executive ego," a central overarching control system. According to Hilgard (1986), increased task interference could result from the cognitive effort required to erect and maintain an amnesic-like barrier designed to "maintain one task as subconscious" (p. 147).

Hilgard's position was based on hypnosis research contrasting apparently subconscious performance (typically through the use of automatic writing suggestions) with conscious performance of an individual task. Studies indicated that keeping a task out of conscious awareness does indeed tax attentional resources (see Knox, Crutchfield, & Hilgard, 1975; Stevenson, 1976). Bowers and Brenneman (1981) found that performance on a dichotic listening task was not compromised by a competing task. However, a second study suggested that the initial results were not attributable to dissociation, but rather to participants adopting a passive response style whereby they focused attention primarily on the target stimuli. This interpretation was later supported by Green and Lynn's (1995) task interference study. In summary, studies of competing task performance cast doubt on the existence of a dissociative mechanism that creates two "streams of consciousness" that function independently without interference.

HIDDEN OBSERVER OR FLEXIBLE OBSERVER?

Hilgard introduced the metaphor of a "hidden observer" to describe the phenomenon by which a person registers and stores information in memory, without awareness that the information had been processed. Hilgard (1977) noted that the phenomenon was analogous to a situation in which an observer stands in the wings of a theater watching a center stage performance. For Hilgard, the hidden observer phenomenon represented a division of the monitoring function of consciousness, separated by an amnesic-like barrier.

Hilgard and associates (e.g., Crawford, Macdonald, & Hilgard, 1979; Hilgard, 1973, 1977; Hilgard, Hilgard, Macdonald, Morgan, & Johnson, 1978; Hilgard, Morgan, & McDonald, 1975; Knox, Morgan, & Hilgard, 1974) attempted to study the hidden observer phenomenon with tasks involving pain and hearing. In a typical study, highly suggestible subjects are first given hypnotic suggestions for analgesia, followed by instructions that they possess a "hidden part" that can experience high levels of pain when the hypnotist communicates directly with that hidden part by way of a prearranged cue. Research conducted in Hilgard's laboratory has demonstrated that hidden observer reports can penetrate hypnotic blindness, hypnotic deafness, and positive hallucinations in about 50% of subjects (see Kirsch & Lynn, 1998, for a review).

Supporters of neodissociation theory have interpreted the hidden observer phenomenon as reflecting the emergence of a hidden part of consciousness that exists independent of instructions or imaginative suggestions. Research has shown this is not the case, and the hidden observer phenomenon is reactive to the shaping influences of suggestion. Depending on instructions, the hidden observer can experience more pain or less pain or perceive things normally or in reverse. There can even be two hidden observers, one storing memories of abstract words, the other storing memories of concrete words (Spanos, Flynn, & Gwynn, 1988; Spanos, Gwynn, & Stam, 1983; Spanos & Hewitt, 1980; Spanos & McLean, 1986; Spanos, Radtke, & Bertrand, 1984). Accordingly, reports of "hidden entities" appear to be byproducts of suggestions and contextual demands, rather than spontaneously occurring dissociated aspects of the personality (see Laurence, Perry, & Kihlstrom, 1983; Nogrady, McConkey, Laurence, & Perry, 1983, for a defense of the "hidden observer" and a rebuttal by Spanos, 1983, 1991). Such findings led Kirsch and Lynn (1998) to dub the hidden observer a "flexible observer."

The hidden observer phenomenon is analogous to the trauma-engendered "hidden" alters that are the hallmark of DID, and that can purportedly be accessed by hypnotic suggestion. Bliss (1980) noted in the hypnotic treatment of DID that "alter egos are summoned, and usually asked to speak freely. When they appear, the subject is asked to listen. [The subject] is then introduced to some of the personalities" (p. 1393). However, the flexible observer research underscores how easy it is to suggest seemingly independent "parts" of the personality in individuals culled from a non-pathological, college student population. Such findings are consistent with the idea that the putative personalities of DID patients are likewise the products of suggestion rather than spontaneously discovered entities. Finally, flexible observer studies do not support the idea that dissociations are due to an amnesic barrier separating consciousness into two simultaneous streams (Kirsch & Lynn, 1998). Rather, a single, undivided stream of consciousness changes in a manner consistent with instructional cues.

Hypnotic amnesia is central to Hilgard's neodissociation theory, and there are noteworthy parallels between dissociative amnesia and the subsequent recall of purportedly dissociated memories. Although spontaneous amnesia during or after hypnosis was once considered a common phenomenon, contemporary research has focused primarily on suggestion-induced amnesia. Typically, a suggestion is given to forget an event (e.g., one or more suggestions received), after which a reversal cue is administered to cancel the effects of the suggestion (e.g., "Now you can remember everything"). According to neodissociation theory, the temporarily forgotten material is isolated in a dissociated stream of consciousness, until rendered accessible to a second, non-dissociated stream of consciousness, by the retrieval cue. In the single experimental assessment of hypnotic amnesia by way of the hidden observer, Spanos et al. (1984) produced two hidden observers in each of eight, highly hypnotizable participants. After individuals learned a list of concrete and abstract words, they received an amnesia suggestion to forget the words. Half of the participants were told that abstract words were stored in their right hemisphere and that concrete words were stored in their left. The remaining individuals received the opposite instructions regarding information storage. When the hypnotist contacted the hidden observer associated with the right hemisphere, individuals recalled all of the words purportedly stored there (e.g., concrete words), but none of the words stored in the left hemisphere (e.g., abstract words), and vice versa. Kirsch and Lynn (1998) observed that it was extremely unlikely that amnesia suggestions would generate such divisions of consciousness. Instead, the apparent division of consciousness is likely to have been produced by the hidden observer instructions.

The hypothesis that suggested amnesia is produced by a division of consciousness into two or more simultaneous streams is without an evidential base. Rather, the selective recall of information after hidden observer instructions is consistent with motivated forgetting, a phenomenon that may be associated with forgetting important information in non-hypnotic contexts.

REPORTS OF AMNESIA FOR LIFE EVENTS

According to the DSM-IV, individuals with DID report significant episodes of amnesia for important personal information. They may report frequent periods of "lost time," lasting hours or days, in which they cannot recall where they were or what they were doing. This amnesia is often reported to be asymmetrical, whereby the host personality knows little about the behaviors of the alters, but not vice versa (APA, 1994). The traditional treatment of DID involves liberating or recovering memories of traumatic abuse that are ostensibly ensconced within alter personalities. When these recovered memories become available to the host personality, they can be melded into an overarching personality structure.

A key question for conceptual models of DID is whether traumatic memories can be dissociated or repressed for many years, and then recovered in pristine form during psychotherapy. Some believe the matter is resolved. Karon and Widener (1997), for example, maintained that "Laboratory experiments from the 1930s . . . to the present . . . have shown evidence for repression" (p. 338). Others believe a considerably more tempered appraisal is warranted (see Lilienfeld & Loftus, 1998), observing that anecdotal data may provide suggestive support for repression (Cohen, 1996; Schachter & Kihlstrom, 1989), but over 60 years of laboratory research has failed to yield compelling support for this defense mechanism (Holmes, 1974, 1990). These observers note that, if anything, stressful experiences, because of their salience, should be easier to recall than emotionally sterile memories (Shobe & Kihlstrom, 1997).

Clinical anecdotes of reportedly recovered memories remain compelling to some workers in the field. Rieker and Carmen (1986) reported that a woman who entered psychotherapy for sexual dysfunction recovered memories of incest committed by her father. Schuker (1979) described a woman who entered psychotherapy for chronic insomnia, low self-esteem, and other problems, eventually coming to believe that she was sexually assaulted by her father. Williams (1987) described a man who entered therapy for depression and sleep disturbances, and had "recovered memories" of a servant molesting him. Such anecdotal reports are taken by some clinicians as "evidence" that clients can remember previously inaccessible painful experiences (Erdelyi, 1985). Others find these cases unconvincing "clinical speculations" (Holmes, 1990, p. 97).

Studies often cited (see Karon & Widener, 1997) as providing evidence for repression or dissociation are vulnerable to alternative explanations and criticisms. For example, Diven (1937) and Haggard (1943) associated electric shock with poorer recall of words, a finding potentially attributable to the interfering effects of stress on memory (Holmes, 1990). "Perceptual defense studies," in which participants demonstrate greater reluctance to report emotional than non-emotional words, may be attributable to differences in familiarity between these two classes of words (Holmes, 1990). Other studies suggest the possibility that some cognitive processing of simple stimuli may occur below the threshold of awareness (e.g., Shevrin, Williams, Marshall, & Hertel, 1992), but this does not provide direct evidence for the existence of repression, dissociation, or any other special mechanism. After reviewing 60 years of research and finding no controlled laboratory support for the concept of repression, Holmes (1990) wryly suggested that any use of the concept be preceded by a caveat: "Warning. The concept of repression has not been validated with experimental research and its use may be hazardous to the accurate interpretation of clinical behavior" (p. 97).

Current research findings have not quelled the debates. Scheflin and Brown (1996) reviewed 25 studies and concluded that amnesia for childhood abuse was a robust finding. Piper (1997) proffered a critique of the same literature and observed that concepts of dissociation and dissociative amnesia were ambiguous and over-inclusive. Additionally, many of the studies reviewed by Scheflin and Brown (1996) failed to provide compelling verification that the reported abuse occurred. Piper observed that the failure to report past abuse provided no guarantee that the individual had actually forgotten, nor did the inability to recall a particular event implicate dissociation or repression as the causative mechanism.

Several studies provide support for Piper's position. For example, Goodman and colleagues (2003) repeatedly interviewed 175 individuals with documented child sexual abuse, approximately 13 years after the target case. Of the individuals interviewed over three phases of the study, 18.9% of the respondents did not report the documented target case on initial report. In a subsequent phone interview, 15.5% did not report the target case, and by the third (in person) interview phase, only 8% of the participants failed to report the target case. Goodman and colleagues (2003) observed that their findings highlight the importance of social factors in child sexual abuse disclosure. Other studies have shown that as many as 25% of individuals sampled failed to remember significant life events (e.g., injury-producing motor vehicle accidents, hospitalizations), even a year after they occurred (see Lilienfeld & Loftus, 1998).

Read and colleagues (see, for example, Read & Lindsay, 2000) demonstrated that one can readily induce reports of autobiographical memory gaps in normal subjects simply by asking them to recall multiple events from early childhood. When individuals are then asked, "Was there ever a period of time when you remembered less of your childhood than you do now?," they typically respond "Yes," believing that they now recall more of their childhood history than they once did. Ross (1997) has observed that similar questions are used commonly in investigations of DID to verify the presence of amnesia. Therefore, self-reports of autobiographical memory gaps in DID patients must be interpreted with caution, particularly when patients have been asked repeatedly to recall childhood memories.

DISSOCIATION, TRAUMA, AND MEMORY

The traditional notion of dissociation implies that memories can split off from ordinary consciousness in childhood yet remain preserved with minimal or no distortion for later recall in adulthood. Thus, van der Kolk, van der Hart, and Marmar (1996) suggested that dissociated imprints of memories are retrieved as sensory fragments that have little or no linguistic component. These hypothesized fragments then must be woven together to construct a coherent narrative memory of the traumatic event. Challenging this viewpoint,

Eisen and Lynn (2001) expressed skepticism regarding whether a memory that was never encoded as a coherent narrative could be retrieved and accurately reported at a later date. Further, the reconstruction of events from memory fragments, feelings, and intuition are among the most common contributing factors in the creation of false memory formation (see Loftus, 1993, 2003, for a review).

Additional considerations belie the notion that initially incomplete and fragmented memories can be made whole years later (Eisen & Lynn, 2001). For example, even when there are no manifest memory problems such as profound amnesia for experienced traumas, the recovery of traumatic memories would be expected to vary from time to time, be more or less complete, and reflect contextual and defensive influences. Further, it is well known that normal forgetting takes place when a memory is isolated and never rehearsed. If dissociation involves the compartmentalization and subsequent avoidance of memories during a stressful experience, then rehearsal of memories should be effectively abolished. Even if isolated elements of the event were encoded and retained in declarative memory, the details of these decontextualized fragments would fade over time, like "ordinary" memories. If so, it would undermine the contention that dissociated memories can be recovered intact—often many years after the event—by such techniques as hypnosis (see Spiegel, 1995).

DISSOCIATION AND SUGGESTIBILITY

Appreciable individual differences exist in dissociative experiences (see Lynn & Rhue, 1994), as demonstrated by valid and reliable measures of dissociative tendencies (e.g., Dissociative Experiences Scale/DES, Bernstein & Putnam, 1986). Based on the DES and related instruments, an accumulating literature, albeit not entirely consistent, suggests a modest relationship between dissociation and inaccurate memories in children and adults. For example, the association between inaccurate memories and dissociation has been demonstrated in adults across several memory paradigms, with correlations in the range of $r = .18$ to $r = .53$. These paradigms have included a staged event followed by highly suggestive misleading questions a week later (Eisen & Carlson, 1998; Eisen, Morgan, & Mickes, 2002); a video of a crime followed by misleading information (Wright & Livingston-Raper, 2002); acceptance of early autobiographical memories using a memory implantation paradigm (Hyman & Billings, 1998; Porter, Birt, Yuille, & Lehman, 2000; Qin, 1999; Wilkinson & Hyman, 1998); repeated imagining of events that did not actually occur (Heaps & Nash, 2001; Paddock et al., 1998); errors in response to misleading questions on the Gudjonsson Scale of Interrogative Suggestibility (Merckelbach, Muris, Rassin, & Horselenberg, 2000; Wolfradt & Meyer, 1998); listening to an aversive story (Candel, Merckelbach, & Kuijpers, 2003); the inability to distinguish dreams and reality (Rassin, Merckelbach, & Spaan, 2001); and the DRM paradigm that involves the (false) recall of words that are not actually presented during the experiment (e.g., sleep) when a list of highly associated words (e.g., dream, bed) is presented to participants (Winograd, Peluso, & Glover, 1998).

A number of studies have failed to replicate these findings in the context of the DRM (Eisen, Cardeneas, Kistorian, Yu, & Tirtibudi, 1999; Platt, Lacey, Iobst, & Finkelman, 1998; Qin, 1999; Wilkinson & Hyman, 1998), and memory implantation paradigms (Mazzoni, Loftus, Seitz, & Lynn, 1999; Mazzoni & Memom, in press). However, in aggregate, the reviewed studies indicate that individuals with dissociative tendencies are at a somewhat heightened risk of developing false memories. Clearly, suggestive procedures should be scrupulously avoided with patients who demonstrate dissociative tendencies.

THE SOCIOCOGNITIVE MODEL OF DID

The sociocognitive model stands in contradistinction to traditional posttraumatic models, and proffers no special mechanism such as dissociation to account for the dramatic symptoms of DID. Rather, proponents of the sociocognitive model (Spanos, 1994, 1996; see also Aldridge-Morris, 1989; Lilienfeld et al., 1999; Lynn & Pintar, 1997; McHugh, 1992) contend that DID is a socially constructed condition that results from: (1) inadvertent therapist cueing such as suggestive questioning regarding the existence of possible alters; (2) media influences including film and television portrayals of DID like *Sybil*; and (3) broader sociocultural expectations regarding the presumed clinical features of DID.

The sociocognitive model does not maintain that DID can typically be created in vacuum by iatrogenic or sociocultural influences. A large proportion of DID patients have histories of co-occurring psychopathology, particularly depression and borderline personality disorder (Ganaway, 1995). In the case presented at the outset of our discussion, it is virtually inconceivable but true that "Ms. M." 's depression was not a target of treatment, and she was never treated with antidepressant medications. Nor did her therapist realize that relatively common sleep-related phenomena, such as hypnagogic hallucinations and sleep paralysis, have been associated with false memories of abuse (Powell & Nielsen, 1998). It seems plausible that iatrogenic and sociocultural influences often operate on a backdrop of preexisting psychopathology, and exert their impact primarily on individuals who are seeking a causal explanation ("effort after meaning") for their instability, identity problems, impulsiveness, and seemingly inexplicable behaviors. It is possible that fantasy proneness (see Lynn, Rhue, & Green, 1989) and the inability to distinguish reality and dream experiences (Kemp, Burt, & Sheen, 2003; Rassin et al., 2001) also increase vulnerability to DID.

SUGGESTING COMPLEX MEMORIES

According to the sociocognitive model, the presentation of DID is shaped by beliefs, expectancies, and suggestions regarding the symptoms of DID and early life events. Research has demonstrated that complex memories can be formed by way of subtle and not so subtle suggestions. Loftus and colleagues (Loftus, 1993; Loftus & Ketcham, 1994; Loftus & Pickrell, 1995) were among the first to demonstrate that people can be led to integrate an entirely fabricated event into their personal histories. In this line of research, participants were asked by an older sibling to remember real and fictitious events. The older sibling initially provided a few details about the false event, such as getting lost in a shopping mall. All subjects then participated in a series of interviews held over several days, during which some claimed to remember the false event, often providing surprisingly detailed accounts of the fictitious event.

Studies in other laboratories using similar experimental procedures similarly find that a significant minority of people will embrace false events. Hyman, Husband, and Billings

(1995) conducted interviews that included one unlikely event among several true events. The false events used in the study were: (1) spilling a punch bowl at a wedding reception; (2) evacuating a grocery store when the sprinklers went off; and (3) releasing the parking brake of a car in a parking lot and hitting another car. Hyman and colleagues were interested in any elaboration that participants might provide to the false event. Results indicated that recall was very high for true events, and significantly lower for the false events. Nevertheless, by the time of a third interview, 25% of the participants exhibited some recall for the false event.

Pezdek, Finger, and Hodge (1997) asked adolescents to recall details regarding both true and false events. The false events involved the participants engaging in religious activities that were either consistent or inconsistent with their religious denomination (Catholic or Jewish). Ten out of 29 Catholics and 3 out of 22 Jews reported memories for at least one of the false events. Three of the participants exhibited memories for religious activities that were inconsistent with their denomination. Porter, Yuille, and Lehman (1999) recently found that 26% of participants reported at least one "complete" false memory of six suggested emotional childhood events (animal attack, indoor accident, outdoor accident, getting lost, medical procedure, and being injured by another child). The events were suggested in three different interviews over a two-week period in which the interviewer attempted to elicit false memories using guided imagery, context reinstatement, mild social pressure, and the encouragement of repeated recall attempts. In addition to the substantial minority of participants who reported a "complete" false memory, 30% reported a "partial" false memory in which some information was recalled or the individual was uncertain about whether the memory was false. In short, more than half of individuals exposed to a variety of memory recovery techniques were led to report an emotional false memory.

One recurring issue for memory distortion research is the question of whether purportedly "false" events actually might have happened. Perhaps the subject was, in fact, injured by another child, or lost in a mall, and the imagination exercise triggered a true memory rather than planting a false one. To demonstrate more convincingly that false memories can be insinuated into memory with suggestive techniques, researchers have tried to plant memories of events that are highly implausible, if not impossible. For example, very early memories dating from age 2 or earlier are implausible because infantile amnesia covers these early years. Yet, several studies demonstrate how easy it is to manipulate reports of early recollections. Malinoski and Lynn (1997) examined the influence of several techniques used by memory recovery therapists (e.g., Farmer, 1989; Meiselman, 1990) on reports of memories earlier than age 2. These techniques include compliments for increasingly early memory reports, the provision of information that most young adults can retrieve memories of very early events, and instructions to see events "in their mind's eye" as toddlers or infants. Prior to the introduction of such techniques, the mean age of initial reported memory was 3.7 years, with only 11% of participants reporting initial memories at or before age 24 months. After memory recovery procedures were implemented, 59% of participants reported a memory of their second birthday, 78.2% reported at least one memory that occurred by 24 months, and 33% reported a memory at age 12 months or earlier. In a second study (Lynn & Malinoski, 1997), a slight change in the wording of the question used to elicit early memories (High demand condition: "Tell me when you get an earlier memory", versus Low demand condition: "If you don't remember it's all right") resulted in a difference of average recall of nearly 1 year (low demand M = 3.45 years versus high demand M = 2.48 years).

The material reviewed thus far underscores the malleability of early memory reports and calls into question the veracity of at least some reports of child abuse in studies of DID. In one study, for example, Ross, Miller, Bjornson, and Reagor (1991) found that 26% of DID patients reported being abused prior to age 3, while 10.6% reported being abused prior to age 1. Dell and Eisenhower (1990) reported that 4 of 11 adolescent patients with DID reported that their first alter emerged at age 2 or earlier. Of course, skeptics might still insist that memory recovery procedures access memories of actual events, no matter how early they are claimed to have occurred. To address this concern, investigators have demonstrated that participants can be led to report memories of events that could not possibly have occurred. For example, Sivec, Lynn, and Malinoski (1997) used hypnosis to regress participants to the age of 5. Some 20% of these participants then recalled playing with a toy that was not yet released at the time they would have been so young. Mazzoni and Memom (in press) implanted "impossible" memories in British students. The false event was "having a nurse remove a skin sample from my little finger." This medical procedure was not carried out in the United Kingdom, according to extensive investigation of health policy records.

In another line of research (Braun, Ellis, & Loftus, 2002), people evaluated advertising copy that featured Bugs Bunny at Disneyland, a scene that never could have occurred because Bugs Bunny is a Warner Bros cartoon character. Later, when asked about their own experiences at Disneyland, 16% of these subjects said that they remembered meeting and shaking hands with Bugs Bunny. In follow-up research carried out by Grinley (cited in Loftus, 2003), several presentations of fake advertisements involving Bugs Bunny at Disneyland resulted in 25–35% of subjects claiming to have met Bugs Bunny at the Disney theme park. Moreover, when subjects were subsequently asked for precise reports on their encounter with Bugs Bunny, 62% remembered shaking his hand and 46% remembered hugging him.

One of the most powerful techniques for planting implausible false memories has involved the use of fake photographs (Wade, Garry, Read, & Lindsay, 2002). Subjects were shown a falsified photograph of a hot-air balloon, in which the subject and a relative had been pasted. Family members had confirmed that an actual hot-air balloon ride had never occurred for the subjects, who were shown the fake photograph and asked to tell "everything you can remember without leaving anything out, no matter how trivial it may seem." After two further interviews, 50% of subjects recalled the fictitious hot-air balloon ride, at least in part, with some embellishing their reports with sensory details.

Yet another set of findings concerns individuals who genuinely believe in memories of traumatic events that are extremely unlikely to have occurred. For example, there have been reports of satanic ritual abuse, often associated with diagnoses of DID, and often arising in the context of psychotherapy (Mulhern, 1992; Qin, Goodman, Bottoms, & Shaver, 1998). Following years of investigation into claims of horrific child abuse (e.g., human sacrifice, baby-breeding), American law enforcement agencies, including the FBI (Lanning & Burgess, 1989), were unable to garner any evidence to support the allegations. Mulhern (1992) conducted a sociohistorical analysis and concluded that there is no credible evidence to suggest that memories of ritualistic torture and abuse are veridical. Spanos,

Burgess, and Burgess (1994) drew similar conclusions concerning the veracity of reports on alleged abductions by aliens. Surveys of therapists conducted by Qin et al. (1998) reveal that satanic ritual abuse reports are associated with a relatively small group of therapists who, the authors speculate, may "accept, and even help to create, 'false memories' of satanic ritual abuse" (p. 279).

ADDITIONAL FINDINGS SUPPORTING THE SOCIOCOGNITIVE MODEL

According to the sociocognitive model, the dramatic rise in DID cases in the 1980s occurred largely as a result of iatrogenic (therapist-induced) influences, coupled with increased media attention accorded to the diagnosis. Specifically, as DID became familiar to both psychotherapists and the general public, an autocatalytic feedback loop was set in motion (see Shermer, 1997, for examples). In this feedback loop, therapeutic and societal expectations regarding the features of DID gave rise to greater numbers of cases; in turn influencing therapeutic and societal expectations regarding the features of DID; in turn giving rise to greater number of cases of DID, and so on. In short, the features of DID (e.g., "separate" personalities that house dissociated memories) do not necessarily arise spontaneously in the aftermath of a devastating history of trauma. Rather, they represent "creations," much like the hidden observer. Multiple findings support this view including the following:

1 The number of patients with DID has increased dramatically over the past few decades (Elzinga, van Dyck, & Spinhoven, 1998).
2 The number of alters per DID individual has similarly increased over the past few decades (North, Ryall, Ricci, & Wetzel, 1993), although the number of alters at the time of initial diagnosis appears to have remained constant (Ross, Norton, & Wozney, 1989).
3 Both of these increases coincide with dramatically increased therapist and public awareness of the major features of DID (Fahy, 1988).
4 It has been well established (see Loftus, 1992; Spanos, 1994) that individuals can be led to report a wide range of fabricated memories that are held with conviction.
5 Mainstream treatment techniques for DID appear to reinforce patients' displays of multiplicity, reify alters as distinct personalities, and encourage patients to establish contact with presumed latent alters (Spanos, 1994, 1996).
6 Many or most DID patients show few or no clear-cut signs of this condition (e.g., alters) prior to psychotherapy (Kluft, 1984).
7 The number of alters per DID individual tends to increase substantially over the course of DID-oriented psychotherapy (Piper, 1997).
8 Psychotherapists who use hypnosis tend to have more DID patients in their caseloads than do psychotherapists who do not use hypnosis (Powell & Gee, 1999).
9 The majority of diagnoses of DID derive from a relatively small number of psychotherapists, many of whom are specialists in DID (Mai, 1995).
10 Laboratory studies suggest that non-clinical participants who are provided with appropriate cues and prompts can reproduce many of the overt features of DID (Spanos, Weekes, & Bertrand, 1985; Stafford & Lynn, 2002).

11 Until fairly recently, diagnoses of DID were limited largely to North America, where the condition has received widespread media publicity (Spanos, 1996), although DID is now being diagnosed with considerable frequency in some countries (e.g., Holland) in which it has recently become more widely publicized.

SUGGESTIVE THERAPEUTIC TECHNIQUES

According to the sociocognitive model, certain psychotherapeutic techniques are viewed as highly "risky," insofar as they can induce false memories (see Lynn, Lock, Loftus, Lilienfeld, & Krackow, 2003, for a more expansive treatment of the issue). These techniques are now discussed.

GUIDED IMAGERY

According to a survey by Poole, Lindsay, Memom, and Bull (1995), 32% of US therapists report using "imagery-related" techniques to reveal past abuse. Roland (1993), for example, used visualization to jog "blocked" memories, and a "reconstruction" technique to recover repressed memories. The use of imagery to uncover allegedly repressed memories warrants concern because people frequently confuse real and imagined memories, particularly when memories are initially hazy or unavailable. Hyman and Pentland (1996) found that participants who engaged in guided imagery reported more false memories of attending a wedding and knocking over a punchbowl than did individuals in a control group with instructions to do their best to remember childhood events. This finding is not surprising given that a sizable body of research has shown that simply having participants imagine an event can lead to the formation of false memories. Typically, confidence in the occurrence of fictitious events increases after those events have been imagined. This phenomenon is called imagination inflation, and has been demonstrated repeatedly (reviewed in Garry & Polaschek, 2000).

DREAM ANALYSIS

The imagination inflation paradigm has been extended to dream experiences. Viewed by Freud as the "royal road to the unconscious," dreams have been used to provide a window on past experiences, including repressed traumatic events. For example, van der Kolk, Britz, Burr, Sherry, and Hartmann (1994) claimed that dreams can represent "exact replicas" of traumatic experiences (p. 188), a view not unlike that propounded by Frederickson (1992), who argued that dreams are a vehicle by which "Buried memories of abuse intrude into . . . consciousness" (p. 44). In the case study presented at the outset of this chapter, the patient's dreams were interpreted in this manner. Survey research indicates that upwards of a third of US psychotherapists (37–44%) use dream interpretation (see also Brenneis, 1997; Polusny & Follette, 1996), despite the fact that no data exist to support the claim that dreams are indicative of a history of child abuse (Lindsay & Read, 1994).

In several studies by Mazzoni and colleagues (Loftus & Mazzoni, 1998; Mazzoni, Lombardo, Malvagia, & Loftus, 1997; Mazzoni et al., 1999), participants reported childhood experiences on two occasions, 3–4 weeks apart. Between sessions, some subjects were exposed to a 30-minute therapy simulation in which an expert clinician analyzed dream reports. No matter what participants dreamed, they received the suggestion that their dream was indicative of having experienced certain events (e.g., being lost in a public place or abandoned by parents) before the age of 3. Although subjects previously had indicated that they had not experienced these events before age 3, many individuals revised their accounts of the past.

HYPNOSIS

For many years, hypnosis has been a mainstream treatment of DID (e.g., see Ross, 1997), employed in an effort to discover or call forth presumed latent alters (Spanos, 1994, 1996). Hypnotic techniques frequently employ suggestions that clearly resemble those used to elicit the hidden observer in an effort to recover purportedly repressed or dissociated memories. Nevertheless, there is strong evidence that hypnosis does not improve recall, although it often increases respondents' confidence in their recall (Lynn, Lock, Myers, & Payne, 1997; Steblay & Bothwell, 1994). Lynn et al. reviewed data from several studies indicating that hypnotized participants performed either no better or worse than non-hypnotized participants on both structured and unstructured tests of recall. Moreover, a meta-analysis demonstrated that hypnotized participants exhibit higher rates of false memories than non-hypnotized participants following misinformation and leading questions (Steblay & Bothwell, 1994).

"Hypnotic age-regression" is the use of hypnosis to take a person back in time to recover traumatic and non-traumatic memories. According to Nash (1987), adults who ostensibly age-regressed to childhood do not show expected patterns associated with early development. For example, adults who age-regressed to childhood fall prey to the famous Ponzo (railroad tracks) illusion, even though this perceptual phenomenon occurs among adults, but not most children. This finding, and others reviewed by Nash (1987), strongly suggest that the perceptions of adults purportedly regressed to childhood continue to function like that of adults, not children. No matter how compelling "age-regressed experiences" may be to the hypnotized subject, they do not represent literal reinstatements of childhood experiences, behaviors, or feelings.

Hypnosis also can be used to induce "Past life regression," based on the premise that current psychological and physical symptoms are related to traumas that occurred in previous lives (see Mills & Lynn, 2000). However, Spanos, Menary, Gabora, DuBreuil, and Dewhirst (1991) demonstrated that information provided during hypnotic age regression was almost invariably incorrect. For example, one participant who was regressed to ancient times claimed to be Julius Caesar, emperor of Rome, in 50 BC, even though the designations of BC and AD were not adopted until centuries later, and Julius Caesar had died decades prior to the first Roman emperor. Spanos and colleagues found that past life experiences were elaborate, conformed to induced expectancies, and varied in accordance with pre-hypnotic information participants received regarding past historical periods (Spanos, 1996). Hypnotically induced past life experiences appear to be fantasies constructed from available cultural narratives, as well as from cues present in the hypnotic situation.

Finally, hypnosis can be used to implant false traumatic memories, a phenomenon demonstrated more than 100 years ago (Rosen, Sageman, & Loftus, 2003).

SYMPTOM AND PERSONALITY INTERPRETATIONS

Poole et al. (1995) surveyed US practitioners and found that more than one-third used symptom interpretation to recover suspected memories of abuse. Some popular self-help books for incest survivors follow this approach and provide symptom lists whose items are touted as possible or probable correlates of childhood incest (e.g., "Do you use work or achievements to compensate for inadequate feelings in other parts of your life?"). Blume's Incest Survivors' Aftereffects Checklist consists of 34 such correlates. The scale instructions read: "Do you find many characteristics of yourself on this list? If so, you could be a survivor of incest." Many of the characteristics of such checklists are vague and applicable to non-abused individuals; an observation that calls to mind the "P. T. Barnum effect," wherein highly general statements are perceived as true when applied specifically to oneself (Emery & Lilienfeld, 2002; Rosen, 1975). Additionally, no known constellation of specific symptoms related to a history of abuse actually exists, and non-victims experience many of the same symptoms contained on survivor checklists (Tavris, 1993).

Like bogus symptom interpretation, bogus personality interpretation can be used to create highly implausible or false memories. Spanos, Burgess, Burgess, Samuels, and Blois (1999) informed participants that their personality indicated certain experiences during the first week of life. After participants completed a questionnaire, they were told that a computer-generated personality profile based on their responses indicated they were "High Perceptual Cognitive Monitors," and that people with this profile had experienced special visual stimulation by a mobile within the first week of life. Participants were told falsely that the study was designed to recover memories to confirm the personality test scores. The participants were age-regressed to the crib; half of the participants were hypnotized and half received non-hypnotic age regression instructions. In the non-hypnotic group, 95% of the participants reported infant memories and 56% reported the target mobile. However, all of these participants indicated that the memories were fantasy constructions or that they were unsure if the memories were real. In the hypnotic group, 79% of the participants reported infant memories and 46% reported the target mobile. Some 49% of these participants believed the memories were real, and only 16% classified the memories as fantasies.

DuBreuil, Garry, and Loftus (1998) used the bogus personality interpretation paradigm and non-hypnotic age regression to implant memories of the second day of life (crib group) or the first day of kindergarten (kindergarten group). College students were administered a test that purportedly measured personality. These students were told that their test scores indicated it was likely they had participated in a nationwide program designed to enhance development through the use of red and green moving mobiles. A "crib" group was told that their enrichment program had occurred in the hospital immediately after birth, while a "kindergarten" group was told that mobiles had been placed in kindergarten classrooms. Participants were given the false information that memory functions "like a videotape recorder" and that age-regression can access otherwise inaccessible memories. Participants were age-regressed without hypnosis and given suggestions to visualize themselves at the target age. Some 25% of the kindergarten group and 55% of the crib group reported the target memory. All kindergarten participants believed that their memories corresponded to real events. In the crib group, 33% believed in the reality of their memories, 17% did not, and 50% were unsure.

BIBLIOTHERAPY

Many therapists who treat patients with suspected abuse histories prescribe "survivor books" or self-help books that provide "confirmation" of an individual's signs and symptoms from past abuse. The issue of symptom lists and interpretation of these symptoms already has been discussed. In some cases, the survivor self-help books purport to provide a means of gaining access to memories (e.g., Bass & Davis, 1988, *The Courage to Heal*), providing imaginative exercises, stories of other survivors' struggles, and sources of potential support for with other abuse survivors. These instructional materials can lead readers to develop false memories, as demonstrated by Mazzoni, Loftus, and Kirsch (2001) with regard to beliefs pertaining to whether individuals witnessed a case of demonic possession during early childhood. Events that were not experienced during childhood and initially deemed to be highly implausible can, with sufficient credibility-enhancing information, come to be viewed as having occurred in real life.

CONCLUDING COMMENTS AND CLINICAL IMPLICATIONS

Some authors (e.g., Karon & Widener, 1997) have been quick to invoke the existence of special memory processes, particularly dissociation and repression, to account for certain seemingly striking cases of memory loss among psychiatric patients. Several of these authors have dismissed evidence that well-established memory phenomena, such as ordinary forgetting or infantile amnesia, can account for such cases. Nevertheless, careful examination of these cases reveals that strong claims of special memory mechanisms are susceptible to a host of alternative explanations (Lilienfeld & Loftus, 1998).

A review of the research literature finds little empirical support for a dissociative mechanism that is responsible for the forgetting of traumatic events. Nor is there much support for the capacity of memory recovery techniques to excavate remembrances that somehow remain unadulterated by the passage of time. These conclusions are based largely on: (1) the lack of support for separate yet co-occurring streams of consciousness; (2) the fact that apparent divisions in the personality (e.g., the hidden observer phenomenon) can be created and shaped by suggestions; (3) the dubious nature of claims of psychogenic amnesia for salient life events; and (4) the fact that high scores on measures of dissociation are related to false rather than accurate memories. Further, there are findings to suggest that the very techniques used to recover memories may sully them and provide the fodder for both the creation of alter personalities in DID and the traumatic memories that are so frequently associated in clinical lore with multiple identities. Moreover, the evidence in support of the operation of a special dissociative mechanism that isolates and preserves memories is less than convincing.

The convergence of evidence provides a potent argument for the validity of the sociocognitive model (Lilienfeld et al., 1999; see also Lynn & Pintar, 1997). Although it would be premature to exclude all possibility that early trauma plays at least some role in the genesis of DID (see Lilienfeld & Lynn, 2003), compelling evidence indicates that the multiple identities are shaped substantially by suggestive therapeutic practices and broader sociocultural expectations regarding the features of multiple personality disorder (cf. Gleaves, 1996).

Unquestionably, the suffering of DID patients is entirely genuine. In this respect, the oft-asked question of whether DID "exists," misses the mark (Lilienfeld et al., 1999; McHugh, 1992). Ironically, however, at least some of this suffering appears to be brought on by well-intentioned psychotherapists. The history of DID, its rise in the 1980s, alarm that suggestive techniques could be causing the phenomena, followed by a decline in clini- cal presentations of the disorder, along with successful litigation against clinicians alleged to have created "multiples," should give pause to all concerned clinicians. Today, informed practice demands vigilance regarding the use of even mildly suggestive procedures in psychotherapy.

While the existence of special memory processes cannot be ruled out conclusively, given the state of the research evidence, a basic principle in philosophy of science is that the burden of proof falls squarely on the shoulders of those advancing affirmative claims. At this point, the ball now lies in the court of those who invoke dissociation, repression, or both to account for DID and related clinical phenomena. Moreover, the logical principle of Occham's Razor (the principle of parsimony) suggests that we should be reluctant to invoke special explanations for phenomena in the absence of strong evidence, when more mundane explanations work equally well, or better. Whether the advocates of special memory mechanisms will be able to meet this test remains to be seen.

REFERENCES

Aldridge-Morris, R. (1989). *Multiple personality: An exercise in deception*. Hillsdale, NJ: Lawrence Erlbaum Associates.

American Psychiatric Association. (1994). *Diagnostic and statistical manual of mental disorders* (4th edn). Washington, DC: Author.

Bass, E., & Davis, L. (1988). *The courage to heal*. New York: Harper & Row.

Bernstein, E. M., & Putnam, F. W. (1986). Development, reliability, and validity of a dissociation scale. *Journal of Nervous and Mental Disease, 174*, 727–735.

Bliss, E. L. (1980). Multiple personalities: A report of 14 cases with implications for schizophrenia and hysteria. *Archives of General Psychiatry, 37*, 1388–1397.

Blume, S. E. (1990). *Secret survivors: Uncovering incest and its aftereffects in women*. Chichester: John Wiley & Sons.

Bowers, K. S., & Brenneman, H. A. (1981). Hypnotic dissociation, dichotic listening, and active versus passive modes of attention. *Journal of Abnormal Psychology, 90*, 55–67.

Braun, K. A., Ellis, R., & Loftus, E. L. (2002). Make my memory: How advertising can change our memories of the past. *Psychology and Marketing, 19*, 1–23.

Brenneis, C. B. (1997). On the relationship of dream content, trauma, and mind: A view from inside out or outside in? In E. R. Shapiro (ed.), *The inner world in the outer world: Psychoanalytic perspectives* (pp. 59–76). New Haven, CT: Yale University Press.

Bruhn, A. R. (1990). *Earliest childhood memories*, Vol. 1: *Theory and application to clinical practice*. New York: Praeger.

Candel, I., Merckelbach, H., & Kuijpers, M. (2003). Dissociative experiences are related to commissions in emotional memory. *Behaviour Research and Therapy*, *41*, 719–725.

Cioffi, F. (1974). Was Freud a liar? *The Listener*, *91*, 172–174.

Cohen, N. J. (1996). Functional retrograde amnesia as a model of amnesia for childhood sexual abuse. In K. Pezdek & W. P. Banks (eds), *The recovered memory/false memory debate* (pp. 81–95). San Diego: Academic Press.

Crawford, H. J., Macdonald, H., & Hilgard, E. R. (1979). Hypnotic deafness: A psychophysical study of responses to tone intensity as modified by hypnosis. *American Journal of Psychology*, *92*, 193–214.

Crews, F. C. (1998). *Unauthorized Freud*. New York: Penguin Books.

Dell, P. F., & Eisenhower, J. W. (1990). Adolescent multiple personality disorder: A preliminary study of eleven cases. *Journal of the American Academy of Child and Adolescent Psychiatry*, *29*, 359–366.

Diven, K. (1937). Certain determinants in the conditioning of anxiety reactions. *Journal of Psychology*, *3*, 291–308.

DuBreuil, S. C., Garry, M., & Loftus, E. F. (1998). Tales from the crib: Age regression and the creation of unlikely memories. In S. J. Lynn & K. M. McConkey (eds), *Truth in memory* (pp. 137–160). New York: Guilford Press.

Eisen, M. L., Cardeneas, E., Kistorian, V., Yu, T., & Tirtibudi, P. (1999). Individual differences in college students' resistance to misleading information. In M. L. Eisen (Chair), Individual Differences in Suggestibility and Memory Distortion. Paper presented at the 3rd biennial meeting of the Society of Applied Research in Memory and Cognition, Boulder, Colorado.

Eisen, M. L., & Carlson, E. B. (1998). Individual differences in suggestibility: Examining the influence of dissociation, absorption, and a history of childhood abuse. *Applied Cognitive Psychology*, *12*, S47–S61.

Eisen, M. L., & Lynn, S. J. (2001). Dissociation, memory and suggestibility in adults and children. *Applied Cognitive Psychology*, *15*, S49–S73.

Eisen, M. L., Morgan, D. Y., & Mickes, L. (2002). Individual differences in eyewitness memory and suggestibility: Examining the relations between acquiescence, dissociation, and resistance to misleading information. *Personality and Individual Differences*, *33*, 553–571.

Elzinga, B. M., van Dyck, R., & Spinhoven, P. (1998). Three controversies about dissociative identity disorder. *Clinical Psychology and Psychotherapy*, *5*, 13–23.

Emery, C. L., & Lilienfeld, S. O. (2002). The validity of childhood sexual abuse victim checklists in popular psychology literature: A Barnum effect. Unpublished manuscript, Emory University, Atlanta, GA.

Erdelyi, M. H. (1985). *Psychoanalysis: Freud's cognitive psychology*. New York: W. H. Freeman/ Times Books/Henry Holt & Co.

Fahy, T. A. (1988). The diagnosis of multiple personality disorder: A critical review. *British Journal of Psychiatry*, *153*, 597–606.

Farmer, S. (1989). *Adult children of abusive parents: A healing program for those who have been physically, sexually, or emotionally abused*. Los Angeles: Lowell House.

Frederickson, R. (1992). *Repressed memories*. New York: Fireside.

Freud, S. (1894). *The psycho-neuroses of defense. Standard Edition*, *3*, 43–62.

Galatzer-Levy, R. M. (1997). *Psychoanalysis, memory, and trauma*. London: Oxford University Press.

Ganaway, G. K. (1995). Hypnosis, childhood trauma, and dissociative identity disorder: Toward an integrative theory. *International Journal of Clinical and Experimental Hypnosis*, *43*, 127–144.

Garry, M., & Polaschek, D. L. L. (2000). Imagination and memory. *Current Directions in Psychological Science*, *9*, 6–10.

Gleaves, D. H. (1996). The evidence for "repression": An examination of Holmes (1990) and the implications for the recovered memory controversy. *Journal of Child Sexual Abuse, 5*, 1–19.

Gleaves, D. H., May, M. C., & Cardena, E. (2001). An examination of the diagnostic validity of dissociative identity disorder. *Clinical Psychology Review, 21*, 577–608.

Gold, S. N., Hughes, D., & Hohnecker, L. (1994). Degrees of repression of sexual abuse memories. *American Psychologist, 49*, 441–442.

Goodman, G. S., Ghetti, S., Quas, J. A., Edelstein, R. S., Alexander, K. W., Redlich, A. D. et al. (2003). A prospective study of memory for child sexual abuse: New findings relevant to the repressed-memory controversy. *Psychological Science, 14*, 113–118.

Green, J. P., & Lynn, S. J. (1995). Hypnosis, dissociation, and simultaneous task performance. *Journal of Personality and Social Psychology, 69*, 728–735.

Grinley, M. J. (2002). Effects of advertising on semantic and episodic memory. Unpublished Masters thesis, University of Washington.

Haggard, E. A. (1943). Experimental studies in affective processes: I. Some effects of cognitive structure and active participation on certain autonomic reactions during and following experimentally induced stress. *Journal of Experimental Psychology, 33*, 257–284.

Heaps, C. M., & Nash, M. (2001). Comparing recollective experience in true and false autobiographical memories. *Journal of Experimental Psychology: Learning, Memory, and Cognition, 27*, 920–930.

Hilgard, E. R. (1973). The neodissociation interpretation of pain reduction in hypnosis. *Psychological Review, 80*, 396–411.

Hilgard, E. R. (1977). *Divided consciousness: Multiple controls in human thought and action.* New York: John Wiley & Sons.

Hilgard, E. R. (1986). *Divided consciousness: Multiple controls in human thought and action* (expanded edition). New York: John Wiley & Sons.

Hilgard, E. R. (1994). Neodissociation theory. In S. J. Lynn & J. W. Rhue (eds), *Dissociation: Clinical, theoretical and research perspectives* (pp. 32–51). New York: Guilford Press.

Hilgard, E. R., Hilgard, J., Macdonald, H., Morgan, A. H., & Johnson, L. S. (1978). Covert pain in hypnotic analgesia: Its reality as tested by the real-simulator design. *Journal of Abnormal Psychology, 87*, 655–663.

Hilgard, E. R., Morgan, A. H., & Macdonald, H. (1975). Pain and dissociation in the cold pressor test: A study of hypnotic analgesia with "hidden reports" through automatic key pressing and automatic talking. *Journal of Abnormal Psychology, 84*, 280–289.

Holmes, D. S. (1974). Investigations of repression: Differential recall of material experimentally or naturally associated with ego threat. *Psychological Bulletin, 81*, 632–653.

Holmes, D. S. (1990). The evidence for repression: An examination of sixty years of research. In J. L. Singer (ed.), *Repression and dissociation: Implications for personality theory, psychopathology, and health* (pp. 85–102). Chicago, IL: University of Chicago Press.

Hull, C. L. (1933). *Hypnosis and suggestibility: An experimental approach.* New York: Appleton-Century-Crofts.

Hyman, I. E., Jr, & Billings, J. F. (1998). Individual differences and the creation of false childhood memories. *Memory, 6*, 1–20.

Hyman, I. E., Jr, Husband, T. H., & Billings, F. J. (1995). False memories of childhood experiences. *Applied Cognitive Psychology, 9*, 181–197.

Hyman, I. E., Jr, & Pentland, J. (1996). The role of mental imagery in the creation of false childhood memories. *Journal of Memory and Language, 35*, 101–117.

Israels, H., & Schatzman, M. (1993). *History of psychiatry.* United Kingdom: Alpha Academic.

Janet, P. (1889). *Psychological automatisms.* Paris: Alcan.

Karon, B. P., & Widener, A. J. (1997). Repressed memories and World War II: Lest we forget! *Professional Psychology: Research and Practice, 28,* 338–340.

Kemp, S., Burt, C. D. B., & Sheen, M. (2003). Remembering dreamt and actual experiences. *Applied Cognitive Psychology, 17,* 577–591.

Kirsch, I., & Lynn, S. J. (1998). Dissociation theories of hypnosis. *Psychological Bulletin, 123,* 100–115.

Kluft, R. P. (1984). Treatment of multiple personality disorder. *Psychiatric Clinics of North America, 7,* 9–29.

Knox, V. J., Crutchfield, L., & Hilgard, E. R. (1975). The nature of task interference in hypnotic dissociation: An investigation of hypnotic behavior. *International Journal of Clinical and Experimental Hypnosis, 23,* 305–323.

Knox, V. J., Morgan, A. H., & Hilgard, E. R. (1974). Pain and suffering in ischemia: The paradox of hypnotically suggested anesthesia as contradicted by reports from the "hidden observer." *Archives of General Psychology, 30,* 840–847.

Lanning, K. V., & Burgess, A. W. (1989). Child pornography and sex rings. In D. Zillmann & J. Bryant (eds), *Pornography: Research advances and policy considerations* (pp. 235–255). Hillsdale, NJ: Lawrence Erlbaum Associates.

Laurence, J. R., Perry, C. W., & Kihlstrom, J. F. (1983). "Hidden observer" phenomenon in hypnosis: An experimental creation? *Journal of Personality and Social Psychology, 44,* 163–169.

Lilienfeld, S. O., & Loftus, E. F. (1998). Repressed memories and World War II: Some cautionary notes. *Professional Psychology: Research and Practice, 29,* 471–475.

Lilienfeld, S. O., & Lynn, S. J. (2003). Dissociative identity disorder: Multiple personalities, multiple controversies. In S. O. Lilienfeld, S. J. Lynn, & J. M. Lohr (eds), *Science and pseudoscience in clinical psychology* (pp. 109–142). New York: Guilford Press.

Lilienfeld, S. O., Lynn, S. J., Kirsch, I., Chaves, J., Sarbin, T., & Ganaway, G. (1999). Dissociative identity disorder and the sociocognitive model: Recalling lessons of the past. *Psychological Bulletin, 125,* 507–523.

Lindsay, D. S., & Read, D. (1994). Psychotherapy and memories of childhood abuse: A cognitive perspective. *Applied Cognitive Psychology, 8,* 281–338.

Loftus, E. F. (1992). When a lie becomes memory's truth: Memory distortion after exposure to misinformation. *Current Directions in Psychological Science, 1,* 121–123.

Loftus, E. F. (1993). The reality of repressed memories. *American Psychologist, 48,* 518–537.

Loftus, E. F. (2003). Our changeable memories: Legal and practical implications. *Nature Reviews: Neuroscience, 4,* 231–234.

Loftus, E. F., & Ketcham, K. (1994). *The myth of repressed memories.* New York: Plenum.

Loftus, E. F., & Mazzoni, G. (1998). Using imagination and personalized suggestion to change behavior. *Behavior Therapy, 29,* 691–708.

Loftus, E. F., & Pickrell, J. E. (1995). The formation of false memories. *Psychiatric Annals, 25,* 720–725.

Lynn, S. J., Lock, T., Loftus, E. F., Lilienfeld, S. O., & Krackow, E. (2003). The remembrance of things past: Problematic memory recovery techniques in psychotherapy. In S. O. Lilienfeld, S. J. Lynn, & J. M. Lohr (eds), *Science and pseudoscience in clinical psychology* (pp. 205–239). New York: Guilford Press.

Lynn, S. J., Lock, T., Myers, B., & Payne, D. G. (1997). Recalling the unrecallable: Should hypnosis be used to recover memories in psychotherapy? *Current Directions in Psychological Science, 6,* 79–83.

Lynn, S. J., & Malinoski, P. (1997). Early memory reports as a function of high versus low situational influence. Unpublished manuscript, Ohio University, Athens, OH.

Lynn, S. J., & Pintar, J. (1997). The social construction of multiple personality disorder. In J. D.

Read & D. S. Lindsay (eds), *Recollections of trauma: Scientific studies and clinical practice* (pp. 483–491). New York: Plenum.

Lynn, S. J., & Rhue, J. W. (1994). *Dissociation: Clinical, theoretical and research perspectives.* New York: Guilford Press.

Lynn, S. J., Rhue, J. W., & Green, J. P. (1989). Multiple personality and fantasy proneness: Is there an association or dissociation? *British Journal of Experimental and Clinical Hypnosis, 5,* 138–142.

Mai, F. M. (1995). Psychiatrists' attitudes to multiple personality disorder: A questionnaire study. *Canadian Journal of Psychiatry, 40,* 154–157.

Malinoski, P. T., & Lynn, S. J. (1997). The plasticity of early memory reports: Social pressure, hypnotizability, compliance, and interrogative suggestibility. *International Journal of Clinical and Experimental Hypnosis, 47,* 320–345.

Mazzoni, G. A. L., Loftus, E. F., & Kirsch, I. (2001). Changing beliefs about implausible autobiographical events: A little plausibility goes a long way. *Journal of Experimental Psychology: Applied, 7,* 51–59.

Mazzoni, G. A. L., Loftus, E. F., Seitz, A., & Lynn, S. J. (1999). Changing beliefs and memories through dream interpretation. *Applied Cognitive Psychology, 13,* 125–144.

Mazzoni, G. A., Lombardo, P., Malvagia, S., & Loftus, E. F. (1997). Dream interpretation and false beliefs. Unpublished manuscript, University of Florence and University of Washington.

Mazzoni, G. A., & Memom, A. (in press). Imagination can create false memories. *Psychological Science.*

McHugh, P. R. (1992). Psychiatric misadventures. *American Scholar, 61,* 497–510.

McNally, R. J. (2003). *Remembering trauma.* Cambridge, MA: Harvard University Press.

Meiselman, K. (1990). *Resolving the trauma of incest: Reintegration therapy with survivors.* San Francisco: Jossey-Bass.

Merckelbach, H., Muris, P., Rassin, E., & Horselenberg, R. (2000). Dissociative experiences and interrogative suggestibility in college students. *Personality and Individual Differences, 29,* 1133–1140.

Messerschmidt, R. (1927–1928). A quantitative investigation of the alleged independent operation of conscious and subconscious processes. *Journal of Abnormal and Social Psychology, 22,* 325–340.

Mills, A., & Lynn, S. J. (2000). Past-life experiences. In E. Cardena, S. J. Lynn, & S. Krippner (eds), *The varieties of anomalous experience* (pp. 283–314). New York: Guilford Press.

Mitchell, M. B. (1932). Retroactive inhibition and hypnosis. *Journal of General Psychology, 7,* 343–359.

Mulhern, S. A. (1992). Ritual abuse: Defining a syndrome versus defending a belief. *Journal of Psychology and Theology, 20,* 230–232.

Nash, M. R. (1987). What, if anything, is regressed about hypnotic age regression? A review of the empirical literature. *Psychological Bulletin, 102,* 42–52.

Nogrady, H., McConkey, K. M., Laurence, J. R., & Perry, C. (1983). Dissociation, duality, and demand characteristics in hypnosis. *Journal of Abnormal Psychology, 92,* 223–235.

North, C. S., Ryall, J. M., Ricci, D. A., & Wetzel, R. D. (1993). *Multiple personalities, multiple disorders: Psychiatric classification and media influence.* London: Oxford University Press.

Paddock, J. R., Joseph, A. L., Chan, F. M., Terranova, S., Manning, C., & Loftus, E. F. (1998). When guided visualization procedures may backfire: Imagination inflation and predicting individual differences in suggestibility. *Applied Cognitive Psychology, 12,* S63–S75.

Pezdek, K., Finger, K., & Hodge, D. (1997). Planting false childhood memories: The role of event plausibility. *Psychological Science, 8,* 437–441.

Piper, A. (1997). What science says—and doesn't say—about repressed memories: A critique of Scheflin and Brown. *Journal of Psychiatry and Law, 25,* 614–639.

Platt, R. D., Lacey, S. C., Iobst, A. D., & Finkelman, D. (1998). Absorption, dissociation, and fantasy-proneness as predictors of memory distortion in autobiographical and laboratory generated memories. *Applied Cognitive Psychology, 12,* 77–89.

Polusny, M. A., & Follette, V. M. (1996). Remembering childhood sexual abuse: A national survey of psychologists' clinical practices, beliefs, and personal experiences. *Professional Psychology: Research and Practice, 27,* 41–52.

Poole, D. A., Lindsay, D. S., Memom, A., & Bull, R. (1995). Psychotherapists' opinions, practices, and experiences with recovery of memories of incestuous abuse. *Journal of Consulting and Clinical Psychology, 68,* 426–437.

Porter, S., Birt, A. R., Yuille, J. C., & Lehman, D. R. (2000). Negotiating false memories: Interviewer and rememberer characteristics relate to memory distortion. *Psychological Science, 11,* 507–510.

Porter, S., Yuille, J. C., & Lehman, D. R. (1999). The nature of real, implanted, and fabricated memories for emotional childhood events: Implications for the false memory debate. *Law and Human Behavior, 23,* 517–537.

Powell, R. A., & Boer, D. P. (1994). Did Freud mislead patients to confabulate memories of abuse? *Psychological Reports, 74,* 1283–1298.

Powell, R. A., & Boer, D. P. (1995). Did Freud misinterpret reported memories of sexual abuse as fantasies? *Psychological Reports, 77,* 563–570.

Powell, R. A., & Gee, T. L. (1999). The effects of hypnosis on dissociative identity disorder: A reexamination of the evidence. *Canadian Journal of Psychiatry, 44,* 914–916.

Powell, R. A., & Nielsen, T. A. (1998). Was Anna O.'s black snake hallucination a sleep paralysis nightmare? Dreams, memories, and trauma. *Psychiatry: Interpersonal and Biological Processes, 61,* 239–248.

Prince, M. (1929). *Clinical and experimental studies in personality.* Cambridge, MA: Harvard University Press.

Qin, J. J. (1999). Adults' memories of childhood: True versus false reports. Dissertation, University of California, Davis.

Qin, J. J., Goodman, G. S., Bottoms, B. L., & Shaver, P. R. (1998). Repressed memories of ritualistic and religion-related child abuse. In S. J. Lynn & K. M. McConkey (eds), *Truth in memory* (pp. 284–303). New York: Guilford Press.

Rassin, E., Merckelbach, H., & Spaan, V. (2001). When dreams become a royal road to confusion: Realistic dreams, dissociation, and fantasy proneness. *Journal of Nervous and Mental Disease, 189,* 478–481.

Read, D. J., & Lindsay, S. D. (2000). "Amnesia" for summer camps and high school graduation: Memory work increases reports of prior periods of remembering less. *Journal of Traumatic Stress, 13,* 129–147.

Rieker, P. P., & Carmen, E. H. (1986). The victim-to-patient process: The disconfirmation and transformation of abuse. *American Journal of Orthopsychiatry, 56,* 360–370.

Roland, C. B. (1993). Exploring childhood memories with adult survivors of sexual abuse: Concrete reconstruction and visualization techniques. *Journal of Mental Health Counseling, 15,* 363–372.

Rosen, G. M. (1975). Effects of source prestige on subjects' acceptance of the Barnum effect: Psychologist vs. astrologer. *Journal of Consulting and Clinical Psychology, 43,* 95.

Rosen, G. M., Sageman, M., & Loftus, E. (2003). A historical note on false traumatic memories. *Journal of Clinical Psychology, 60,* 137–139.

Ross, C. A. (1997). *Dissociative identity disorder: Diagnosis, clinical features, and treatment of multiple personality.* New York: John Wiley & Sons.

Ross, C. A., Miller, S. D., Bjornson, L., & Reagor, P. (1991). Abuse histories in 102 cases of multiple personality disorder. *Canadian Journal of Psychiatry, 36,* 97–101.

Ross, C. A., Norton, G. R., & Wozney, K. (1989). Multiple personality disorder: An analysis of 236 cases. *Canadian Journal of Psychiatry, 34*, 413–418.

Schachter, D., & Kihlstrom, J. F. (1989). Functional amnesia. In F. Boller & J. Grafman (eds), *Handbook of neuropsychology* (Vol. 3, pp. 209–231). New York: Elsevier.

Scheflin, A. W., & Brown, D. (1996). Repressed memory or dissociative amnesia: What the science says. *Journal of Psychiatry and Law, 24*, 143–188.

Schuker, E. (1979). Psychodynamics and treatment of sexual assault victims. *Journal of the American Academy of Psychoanalysis and Dynamic Psychiatry, 7*, 553–573.

Shermer, M. (1997). *Why people believe weird things: Pseudoscience, superstition, and other confusions of our time.* New York: W. H. Freeman/Times Books/Henry Holt & Co.

Shevrin, H., Williams, W. J., Marshall, R. E., & Hertel, R. K. (1992). Event-related potential indicators of the dynamic unconscious. *Consciousness and Cognition: An International Journal, 1*, 340–366.

Shobe, K. K., & Kihlstrom, J. F. (1997). Is traumatic memory special? *Current Directions in Psychological Science, 6*, 70–74.

Sivec, H. J., Lynn, S. J., & Malinoski, P. T. (1997). Hypnosis in the cabbage patch: Age regression with verifiable events. Unpublished manuscript, Ohio University, Athens, OH.

Spanos, N. P. (1983). The hidden observer as an experimental creation. *Journal of Personality and Social Psychology, 44*, 170–176.

Spanos, N. P. (1991). A sociocognitive approach to hypnosis. In S. J. Lynn & J. W. Rhue (eds), *Theories of hypnosis: Current models and perspectives* (pp. 324–361). New York: Guilford Press.

Spanos, N. P. (1994). Multiple identity enactments and multiple personality disorder: A sociocognitive perspective. *Psychological Bulletin, 116*, 143–165.

Spanos, N. P. (1996). *Multiple identities and false memories: A sociocognitive perspective.* Washington, DC: American Psychological Association.

Spanos, N. P., Burgess, C. A., & Burgess, M. F. (1994). Past-life identities, UFO abductions, and satanic ritual abuse: The social construction of memories. *International Journal of Clinical and Experimental Hypnosis, 42*, 433–446.

Spanos, N. P., Burgess, C. A., Burgess, M. F., Samuels, C., & Blois, W. O. (1999). Creating false memories of infancy with hypnotic and nonhypnotic procedures. *Applied Cognitive Psychology, 13*, 201–218.

Spanos, N. P., Flynn, D. M., & Gwynn, M. I. (1988). Contextual demands, negative hallucinations, and hidden observer responding: Three hidden observers observed. *British Journal of Experimental and Clinical Hypnosis, 5*, 5–10.

Spanos, N. P., Gwynn, M., & Stam, H. J. (1983). Instructional demands and ratings of overt and hidden pain during hypnotic analgesia. *Journal of Abnormal Psychology, 92*, 479–488.

Spanos, N. P., & Hewitt, E. C. (1980). The hidden observer in hypnotic analgesia: Discovery or experimental creation? *Journal of Personality and Social Psychology, 39*, 1201–1214.

Spanos, N. P., & McLean, J. (1986). Hypnotically created pseudomemories: Memory distortions or reporting biases? *British Journal of Experimental and Clinical Hypnosis, 3*, 155–159.

Spanos, N. P., Menary, R., Gabora, M. J., DuBreuil, S. C., & Dewhirst, B. (1991). Secondary identity enactments during hypnotic past-life regression: A sociocognitive perspective. *Journal of Personality and Social Psychology, 61*, 308–320.

Spanos, N. P., Radtke, H. L., & Bertrand, L. D. (1984). Hypnotic amnesia as a strategic enactment: Breaching amnesia in highly susceptible subjects. *Journal of Personality and Social Psychology, 46*, 1155–1169.

Spanos, N. P., Weekes, J. R., & Bertrand, L. D. (1985). Multiple personality: A social psychological perspective. *Journal of Abnormal Psychology, 94*, 362–376.

Spiegel, D. (1995). Hypnosis, dissociation, and trauma: Hidden and overt observers. In J. L. Singer (ed.), *Repression and dissociation: Implications for personality theory, psychopathology, and health*. Chicago, IL: University of Chicago Press.

Stafford, J., & Lynn, S. J. (2002). Cultural scripts, memories of childhood abuse, and multiple identities: A study of role-played enactments. *International Journal of Clinical and Experimental Hypnosis, 50,* 67–85.

Steblay, N. M., & Bothwell, R. K. (1994). Evidence for hypnotically refreshed testimony: The view from the laboratory. *Law and Human Behavior, 18,* 635–651.

Stevenson, J. H. (1976). The effect of posthypnotic dissociation on the performance of interfering tasks. *Journal of Abnormal Psychology, 85,* 398–407.

Tavris, C. (1993). Beware the incest survivor machine. *New York Times Book Review,* January 3, pp. 1, 16–17.

van der Kolk, B. A., Britz, R., Burr, W., Sherry, S., & Hartmann, E. (1994). Nightmares and trauma: A comparison of nightmares after combat with life-long nightmares in veterans. *American Journal of Psychiatry, 141,* 187–190.

van der Kolk, B. A., van der Hart, O., & Marmar, C. R. (1996). Dissociation and information processing in posttraumatic stress disorder. In B. A. van der Kolk & A. C. McFarlane, & L. Weisaeth (eds), *Traumatic stress: The effects of overwhelming experience on mind, body, and society* (pp. 303–327). New York: Guilford Press.

Wade, K. A., Garry, M., Read, J. D., & Lindsay, D. S. (2002). A picture is worth a thousand lies: Using false photographs to create false childhood memories. *Psychonomic Bulletin and Review, 9,* 597–603.

Wilkinson, C., & Hyman, I. E. (1998). Individual differences related to two types of memory errors: Word lists may not generalize to autobiographical memory. *Applied Cognitive Psychology, 12,* S29–S46.

Williams, M. (1987). Reconstruction of an early seduction and its aftereffects. *Journal of the American Psychoanalytic Association, 35,* 145–163.

Winograd, E., Peluso, J. P., & Glover, T. A. (1998). Individual differences in susceptibility to memory illusions. *Applied Cognitive Psychology, 12,* 5–27.

Wolfradt, U., & Meyer T. (1998). Interrogative suggestibility, anxiety and dissociation among anxious patients and normal controls. *Personality and Individual Differences, 25,* 425–432.

Wright, D. B., & Livingston-Raper, D. (2002). Memory distortion and dissociation: Exploring the relationship in a non-clinical sample. *Journal of Trauma and Dissociation, 3,* 97–109.

10 In the Aftermath of Trauma: Normative Reactions and Early Interventions

RICHARD A. BRYANT

School of Psychology, University of New South Wales, Sydney, Australia

One of the major controversies in the field of traumatic stress involves how people should be managed in the acute aftermath of trauma exposure. This issue is marked by strong debate over two significant questions. First, what is the role of dissociation, if any, in acute trauma responses? Second, what is the utility of providing psychological debriefing to all trauma survivors? These two areas of debate have attracted much attention in recent years, increasingly polarizing the views of researchers and practitioners. This chapter approaches these areas of concern by initially focusing on the normative course of post-traumatic adjustment, reviewing recent developments in early identification of people at high psychiatric risk after trauma, discussing the diagnosis of acute stress disorder, and evaluating evidence for dissociation occurring at the time of trauma as an important precursor of subsequent psychopathology. The chapter then addresses current alternatives to managing acute stress reactions by appraising the evidence for psychological debriefing, and alternative cognitive behavioural approaches. This review attempts to provide a balanced account of highly contentious matters through an evidence-based evaluation, with the goal of identifying an optimal approach for the management of initial posttraumatic reactions.

DISSOCIATION AND ASD IN THE AFTERMATH OF TRAUMA

There is a need to understand the typical adjustment course following trauma. Throughout the literature, there are reports of high rates of emotional numbing (Feinstein, 1989; Noyes, Hoenk, Kuperman, & Slymen, 1977), reduced awareness of one's environment (Berah, Jones, & Valent, 1984; Hillman, 1981), derealization (Cardeña & Spiegel, 1993; Freinkel, Koopman, & Spiegel, 1994; Noyes & Kletti, 1977; Sloan, 1988), depersonalization (Cardeña & Spiegel, 1993; Freinkel et al., 1994; Noyes et al., 1977; Sloan, 1988), intrusive thoughts (Cardeña & Spiegel, 1993; Feinstein, 1989; Sloan, 1988), avoidance behaviors (Bryant & Harvey, 1996; Cardeña & Spiegel, 1993; North, Smith, McCool, & Lightcap, 1989), insomnia (Cardeña & Spiegel, 1993; Feinstein, 1989, Sloan, 1988), concentration deficits (Cardeña & Spiegel, 1993; North et al., 1989), irritability (Sloan, 1988), and autonomic arousal (Feinstein, 1989; Sloan, 1988). It is apparent that psychological distress is commonplace in the weeks after a traumatic experience.

Posttraumatic Stress Disorder: Issues and Controversies. Edited by G. M. Rosen.
© 2004 John Wiley & Sons, Ltd. ISBN 0-470-86284-X/0-470-86285-8.

Although acute stress reactions are common, there is strong evidence that they usually are transient. That is, the majority of people who initially display distress will naturally adapt in the following months. For example, whereas 94% of rape victims displayed sufficient PTSD symptoms two weeks posttrauma to meet criteria (excluding the one-month time requirement), this rate dropped to 47% eleven weeks later (Rothbaum, Foa, Riggs, Murdock, & Walsh, 1992). In another study 70% of women and 50% of men were diagnosed with PTSD at an average of 19 days after an assault; at four-month follow-up, the rate of PTSD dropped to 21% for women and zero for men (Riggs, Rothbaum, & Foa, 1995). Similarly, half of a sample meeting criteria for PTSD shortly after a motor vehicle accident had remitted by six months, and two-thirds had remitted by one year posttrauma (Blanchard et al., 1996). There also is evidence that most stress responses after the terrorist attacks of September 11 constituted temporary reactions. Galea et al. (2002) surveyed residents of New York City to gauge responses to the attacks. Five to eight weeks post-incident, 7.5% of a random sample of adults living south of 110th Street in Manhattan met criteria for PTSD, while among those living south of Canal Street, 20% met criteria. In February 2002, Galea's group conducted a follow-up assessment on another group of adults living south of 110th Street, and found only 1.7% of the sample meeting PTSD criteria (Galea, Boscarino, Resnick, & Vlahov, in press). Available evidence suggests that the normative initial response to trauma involves a range of PTSD symptoms, but the majority of acute reactions remit in the first few months.

ACUTE STRESS DISORDER

In 1994 the fourth edition of the *Diagnostic and Statistical Manual of Mental Disorders* (DSM-IV; American Psychiatric Association, 1994) introduced the diagnosis of acute stress disorder (ASD). There were two primary goals of this diagnosis. First, the diagnosis was intended to describe initial traumatic stress reactions that occur during the first month after trauma exposure. There was the perception that these initial reactions needed to be described in diagnostic terms because DSM-IV stipulated that PTSD could only be recognized at least one month posttrauma. Second, the diagnosis was meant to identify people who shortly after trauma were at high risk to develop later PTSD (Koopman, Classen, Cardeña, & Spiegel, 1995). It is worth noting that the goal of the ASD diagnosis to predict PTSD contrasted significantly with the conceptualization of acute stress reactions described in the tenth edition of the *International Classification of Diseases* (ICD-10; World Health Organization, 1992). ICD-10 describes acute stress reaction as a transient condition that occurs in the initial 48 hours after trauma, and encompasses a broad range of anxiety and depressive reactions. Some commentators have noted that the ICD-10 approach is more clinically friendly and flexible in describing acute trauma reactions (Solomon, Laor, & McFarlane, 1996).

DSM-IV stipulates that ASD can occur after a fearful response to experiencing or witnessing a threatening event (Criterion A). The requisite criteria for a diagnosis of ASD include three dissociative symptoms (Criterion B), one reexperiencing symptom (Criterion C), marked avoidance (Criterion D), marked anxiety or increased arousal (Criterion E), and evidence of significant distress or impairment (Criterion F). The disturbance must last for a minimum of two days and a maximum of four weeks (Criterion G) after which time a diagnosis of PTSD can be considered. With respect to the Criterion B dissociative symptoms, ASD requires at least three of the following: (1) a subjective sense of numbing or detachment; (2) reduced awareness of one's surroundings; (3) derealization; (4) depersonalization; or (5) dissociative amnesia. The primary difference between the criteria for ASD and PTSD is the timeframe (ASD refers to symptoms manifested during the period from two days to four weeks posttrauma, while PTSD can only be diagnosed one month post-incident), and ASD's emphasis on dissociative reactions.

Numerous studies have now reported the incidence of ASD following a range of traumatic events. ASD has been reported between 13% and 21% following MVAs (Harvey & Bryant, 1998a; Holeva, Tarrier, & Wells, 2001); 14% following mild brain injury (Harvey & Bryant, 1998b); between 16% and 19% following assault (Brewin, Andrews, Rose, & Kirk, 1999; Harvey & Bryant, 1999a); 16% following traumatic loss (Green, Krupnick, Stockton, & Goodman, 2001); 10% following burns (Harvey & Bryant, 1999a); between 6% and 12% following industrial accident (Creamer & Manning, 1998; Harvey & Bryant, 1999a); 33% following a mass shooting (Classen, Koopman, Hales, & Spiegel, 1998); and 7% following a typhoon (Staab, Grieger, Fullerton, & Ursano, 1996).

MECHANISMS OF ASD

The defining criteria for ASD were strongly influenced by the notion that dissociative reactions are a crucial mechanism in posttraumatic adjustment. This perspective originated in work conducted at the Salpêtrière Infirmary in Paris over 100 hundred years ago. Charcot (1889) proposed that traumatic shock could evoke responses that were phenomenologically similar to hypnotic states. In this sense Charcot believed that traumatic experiences resulted in dissociative states that were evident in hysteria and could be elicited during hypnosis. Extending this argument, Janet (1907) proposed that traumatic experiences led to dissociated awareness when they were incongruent with existing cognitive schema. Janet argued that although this "splitting" of traumatic memories from awareness led to a reduction in distress, there was a loss of mental functioning because mental resources were not available for other processes. Janet proposed that adaptation following trauma required the integration of fragmented memories into awareness. These views have enjoyed renewed attention in the past 20 years, and represent the basis for the current notion that trauma-induced dissociation is a pivotal trauma response (Nemiah, 1989; van der Kolk & van der Hart, 1989).

In recent years, the focus of attention has been on cognitive and biological responses in the period shortly after trauma exposure. With regard to cognitive responses, current models posit that psychopathological responses may be mediated by two core factors: (1) maladaptive appraisals of the trauma and its aftermath; and (2) disturbances in autobiographical memory that involve impaired retrieval and strong associative memory (Ehlers & Clark, 2000). Consistent with the first factor is evidence that people with ASD exaggerate both the probability that future negative events may occur and the adverse effects of such events (Warda & Bryant, 1998a). Moreover, ASD-diagnosed individuals display cognitive biases for events related to external harm, somatic sensations, and social concerns (Smith & Bryant, 2000). Experimental studies indicate that ASD individuals respond to a hyperventilation task with more dysfunctional interpretations about their reactions than non-ASD individuals (Nixon & Bryant, 2003). There also is evidence that catastrophic appraisals about oneself in the period after trauma exposure predict subsequent

PTSD (Ehlers, Mayou, & Bryant, 1998; Engelhard, van den Hout, Arntz, & McNally, 2002). Relatedly, the nature of attributions about the trauma shortly after the event apparently influences longer-term functioning. Prospective studies indicate that early attributions of responsibility to another person (Delahanty et al., 1997) and attributions of shame (Andrews, Brewin, Rose, & Kirk, 2000) in the acute phase posttrauma can be associated with later PTSD.

Additional evidence suggests that people with ASD manage trauma-related information differently from other trauma survivors. Specifically, individuals with ASD tend to avoid aversive information. One study employed a directed-forgetting paradigm that required ASD, non-ASD, and non-trauma-exposed control participants to read a series of trauma-related, positive, or neutral words, which participants were instructed to either remember or forget (Moulds & Bryant, 2002). The finding that ASD participants recalled fewer trauma-related to-be-forgotten words than non-ASD participants suggests that they have an aptitude for forgetting aversive material. In a similar study that employed a method of directed forgetting that indexes retrieval patterns, ASD participants displayed poorer recall of to-be-forgotten trauma words than non-ASD participants (Moulds & Bryant, in press). These findings suggest that people with ASD possess a cognitive style that avoids awareness of aversive or distressing information. This interpretation accords with findings that people with ASD use avoidant cognitive strategies to manage trauma memories (Guthrie & Bryant, 2000; Warda & Bryant, 1998b). Avoidance of distressing information or memories may be associated with psychopathological responses because it can lead to impaired processing of trauma-related memories and affect. In terms of autobiographical memory, one study has found that ASD participants report fewer specific positive memories than non-ASD participants (Harvey, Bryant, & Dang, 1998). This finding concurs with difficulty in retrieving specific positive memories in other clinical disorders, particularly depression (Williams, 1996). More importantly, Harvey et al. (1998) found that this deficit for retrieval of positive memories in the acute trauma phase contributes to subsequent PTSD severity. This pattern suggests that problems in retrieving positive memories about one's personal past may limit access to information that is useful when appraising the trauma and its consequences (Ehlers & Clark, 2000).

Biological perspectives on factors that mediate reactions in the aftermath of trauma have focused on fear conditioning and progressive neural sensitization (Kolb, 1987; Pitman, Shalev, & Orr, 2000). One hypothesis is that sensitization occurs as a result of repetitive activation by trauma reminders that elevate sensitivity of limbic networks (Post, Weiss, & Smith, 1995); as time progresses, these responses become increasingly conditioned to trauma-related stimuli (LeDoux, Iwata, Cicchetti, & Reis, 1988). In support of these proposals, there is evidence that people who eventually develop PTSD display elevated resting heart rates in the initial week after trauma (Bryant, Harvey, Guthrie, & Moulds, 2000a; Shalev et al., 1998; see also Blanchard, Hickling, Galovski, & Veazey, 2002). There also is evidence that lower cortisol levels shortly after trauma predict subsequent PTSD (Delahanty, Raimonde, & Spoonster, 2000; McFarlane, Atchison, & Yehuda, 1997). Cortisol may act as an "anti-stress" hormone that regulates initial activation, such that lower cortisol levels reflect an incapacity to lower posttrauma arousal (Yehuda, 1997). The importance of increased arousal in the acute phase also is indicated by the prevalence of panic attacks in people with ASD (Bryant & Panasetis, 2001; Nixon & Bryant, 2003). ASD-diagnosed individuals also display greater theta EEG activity than non-ASD participants (Felmingham, Bryant, & Gordon, in press). Theta activity is linked to encoding new memories (Klimesch, Doppelmayr, Pachinger, & Ripper, 1997) and associative learning (Sakowitz, Schurmann, & Basar, 2000), a finding consistent with conditioning models that relate overconsolidation of acute trauma memories to subsequent development of PTSD (Pitman et al., 2000). A promising finding emerged from a pilot study that attempted to prevent PTSD by administering propranolol (a b-adrenergic blocker) within six hours of trauma exposure (Pitman et al., 2002). This intervention was based on evidence that propranolol abolishes the epinephrine enhancement of conditioning (Cahill, Prins, Weber, & McGaugh, 1994). Although propranolol did not result in reduced PTSD relative to a placebo condition, patients receiving propranolol displayed less reactivity to trauma reminders three months later. This outcome suggests that propranolol administration shortly after trauma exposure may limit fear conditioning, thereby influencing subsequent PTSD development. This proposal is supported by a recent finding that propranolol administered in the initial week after trauma exposure resulted in reduced PTSD two months later (Vaiva et al., 2003).

CRITICAL ISSUES WITH THE ASD DIAGNOSIS

There have been many criticisms of the ASD diagnosis (see Bryant & Harvey, 2000; Butler, 2000; Harvey & Bryant, 2002; Keane, Kaufman, & Kimble, 2001; Koopman, 2000; Marshall, Spitzer, & Liebowitz, 2000; Simeon & Guralnik, 2000; Spiegel, Classen, & Cardeña, 2000). First, the new diagnosis was introduced with little evidence to support its inclusion in the DSM-IV. At the time of its introduction, even proponents of the diagnosis admitted that the hypothesized relationship between ASD and PTSD was "based more on logical arguments than on empirical research" (Koopman et al., 1995, p. 38). Whereas inclusion of other diagnoses in the DSM-IV required satisfaction of a number of standards (e.g., literature reviews, statistical analyses of established datasets, and field trials), the ASD diagnosis did not undergo this rigorous scrutiny (Bryant, 2000). A second criticism of ASD has concerned the emphasis on dissociation as an acute trauma response, when evidence was insufficient to support such a pivotal role for this construct (Bryant & Harvey, 1997; Keane et al., 2001; Marshall et al., 2000). Third, some objected to the notion that the primary role of the ASD diagnosis was to predict another diagnosis (McNally, 2003). Fourth, there was concern that the diagnosis may pathologize transient reactions (Wakefield, 1996). Fifth, it was argued that distinguishing between two diagnoses that have comparable symptoms (ASD and PTSD) on the basis of symptom duration was not justified (Marshall, Spitzer, & Leibowitz, 1999).

Research has reinforced these concerns. For example, there are now 12 studies that have prospectively assessed the relationship between ASD in the initial month after trauma, and subsequent development of PTSD (Brewin et al., 1999; Bryant & Harvey, 1998; Creamer, O'Donnell, & Pattison, 2004; Difede et al., 2002; Harvey & Bryant, 1998a, 1999b, 2000a; Holeva et al., 2001; Kangas, Henry, & Bryant, in press; Murray, Ehlers, & Mayou, 2002; Schnyder, Moergeli, Klaghofer, & Buddeberg, 2001; Staab et al., 1996). A number of these studies have found that approximately three-quarters of trauma survivors who display ASD go on to develop PTSD (Brewin et al., 1999; Bryant & Harvey, 1998; Difede et al., 2002; Harvey & Bryant, 1998a, 1999b, 2000a; Holeva et al., 2001; Kangas et al., in press; Murray et al., 2002). Compared to the expected remission of most people who display initial posttrauma reactions, these studies indicate that the ASD diagnosis performs reasonably well in predicting PTSD.

The utility of ASD is less encouraging when one considers the proportion of PTSD-diagnosed individuals who initially displayed the defining criteria of ASD. This is because the minority of people who eventually develop PTSD initially meet ASD criteria. That is, whereas the majority of people who develop ASD are at high risk for developing subsequent PTSD, there are many people who develop PTSD but do not initially meet ASD criteria. The major reason for this finding is the requirement of three dissociative symptoms for a diagnosis of ASD to be made. In one study, 60% of people who met all ASD criteria except for the dissociation cluster met PTSD criteria six months later (Harvey & Bryant, 1998a), and 75% of these people still had PTSD two years later (Harvey & Bryant, 1999b). This pattern suggests that emphasizing dissociation as a critical factor in predicting subsequent PTSD leads to the neglect of other acute stress reactions that serve as risk factors.

It is important to note that our understanding of the relationship between ASD and PTSD is limited by methodological variability across studies. Selected populations, assessment tools, and inclusion/exclusion criteria vary markedly. Different studies have employed different criteria that variably include or exclude participants who sustained a mild brain injury, or used medications that can mimic dissociative reactions (Creamer et al., 2004). These discrepancies have potentially influenced the extent to which ASD was identified, and accordingly the reported relationship between ASD and subsequent PTSD. Similarly, there is considerable disparity in terms of how ASD has been assessed. Whereas some researchers have used tools specifically developed to index ASD (e.g., Acute Stress Disorder Interview; Bryant, Harvey, Dang, & Sackville, 1998a), others derived ASD diagnoses on the basis of various measures that indexed symptoms only comparable to ASD (Brewin et al., 1999; Staab et al., 1996). Variability across studies points to the need for multi-site, and multinational studies that employ standardized methodologies across a range of trauma populations.

DOES ACUTE DISSOCIATION PREDICT PTSD?

Early reports on "peritraumatic" dissociation (reactions that occur during the event) found a relationship between dissociation and subsequent psychopathology, but these studies typically involved retrospective accounts that were obtained months after trauma exposure (e.g., Barton, Blanchard, & Hickling, 1996; Holen, 1993; Marmar et al., 1994; McFarlane, 1986). This practice was flawed in light of increasing evidence that recollections of acute reactions to trauma are often inaccurate and are influenced by an individual's psychological state at the time of the recollection (Harvey & Bryant, 2000b; Marshall & Schell, 2002; Southwick, Morgan, Nicolaou, & Charney, 1997). Fortunately, there are a number of prospective studies, and several of these indicate that peritraumatic dissociation is a strong predictor of PTSD (Ehlers et al., 1998; Koopman, Classen, & Spiegel, 1994; Murray et al., 2002; Shalev, Freedman, Peri, Brandes, & Sahar, 1997; for a review, see a meta-analysis by Ozer, Best, Lipsey, & Weiss, 2003). At the same time, however, there is evidence against a linear relationship between acute dissociation and longer-term PTSD. Thus, a number of prospective studies have found that peritraumatic dissociation does not predict PTSD (Dancu, Riggs, Hearst-Ikeda, Shoyer, & Foa, 1996; Marshall & Schell, 2002).

There are several mechanisms that may account for the mixed findings regarding peritraumatic dissociation and subsequent PTSD. One possibility is that dissociation plays a role in PTSD development in some individuals but not others. Diathesis-stress models of dissociative disorders suggest that only people who possess dissociative tendencies respond to trauma with dissociative reactions (Butler, Duran, Jasiukaitis, Koopman, & Spiegel, 1996; Kihlstrom, Glisky, & Angiulo, 1994). Consistent with this view, Davidson and Foa (1991) suggest that dissociative responses are coping mechanisms only for individuals who can utilize these skills. Accordingly, only people who possess dissociative tendencies prior to a traumatic experience will display acute dissociation in response to trauma (Atchison & McFarlane, 1994). This notion is supported by evidence that higher levels of hypnotizability are demonstrated in people with ASD, as compared to individuals with equivalent stress reactions who lack dissociative symptoms (Bryant, Moulds, & Guthrie, 2001). Although both groups may have high risk for developing PTSD, only the subset of people with dissociative tendencies respond with acute dissociative symptoms.

Another mechanism to account for research findings on peritraumatic dissociation and subsequent PTSD concerns relationships with other known risk factors. For example, there is a documented relationship between a history of childhood trauma and subsequent dissociation tendencies (Spiegel & Cardeña, 1991). Moreover, childhood trauma is a known risk factor for adult PTSD (Brewin, Andrews, & Valentine, 2000). Accordingly, it is possible that peritraumatic dissociation is linked to PTSD because of its association with childhood trauma (Keane et al., 2001). This view suggests that our understanding of PTSD development will be enhanced by including childhood trauma, prior dissociation, and peritraumatic dissociation in mathematical models that recognize the relative influences of pretrauma, peritraumatic, and posttrauma factors (Keane et al., 2001).

Another potential role of dissociation is its association with hyperarousal in the acute phase after trauma exposure. Peritraumatic dissociation may be a consequence of elevated arousal that occurs during trauma. Indirect support for this proposal comes from evidence that dissociative phenomenon (e.g., flashbacks) occur in PTSD individuals with yohimbine-induced arousal (Southwick et al., 1993). Further, dissociative reactions are commonly reported during panic attacks (Krystal, Woods, Hill, & Charney, 1991), which frequently occur during the trauma itself (Bryant & Panasetis, 2001; Resnick, Falsetti, Kilpatrick, & Foy, 1994). Moreover, dissociative responses can be induced with hyperventilation in recent trauma-exposed individuals (Nixon & Bryant, 2003). There also is evidence that panic during trauma is associated with ongoing panic (Nixon & Bryant, 2003), and hyperarousal in the acute phase following trauma has been associated with subsequent PTSD (Shalev, 1992). Thus, it is possible that peritraumatic dissociation may be associated with later PTSD because it is linked to hyperarousal, which contributes directly to PTSD development.

Another possibility is that appraisals of peritraumatic dissociation, rather than peritraumatic dissociation itself, may influence subsequent PTSD. Cognitive theories of PTSD place much emphasis on the role of appraisals of the trauma and of resulting symptoms in the development and maintenance of PTSD (Ehlers & Clark, 2000). There is evidence that psychopathological responses to trauma are characterized by catastrophic interpretations of events. It may be that catastrophic appraisals of peritraumatic dissociation predict subsequent PTSD more than actual dissociative reactions. For example, a woman who interprets emotional numbing towards her child as a normal response to an assault may be less distressed than the woman who misinterprets emotional numbing as an indication of an uncaring mother.

IS DISSOCIATION PATHOLOGICAL?

Alterations in awareness can occur under many circumstances in which there is increased arousal or perceived threat, and many of these dissociative responses do not develop into pathological states. For example, weapon-focus studies in non-clinical populations have found that there are marked alterations in attentional focus towards the narrow source of threat; that is, there is reduced awareness of peripheral events during mildly stressful experiences (Kramer, Buckhout, & Eugenio, 1990; Maas & Kohnken, 1989). Further, novice skydivers display elevated levels of dissociative reactions during their skydive, even though they do not develop subsequent disorder (Sterlini & Bryant, 2002). Some commentators have suggested that dissociation during trauma may actually be adaptive because it protects the individual, to some degree, from encoding many distressing features of a traumatic experience (Horowitz, 1986; Noyes & Kletti, 1977). In this sense, dissociation may serve a function similar to traumatic brain injury, wherein unconscious trauma survivors are spared awareness of many potentially distressing experiences (Bryant, 2001).

THE FUTURE OF ASD

It has been suggested that an important role of the ASD diagnosis is to describe people who are currently experiencing severe stress reactions. Yet, describing these individuals can be achieved by applying the PTSD diagnosis in the initial period, or by describing acute reactions that require clinical attention without applying the label of a mental disorder (Blank, 1993). Further, it seems that introducing the new diagnosis of ASD to describe initial posttraumatic reactions has caused a number of problems that include (1) use of one diagnosis to predict another and (2) attempts to distinguish between two diagnoses primarily in terms of their timeframe.

Should the ASD diagnosis be retained in future editions of the DSM? It is apparent from the available evidence that the ASD diagnosis does not accurately identify the majority of people who eventually develop PTSD. Further, embodying risk factors for chronic PTSD into a single diagnostic category may limit accurate identification of people likely to develop PTSD. There are many factors that predict PTSD: a sensible approach would be to identify individuals at risk of developing PTSD by using a range of empirically supported indicators, rather than by relying on a diagnostic label. Developing formulae that include pretrauma factors, acute symptoms, biological responses, and cognitive styles may better identify people at risk than the current diagnosis of ASD.

PSYCHOLOGICAL DEBRIEFING

If most people show resilience after traumatic events, but a minority go on to develop significant posttraumatic problems, how should professionals and communities best respond in the aftermath of trauma? One approach to early intervention for posttraumatic stress has been termed "psychological debriefing." This approach encompasses a number of techniques that attempt to reduce posttraumatic stress by intervening in the initial days after trauma exposure. Historically, psychological debriefing can be traced to military settings in World War I, where commanders allowed their troops to review a battle (Litz, Gray, Bryant, & Adler, 2002). The modern form of debriefing has been popularized by Mitchell (1983), who termed the intervention "Critical Incident Stress Debriefing" (CISD). According to Mitchell, a single debriefing session "will generally alleviate the acute stress responses which appear at the scene and immediately afterwards and will eliminate, or at least inhibit, delayed stress reactions" (1983, p. 36). Although CISD is not the only form of debriefing, it is probably the most commonly used method and is conceptually very similar to other debriefing practices that are currently available (Raphael & Wilson, 2000).

The CISD approach was initially developed for emergency service personnel (e.g., firefighters, paramedics, police), then extended to a wide variety of trauma victims (Everly & Mitchell, 1999, p. 85), and then criticized by its proponents for these very extensions (Mitchell, 2002). There also have been modifications to the procedural components of CISD. In fact, it is difficult to operationalize CISD because its definition has changed over time. Whereas it was initially described as being beneficial for individuals or groups (Mitchell, 1983), CISD is now recommended only for groups. Further, whereas Mitchell (1983) initially believed that CISD should be mandatory for all trauma-exposed personnel, he has subsequently suggested that voluntary participation may be beneficial (Everly & Mitchell, 1999). Whereas the initial conceptualization of CISD focused on the initial debriefing, Everly and Mitchell (1999) have more recently suggested that Critical Incident Stress Management (CISM) is the overarching framework within which a range of techniques is offered, including initial diffusings, debriefings, and referral to structured therapy. This variable definition of debriefing is a problem for attempts to evaluate its effectiveness. Further, the CISM framework is not amenable to controlled evaluation because of its multifaceted and unstructured content. Accordingly, all attempts to evaluate the debriefing model can only approximate Mitchell's CISD/CISM approach.

According to Mitchell, a CISD session typically comprises seven phases. In an Introduction Phase, the debriefer explains the session as an opportunity to reduce stress reactions, informs participants that speaking in the group is voluntary, explains that it is not a therapeutic exercise, and answers questions about the session. In the Fact Phase, the debriefer asks participants to describe what they saw and heard during the event. In the Thought Phase, the debriefer inquires about thoughts that occurred during and after the event. In the Reaction Phase, participants are invited to express their emotional responses to the event. According to Mitchell (1983), "everyone has feelings which need to be shared and accepted" (p. 38). In the Symptom Phase, the debriefer asks participants about psychological or physical symptoms to ascertain stress reactions. In the Teaching Phase, the debriefer instructs participants about normal reactions and provides suggestions for stress reduction. In the Reentry Phase, the debriefer summarizes the session, answers questions, and makes referral suggestions if warranted. Debriefing sessions can last between three and four hours, and occur between two and ten days after a critical incident.

Psychological debriefing is enormously popular in many western countries. Throughout North America, the United Kingdom, and Australia, it is commonplace for government and private sector agencies to routinely employ debriefing practices for personnel. An impetus for providing debriefings is the concern that if a debriefing is not conducted, the employer will have breached a duty of care, thereby incurring liability for subsequent psychiatric disorder (Rose, Bisson, & Wessely, 2001). The popularity of debriefing practices is underscored by reports that following the attacks on the World Trade Center, over 9,000 counselors arrived in New York City to provide aid to people affected by the incident (Kadet, 2002).

There have been many claims that CISD is a highly effective method. The argument is made that social support, expression of emotions, and provision of coping skills contribute to better mental health after trauma exposure. Proponents of debriefing claim that there is convergent evidence to support the efficacy of the practice. Mitchell and Bray (1990) cited estimates, based on anecdotal reports, that CISD results in diminished mental health problems. Robinson and Mitchell (1993) reported a survey of 172 emergency service, welfare, and hospital personnel who participated in debriefings, with 60% of participants reporting stress reduction. It has been demonstrated that many people appreciate debriefings and perceive them as beneficial (e.g., Carlier, Voerman, & Gersons, 2000; Small, Lumley, Donohue, Potter, & Waldenstrom, 2000). Mitchell and Everly have concluded that available research on debriefings "proves their clinical effectiveness far beyond reasonable doubt" (2001, p. 84).

It is important to note that perceived benefit does not equate with better mental health. The critical question for debriefing practices is the extent to which they result in reduced psychological problems relative to trauma survivors who are not debriefed. How we answer this question has itself become the subject of debate. The standard for assessing the merits of any intervention is the randomized control trial, which involves random allocation of eligible participants to interventions or control conditions, and administration of standardized measures before and following the intervention period. Some proponents of debriefing have suggested that this approach is not suitable for assessment of debriefing practices, because one cannot adequately impose experimental controls in a disaster scene (Everly & Mitchell, 1999). It is true that random allocation, standardization of treatments, treatment fidelity checks, and other criteria usually applied to controlled trials (Foa & Meadows, 1997) are difficult to apply in the immediate aftermath of trauma. Nevertheless, when proponents of debriefing cite uncontrolled studies (e.g., Everly, Flannery, & Mitchell, 2000), it becomes imperative to consider attempts at random allocation, assessment of participants before and after intervention, and independent assessments of eventual functioning (Litz et al., 2002).

Several studies purportedly support the alleged benefits of debriefing practices (for comprehensive reviews, see Litz et al., 2002; McNally, Bryant, & Ehlers, 2003). In one study of 15 terrorist attack survivors, participants received a group debriefing two days after the attack, followed by six group therapy sessions during the following two months (Amir, Weil, Kaplan, Tocker, & Witztum, 1998). Although reported PTSD symptoms declined at two months follow-up, the absence of a control condition precludes inferences about natural remission versus interventions. In an application of CISD, Campfield and Hills (2001) randomly assigned robbery victims to either immediate (within ten hours of the crime) or delayed debriefing (more than two days after the crime). Whereas the delayed-intervention group reported no decline, the immediate-intervention group reported diminished symptoms two weeks later. The lack of a no-treatment control group and a longer-term follow-up precludes firm inferences from this study. Wee, Mills, and Koehler (1999) obtained a record of PTSD symptoms from emergency medical service personnel who had, or had not, received CISD, after involvement in the 1992 Los Angeles riot. Three months after the riots, the debriefed participants reported fewer PTSD symptoms than those who were not debriefed. In this study, the non-random allocation of participants and lack of pre-debriefing assessments limit conclusions.

In a study of 106 troops who had returned from peacekeeping duties, half of the troops were assigned to a single session of debriefing, with allocation based on logistical factors (Deahl et al., 2000). Whereas the control group reported a significant decrease in self-reported PTSD symptoms by the six-month assessment, the debriefed group did not. PTSD symptoms assessed by clinical interview did not differ between the two groups at any time point. At 12 months, the debriefed group reported fewer symptoms than the control group on self-report measures of anxiety and depression. Most interestingly, troops who received debriefing reported a decrease in alcohol use. Although these findings are encouraging, the results are again limited by the non-random allocation of troops, and low rates of reported psychiatric disturbance; only three soldiers reported PTSD at any point during the study.

Yule (1992) assessed child survivors of a ship sinking who were debriefed ten days after the event, and compared them to children who did not receive debriefing. Although the children who received debriefing reported fewer symptoms on a range of measures relative to the control group, the absence of random allocation and pretreatment measures limits firm conclusions. Nurmi (1999) reported on a single debriefing of rescue workers three to seven days after a ship sinking, and found that self-reported symptoms were lower among debriefed personnel. This study was flawed by the absence of randomization, no pre-debriefing measures, and gender bias in the different groups. In a departure from normal debriefing practice, Chemtob, Tomas, Law, and Cremniter (1997) reported the results of a debriefing session conducted six months after a hurricane. Although debriefing was associated with a reduction in reported PTSD symptoms, the delayed intervention and absence of a control group render the study's findings difficult to interpret. Numerous other studies also reported on reduced symptoms or increased functioning following debriefing, but once again, the absence of adequate methodologies limit interpretation of results (Bohl, 1995; Flannery, 2001; Jenkins, 1996; Leeman-Conley, 1990.).

Several studies have found that debriefing practices are not beneficial in terms of alleviating posttraumatic stress. Conlon, Fahy, and Conroy (1999) randomly assigned survivors of motor vehicle accidents to either debriefing or assessment only. The debriefing intervention was only three minutes and occurred immediately after the assessment, approximately seven days post-accident. Both groups improved on measures of PTSD symptoms, with no group differences observed at three-month follow-up. Rose, Brewin, Andrews, and Kirk (1999) randomly assigned 157 adult crime victims to either debriefing, an educational intervention, or assessment only. The individually-administered debriefing included discussion of the experience, and direct encouragement to ventilate emotional responses, while the education program only involved information about stress reactions. PTSD was identified at six-month follow-up in 26%, 23%, and 11% in the assessment-only, debriefing, and educational groups, respectively. At an 11-month assessment, all groups reported comparably low rates of PTSD. Carlier, Lamberts, van Uchelen, and Gersons (1998) compared the responses of police officers who received group debriefing after responding to a plane crash, with the responses of officers unable to attend the debriefing. At 18 months, the groups did not differ on psychopathology measures, apart from the debriefed officers reporting more arousal symptoms than non-debriefed partici- pants. This study is limited by the lack of random allocation and the absence of pre- treatment measures. In an adaptation of debriefing approaches, Carlier et al. (2000) administered three CISD sessions to police officers, at 24 hours, 1 month, and 3 months posttrauma exposure. Officers who participated in the debriefings were compared with those who refused participation. Although the debriefed officers reported more PTSD symptoms one week after trauma, there were no group differences at the 24-hour and 6- month assessments. This study was limited by lack of random allocation.

A number of studies have produced evidence that debriefing can have toxic effects by impairing the natural recovery that typically occurs following trauma. Kenardy et al. (1996) assessed earthquake disaster workers who had and had not received debriefing. Responses indicated that the debriefed group reported more symptoms than the non- debriefed group. This finding is limited, however, by the lack of random allocation and some ambiguity about the debriefing practices that were employed. There have been better- controlled studies that also suggest negative effects resulting from debriefings. Bisson, Jenkins, Alexander, and Bannister (1997) randomly assigned burn victims to either debrief- ing or an assessment-only control condition. Debriefing occurred between 2 and 19 days after injuries. At a 13-month follow-up assessment, debriefed participants reported more PTSD, anxiety, and depression than non-debriefed participants, even when controlling for initial severity of symptoms. It should be noted that the debriefed group tended to show more severe injury and distress prior to debriefing than the control participants. It also can be questioned if debriefing should be used with individuals suffering severe burns because they represent a qualitatively distinct group.

Hobbs, Mayou, Harrison, and Worlock (1996) randomly assigned victims of motor vehicle accidents to either a single individually administered debriefing session that occurred between 24 and 48 hours post-accident, or an assessment-only control condition. At four-month follow-up, the debriefing participants reported more distress on selected measures than control participants. As in Bisson et al. (1997), findings were compromised by the debriefed group having more severe injuries than the control group. Three years later these participants were reassessed (Mayou, Ehlers, & Hobbs, 2000). The debriefed participants reported more PTSD symptoms, and more functional difficulties than control participants. Specifically, participants who initially indicated severe PTSD reactions and were not debriefed improved markedly. In contrast, participants who initially indicated severe PTSD reactions and were debriefed remained highly symptomatic. Importantly, this finding was not explained by initial differences in injury severity.

Given current findings, where do we stand in terms of our understanding of early provision of debriefing? First, the better-controlled studies suggest that debriefing does not prevent subsequent disorder. This conclusion is underscored by recent meta-analyses of available studies (Rose et al., 2001; van Emmerik, Kamphuis, Hulsbosch, & Emmelkamp, 2002). Second, there is some evidence that debriefing actually interferes with natural recovery in a subset of individuals. The sum total of current findings suggests that we should not be adopting debriefing interventions as a means of primary prevention.

Proponents of debriefing often claim that critics have made a number of errors in their evaluation of the approach. First, it is argued that debriefing was initially intended to assist emergency service personnel with an intervention in a group format. This is a reasonable comment and there is a need for controlled studies of group debriefing in appropriate settings. It should be noted, however, that individual debriefing is very common (van Emmerik et al., 2002). Further, it is incumbent upon proponents of debriefing to properly evaluate group formats before advancing claims of effectiveness.

Debriefing proponents also argue that critics misinterpret debriefing as a secondary prevention tool and incorrectly use psychopathology measures as dependent variables in their studies of debriefing (Mitchell, 2002). Thus, it is argued that debriefing is best understood as an approach that provides support and assists coping in the initial aftermath of trauma exposure. If this is the intended purpose of debriefing, then it is still requisite to evaluate the extent to which procedures facilitate coping. It also can be noted that proponents of debriefing have argued that debriefing should be considered in the context of a broader range of approaches. For example, Everly and Mitchell (1999) have proposed CISM as an overarching approach that includes numerous educational, preparation, supportive, and counseling techniques. As was previously observed, this framework is so general, and procedural components so poorly operationalized, that it precludes direct evaluation.

ALTERNATIVES TO DEBRIEFING

In contrast to the debriefing model, which generally recommends a single session to all survivors within 72 hours of trauma exposure, there have been attempts to prevent psychological disorder by targeting individuals identified as high risk. The better-controlled studies of these targeted interventions have involved cognitive behavioral therapy (CBT). The typical components of CBT to prevent posttrauma morbidity include education about trauma responses, anxiety management techniques, cognitive restructuring, and planned exposure to trauma cues. Education typically includes information about the common reactions to a traumatic event, the cognitive and behavioral mechanisms that mediate core PTSD reactions, and a rationale for intervening. Anxiety management techniques provide individuals with coping skills to reduce arousal, manage fear reactions, and assist with distressing activities and trauma reminders. These techniques may include Meichenbaum's (1975) stress inoculation training, breathing retraining, muscle relaxation skills, and self-talk. Cognitive restructuring is based on models that emphasize the importance of appraisals in the etiology and maintenance of PTSD (Ehlers & Clark, 2000). Cognitive restructuring helps individuals identify and evaluate the evidence for negative automatic thoughts, while also clarifying beliefs about the trauma, sense of self, the world, and the future (Beck, Rush, Shaw, & Emery, 1979). Prolonged exposure often requires the individual to vividly imagine the trauma for prolonged periods. The individual typically provides a narrative of their traumatic experience in a way that emphasizes all relevant details, including sensory cues and affective responses. The exercise usually occurs for at least 50 minutes, and is often supplemented by daily homework exercises. Most exposure treatments also supplement imaginal exposure with *in vivo* exposure that involves graded exposure to feared, real-life trauma-related stimuli. Exposure may be therapeutic because of habituation of anxiety; integration of corrective information; learning that the trauma is a discrete event that is no longer threatening; and/or self-mastery through management of the exposure itself (Jaycox & Foa, 1996; Rothbaum & Mellman, 2001; Rothbaum & Schwartz, 2002).

Apart from uncontrolled studies (Brom, Kleber, & Hofman, 1993; Viney, Clark, Bunn, & Benjamin, 1985), there have been several attempts at controlled evaluations of CBT in the aftermath of trauma. Kilpatrick and Veronen (1984) randomly allocated 15 rape victims to either early and repeated assessments; delayed assessment; or a brief 4–6 hour behavioral intervention comprised of imaginal reliving of the trauma, education about responses to trauma, cognitive restructuring, and anxiety management. The finding that brief intervention was no more effective than repeated assessments was limited by small sample sizes, lack of rigorous application of exposure, and ambiguity about the degree of post-trauma symptoms (Kilpatrick & Calhoun, 1988).

Foa and colleagues conducted a more rigorous study of CBT by providing a brief intervention to sexual and non-sexual assault victims shortly after their assaults (Foa, Hearst-Ikeda, & Perry, 1995). This study compared a CBT procedure that included exposure, anxiety management, *in vivo* exposure, and cognitive restructuring, with matched participants who received repeated assessments. Each participant received four treatment sessions, and then received assessment by blind assessors at two months posttreatment and five months follow-up. Only 10% of the CBT group met criteria for PTSD at two months, as compared to 70% of the control group. At five months post-assault, no differences between groups were obtained, other than CBT participants reporting less depression. This pilot study suggests that CBT may accelerate natural recovery from trauma. However, inferences from the study are limited by lack of random assignment. In a subsequent study, Foa, Zoellner, and Feeny (2002) randomly allocated survivors of assault who met criteria for PTSD, absent the time requirement of one month, to receive four weekly sessions of CBT, repeated assessment, or supportive counseling. At posttreatment, patients in the CBT and repeated-assessment conditions showed comparable improvements, while supportive counseling was associated with greater PTSD severity and greater general anxiety. At nine-month follow-up, approximately 30% of participants in each group met criteria for PTSD.

Similar to the focus by Foa et al. (2002) on individuals who met PTSD criteria, a stringent test of early interventions may involve targeting individuals with ASD, rather than including the more general population of trauma survivors. Although the ASD diagnosis is flawed, there is reasonable support for the conclusion that people who display ASD in the aftermath of trauma are at high risk for subsequent PTSD (Bryant, 2003). Accordingly, an intervention that focuses on individuals diagnosed with ASD is targeting people whose psychological distress is likely to persist. In an initial study, Bryant and colleagues randomly allocated motor vehicle accident or non-sexual assault survivors with ASD to either CBT or supportive counseling (Bryant, Harvey, Dang, Sackville, & Basten, 1998b). Both interventions consisted of five 1.5-hour weekly individual sessions. CBT included education about posttraumatic reactions, relaxation training, cognitive restructuring, and imaginal and *in vivo* exposure to the traumatic event. The supportive counseling condition included trauma education, general problem-solving skills training, and an unconditionally supportive relationship. At a six-month follow-up, there were fewer participants in the CBT group (20%) who met diagnostic criteria for PTSD, as compared to those who received supportive counseling (67%). In a subsequent study that dismantled the components of CBT, 45 civilian trauma survivors with ASD were randomly allocated to five sessions of either (1) CBT with prolonged exposure, cognitive therapy, and anxiety management; (2) prolonged exposure combined with cognitive therapy; or (3) supportive counseling (Bryant, Sackville, Dang, Moulds, & Guthrie, 1999). This study found that at six months follow-up, PTSD was observed in approximately 20% of both active treatment groups compared to 67% of those receiving supportive counseling. A follow-up of participants indicated that treatment gains for those who received CBT were maintained four years after treatment (Bryant, Moulds, & Nixon, 2003a).

Two recent studies by the same research group have supported the utility of CBT for people with ASD. One study randomly allocated civilian trauma survivors (N = 89) with ASD to either CBT, CBT accompanied by hypnosis, or supportive counseling (Bryant, Moulds, Guthrie, & Nixon, in press). This study added hypnosis to CBT because some commentators have argued that hypnosis may breach the dissociative symptoms that characterize ASD (Spiegel, 1996). To this end, the hypnosis component was provided immediately prior to imaginal exposure in an attempt to facilitate emotional processing of trauma memories. In terms of treatment completers, more participants in the supportive counseling condition (57%) met PTSD criteria at six-month follow-up than those in the CBT (21%) or CBT + Hypnosis (22%) condition. Interestingly, participants in the CBT + Hypnosis condition reported greater reduction of reexperiencing symptoms at posttreatment than those in CBT alone. This finding suggests that hypnosis may facilitate treatment gains in ASD participants. A more recent study replicated Bryant et al. (1998b) with a sample of ASD participants who had sustained mild traumatic brain injury following MVAs, and lost consciousness during the trauma (Bryant, Moulds, Guthrie, & Nixon, 2003b). Consistent with previous studies, fewer participants receiving CBT (8%) met criteria for PTSD at six-months follow-up than those receiving supportive counseling (58%).

A different approach to subject selection was employed by Gidron et al. (2001) who provided a two-session CBT intervention that was intended to promote memory reconstruction in 17 accident survivors. Using an entry criterion of heart rates higher than 94 beats per minute at admission to the emergency room (see Bryant et al., 2000a; Shalev et al., 1998), this study provided a telephone-administered protocol one to three days after the accident. Patients who received the intervention had greater reductions in severity of PTSD symptoms three to four months after the trauma than did those who received two telephone sessions of supportive listening.

It is important to note that there are limitations to current evidence on the effectiveness of CBT shortly after trauma. First, although CBT does lead to significant reductions in symptoms for people who complete treatment, a significant proportion of participants drop out. For example, 20% of participants dropped out of both the Bryant et al. (1999) and Bryant et al. (in press) studies. When "intent-to-treat" analyses are conducted in these studies, more modest benefits for CBT are obtained (Bryant et al., 1999, in press). This pattern clearly points to the need for interventions that are not only efficacious, but also acceptable to recently traumatized individuals. Second, the majority of early intervention studies for ASD have emerged from a handful of treatment centers; there is a need for replication across sites to validate the generalizability of current findings. Further, available studies have been conducted with survivors of assault or accident; we have no data pertaining to CBT shortly after mass violence, disaster, or terrorism. We also have no evidence that early provision of CBT is necessarily superior to later applications, as CBT has been shown effective one to three months after trauma (Ehlers et al., 2003; Öst, Paunovic,

& Gillow, 2002), as well as in the treatment of chronic PTSD (for reviews, see Foa & Meadows, 1997; Harvey, Bryant, & Tarrier, 2003). Of course, even if delayed treatment is eventually as effective as early intervention, there is the obvious benefit of reducing distress sooner rather than later.

WHAT SHOULD WE DO IN THE AFTERMATH OF TRAUMA?

Considering this review of immediate and acute posttraumatic responses, what should our response be in the initial aftermath of trauma? If debriefing can no longer be regarded as an empirically defensible approach to be provided to all who suffer trauma, then what is the alternative? Certainly, in the context of strong and apparent distress following trauma, there is a need to respond in some constructive manner. At the same time, it is imperative that psychological first aid be evaluated to index that it (1) provides desired support and assistance in the initial aftermath of trauma, and (2) does not interfere with natural recovery.

Recent discussions have focused on approaches that provide support and basic education as needed, while addressing the immediate needs of survivors (e.g., providing food, blankets, hospitalization). For example, a consensus meeting of international experts convened shortly after the terrorist attacks on September 11, 2001. The group proposed that psychological first aid should be implemented in the days after mass trauma (National Institute of Mental Health, 2002), to provide shelter, safety, social support, and linkage to appropriate resources. The active facilitation of disclosure of trauma experiences or related emotions was explicitly discouraged. In this sense, psychological first aid adopts a less interventionist approach than debriefing, recognizing the benefit people may receive from support and immediate assistance, without a structured format that encourages disclosure of trauma memories. It can be observed that some commentators have noted that although debriefing may not prevent subsequent psychiatric disorder, it may enhance morale, organizational cohesion, and immediate coping (Litz et al., 2002). In this context, current psychological first aid may be utilizing those components of debriefing practices that are beneficial, while excluding potentially harmful methods.

Current efforts at psychological first aid are not intended to serve a secondary prevention function. These efforts assume that the normative response to trauma is recovery, but also recognize that a proportion of people will develop longer-term disorder. The evidence for empirically supported treatments provided two and four weeks after trauma (e.g., CBT) points to the need for surveillance, and identification of people who are high risk for developing subsequent disorder. At this stage, we have no well-validated instruments to accomplish this early identification. Although there are screening measures based on the ASD diagnosis (Bryant, Moulds, & Guthrie, 2000b; Cardeña, Koopman, Classen, Waelde, & Spiegel, 2000), these instruments suffer the same problems associated with the ASD construct itself. The field needs to prospectively evaluate screening measures that allow us to identify people at high risk for subsequent disorder. It also should be kept in mind that most CBT studies have not provided a formal intervention within two weeks posttrauma. The benefits of allowing the immediate consequences of trauma to subside before considering active interventions may apply here as well.

The current review of issues surrounding posttrauma reactions and interventions in the acute aftermath of trauma highlights some of the most contentious debates in the field of traumatic stress. These issues concern the role of peritraumatic dissociation, the merits of an early posttrauma diagnosis such as ASD, and the efficacy of debriefing or alternative early interventions. Debates have persisted over many years, in part because of the tendency for many commentators and practitioners to neglect the need for strong evidence. Considering the ethical responsibilities that researchers and practitioners have in providing optimal interventions to those who are traumatized, it is imperative that we replace myths with evidence accrued by sound research.

REFERENCES

American Psychiatric Association (1994). *Diagnostic and statistical manual of mental disorders* (4th edn). Washington, DC: Author.

Amir, M., Weil, G., Kaplan, Z., Tocker, T., & Witztum, E. (1998). Debriefing with brief group psychotherapy in a homogenous group of non-injured victims of a terrorist attack: A prospective study. *Acta Psychiatrica Scandinavica, 98*, 237–242.

Andrews, B., Brewin, C. R., Rose, S., & Kirk, M. (2000). Predicting PTSD in victims of violent crime: The role of shame, anger and blame. *Journal of Abnormal Psychology, 109*, 69–73.

Atchison, M., & McFarlane, A. C. (1994). A review of dissociation and dissociative disorders. *Australian and New Zealand Journal of Psychiatry, 28*, 591–599.

Barton, K. A., Blanchard, E. B., & Hickling, E. J. (1996). Antecedents and consequences of acute stress disorder among motor vehicle accident victims. *Behaviour Research and Therapy, 34*, 805–813.

Beck, A. T., Rush, A. J., Shaw, B. F., & Emery, G. (1979). *Cognitive therapy of depression.* New York: Guilford Press.

Berah, E. F., Jones, H. J., & Valent, P. (1984). The experience of a mental health team involved in the early phase of a disaster. *Australian and New Zealand Journal of Psychiatry, 18*, 354–358.

Bisson, J. I., Jenkins, P. L., Alexander, J., & Bannister, C. (1997). Randomised controlled trial of psychological debriefing for victims of acute burn trauma. *British Journal of Psychiatry, 171*, 78–81.

Blanchard, E. B., Hickling, E. J., Barton, K. A., Taylor, A. E., Loos, W. R., & Jones-Alexander, J. (1996). One-year prospective follow-up of motor vehicle accident victims. *Behaviour Research and Therapy, 34*, 775–786.

Blanchard, E. B., Hickling, E. J., Galovski, T., & Veazey, C. (2002). Emergency room vital signs and PTSD in a treatment seeking sample of motor vehicle accident survivors. *Journal of Traumatic Stress, 15*, 199–204.

Blank, A. S. (1993). Suggested recommendations for DSM-IV on course and subtypes. In J. R. Davidson & E. B. Foa (eds), *Posttraumatic stress disorder in review: Recent research and future developments* (pp. 237–240). Washington, DC: American Psychiatric Press.

Bohl, N. (1995). Measuring the effectiveness of CISD: A study. *Fire Engineering, 148*, 125–126.

Brewin, C. R., Andrews, B., Rose, S., & Kirk, M. (1999). Acute stress disorder and posttraumatic stress disorder in victims of violent crime. *American Journal of Psychiatry, 156*, 360–366.

Brewin, C. R., Andrews, B., & Valentine, J. D. (2000). Meta-analysis of risk factors for posttraumatic stress disorder in trauma-exposed adults. *Journal of Consulting and Clinical Psychology, 68*, 748–766.

Brom, D., Kleber, R. J., & Hofman, M. (1993). Victims of traffic accidents: Incidence and prevention of post-traumatic stress disorder. *Journal of Clinical Psychology, 49*, 131–140.

Bryant, R. A. (2000). Acute stress disorder. *PTSD Research Quarterly*, *11*, 1–7.

Bryant, R. A. (2001). Posttraumatic stress disorder and traumatic brain injury: Can they co-exist? *Clinical Psychology Review*, *21*, 931–945.

Bryant, R. A. (2003). Early predictors of posttraumatic stress disorder. *Biological Psychiatry*, *53*, 789–795.

Bryant, R. A., & Harvey, A. G. (1996). Initial post-traumatic stress responses following motor vehicle accidents. *Journal of Traumatic Stress*, *9*, 223–234.

Bryant, R. A., & Harvey, A. G. (1997). Acute stress disorder: A critical review of diagnostic issues. *Clinical Psychology Review*, *17*, 757–773.

Bryant, R. A., & Harvey, A. G. (1998). Relationship of acute stress disorder and posttraumatic stress disorder following mild traumatic brain injury. *American Journal of Psychiatry*, *155*, 625–629.

Bryant, R. A., & Harvey, A. G. (2000). New DSM-IV diagnosis of acute stress disorder. Letter to the Editor, *American Journal of Psychiatry*, *157*, 1889–1890.

Bryant, R. A., Harvey, A. G., Dang, S., & Sackville, T. (1998a). Assessing acute stress disorder: Psychometric properties of a structured clinical interview. *Psychological Assessment*, *10*, 215–220.

Bryant, R. A., Harvey, A. G., Dang, S. T., Sackville, T., & Basten, C. (1998b). Treatment of acute stress disorder: A comparison of cognitive behavior therapy and supportive counseling. *Journal of Consulting and Clinical Psychology*, *66*, 862–866.

Bryant, R. A., Harvey, A. G., Guthrie, R., & Moulds, M. (2000a). A prospective study of acute psychophysiological arousal, acute stress disorder, and posttraumatic stress disorder. *Journal of Abnormal Psychology*, *109*, 341–344.

Bryant, R. A., Moulds, M., & Guthrie, R. (2000b). Acute stress disorder scale: A self-report measure of acute stress disorder. *Psychological Assessment*, *12*, 61–68.

Bryant, R. A., Moulds, M., & Guthrie, R. M. (2001). Hypnotizability in acute stress disorder. *American Journal of Psychiatry*, *158*, 600–604.

Bryant, R. A., Moulds, M. L., Guthrie, R. M., & Nixon, R. D. V. (2003b). Treating acute stress disorder following mild traumatic brain injury. *American Journal of Psychiatry*, *160*, 585–587.

Bryant, R. A., Moulds, M. L., Guthrie, R., & Nixon, R. D. V. (in press). The additive benefit of hypnosis and cognitive behavior therapy in treating acute stress disorder. *Journal of Consulting and Clinical Psychology*.

Bryant, R. A., Moulds, M. A., & Nixon, R. (2003a). Cognitive behaviour therapy of acute stress disorder: A four-year follow-up. *Behaviour Research and Therapy*, *41*, 489–494.

Bryant, R. A., & Panasetis, P. (2001). Panic symptoms during trauma and acute stress disorder. *Behaviour Research and Therapy*, *39*, 961–966.

Bryant, R. A., Sackville, T., Dang, S. T., Moulds, M., & Guthrie, R. (1999). Treating acute stress disorder: An evaluation of cognitive behavior therapy and counselling techniques. *American Journal of Psychiatry*, *156*, 1780–1786.

Butler, L. D. (2000). New DSM-IV diagnosis of acute stress disorder. Letter to the Editor, *American Journal of Psychiatry*, *157*, 1889.

Butler, L. D., Duran, R. E. F., Jasiukaitis, P., Koopman, C., & Spiegel, D. (1996). Hypnotizability and traumatic experience: A diathesis-stress model of dissociative symptomatology. *American Journal of Psychiatry*, *153 (Suppl. 7S)*, 42–63.

Cahill, L., Prins, B., Weber, M., & McGaugh, J. L. (1994). b_Adrenergic activation and memory for emotional events. *Nature*, *371*, 702–704.

Campfield, K. M., & Hills, A. M. (2001). Effect of timing of Critical Incident Stress Debriefing (CISD) on posttraumatic symptoms. *Journal of Traumatic Stress*, *14*, 327–340.

Cardeña, E., Koopman, C., Classen, C., Waelde, L. C., & Spiegel, D. (2000). Psychometric properties of the Stanford Acute Stress Reaction Questionnaire (SASRQ): A valid and reliable measure of acute stress. *Journal of Traumatic Stress, 13*, 719–734.

Cardeña, E., & Spiegel, D. (1993). Dissociative reactions to the San Francisco Bay Area earthquake of 1989. *American Journal of Psychiatry, 150*, 474–478.

Carlier, I. V. E., Lamberts, R. D., van Uchelen, A. J., & Gersons, B. P. R. (1998). Disaster related post-traumatic stress in police officers: A field study of the impact of debriefing. *Stress Medicine, 14*, 143–148.

Carlier, I. V. E., Voerman, A. E., & Gersons, B. P. R. (2000). The influence of occupational debriefing on post-traumatic stress symptomatology in traumatized police officers. *British Journal of Medical Psychology, 73*, 87–98.

Charcot, J.-M. (1889). *Clinical lectures on the diseases of the nervous system*; Vol. III. Trans. by T. Savill. London: The New Sydenham Society.

Chemtob, C. M., Tomas, S., Law, W., & Cremniter, D. (1997). Postdisaster psychosocial intervention: A field study of the impact of debriefing on psychological distress. *American Journal of Psychiatry, 154*, 415–417.

Classen, C., Koopman, C., Hales, R., & Spiegel, D. (1998). Acute stress disorder as a predictor of posttraumatic stress symptoms. *American Journal of Psychiatry, 155*, 620–624.

Conlon, L., Fahy, T. J., & Conroy, R. (1999). PTSD in ambulant RTA victims: A randomized controlled trial of debriefing. *Journal of Psychosomatic Research, 46*, 37–44.

Creamer, M., & Manning, C. (1998). Acute stress disorder following an industrial accident. *Australian Psychologist, 33*, 125–129.

Creamer, M. C., O'Donnell, M. L., & Pattison, P. (2004). The relationship between acute stress disorder and posttraumatic stress disorder in severely injured trauma survivors. *Behaviour Research and Therapy, 42*, 315–328.

Dancu, C. V., Riggs, D. S., Hearst-Ikeda, D., Shoyer, B. G., & Foa, E. B. (1996). Dissociative experiences and posttraumatic stress disorder among female victims of criminal assault and rape. *Journal of Traumatic Stress, 9*, 253–267.

Davidson, J., & Foa, E. B. (1991). Diagnostic issues in posttraumatic stress disorder: Considerations for DSM-IV. *Journal of Abnormal Psychology, 100*, 346–355.

Deahl, M., Srinivasan, M., Jones, N., Thomas, J., Neblett, C., & Jolly, A. (2000). Preventing psychological trauma in soldiers: The role of operational stress training and psychological debriefing. *British Journal of Medical Psychology, 73*, 77–85.

Delahanty, D. L., Herberman, H. B., Craig, K. J., Hayward, M. C., Fullerton, C. S., Ursano, R. J. et al. (1997). Acute and chronic distress and posttraumatic stress disorder as a function of responsibility for serious motor vehicle accidents. *Journal of Consulting and Clinical Psychology, 65*, 560–567.

Delahanty, D. L., Raimonde, A. J., & Spoonster, E. (2000). Initial posttraumatic urinary cortisol levels predict subsequent PTSD symptoms in motor vehicle accident victims. *Biological Psychiatry, 48*, 940–947.

Difede, J., Ptacek, J. T., Roberts, J. G., Barocas, D., Rives, W., Apfeldorf, W. J. et al. (2002). Acute stress disorder after burn injury: A predictor of posttraumatic stress disorder. *Psychosomatic Medicine, 64*, 826–834.

Ehlers, A., & Clark, D. (2000). A cognitive model of posttraumatic stress disorder. *Behaviour Research and Therapy, 38*, 319–345.

Ehlers, A., Clark, D. M., Hackmann, A., McManus, F., Fennell, M., Herbert, C. et al. (2003). A randomized controlled trial of cognitive therapy, self-help, and repeated assessment as early interventions for PTSD. *Archives of General Psychiatry, 60*, 1024–1032.

Ehlers, A., Mayou, R. A., & Bryant, B. (1998). Psychological predictors of chronic PTSD after motor vehicle accidents. *Journal of Abnormal Psychology, 107*, 508–519.

Engelhard, I. M., van den Hout, M. A., Arntz, A., & McNally, R. J. (2002). A longitudinal study of "intrusion-based reasoning" and posttraumatic stress disorder after exposure to a train disaster. *Behaviour Research and Therapy*, *40*, 1415–1424.

Everly, G. S., Flannery, R. B., & Mitchell, J. T. (2000). Critical incident stress management (CISM): A review of the literature. *Aggression and Violent Behavior*, *5*, 23–40.

Everly, G. S., Jr, & Mitchell, J. T. (1999). *Critical Incident Stress Management (CISM): A new era and standard of care in crisis intervention* (2nd edn). Ellicott City, MD: Chevron.

Feinstein, A. (1989). Posttraumatic stress disorder: A descriptive study supporting DSM III-R criteria. *American Journal of Psychiatry*, *146*, 665–666.

Felmingham, K., Bryant, R. A., & Gordon, E. (in press). Tonic arousal in acute stress disorder. *Psychiatry Research*.

Flannery, R. B., Jr (2001). The Assaulted Staff Action Program (ASAP): Ten year empirical support for Critical Incident Stress Management (CISD). *International Journal of Emergency Mental Health*, *3*, 5–10.

Foa, E. B., Hearst-Ikeda, D., & Perry, K. J. (1995). Evaluation of a brief cognitive behavioral program for the prevention of chronic PTSD in recent assault victims. *Journal of Consulting and Clinical Psychology*, *63*, 948–955.

Foa, E. B., & Meadows, E. A. (1997). Psychosocial treatments for post-traumatic stress disorder: A critical review. *Annual Review of Psychology*, *48*, 449–480.

Foa, E. B., Zoellner, L. A., & Feeny, N. C. (2002). An evaluation of three brief programs for facilitating recovery. Manuscript submitted for publication.

Freinkel, A., Koopman, C., & Spiegel, D. (1994). Dissociative symptoms in media witnesses of an execution. *American Journal of Psychiatry*, *151*, 1335–1339.

Galea, S., Boscarino, J., Resnick, H., & Vlahov, D. (in press). Mental health in New York City after the September 11 terrorist attacks: Results from two population surveys. In R. W. Manderscheid & M. J. Henderson (eds), *Mental health, United States, 2002*. Washington, DC: US Government Print Office.

Galea, S., Resnick, H., Kilpatrick, D., Bucuvalas, M., Gold, J., & Vlahov, D. (2002). Psychological sequelae of the September 11 terrorist attacks in New York City. *New England Journal of Medicine*, *346*, 982–987.

Gidron, Y., Gal., R., Freedman, S., Twiser, I., Lauden, A., Snir, Y. et al. (2001). Translating research findings to PTSD prevention: Results of a randomized-controlled pilot study. *Journal of Traumatic Stress*, *14*, 773–780.

Green, B. L., Krupnick, J. L., Stockton, P., & Goodman, L. (2001). Psychological outcomes associated with traumatic loss in a sample of young women. *The American Behavioral Scientist*, *44*, 817–837.

Guthrie, R., & Bryant, R. A. (2000). Attempted thought suppression over extended periods in acute stress disorder. *Behaviour Research and Therapy*, *38*, 899–907.

Harvey, A. G., & Bryant, R. A. (1998a). Relationship of acute stress disorder and posttraumatic stress disorder following motor vehicle accidents. *Journal of Consulting and Clinical Psychology*, *66*, 507–512.

Harvey, A. G., & Bryant, R. A. (1998b). Acute stress disorder following mild traumatic brain injury. *Journal of Nervous and Mental Disease*, *186*, 333–337.

Harvey, A. G., & Bryant, R. A. (1999a). Acute stress disorder across trauma populations. *Journal of Nervous and Mental Disease*, *187*, 443–446.

Harvey, A. G., & Bryant, R. A. (1999b). A two-year prospective evaluation of the relationship between acute stress disorder and posttraumatic stress disorder. *Journal of Consulting and Clinical Psychology*, *67*, 985–988.

Harvey, A. G., & Bryant, R. A. (2000a). A two-year prospective evaluation of the relationship between acute stress disorder and posttraumatic stress disorder following mild traumatic brain injury. *American Journal of Psychiatry*, *157*, 626–628.

Harvey, A. G., & Bryant, R. A. (2000b). Memory for acute stress disorder symptoms: A two-year prospective study. *Journal of Nervous and Mental Disease, 188*, 602–607.

Harvey, A. G., & Bryant, R. A. (2002). Acute stress disorder: A synthesis and critique. *Psychological Bulletin, 128*, 892–906.

Harvey, A. G., Bryant, R. A., & Dang, S. (1998). Autobiographical memory in acute stress disorder. *Journal of Consulting and Clinical Psychology, 66*, 500–506.

Harvey, A. G., Bryant, R. A., & Tarrier, N. (2003). Cognitive behaviour therapy of posttraumatic stress disorder. *Clinical Psychology Review, 23*, 501–522.

Hillman, R. G. (1981). The psychopathology of being held hostage. *American Journal of Psychiatry, 138*, 1193–1197.

Hobbs, M., Mayou, R., Harrison, B., & Worlock, P. (1996). A randomised controlled trial of psychological debriefing for victims of road traffic accidents. *British Medical Journal, 313*, 1438–1439.

Holen, A. (1993). The North Sea oil rig disaster. In J. P. Wilson & B. Raphael (eds), *International handbook of traumatic stress syndromes* (pp. 471–478). New York: Plenum.

Holeva, V., Tarrier, N., & Wells, A. (2001). Prevalence and predictors of acute stress disorder and PTSD following road traffic accidents: Thought control strategies and social support. *Behavior Therapy, 32*, 65–83.

Horowitz, M. J. (1986). *Stress response syndromes* (2nd edn). New York: Aronson.

Janet, P. (1907). *The major symptoms of hysteria*. New York: Macmillan.

Jaycox, L. H., & Foa, E. B. (1996). Obstacles in implementing exposure therapy for PTSD: Case discussions and practical solutions. *Clinical Psychology and Psychotherapy, 3*, 176–184.

Jenkins, S. R. (1996). Social support and debriefing efficacy among emergency medical workers after a mass shooting incident. *Journal of Social Behavior and Personality, 11*, 477–492.

Kadet, A. (2002). Good grief! *Smart Money, 11*, 109–114.

Kangas, M., Henry, J. L., & Bryant, R. A. (in press). The relationship between acute stress disorder and posttraumatic stress disorder following cancer. *Journal of Consulting and Clinical Psychology*.

Keane, T. M., Kaufman, M. L., & Kimble, M. O. (2001). Peritraumatic dissociative symptoms, acute stress disorder, and the development of posttraumatic stress disorder: Causation, correlation or epiphenomena. In L. Sanchez-Planell & C. Diez-Quevedo (eds), *Dissociative states* (pp. 21–43). Barcelona, Spain: Springer-Verlag.

Kenardy, J. A., Webster, R. A., Lewin, T. J., Carr, V. J., Hazell, P. L., & Carter, G. L. (1996). Stress debriefing and patterns of recovery following a natural disaster. *Journal of Traumatic Stress, 9*, 37–49.

Kihlstrom, J. F., Glisky, M. L., & Angiulo, M. J. (1994). Dissociative tendencies and dissociative disorders. *Journal of Abnormal Psychology, 103*, 117–124.

Kilpatrick, D. G., & Calhoun, K. S. (1988). Early behavioral treatment for rape trauma: Efficacy or artifact? *Behavior Therapy, 19*, 421–427.

Kilpatrick, D. G., & Veronen, L. J. (1984). Treatment of rape-related problems: Crisis intervention is not enough. In L. Cohen, W. Clairborn, & G. Specter (eds), *Crisis intervention* (2nd edn). New York: Human Services Press.

Klimesch, W., Doppelmayr, M., Pachinger, T., & Ripper, B. (1997). Brain oscillations and human memory performance: EEG correlates in the upper alpha and theta bands. *Neuroscience Letters, 238*, 9–12.

Kolb, L. C. (1987). A neuropsychological hypothesis explaining post-traumatic stress disorder. *American Journal of Psychiatry, 144*, 989–995.

Koopman, C. (2000). New DSM-IV diagnosis of acute stress disorder. Letter to the Editor, *American Journal of Psychiatry, 157*, 1888.

Koopman, C., Classen, C., Cardeña, E., & Spiegel, D. (1995). When disaster strikes, acute stress disorder may follow. *Journal of Traumatic Stress*, *8*, 29–46.

Koopman, C., Classen, C., & Spiegel, D. (1994). Predictors of posttraumatic stress symptoms among survivors of the Oakland/Berkeley, Calif., firestorm. *American Journal of Psychiatry*, *151*, 888–894.

Kramer, T., Buckhout, R., & Eugenio, P. (1990). Weapon focus, arousal, and eyewitness memory: Attention must be paid. *Law and Human Behavior*, *14*, 167–184.

Krystal, J., Woods, S., Hill, C. L., & Charney, D. S. (1991). Characteristics of panic attack subtypes: Assessment of spontaneous panic, situational panic, sleep panic, and limited symptom attacks. *Comprehensive Psychiatry*, *32*, 4474–4480.

LeDoux, J. E., Iwata, J., Cicchetti, P., & Reis, D. J. (1988). Different projections of the central amygdaloid nucleus mediate autonomic and behavioral correlates of conditioned fear. *Journal of Neuroscience*, *8*, 2517–2529.

Leeman-Conley, M. (1990). After a violent robbery . . . *Criminology Australia*, *1*, 4–6.

Litz, B. T., Gray, M. J., Bryant, R. A., & Adler, A. B. (2002). Early intervention for trauma: Current status and future directions. *Clinical Psychology: Science and Practice*, *9*, 112–134.

Maas, A., & Kohnken, G. (1989). Eyewitness identification. *Law and Human Behavior*, *11*, 397–408.

Marmar, C. R., Weiss, D. S., Schlenger, W. E., Fairbank, J. A., Jordan, K., Kulka, R. A. et al. (1994). Peritraumatic dissociation and posttraumatic stress in male Vietnam theater veterans. *American Journal of Psychiatry*, *151*, 902–907.

Marshall, G. N., & Schell, T. L. (2002). Reappraising the link between peritraumatic dissociation and PTSD symptom severity: Evidence from a longitudinal study of community violence survivors. *Journal of Abnormal Psychology*, *111*, 626–636.

Marshall, R. D., Spitzer, R., & Liebowitz, M. R. (1999). Review and critique of the new DSM-IV diagnosis of acute stress disorder. *American Journal of Psychiatry*, *156*, 1677–1685.

Marshall, R. D., Spitzer, R., & Liebowitz, M. R. (2000). New DSM-IV diagnosis of acute stress disorder. *American Journal of Psychiatry*, *157*, 1890–1891.

Mayou, R. A., Ehlers, A., & Hobbs, M. (2000). Psychological debriefing for road traffic accidents: Three-year follow-up of a randomised controlled trial. *British Journal of Psychiatry*, *176*, 589–593.

McFarlane, A. C. (1986). Posttraumatic morbidity of a disaster. *Journal of Nervous and Mental Disease*, *174*, 4–14.

McFarlane, A. C., Atchison, M., & Yehuda, R. (1997). The acute stress response following motor vehicle accidents and its relation to PTSD. In R. Yehuda & A. C. McFarlane (eds), *Psychobiology of posttraumatic stress disorder* (pp. 433–436). New York: New York Academy of Sciences.

McNally, R. J. (2003). *Remembering trauma*. Cambridge, MA: Harvard University Press.

McNally, R. J., Bryant, R. A., & Ehlers, A. (2003). Psychological debriefing and its alternatives: A critique of early intervention for trauma survivors. *Psychological Science in the Public Interest*, *4*, 45–79.

Meichenbaum, D. (1975). Self-instructional methods. In F. H. Kanfer & A. P. Goldstein (eds), *Helping people change*. New York: Pergamon.

Mitchell, J. T. (1983). When disaster strikes . . . The Critical Incident Stress Debriefing process. *Journal of Emergency Medical Services*, *8*, 36–39.

Mitchell, J. T. (2002, November 11). *CISM research summary*. Retrieved from http:///.licisf.org/articles/cism_research_summary.pdf

Mitchell, J. T., & Bray, G. (1990). *Emergency services stress*. Englewood Cliffs, NJ: Prentice-Hall.

Mitchell, J. T., & Everly, G. S., Jr (2001). *Critical Incident Stress Debriefing: An operations manual for CISD, defusing and other group crisis intervention services* (3rd edn). Ellicott City, MD: Chevron.

Moulds, L. M., & Bryant, R. A. (2002). Directed forgetting in acute stress disorder. *Journal of Abnormal Psychology, 111*, 175–179.

Moulds, M. L., & Bryant, R. A. (in press). Retrieval inhibition of traumatic stimuli in acute stress disorder. *Journal of Traumatic Stress.*

Murray, J., Ehlers, A., & Mayou, R. A. (2002). Dissociation and post-traumatic stress disorder: Two prospective studies of road traffic accident survivors. *British Journal of Psychiatry, 180*, 363–368.

National Institute of Mental Health (2002). *Mental health and mass violence: evidence based early psychological interventions for victims/survivors of mass violence. A workshop to reach consensus on best practices.* NIH Publication No. 02-5138, Washington, DC: US Government Printing Office.

Nemiah, J. C. (1989). Janet redivivus [Editorial]. *American Journal of Psychiatry, 146*, 1527–1529.

Nixon, R., & Bryant, R. A. (2003). Peritraumatic and persistent panic attacks in acute stress disorder. *Behaviour Research and Therapy, 41*, 1237–1242.

North, C. S., Smith, E. M., McCool, R. E., & Lightcap, P. E. (1989). Acute postdisaster coping and adjustment. *Journal of Traumatic Stress, 2*, 353–360.

Noyes, R., Hoenk, P. R., Kuperman, S., & Slymen, D. J. (1977). Depersonalization in accident victims and psychiatric patients. *Journal of Nervous and Mental Disease, 164*, 401–407.

Noyes, R., & Kletti, R. (1977). Depersonalizaton in response to life-threatening danger. *Comprehensive Psychiatry, 18*, 375–384.

Nurmi, L. A. (1999). The sinking of the *Estonia*: The effects of Critical Incident Stress Debriefing (CISD) on rescuers. *International Journal of Emergency Mental Health, 1*, 23–31.

Öst, L.-G., Paunovic, N., & Gillow, E.-M. (2002). Cognitive-behavior therapy in the prevention of chronic PTSD in crime victims. Manuscript submitted for publication.

Ozer, E. J., Best, S. R., Lipsey, T. L., & Weiss, D. S. (2003). Predictors of posttraumatic stress disorder and symptoms in adults: A meta-analysis. *Psychological Bulletin, 129*, 52–73.

Pitman, R. K., Sanders, K. M., Zusman, R. M., Healy, A. R., Cheema, F., Lasko, N. B. et al. (2002). Pilot study of secondary prevention of posttraumatic stress disorder with propranolol. *Biological Psychiatry, 51*, 189–192.

Pitman, R. K., Shalev, A. Y., & Orr, S. P. (2000). Posttraumatic stress disorder: Emotion, conditioning and memory. In M. D. Corbetta & M. Gazzaniga (eds), *The new cognitive neurosciences* (2nd edn). New York: Plenum.

Post, R. M., Weiss, S. R. B., & Smith, M. (1995). Sensitization and kindling: Implication for the evolving neural substrates of posttraumatic stress disorder. In M. J. Friedman, D. S. Charney, & A. Y. Deutch (eds), *Neurobiological and clinical consequences of stress: From normal adaptation to posttraumatic stress disorder.* Philadelphia, PA: Lippincott-Raven.

Raphael, B., & Wilson, J. P. (eds) (2000). *Psychological debriefing: Theory, practice and evidence.* Cambridge: Cambridge University Press.

Resnick, H. S., Falsetti, S. A., Kilpatrick, D. G., & Foy, D. W. (1994). Associations between panic attacks during rape assaults and follow-up PTSD or panic-attack outcomes. Presented at the 10th Annual Meeting of the International Society of Traumatic Stress Studies, Chicago, IL, November.

Riggs, D. S., Rothbaum, B. O., & Foa, E. B. (1995). A prospective examination of symptoms of posttraumatic stress disorder in victims of non-sexual assault. *Journal of Interpersonal Violence, 10*, 201–214.

Robinson, R. C., & Mitchell, J. T. (1993). Evaluation of psychological debriefings. *Journal of Traumatic Stress, 6*, 367–382.

Rose, S., Bisson, J., & Wessely, S. (2001). Psychological debriefing for preventing post traumatic stress disorder (PTSD). *The Cochrane Library (3).* Oxford, England: Update Software.

Rose, S., Brewin, C. R., Andrews, B., & Kirk, M. (1999). A randomized controlled trial of individual psychological debriefing for victims of violent crime. *Psychological Medicine*, *29*, 793–799.

Rothbaum, B. O., Foa, E. B., Riggs, D. S., Murdock, T., & Walsh, W. (1992). A prospective examination of post-traumatic stress disorder in rape victims. *Journal of Traumatic Stress*, *5*, 455–475.

Rothbaum, B. O., & Mellman, T. A. (2001). Dreams and exposure therapy for PTSD. *Journal of Traumatic Stress*, *14*, 481–490.

Rothbaum, B. O., & Schwartz, A. C. (2002). Exposure therapy for posttraumatic stress disorder. *American Journal of Psychotherapy*, *56*, 59–75.

Sakowitz, O. W., Schurmann, M., & Basar, E. (2000). Oscillatory frontal theta responses are increased upon bisensory stimulation. *Clinical Neurophysiology*, *111*, 884–893.

Schnyder, U., Moergeli, H., Klaghofer, R., & Buddeberg, C. (2001). Incidence and prediction of posttraumatic stress disorder symptoms in severely injured accident victims. *American Journal of Psychiatry*, *158*, 594–599.

Shalev, A. Y. (1992). Posttraumatic stress disorder among injured survivors of a terrorist attack. *Journal of Nervous and Mental Disease*, *180*, 505–509.

Shalev, A. Y., Freedman, S., Peri, T., Brandes, D., & Sahar, T. (1997). Predicting PTSD in trauma survivors: Prospective evaluation of self-report and clinician-administered instruments. *British Journal of Psychiatry*, *170*, 558–564.

Shalev, A. Y., Sahar, T., Freedman, S., Peri, T., Glick, N., Brandes, D. et al. (1998). A prospective study of heart rate responses following trauma and the subsequent development of PTSD. *Archives of General Psychiatry*, *55*, 553–559.

Simeon, D., & Guralnik, O. (2000). New DSM-IV diagnosis of acute stress disorder. Letter to the Editor, *American Journal of Psychiatry*, *157*, 1888–1889.

Sloan, P. (1988). Post-traumatic stress in survivors of an airplane crash-landing: A clinical and exploratory research intervention. *Journal of Traumatic Stress*, *1*, 211–229.

Small, R., Lumley, J., Donohue, L., Potter, A., & Waldenstrom, U. (2000). Randomised controlled trial of midwife led debriefing to reduce maternal depression after operative childbirth. *British Medical Journal*, *321*, 1043–1047.

Smith, K., & Bryant, R. A. (2000). The generality of cognitive bias in acute stress disorder. *Behaviour Research and Therapy*, *38*, 709–715.

Solomon, Z., Laor, N., & McFarlane, A. C. (1996). Acute posttraumatic reactions in soldiers and civilians. In B. A. van der Kolk, A. C. McFarlane, & L. Weisaeth (eds), *Traumatic stress: The effects of overwhelming experience on mind, body, and society* (pp. 102–114). New York: Guilford Press.

Southwick, S. M., Krystal, J. H., Morgan, C. A., Johnson, D. R., Nagy, L. M., Nicolaou, A. L. et al. (1993). Abnormal noradrenergic function in posttraumatic stress disorder. *Archives of General Psychiatry*, *50*, 266–274.

Southwick, S. M., Morgan, C. A., Nicolaou, A. L., & Charney, D. S. (1997). Consistency of memory for combat-related traumatic events in veterans of Operation Desert Storm. *American Journal of Psychiatry*, *154*, 173–177.

Spiegel, D. (1996). Dissociative disorders. In R. E. Hales & S. C. Yudofsky (eds), *Synopsis of psychiatry* (pp. 583–604). Washington, DC: American Psychiatric Press.

Spiegel, D., & Cardeña, E. (1991). Disintegrated experience: The dissociative disorders revisited. *Journal of Abnormal Psychology*, *100*, 366–378.

Spiegel, D., Classen, C., & Cardeña, E. (2000). New DSM-IV diagnosis of acute stress disorder. Letter to the Editor. *American Journal of Psychiatry*, *157*, 1890–1891.

Staab, J. P., Grieger, T. A., Fullerton, C. S., & Ursano, R. J. (1996). Acute stress disorder, subsequent posttraumatic stress disorder and depression after a series of typhoons. *Anxiety*, *2*, 219–225.

Sterlini, G., & Bryant, R. A. (2002). Hyperarousal and dissociation: A study of novice skydivers. *Behaviour Research and Therapy, 40,* 431–437.

Vaiva, G., Ducrocq, F., Jezequel, K., Averland, B., Lestavel, P., Brunet, A. et al. (2003). Immediate treatment with propranolol decreases posttraumatic stress disorder two months after trauma. *Biological Psychiatry, 54,* 947–949.

van der Kolk, B. A., & van der Hart, O. (1989). Pierre Janet and the breakdown of adaptation in psychological data. *American Journal of Psychiatry, 146,* 1530–1540.

van Emmerik, A. A. P., Kamphuis, J. H., Hulsbosch, A. M., & Emmelkamp, P. M. G. (2002). Single session debriefing after psychological trauma: A meta-analysis. *Lancet, 360,* 766–771.

Viney, L. L., Clark, A. M., Bunn, T. A., & Benjamin, Y. N. (1985). Crisis intervention counselling: An evaluation of long and short term effects. *Journal of Consulting and Clinical Psychology, 32,* 29–39.

Wakefield, J. C. (1996). DSM-IV: Are we making diagnostic progress? *Contemporary Psychology, 41,* 646–652.

Warda, G., & Bryant, R. A. (1998a). Cognitive bias in acute stress disorder. *Behaviour Research and Therapy, 36,* 1177–1183.

Warda, G., & Bryant, R. A. (1998b). Thought control strategies in acute stress disorder. *Behaviour Research and Therapy, 36,* 1171–1175.

Wee, D. F., Mills, D. M., & Koehler, G. (1999). The effects of Critical Incident Stress Debriefing (CISD) on emergency medical services personnel following the Los Angeles civil disturbance. *International Journal of Emergency Mental Health, 1,* 33–37.

Williams, J. M. G. (1996). Depression and the specificity of autobiographical memory. In D. C. Rubin (ed.). *Remembering our past: Studies in autobiographical memory* (pp. 244–267). Cambridge: Cambridge University Press.

World Health Organization (1992). *The ICD-10 classification of mental and behavioural disorder: Diagnostic criteria for research* (10th revision). Geneva: World Health Organization.

Yehuda, R. (1997). Sensitization of the hypothalamic–pituitary–adrenal axis in posttraumatic stress disorder. *Annals of the New York Academy of Sciences, 821,* 57–75.

Yule, W. (1992). Post-traumatic stress disorder in child survivors of shipping disasters: The sinking of the "Jupiter." *Psychotherapy and Psychosomatics, 57,* 200–205.

11 "First Do No Harm:" Emerging Guidelines for the Treatment of Posttraumatic Reactions

JAMES D. HERBERT
Department of Psychology, Drexel University, Philadelphia, USA

MARC SAGEMAN
Department of Psychiatry, University of Pennsylvania, USA

Despite its many problems, publication of the *Diagnostic and Statistical Manual of Mental Disorders* (DSM-III; American Psychiatric Association, 1980) set the fields of psychiatry and clinical psychology on a solid empirical footing and fostered great advances in epidemiology and in the evaluation of various theories and therapies. But this progress came at a cost, which is perhaps most clearly illustrated by the concept of posttraumatic stress disorder (PTSD). The DSM-III heralded a new positivistic paradigm with imbedded unexamined assumptions that neglected important issues, which then progressively faded from memory. Two decades later, these issues have now resurfaced in therapeutic controversies surrounding PTSD.

PTSD is concerned with a ubiquitous human condition, reaction to adversity. Humans have long tried to cope with adversity, using a multitude of strategies. Modern therapies for PTSD date back to the middle of the nineteenth century with the increased involvement of physicians. A historical perspective on these early therapies will shed light on the nature of current controversies and put contemporary therapies for PTSD in context. In this chapter, we present an overview of this history while also highlighting important findings in the recent scientific literature on posttraumatic reactions. By synthesizing key findings from both the historical and recent scientific literatures, we derive four emergent lessons that we believe may prove fruitful in directing future intervention efforts.

Our central thesis is that the history of adversity-linked emotional disorders has been shaped by the history of medical beliefs about these phenomena. An interaction occurs between professional and patient, who translate their common understandings into physical and mental complaints (Shorter, 1992, 1994). The present positivistic paradigm of mental disorders (the belief that suffering has an objective physical basis independent of the assumptions of the observing healer) neglects the influence of this healer–patient dynamic in raising or lowering expectancy of recovery. The hope is that this chapter will restore an appreciation of the therapeutic and iatrogenic influences of the healer.

Posttraumatic Stress Disorder: Issues and Controversies. Edited by G. M. Rosen.
© 2004 John Wiley & Sons, Ltd.   ISBN 0-470-86284-X/0-470-86285-8.

FROM "RAILWAY SPINE" TO PTSD

Consolation for adversity and suffering in general has long been a jealously guarded religious practice (Bowker, 1970). Physicians and other health care providers cared for physical illness, but only priests could legitimately and meaningfully minister to spiritual suffering. A remnant of this division is the fact that grieving is still a predominantly religious concern. Priests focus on the present situation rather than past events in their consolation of worshippers. Emotional problems, including the sequelae of adversity, came to be viewed as legitimate medical concerns once they were conceived as physical or somatic in nature. The notion became popular in military circles, as military success depended on the morale of the troops. The introduction of firearms in the Renaissance caused widespread fear among soldiers, affecting their ability to fight. The sudden death of soldiers exposed to artillery, but without any apparent outside wound, sent panic among the ranks and affected their will to fight. This gave rise to notions of the "wind of the bullet" (Larrey, 1814a, 1814b; Pare, 1585/1840) and nostalgia (Hofer, 1688/1934). The first signs of this often fatal disease was acute demoralization. Military command did not completely accept these medical concepts; military debates about the nature of troop morale—was it a medical problem or a general lack of discipline?—date back to at least the sixteenth century. Imbedded in this debate was of course the issue of the best way of handling morale problems: military discipline for malingerers versus medical care for legitimate sufferers (see also Da Costa, 1871; Keen, Mitchell, & Morehouse, 1864). The debate about the medical legitimacy of adversity-linked emotional distress continues to plague the military field, as evidenced by the recent history of PTSD following the Vietnam War and the more recent debates over Gulf War Syndrome.

The civilian counterpart of these types of distress arose in the context of legal compensation for industrial accidents. Here, the hand of man was all too visible for such suffering to be blamed on Acts of God. Anglo-Saxon Common Law compensated only physical disabilities that resulted in loss of income, and not mental damages per se (*Baker v. Bolton*, 1808; *Lynch v. Knight*, 1861). It was in this legal context that debates emerged on the nature of emotional distress resulting from industrial accidents. For example, Erichsen (1866, 1875/1882) proposed "railway spine," as a new condition of lower extremities characterized by paralysis of the legs and occasional emotional instability. Erichsen believed the condition to be the result of a concussion of the spine during railway accidents, a physical condition, and he became a champion for victims' claims. His prescribed therapy was massage and physical rehabilitation. Beard (1869, 1880) described a similar condition that he believed was the result of exhaustion of nervous energy, "neurasthenia." Beard advocated mild electric treatment to restore a patient's nervous energy, but he also noted the importance of morbid expectations and advocated that psychotherapy raise expectations of recovery (Beard, 1876, 1877). His colleagues soundly rejected his "mental therapeutics" as "humbuggery," not legitimate for medical practice and best left to shamans and priests.

Although the notions of railway spine and neurasthenia were widely disseminated in the popular press of the time, new developments in the nascent field of neurology and the use of epidemiology suggested a more skeptical approach to these phenomena. Surgeons for the railway companies testified that the victims of railway accidents were suffering from hysteria, a generally derogatory and dismissive term. A well-publicized battle of the experts in court threatened to discredit the medical profession and inspired a multitude of articles and some empirical research in an effort to resolve the dispute. Hodges (1881) challenged the notion of concussion of the spine on both anatomical and epidemiological grounds. Page (1883) conducted a large follow-up of 234 patients injured in railway accidents and concluded that the disorder was mental and not spinal. "The pain in *all* movements may be so great . . . that the patient is really afraid to move at all. This well-grounded *fear of moving* may soon assume the importance of an absolute inability to move" (p. 109, italics in original).

Page's conceptualization of the symptoms produced by railway accidents paralleled those elicited by Charcot in his attempt to demonstrate an anatomical basis for hysteria (Charcot, 1877, 1878). Charcot and his disciples argued that hysteria consisted of a pattern of symptoms traced back to brain physiology, thereby making the disorder a legitimate medical condition to be wrestled from the superstitions of the Church (Charcot & Richer, 1887). In a series of lectures in 1885, Charcot (1889) experimentally demonstrated that the symptoms of railway spine could be produced and eliminated through hypnosis. He concluded that railway spine, which he termed "hystero-traumatism," was "hysteria, nothing but hysteria" (Charcot, 1889, p. 221). The recommended treatment was a series of hypnotic and metallotherapeutic sessions, which gradually eliminated the symptoms. Charcot's project of establishing the anatomical basis of hysteria has strong parallels with the present positivistic paradigm, which emphasizes the presumed biological basis of mental illness. Instead of pharmaceutical agents, Charcot used hypnosis as his therapeutic and investigative tool.

A few physicians actually went a step further than Charcot, arguing that posttraumatic symptoms were due to true brain lesions, resulting in permanent and incurable conditions—"traumatic neurosis" was the nineteenth-century sense of the term, a physical disease of the nerves (Oppenheim, 1889). This was contrary to Charcot's theory of a physiological or functional brain lesion that was temporary and reversible. Although the majority of neurologists rejected this more extreme position, they nevertheless preferred Oppenheim's terminology to Charcot's "hystero-traumatism." This terminological preference set the stage for the use of the term neurosis, now understood as a psychological reaction to an event rather than a physical injury to the nerves.

New experimental evidence quickly challenged the medical positivism of Charcot and Oppenheim. Bernheim (1889) and Delboeuf (1890) argued that hysterical symptoms were only the result of suggestion or expectancy, produced by popular culture and/or the examining physician. Charcot's patients were simply the victims of the positivism of expert institutional suggestion. Using care not to suggest any symptoms to their patients, they could not duplicate Charcot's demonstrations of hysterical symptoms. Charcot's critics also argued that hypnosis did not produce a distinctive physical condition but represented, instead, a self-generated subjective mental condition of the patient. In other words, hypnosis was simply self-suggestion, and some healers were better than others at inducing suggestions. The critical issue, therefore, was what the patient believed. The new treatments proposed by Bernheim and Delboeuf, whose goals were to foster healthy self-suggestions, were termed "psychotherapy."

By the end of his life, Charcot had moved from a strictly somatic position to one between mental and physical disorders. Nevertheless, Charcot maintained that the somatic grounding for this condition was necessary for medical legitimacy. While Charcot was alive, his disciples did not pursue the possibility that hysteria, now a fully legitimate medical condition, was psychological in origin. Charcot's death gave two of his students the latitude to explore psychological dimensions of traumatic neurosis through individual case studies. One of these was Janet (e.g., 1889, 1898, 1911, 1928), who used hypnosis for investigation and treatment, but was careful to avoid the inadvertent suggestions that had undermined Charcot's work. He continued Charcot's project and argued that emotional trauma caused numbness of the mind, diminishing the field of consciousness, and allowing hysterical symptoms to exist disaggregated from the rest of consciousness. He used hypnotic suggestion to change the memories and beliefs of his patients, thereby normalizing these psychological processes and producing dramatic improvements.

Charcot's second influential student was Freud (e.g., 1893, 1894, 1895a, 1895b, 1896a, 1896b, 1896c, 1898; Breuer & Freud, 1895), who explored traumatic neurosis but quickly got lost in ever more elaborate theories of repression of childhood seduction. Freud later changed his position and came to view hysterical symptoms as a result of problematic psychosexual development, associated with memories of poorly processed emotional trauma (Freud, 1905). Freud believed that trauma, experienced through a process of catharsis, had to be abreacted in order to heal. Despite public claims of success (Freud, 1896c), Freud privately admitted that psychoanalytic treatment failed in each of his cases (Freud, 1995).

Prince (1891, 1898a–e) extended Janet's theories and attributed traumatic neuroses to the strong aggregation of two mental phenomena outside of consciousness, which he called "association neuroses." Prince advocated his "educational treatment," a multicomponent intervention that resembled many of the strategies associated with modern behavior therapy, and which included psychoeducation, correction of erroneous fixed ideas and faulty habits, suppression of symptoms by electricity and suggestion, good hygiene, and substitution of healthy habits for morbid ones. Studies of large numbers of railway accident victims supported the mental etiology of traumatic neuroses, now conceptualized as a purely psychological disorder (Bevan, 1900; Outten, 1894, 1907).

Babinski, another of Charcot's disciples, was finally the one to draw the ultimate implication of a decade of accumulated evidence by demonstrating the importance of suggestion in the development of hysteria and its traumatic variant. He argued that hysteria was a result of inadvertent iatrogenic suggestions, even non-verbal ones such as paying undue attention to certain parts of the body. The proposed cure was persuasion. He made a plea for his colleagues not to elicit or suggest possible pathological symptoms (Babinski, 1934). Although the weak form of Babinski's argument was generally accepted, some challenged that the sole basis of hysteria was iatrogenic subjective symptoms (e.g., Dejerine & Gaukler, 1913; see also debates at the 1909/1910 Paris Neurological and Psychiatric Societies meetings in Compte-rendu, 1909). Babinski's argument that such disorders could be cured through persuasion gave rise to multiple moralizing persuasive therapies, which self-consciously avoided any hint of harmful suggestion that might give rise to abnormal symptoms. The use of logical questioning somewhat anticipated modern cognitive therapy. Dubois (1905) and Dejerine (Dejerine & Gaukler, 1913), who also advocated isolation to protect patients from suggestions by other patients and sympathetic family members, developed the most popular of the persuasive therapies.

Thus, by the early twentieth century, reactions to trauma had become legitimate topics of medical intervention. At the same time, the study of posttraumatic reactions had come full circle, with a growing appreciation of the psychological origins and psychosocial treatments for adversity-linked emotional distress.

LESSONS FROM THE WORLD WARS

When World War I degenerated into static trench warfare in which soldiers became passive recipients of intense artillery barrages, the emotional toll of these bombardments threatened to disable armies on both sides. The French were the first to react to this danger when, in the fall of 1914, consultant neurologists agreed to implement Babinski's ideas on how to treat emotional casualties. It was deemed most important not to suggest morbid ideas in the minds of victims, who were instead to be treated as experiencing a normal reaction to extreme events. Most of the treatment would take place close to the front so as not to suggest unnecessary seriousness of the situation. After some comfort care, soldiers were returned to the front if improved or evacuated to special army hospitals, where sympathy and firmness were applied. More severe cases were treated with more aggressive forms of persuasion and reeducation. The most severe required drastic measures of persuasion, such as the use of electricity (Southard, 1919). Although these painful treatments were quite effective in eliminating hysterical symptoms, they came close to appearing like torture.

England took longer to develop a strategy to deal with emotional casualties of the war. The second half of 1916 brought about 16,000 cases of "shell-shock," who were evacuated back to England and did not improve with treatment (Shephard, 2000). Charles Myers (1940) took the French line and argued that they should be treated promptly with psychotherapeutic measures in special treatment centers near the front line. The implementation of these recommendations, and the adoption of a new term "not yet diagnosed nervous" to avoid all hint of a diagnostic label, succeeded in dramatically lowering mental casualties in the last two years of the war (Shephard, 2000).

Before the entrance of the United States into the war, the American doctor Salmon visited England and France to learn from their experience and to formulate a strategy for dealing with the anticipated mental casualties from the war. Salmon (1917) recognized that the main goal was the prevention of secondary mental symptoms that could lead to permanent invalidism. He recommended that emotional casualties be treated immediately and close to the front, with personnel familiar with the nature of functional nervous disorders, and with the expectation of rapid improvement. After an initial brief rest, casualties were to be given meaningful work and returned to duty as soon as possible before morbid habits and thoughts could develop (Salmon, 1917). The acronym PIE was later coined to memorialize the three prongs of Proximity, Immediacy, and Expectancy.

In retrospect, relatively absent from the voluminous literature on treatment of mental casualties from the war was any mention of Freudian psychoanalysis (e.g., Bailey, Williams, & Komora, 1929; Brown, 1918; Southard, 1919). Psychodynamic methods (Rivers, 1924) were available only to a few select officers, and were not suited for large numbers of victims. Despite the insignificant contributions of psychoanalysis during World War I, the method won attention in the United States between the two world wars because of promises that caught the popular imagination. American psychoanalysts revived Freud's concept of traumatic hysterical symptoms as undischarged repressed emotional energy converted into physical symptoms, and claimed that they could cure these symptoms through cathartic release of the repressed energy. The claims had two variants. Dunbar (1935) first linked specific personality types with specific chronic illnesses. When these links failed to be detected, Alexander (1950) argued that specific conflicts resulted in specific symptoms. In both cases, therapeutic claims were anecdotal but were asserted with a great deal of authority. The lack of empirical specificity between physical symptoms and personality or conflict characteristics eventually led to the demise of the psychosomatic paradigm. Nevertheless, the influence of the psychoanalytic program continues to be felt today in at least three important ways. First, the idea of cathartic release of repressed emotional energy from past trauma has become central to certain modern therapies for PTSD. Second, the Freudian theory of symptoms arising objectively from childhood trauma and independent of the observer ushered in a new therapeutic positivism, which anticipated current paradigms in psychiatry and clinical psychology. Third, as discussed below, the specific symptoms that define PTSD in the third and subsequent editions of the DSM are largely a product of psychoanalytic theory.

Due to the influence of psychoanalytic theories, the role of suggestion in the generation of adversity-linked distress was all but forgotten, leaving the United States totally unprepared for the traumas of World War II. The first campaigns of the war brought alarming emotional casualty rates, which at one time exceeded the rate of mobilization (Glass, 1973; Glass & Bernucci, 1966). Responding to this situation, old military psychiatric consultants reinstated Salmon's policy of Proximity, Immediacy, and Expectancy with great improvement in the situation (Glass, 1973). With Freudian psychiatrists at the front, Salmon's strategy was slightly modified to include emotional abreaction with hypnosis (Kardiner & Spiegel, 1947), sodium pentothal, sodium amytal (Grinker & Spiegel, 1943; Sargant, 1967), ether, and so on (Glass, 1973; Lewis & Engle, 1954). However, Hanson (1949) argued that abreaction was not necessary as he achieved superior results with sedation alone. This proved to be the crucial element, allowing the exhausted body to recover. Indeed, by 1943, the official terminology reflected this idea, and war neurosis in World War II was officially termed "battle fatigue," reflecting a normal reaction to abnormal circumstances. In terms of psychotherapeutic intervention, quick well-timed directions, persuasion, and counseling, without the customary psychological exploration, were viewed as critical to prevent secondary gain and adoption of a chronic sick role (Spiegel, 2000). Again, the key was to prevent these morbid psychological symptoms from forming (Spiegel, 2000). Shephard (1999) has characterized treatment approaches emerging from the world wars as "Pitiless Psychology," wherein adopted policies where characterized by "deterrence" strategies that included avoidance of diagnostic terms, rest with an expectation of return to battle, and elimination of pensions for war neuroses.

The lessons from the two world wars have now been completely incorporated into military psychiatry and clinical psychology, and battle fatigue (or combat stress under whatever label) has not been a significant *military* problem in the Korean, Vietnam, or Gulf I Wars (Jones, 1995). Much of our present knowledge of treatment for emotional trauma in the acute phase (ten days or less) derives from these military experiences. Although not based on methods of prospective randomized controlled trials, experience from the two world wars was extensive, covering over 100,000 victims. The resulting PIE recommendations suggested recuperative measures with sedation, quickly instituted in the vicinity of a supportive community with strong expectation of recovery and prevention or elimination of potential morbid beliefs. This experience led to an emphasis on expectancies, the "E" in Salmon's PIE strategy (Babinski & Froment, 1918; Salmon, 1917; Southard, 1919; see also Spiegel, 2000), an emphasis consistent with recent findings on expectancy effects in psychotherapy (e.g., Kirsch, 1999; in press) and antidepressant medications (Gaudiano & Herbert, in press). Front-line military clinicians went to great pains to avoid inadvertently suggesting pathological symptoms that might contribute to suffering. On the contrary, they were taught to be optimistic about patient recovery. As discussed below, this emphasis has been largely forgotten in modern approaches to treating posttraumatic reactions.

EMERGENCE OF PTSD IN THE DSM

PTSD is a recent addition to the history of the concept of adversity-linked distress. In 1980, it was accepted as a new diagnostic entity in the DSM III, as much, if not more, as a result of political activism (Scott, 1993) than compelling data. In defining PTSD, the responsible APA Committee adopted Horowitz's (1976) modification of Freud's (1920) repetition compulsion, making as the core characteristic of this new disorder the alternation between numbness and arousal. One implication of this framework was that treatment would consist of Freudian abreaction of the traumatic memory. Forgotten from the putatively "objective" list of symptoms defining PTSD were concerns from the first century of medical study on adversity-linked distress, namely the role of the expert healer in determining both the magnitude and nature of reactions to trauma.

The inclusion of PTSD in the DSM inserted the issue of adversity-linked distress into an ambitious program to put mental disorders on a purely objective basis. This positivist program has led to many advances in the past quarter century. Objective methods such as epidemiological surveys have been able to approximate the incidence and prevalence of disorders. The objectification of psychopathology has opened the door to physiological investigation of specific disorders, carefully defined according to specific criteria. Intensity of suffering has been objectified to evaluate the relative efficacy of treatment methods. The development of treatment manuals has permitted replication of intervention programs across sites. The apparently objective structure of the DSM coincided with pharmaceutical successes in taming previously intractable disorders. The success of treating *some* disorders held the promise of treating *all* disorders with medication.

Ironically, the present situation is similar to that of exactly a century ago, before Babinski warned that much of post-traumatic distress might be the result of well-intentioned suggestion. Further, the modern situation has forgotten lessons of the world wars (Shephard, 1999). Rather than self-consciously avoiding the effects of medical diagnoses, we have given adversity-linked distress its own terminology: posttraumatic stress disorder. Accompanying the creation of this diagnosis, we have widely publicized the symptomatology of PTSD to the point that the concept is increasingly a part of the social consciousness. Third, we pay compensation to military and civilian victims of trauma, often providing grounds for retirement in many professions. These developments are opposite the policies of deterrence that arose from military experiences in the world wars.

The current belief in a universal physical reaction to emotional trauma implies a universality of symptoms that should be invariant both geographically and historically. On the other hand, the importance of the role of suggestion would predict strong variance of these symptoms according to prevailing cultural and expert beliefs. Most cross-cultural epidemiological studies have been of limited value in addressing this question, since they presuppose the universal validity of PTSD, and force indigent peoples to endorse decontextualized statements that might not even make sense. On the other hand, medical anthropologists allow victims to talk spontaneously about their distress. These studies reveal a wide variety of symptoms, and reflect the importance of present conditions over past events in fostering distress (Bracken & Petty, 1998; Kirmayer, Doa, & Smith, 1998; Kleinman, 1995; Kleinman, Das, & Lock, 1997). For instance, the absence of parents or children—a present, enduring, and unchanging condition—is more important than having witnessed their death, a single past event (Summerfield, 1999). Depression may well be a more universal result of war than PTSD in the DSM sense (Bolton, Neugebauer, & Ndogoni, 2002).

Furthermore, historical analyses of symptom expression demonstrate changes even within a relatively short period of time among Western cultures. American and European psychiatry has gone from paralysis (railway spine) to seizure and hemianesthesia (hysterotraumatism), fatigue (neurasthenia), mutism and intractable trembling (shell-shock and *Kriegszitterer*), to purely mental symptoms of "repetition compulsion" (flashbacks, nightmares) accompanied by alternating arousal and numbness. The lack of geographical and temporal universality of symptoms argues for an explanatory framework that does not rely on a universal chronic human response to emotional trauma. A more parsimonious explanation is that the specific nature of posttraumatic reactions reflects prevailing cultural beliefs of the time.

THERAPEUTIC IMPLICATIONS OF THE POSITIVISTIC PARADIGM

The current positivistic neglect of the powerful effects of expectancies in favor of a search for permanent biological markers of trauma and pharmacologic interventions has significant therapeutic implications. The approach tends to lead to a pessimistic sense of therapeutic fatalism, and may result in permanent disability and distress in patients. A recent example is the intensive search for permanent physical damage to the brain from emotional trauma, in a research program reminiscent of Charcot's project. Postulated excessive secretion of glucocorticoids produced by exposure to trauma was assumed to cause damage to the hippocampus, a brain structure necessary for the encoding of new autobiographical memories. Indeed, several studies found apparent hippocampal atrophy in patients with PTSD (e.g., Bremner et al., 1995; Gurvits et al., 1996). However, a recent controlled study showed that twins not exposed to emotional trauma showed the same amount of "shrinkage" in their hippocampus (Gilbertson et al., 2002; see also McNally, 2003b, pp. 136–145, for an extensive discussion of this issue). In other words, small hippocampal volume represented a pre-incident risk factor rather than a permanent brain "scar" from the emotional trauma. Nevertheless, some clinicians and researchers continue to use the metaphor of "brain damage." Perhaps the lack of effectiveness of treatment in "difficult" patients results from the inadvertent messages and iatrogenic suggestions contained in such metaphors, as well as the perversity of prevailing social and economic incentives that reward suffering.

Fortunately, the situation need not be so bleak. An appreciation of the lessons derived from military experiences over the past century, combined with recent data on the effects of cognitive-behavioral interventions for PTSD, suggest considerable grounds for optimism.

THERAPIES IN THE ACUTE PHASE FOLLOWING TRAUMA

As discussed above, most of what we know about the efficacy of interventions targeting the immediate after-effects of trauma derives from the considerable accumulated experience of the two world wars. The only modern study on the benefits of PIE in the military context was supportive of its efficacy (Solomon & Benbenishty, 1986). As symptoms of distress in the immediate aftermath of combat may simply reflect physical and emotional exhaustion, immediate and proximal restorative measures combined with expectancy of improvement may be all that is needed. We hypothesize that immediately after intense emotional trauma the individual may be particularly vulnerable to morbid suggestion, which may interfere with natural resiliency. There is evidence that this early reaction may be a universal physiological reaction to stress (Sapolsky, 1998). Perhaps this physiological state of noradrenergic and steroid arousal renders the individual particularly receptive to suggestion. Therefore, it may be especially important to avoid any inadvertent morbid suggestion that may then contribute to chronic distress and disability.

Based on this military experience, it appears that, at present, the most efficacious treatment in the immediate wake of trauma is to allay the early sleep and anxiety problems with immediate recuperative and restorative measures within a supportive social context, including provision of food, shelter, and, if indicated, sedation. Individuals need to be actively involved in some form of meaningful activity to prevent self-absorption with the trauma. The emergence of somatic symptoms must be immediately addressed, before they become chronic. Especially critical therapeutic elements appear to be assurance that the individual's reaction is normal, and prevention of pathological beliefs about the possibility of permanent damage and disability.

THERAPIES IN THE SUBACUTE PHASE FOLLOWING TRAUMA

There is a nascent research literature on the effects of brief psychotherapy programs provided in the subacute phase following a traumatic experience. Two studies recently evaluated the ability of cognitive behavior therapy (CBT) to prevent the development of chronic and severe posttraumatic symptoms in vulnerable individuals. Foa, Hearst-Ikeda, and Perry (1995) provided a four-session, multi-component CBT program to ten victims of sexual assault, all of whom met diagnostic criteria for PTSD. Most of the women were referred to the study approximately two weeks following the assault (although one participant was referred after 21 days, and another after 60 days). Two months posttreatment the women had significantly less severe PTSD symptoms relative to a matched, untreated group. Bryant, Harvey, Dang, Sackville, and Basten (1998) reported a similar study, in which 24 victims of various civilian traumas, all of whom met DSM-IV criteria for acute stress disorder (ASD), were randomly assigned to receive five sessions of either CBT or supportive counseling within two weeks of the traumatic event. Relative to those who received supportive counseling, participants treated with CBT had fewer symptoms and lower rates of PTSD at both posttreatment and at six months posttrauma. At posttreatment, for example, only 8% of the CBT group met diagnostic criteria for PTSD, compared to 83% of those who received supportive counseling.

There are two noteworthy features of these studies that should be highlighted. First, all participants were reporting clinically significant symptoms and impairment in functioning, as evidenced by their meeting diagnostic criteria for ASD or PTSD. Because most individuals do not develop ASD or PTSD subsequent to trauma (Yehuda & McFarlane, 1995), the participants represented a select sample. Second, treatment was not initiated for several days, and in some cases several weeks, following the traumatic event. Therefore, we do not know what happened in the hours and days immediately following the trauma. The question of whether well-intentioned helping efforts in the immediate aftermath of the event might have contributed to the development of ASD or PTSD in some individuals, as well as the related question of whether early intervention programs focused on acknowledgment and normalization of symptoms along with physical recuperation might have arrested the initial development of the disorders, remains unanswered. Nevertheless, for those who do develop impairing symptoms that last at least two weeks, these studies, and more recent ones (e.g. Bryant, Moulds, Guthrie, & Nixon, 2003, in press; Bryant, Sackville, Dang, Moulds, & Guthrie, 1999) strongly suggest that short-term CBT programs may be effective in arresting the development of chronic symptoms and disability.

THERAPIES OF CHRONIC CONDITIONS

The present therapeutic positivism encourages the use of medication in treating chronic PTSD. Only a few randomized controlled trials have been conducted with medications. Open label studies have been conducted with a variety of medications including the selective serotonin reuptake inhibitors, alternative classes of antidepressants including the monoamine oxidase inhibitors and novel agents, mood stabilizers such as carbamazepine, and benzodiazepines. The general finding from uncontrolled studies is that all of these agents lead to general improvement of symptoms. Given the general comorbidity with other forms of psychopathology (e.g., depression, panic disorder), it is unclear whether drug therapy directly addresses symptoms specific to PTSD, or whether these symptoms improve concurrently with improvement in comorbid conditions. Despite the growing use of drug therapy for PTSD, the FDA has only approved two medications, Sertraline and Paroxetine, for treatment of the condition. Because subject selection eliminates people involved in litigation or receiving pensions for PTSD, it is unclear whether these medications are effective in these two important populations. Moreover, the vast majority of medication studies have failed to comment on any potential harmful effects of treatment.

Aside from medications, a growing literature supports the effectiveness of exposure-based psychotherapeutic treatments for posttraumatic symptoms. Using various techniques, such treatments systematically expose the individual to distressing thoughts, images, and memories associated with the trauma (imaginal exposure), as well as associated environmental stimuli (in vivo exposure), while also encouraging resumption of normal activities. Exposure-based interventions are often conducted under the general rubric of CBT, in which other techniques such as cognitive restructuring and relaxation training are integrated into the program. A number of studies support the efficacy of exposure-based therapies in various traumatized populations, including victims of accidents, natural disasters, and non-sexual assault (Bryant et al., 1999; Devilly & Spence, 1999; Marks, Lovell, Noshirvani, Livanou, & Thrasher, 1998), military combat (Keane, Fairbank, Caddell, & Zimering, 1989), and rape (Foa, Rothbaum, Riggs, & Murdoch, 1991; Foa et al., 1999).

Although the literature on the efficacy of exposure-based treatments is impressive, the precise mechanisms by which exposure operates remain unclear. Learning theorists stress habituation of classically-conditioned fear responses, whereas cognitive theorists stress the modification of internal fear structures. Some data even suggest that the effects of exposure are mediated by expectancies. Southworth and Kirsch (1988) randomly divided agoraphobic patients into two exposure conditions: one defined as "treatment" and the other as "assessment." Subjects in both groups were given ten identical *in vivo* exposure sessions. Subjects provided with therapeutic expectancies demonstrated greater and more rapid improvement than those in the assessment expectancy condition. These results once again highlight the importance of promoting optimistic therapeutic expectancies even when conducting well-established treatments.

A common theme of all exposure-based treatments is the importance of addressing the natural tendency to avoid distressing material. In fact, the newest forms of CBT highlight emotional avoidance as the key feature underlying much psychopathology (e.g., Hayes, Strosahl, & Wilson, 1999). Similarly, recent interest in incorporating principles derived from Buddhism into psychotherapy illustrates an emerging recognition of the importance of directly facing one's pain and the damaging effects of avoidance (Campos, 2002; Kumar, 2002).

The past decade has witnessed the rapid growth of so-called "power" therapies, which claim to offer unprecedented results in terms of both speed and efficacy for the treatment of PTSD and related conditions. By far the most popular of these innovative therapies is Eye Movement Desensitization and Reprocessing (EMDR; Shapiro, 2001). Essentially, EMDR involves imaginal exposure exercises combined with bilateral stimulation, typically achieved by having the patient visually track the therapist's finger back and forth across his or her field of vision. A review of this controversial treatment is beyond the scope of this chapter; interested readers are referred to recent reviews by Davidson and Parker, 2001; Devilly, 2002b; Herbert et al., 2000; and McNally, 1999. These reviews of EMDR have consistently reached two general conclusions: (1) the technique is no more effective than standard exposure-based treatments, and perhaps even less so in the long term; and (2) the distinctive feature of EMDR—eye movements or other bilateral stimulation—is superfluous to its effects. That is, dismantling studies that compare the EMDR program *sans* eye movements to the full EMDR protocol consistently reveal no differences in efficacy. Thus, EMDR's effectiveness appears to lie in the so-called non-specific effects common to most psychotherapies (e.g., positive expectations for improvement) combined with imaginal exposure. There is no need for unnecessary rituals such as inducing eye movements in patients, and no support for unwarranted claims of unique efficacy.

Finally, there is no evidence that traditional forms of psychotherapy such as supportive counseling or psychoanalytic psychotherapy are helpful for patients with chronic post-traumatic symptoms. Many psychoanalytic and "power" therapies share the idea that memories of traumatic experiences are often dissociated or repressed, and must be "recovered" and "worked through" in order to promote healing. Aside from the dubious scientific status of "recovered" traumatic memories (McNally, 2003b), this model can contribute to patient pessimism since there can always be more material to uncover, leading to a potentially never-ending process.

EMERGING GUIDELINES FOR TREATING POSTTRAUMA REACTIONS

The history of efforts to treat the aftermath of trauma, together with recent research findings, suggest four emergent principles or guidelines that are important in the treatment of the sequelae of trauma.

THE IMPORTANCE OF EXPECTANCIES

The first area of concern is the critical role of expectations as related to the nature of PTSD and the likely course of this condition. The current conceptualization of PTSD and its treatment tends to contribute to pessimistic expectations about prognosis, at least without intensive treatment efforts. A diagnosis of PTSD results in the pathologizing of reactions to adversity, and suggests that intervention efforts should focus on emotional abreaction related to the traumatic event. Biological psychiatrists attempt to legitimize PTSD as a "real" medical condition by searching for biological markers associated with the condition. The range of conditions that qualify as traumatic keeps growing (McNally, 2003a), as do estimates of the number of people likely to experience pathological reactions to such traumatic events (e.g., McDonald, 2003). These diagnostic practices and views on adversity conspire to create an expectation among clinicians that even relatively common traumatic events produce quasi-permanent pathological symptoms mediated by scarring of the brain, which result in severe and lasting impairments in functioning. Moreover, the current *Zeitgeist* of therapeutic positivism neglects the therapist's critical role in passing such expectations to the patient. Well-intentioned intervention efforts within this therapeutic framework may contribute to a victim mentality that undercuts coping efforts and contributes to increased suffering. A growing body of evidence supports this concern. For example, certain forms of psychological debriefing in the immediate aftermath of trauma are not only ineffective, but actually lead to increased symptoms (Gist & Devilly, 2002; Kenardy, 2000; Rose, Bisson, & Wessley, 2001; van Emmerik, Kamphuis, Hulsbosch, & Emmelkamp, 2002). Although the mechanism through which such effects occur is unclear, we speculate that an important factor involves the communication of pathological expectations. This is ironic since normalization of reactions to trauma is one of the stated goals of debriefing. Nevertheless, by emphasizing the need for specialized intervention by a mental health professional, the procedure may communicate a contrary message.

The extensive military experience previously discussed suggests an alternative: intervention efforts should seek to normalize reactions to trauma and to foster expectations that the individual will be able to cope effectively without elaborate intervention. This perspective is further supported by recent research finding surprisingly good long-term functioning in most individuals exposed to trauma. For example, in one of the very few long-term prospective studies of a whole cohort born on Kauai, Hawaii, the dominant finding was one of resilience in people exposed to various emotional traumas (Werner & Smith, 1982, 1992). Similarly, in a comprehensive meta-analysis of studies on the long-term effects of childhood sexual abuse, Rind, Tromovitch, and Bauserman (1998) found that the vast majority of victimized individuals went on to lead normal, productive lives, with little evidence of long-term psychological damage. Finally, Schlenger et al. (2002) assessed symptoms of psychological distress in a representative sample of 2,273 Americans following the terrorist attacks on New York City and Washington, DC, on September 11, 2001. By four to eight weeks following the attacks, Schlenger et al. found that "overall distress levels in the country were within normal ranges" (2002, p. 581). Given appropriate expectations and sufficient support, people are surprisingly resilient in the face of adversity.

Also following from past military experience is the need to avoid social and economic incentives that serve to maintain disability. For example, ongoing pensions contingent upon continuing psychiatric impairment serve as powerful incentives for extended disability (McNally, 2003b). Appreciation of this point suggests specific strategies to promote positive expectancies for healing. First, programs that provide monetary com-pensation contingent on ongoing symptoms and/or disability, such as the present pension program of the US Veteran's Administration, should be restructured. As early as the 1890s German physicians recognized the dangers inherent in such programs, which were banned between the two world wars. This is not to suggest that soldiers should not be compen-sated for their disability. Rather, the argument is for rapid provision of a single lump sum payment. Likewise, efforts should be made to speed up litigation that encourages or even depends upon maintenance of symptoms. The litigant has obvious incentives to convince others of his or her suffering. Winning the case often assumes moral characteristics, such that legal victory represents a sort of vindication over the trauma itself (Herman, 1992). Once again, this system stands in the way of recovery.

SHORT-TERM COPING AND CARING FOR BASIC NEEDS

The second principle is the importance of fostering short-term coping in the immediate aftermath of adversity. Effective coping in this phase depends on two general factors: (1) validation of the individual's suffering as real and painful, on the one hand, yet normal and temporary on the other; and (2) short-term interventions aimed at meeting basic bio-logical needs, including shelter, food, and sleep (Gist & Lubin, 1999). It is completely normal to experience a variety of symptoms immediately following an adverse or trau-matic event, and human societies have developed various rituals to acknowledge many of these events (e.g., funerals following the death of a loved one), and to assist with coping in their immediate aftermath (e.g., neighbors helping each other by rebuilding homes or providing food following natural disasters). As much as possible, persons who experience a traumatic event should be encouraged to participate in such rituals in the context of their particular culture. For example, police and firefighters often witness horrific events. The relatively "machismo" culture of these professions emphasizes private support among trusted colleagues rather than emotional discussions with mental health professionals. Clinicians must appreciate the typical ways of acknowledging loss and distress in an indi-vidual's culture, rather than insisting on a monolithic formula inspired by theories of psychotherapy.

PROVISION OF EXPOSURE-BASED THERAPIES WHEN INDICATED

The third principle derived from our review concerns the pernicious effects of avoidance, and its treatment with exposure-based psychotherapies when indicated. Historical military experience and recent studies on the effects of trauma reveal that whereas most individuals return to premorbid levels of functioning relatively quickly without specialized intervention, some develop persistent symptoms and impairments in functioning. Although the expectation of rapid normalization following a recuperative period should be the rule, tracking mechanisms must be established to identify those individuals who may require further intervention.

Devilly (2002a) highlights the importance of providing professional services only to those who actually request them, and who also present clinically significant symptoms. These recommendations stand in contrast to debriefing programs, in which services are typically provided regardless of symptom status and the individual's desire to participate. Although Devilly's recommendations are generally sound, they beg the question of exactly what constitutes "clinically significant symptoms." As discussed above, most persons who experience a traumatic event will experience some short-term distress and impairment in daily activities. It is in this context that the clinician must balance the potential dangers of unnecessary intervention, on the one hand, with the possibility of effective early intervention using state-of-the-art empirically supported methods, on the other. To date, little research outside of debriefing has compared different interventions against no-intervention conditions for persons displaying varying degrees of symptoms in the immediate aftermath of trauma. Although the research by Foa and colleagues, and Bryant and colleagues reviewed above offers some preliminary suggestions, the question of when the magnitude and duration of symptoms warrant psychotherapeutic intervention awaits further research.

When professional intervention is provided, it should of course be based on methods with the most scientific support. As noted above, CBT programs, particularly those incorporating exposure, are currently the most empirically supported treatments for individuals who experience persistent symptoms following a traumatic event. To be maximally effective, such treatments should be conducted within the context of strong expectations for improvement. Furthermore, exposure should be carefully titrated to confront the individual with previously avoided material, while simultaneously encouraging specific activities consistent with healthy functioning.

COGNITIVE REFRAMING

The fourth and final principle to emerge from our review is the importance of cognitive framing that fosters moving forward with life. This entails brief and focused interventions to help an individual move as quickly as possible beyond the trauma as the central focus of one's life, while resuming other roles and activities. The lack of effectiveness of both traditional psychotherapy and psychological debriefing for posttraumatic symptoms may be related in part to perverse social incentives that serve to maintain suffering and disability. Ongoing attention and help from both professionals and even loved ones can backfire, leading to the development of a self-identity centered on being a victim of trauma. In this context, prolonged psychotherapy focused on the trauma should be abandoned, except perhaps in the most treatment refractory cases. Long-term psychotherapy fixes and maintains the trauma as the central focus of the individual's life. Even in refractory cases, the emphasis should be on enhancing coping strategies and decreasing avoidance, rather than on "working through" the trauma. In addition to fostering the enhancement of specific coping skills, the creative psychotherapist can help with a narrative that puts the trauma in perspective. History cannot be undone: one can only accept the past, including distressing or traumatic experiences, and commit to moving forward with a meaningful life.

Cases cited

Baker v. Bolton and Others (1808) 1 Campbell 493, 170 Eng. Rep. 1033 (Nisi Prius).

Lynch v. Knight (1861) 9 H.L.C. 577.

REFERENCES

Alexander, F. (1950). *Psychosomatic medicine: Its principles and applications*. New York: W. W. Norton & Co.

American Psychiatric Association (1980). *Diagnostic and statistical manual of mental disorders* (3rd edn). Washington, DC: Author.

Babinski, J. (1934). *Œuvre scientifique*. Paris: Massons et Cie.

Babinski, J., & Froment, J. (1918). *Hystérie, pithiatisme et troubles nerveux d'ordre réflexes en neurologie de guerre*. Paris: Massons et Cie.

Bailey, P., Williams, F., & Komora, P. (1929). *The Medical Department of the United States Army in the world war*, Vol. X: *Neuropsychiatry*. Washington, DC: US Government Printing Office.

Beard, G. (1869). Neurasthenia, or nervous exhaustion. *Boston Medical and Surgical Journal, 80*, 217–221.

Beard, G. (1876). The influence of mind in the causation and cure of disease: The potency of definite expectation. *Journal of Nervous and Mental Disease, 3*, 429–434.

Beard, G. (1877). Mental therapeutics. *Journal of Nervous and Mental Disease, 4*, 581–582.

Beard, G. (1880). *A practical treatise on nervous exhaustion (neurasthenia): Its symptoms, nature, sequences, treatment* (2nd and rev. edn). New York: William Wood & Co.

Bernheim, H. (1889). *Suggestive therapeutics: A treatise on the nature and uses of hypnotism*. New York: G. P. Putnam's Sons.

Bevan, A. D. (1900). Traumatic neuroses from the standpoint of a surgeon. *Journal of the American Medical Association, 35*, 728–733 (and discussion: 736–739).

Bolton, P., Neugebauer, R., & Ndogoni, L. (2002). Prevalence of depression in rural Rwanda based on symptom and functional criteria. *Journal of Nervous and Mental Diseases, 190*, 631–637.

Bowker, J. (1970). *Problems of suffering in religions of the world*. Cambridge: Cambridge University Press.

Bracken, P., & Petty, C. (1998). *Rethinking the trauma of war*. London: Free Association Books.

Bremner, J. D., Randall, P., Scott, T. M., Bronen, R. A., Seibyl, J. P., Southwick, S. M. et al. (1995). MRI-based measurement of hippocampal volume in patients with combat-related posttraumatic stress disorder. *American Journal of Psychiatry, 152*, 973–981.

Breuer, J., & Freud, S. (1895). *Studies on Hysteria*. In S. Freud (1953–1974). *The standard edition of the complete psychological works of Sigmund Freud*, 24 Vols. London: The Hogarth Press and the Institute of Psycho-analysis. (Henceforth referred to as *Standard Edition*), Vol. 2.

Brown, M. W. (1918). *Neuropsychiatry and the war: A bibliography with abstracts*. New York: War Work Committee, The National Committee for Mental Hygiene.

Bryant, R. A., Harvey, A. G., Dang, S. T., Sackville, T., & Basten, C. (1998). Treatment of acute stress disorder: A comparison of cognitive-behavioral therapy and supportive counseling. *Journal of Consulting and Clinical Psychology, 66*, 862–866.

Bryant, R. A., Moulds, M. L., Guthrie, R. M., & Nixon, R. D. V. (2003). Treating acute stress disorder following mild traumatic brain injury. *American Journal of Psychiatry, 160*, 585–587.

Bryant, R. A., Moulds, M. L., Guthrie, R., & Nixon, R. D. V. (in press). The additive benefit of hypnosis and cognitive behavior therapy in treating acute stress disorder. *Journal of Consulting and Clinical Psychology*.

Bryant, R. A., Sackville, T., Dang, S. T., Moulds, M., & Guthrie, R. (1999). Treating acute stress disorder: An evaluation of cognitive behavior therapy and supportive counseling techniques. *American Journal of Psychiatry, 156*, 1780–1786.

Campos, P. E. (2002). Introduction. *Cognitive and Behavioral Practice, 9*, 38–40.

Charcot, J.-M. (1877). *Lectures on the diseases of the nervous system*. Trans. G. Sigerson. London: The New Sydenham Society.

Charcot, J.-M. (1878). De l'influence des lésions traumatiques sur le développement des phénomènes d'hystérie locale. *Le Progrès Médicale, 6*, 335–338.

Charcot, J.-M. (1889). *Clinical lectures on diseases of the nervous system*, Vol. III. Trans. T. Savill. London: The New Sydenham Society.

Charcot, J.-M., & Richer, P. (1887). *Les démoniaques dans l'art*. Paris: Delaye & Lecrosnier.

Compte-rendu Officiel de la Réunion Annuelle de la Société de Neurologie de Paris et de la Société de Psychatrie de Paris (1909). Du rôle de l'émotion dans la genèse des accidents neuropathiques et psychopathiques. *Revue Neurologique, 17*, 1549–1687.

Da Costa, J. M. (1871). On irritable heart: A clinical study of the form of functional cardiac disorder and its consequences. *American Journal of the Medical Sciences, 121*, 17–52.

Davidson, P. R., & Parker, K. C. H. (2001). Eye movement desensitization and reprocessing (EMDR): A meta-analysis. *Journal of Consulting and Clinical Psychology, 69*, 305–316.

Dejerine, J., & Gauckler, E. (1913). *The psychoneuroses and their treatment by psychotherapy* (2nd English edn). Philadelphia, PA: J. B. Lippincott.

Delboeuf, J. (1890). *Le magnétisme animal*. Paris: Librairie Félix Alcan.

Devilly, G. J. (2002a). Clinical intervention, supportive counseling, and therapeutic methods: A clarification and direction for restorative treatment. *International Review of Victimology, 9*, 1–14.

Devilly, G. J. (2002b). Eye movement desensitization and reprocessing: A chronology of its development and scientific standing. *The Scientific Review of Mental Health Practice, 1*, 113–138.

Devilly, G. J., & Spence, S. H. (1999). The relative efficacy and treatment distress of EMDR and a cognitive behavioral trauma treatment protocol in the amelioration of posttraumatic stress disorder. *Journal of Anxiety Disorders, 13*, 131–157.

Dubois, P. (1905). *The psychic treatment of nervous disorders*. New York: Funk & Wagnalls.

Dunbar, H. F. (1935). *Emotions and bodily changes: A survey of literature on psychosomatic interrelationships, 1910–1933*. New York: Columbia University Press.

Erichsen, J. (1866). *On railway and other injuries of the nervous system*. London: Walton & Maberly.

Erichsen, J. (1875/1882). *On concussion of the spine, nervous shock, and other obscure injuries of the nervous system in their clinical and medico-legal aspects*. New York: William Wood & Co.

Foa, E. B., Dancu, C. V., Hembree, E., Jaycox, L. H., Meadows, E. A., & Street, G. P. (1999). The efficacy of exposure therapy, stress inoculation training and their combination in ameliorating PTSD for female victims of assault. *Journal of Consulting and Clinical Psychology*, *67*, 194–200.

Foa, E. B., Hearst-Ikeda, D., & Perry, K. J. (1995). Evaluation of a brief cognitive-behavioral program for the prevention of chronic PTSD in recent assault victims. *Journal of Consulting and Clinical Psychology*, *63*, 948–955.

Foa, E. B., Rothbaum, B. O., Riggs, D. S., & Murdoch, T. B. (1991). Treatment of posttraumatic stress disorder in rape victims: A comparison between cognitive-behavioral procedures and counseling. *Journal of Consulting and Clinical Psychology*, *59*, 715–723.

Freud, S. (1893). On the psychical mechanism of hysterical phenomena: Preliminary communication. In *Standard Edition*, *3*, 27–39.

Freud, S. (1894). The neuro-psychoses of defense. In *Standard Edition*, *3*, 45–61.

Freud, S. (1895a). Anxiety neurosis. In *Standard Edition*, *3*, 90–115.

Freud, S. (1895b). A reply to criticisms of my paper on anxiety neurosis. In *Standard Edition*, *3*, 123–139.

Freud, S. (1896a). Heredity and the aetiology of the neuroses. In *Standard Edition*, *3*, 143–156.

Freud, S. (1896b). Further remarks on the neuro-psychoses of defense. In *Standard Edition*, *3*, 162–185.

Freud, S. (1896c). The aetiology of hysteria. In *Standard Edition*, *3*, 191–221.

Freud, S. (1898). Sexuality in the aetiology of the neuroses. In *Standard Edition*, *3*, 263–285.

Freud, S. (1905). Three essays on the theory of sexuality. In *Standard Edition*, *7*, 135–243.

Freud, S. (1920). Beyond the pleasure principle. In *Standard Edition*, *18*, 3–143.

Freud, S. (1995). *The complete letters of Sigmund Freud to Wilhelm Fliess, 1887–1904*. Trans. and ed. by J. M. Masson. Cambridge, MA: Harvard University Press.

Gaudiano, B. A., & Herbert, J. D. (in press). Methodological issues in clinical trials of antidepressant medications: Perspectives from psychotherapy outcome research. *Psychotherapy and Psychosomatics*.

Gilbertson, M. W., Shenton, M. E., Ciszewski, A., Kasai, K., Lasko, N. B., Orr, S. P. et al. (2002). Smaller hippocampal volume predicts pathologic vulnerability to psychological trauma. *Nature Neuroscience*, *5*, 1242–1247.

Gist, R., & Devilly, G. J. (2002). Post-trauma debriefing: The road too frequently traveled. *The Lancet*, *360*, 741–742.

Gist, R., & Lubin, B. (1999). *Response to disaster: Psychosocial, community, and ecological approaches*. Philadelphia: Brunner/Mazel.

Glass, A. (1973). *Neuropsychiatry in World War II*, Vol. II: *Overseas theaters*. Washington, DC: Office of the Surgeon General, Department of the Army.

Glass, A., & Bernucci, R. J. (1966). *Neuropsychiatry in World War II*, Vol. I: *Zone of interior*. Washington, DC: Office of the Surgeon General, Department of the Army.

Grinker, R., & Spiegel, J. (1943). *War neuroses in North Africa: The Tunisian campaign (January–May 1943)*. New York: Josiah Macy, Jr, Foundation.

Gurvits, T. V., Shenton, M. E., Hokama, H., Ohta, H., Lasko, N. B., Gilbertson, M. W. et al. (1996). Magnetic resonance imaging study of hippocampal volume in chronic, combat-related posttraumatic stress disorder. *Biological Psychiatry*, *40*, 1091–1099.

Hanson, F. R. (1949). The factor of fatigue in the neuroses of combat. *Bulletin of US Army Medical Department*, *9*, 147–150.

Hayes, S. C., Strosahl, K., & Wilson, K. G. (1999). *Acceptance and commitment therapy: An experiential approach to behavior change*. New York: Guilford Press.

Herbert, J. D., Lilienfeld, S. O., Lohr, J. M., Montgomery, R. W., O'Donohue, W. T., Rosen, G. M. et al. (2000). Science and pseudoscience in the development of eye movement desensitization and reprocessing: Implications for clinical psychology. *Clinical Psychology Review, 20,* 945–971.

Herman, J. (1992). *Trauma and recovery: The aftermath of violence—from domestic abuse to political terror.* New York: Basic Books.

Hodges, R. M. (1881). So-called concussion of the spinal cord. *Boston Medical and Surgical Journal, 104,* 361–365, 386–389.

Hofer, J. (1688/1934). Medical dissertation on nostalgia or homesickness. Trans. C. K. Anspach. *Bulletin of the History of Medicine, 2,* 376–391.

Horowitz, M. (1976). *Stress response syndromes.* New York: Aronson.

Janet, P. (1889/1989). *L'automatisme psychologique: Essai de psychologie expérimentale sur les formes inférieures de l'activité humaine.* Paris: Presses de la Société d'Imprimerie Périodiques et d'Editions.

Janet, P. (1898). *Neuroses et idées fixes* (troisième edn). Paris: Librairie Félix Alcan.

Janet, P. (1911). *L'état mental des hystériques* (deuxième edn). Paris: Librairie Félix Alcan.

Janet, P. (1928). *Les médications psychologiques: Etudes historiques, psychologiques et cliniques sur les méthodes de la psychotherapie* (deuxième edn). Paris: Librairie Félix Alcan.

Jones, F. (1995). Psychiatric lessons of war. In F. Jones, L. Sparacino, V. Wilcox, J. Rothberg, & J. Stokes (eds), *Textbook of military medicine: War psychiatry.* Falls Church, VA: Office of the Surgeon General, United States Army.

Kardiner, A., & Spiegel, H. (1947). *War stress and neurotic illness.* New York: Paul B. Hoeber.

Keane, T. M., Fairbank, J. A., Caddell, J. M., & Zimering, R. T. (1989). Implosive (flooding) therapy reduces symptoms of PTSD in Vietnam combat veterans. *Behavior Therapy, 20,* 245–260.

Keen, W. W., Mitchell, S. W., & Morehouse, G. R. (1864). On malingering, especially in regard to simulation of diseases of the nervous system. *American Journal of the Medical Sciences, 96,* 367–394.

Kenardy, J. (2000). The current status of psychological debriefing: It may do more harm than good. *British Medical Journal, 321,* 1032–1033.

Kirmayer, L., Doa, T. H. T., & Smith, A. (1998). Somatization and psychologization: Understanding cultural idioms of distress. In S. Okpaku (ed.), *Clinical methods in transcultural psychiatry.* Washington, DC: American Psychiatric Press.

Kirsch, I. (1999). *How expectancies shape experience.* Washington, DC: American Psychological Association.

Kirsch, I. (in press). Placebo psychotherapy: Synonym or oxymoron? *Journal of Clinical Psychology.*

Kleinman, A. (1995). *Writing at the margin: Discourse between anthropology and medicine.* Berkeley, CA: University of California Press.

Kleinman, A., Das, V., & Lock, M. (1997). *Social suffering.* Berkeley, CA: University of California Press.

Kumar, S. M. (2002). An introduction to Buddhism for the cognitive-behavioral therapist. *Cognitive and Behavioral Practice, 9,* 40–43.

Larrey, B. D. (1814a). *Memoirs of military surgery and campaigns of the French armies,* Vol. I. Trans. R. W. Hall from the second Paris edition. Baltimore, MD: Joseph Cushing.

Larrey, B. D. (1814b). *Memoirs of military surgery and campaigns of the French armies,* Vol. II. Trans. R. W. Hall from the second Paris edition. Baltimore, MD: Joseph Cushing.

Lewis, N., & Engle, B. (1954). *Wartime psychiatry: A compendium of the international literature.* New York: Oxford University Press.

Marks, I., Lovell, K., Noshirvani, H., Livanou, M., & Thrasher, S. (1998). Treatment of posttraumatic stress disorder by exposure and/or cognitive restructuring. *Archives of General Psychiatry, 55,* 317–325.

McDonald, J. J. (2003). Posttraumatic stress dishonesty. *Employee Relations Law Journal*, *28*, 93–111.

McNally, R. J. (1999). Research on eye movement desensitization and reprocessing (EMDR) as a treatment for PTSD. *PTSD Research Quarterly*, *10*, 1–3.

McNally, R. J. (2003a). Progress and controversy in the study of posttraumatic stress disorder. *Annual Review of Psychology*, *54*, 229–252.

McNally, R. J. (2003b). *Remembering trauma*. Cambridge, MA: Harvard University Press.

Myers, C. S. (1940). *Shell shock in France 1914–1918*. Cambridge: Cambridge University Press.

Oppenheim, H. (1889). *Die traumatische Neurosen nach den in der Nervenklinik der Charité in dem lezten 5 Jahren gesammelten Beobachtungen*. Berlin: Verlag von Hirschwald.

Outten, W. (1894). Railway injuries: Their clinical and medico-legal features. In R. A. Withaus & T. Becker (eds), *Medical jurisprudence: Forensic medicine and toxicology* (pp. 519–698). New York: William Wood & Co.

Outten, W. (1907). Railway injuries: Their clinical and medico-legal features. In R. A. Withaus & T. Becker (eds), *Medical jurisprudence: Forensic medicine and toxicology* (2nd edn) (pp. 763–979). New York: William Wood & Co.

Page, H. (1883). *Injuries of the spine and spinal cord without apparent mechanical lesions and nervous shock, in their surgical and medico-legal aspects*. London: J. & A. Churchill.

Pare, A. (1585/1840). *Œuvres complètes*. Edité par J. Malgaigne. Tome III. Paris: J.-B. Baillière.

Prince, M. (1891). Association neuroses: A study of the pathology of hysterical joint affections, neurasthenia and allied forms of neuro-mimesis. *Journal of Nervous and Mental Disease*, *18*, 257–282.

Prince, M. (1898a). The pathology, genesis and development of some of the more important symptoms in traumatic hysteria and neurasthenia. *Boston Medical and Surgical Journal*, *138*, 511–514, 536–540, 560–562.

Prince, M. (1898b). The educational treatment of neurasthenia and certain hysterical states. *Boston Medical and Surgical Journal*, *139*, 332–337.

Prince, M. (1898c). Habit neuroses as true functional diseases. *Boston Medical and Surgical Journal*, *139*, 589–592.

Prince, M. (1898d). Fear neurosis. *Boston Medical and Surgical Journal*, *139*, 613–616.

Prince, M. (1898e). Hysterical neurasthenia. *Boston Medical and Surgical Journal*, *139*, 652–655.

Rind, B., Tromovitch, P., & Bauserman, R. (1998). A meta-analytic examination of assumed properties of child sexual abuse using college samples. *Psychological Bulletin*, *124*, 22–53.

Rivers, W. H. R. (1924). *Instinct and the Unconscious* (2nd edn). Cambridge: Cambridge University Press.

Rose, S., Bisson, J., & Wessley, S. (2001). Psychological debriefing for preventing post-traumatic stress disorder (PTSD) (Cochrane Review). *The Cochrane Library* (*3*). Oxford: Update Software.

Salmon, T. (1917). *The care and treatment of mental diseases and war neuroses ("shell shock") in the British army*. New York: War Work Committee of the National Committee for Mental Hygiene, Inc.

Sapolsky, R. (1998). *Why zebras don't get ulcers*. New York: W. H. Freeman & Co.

Sargant, W. (1967). *The unquiet mind*. Boston: Little, Brown & Co.

Schlenger, W. E., Caddell, J. M., Ebert, L., Jordan, B. K., Rourke, K. M., Wilson, D. et al. (2002). Psychological reactions to terrorist attacks: Findings from the National Study of Americans' reactions to September 11. *JAMA*, *288*, 581–588.

Scott, W. (1993). *The politics of readjustment: Vietnam veterans since the war*. New York: Aldine de Gruyter.

Shapiro, F. (2001). *Eye movement desensitization and reprocessing: Basic principles, protocols, and procedures* (2nd edn). New York: Guilford Press.

Shephard, B. (1999). "Pitiless psychology:" The role of prevention in British military psychiatry in the Second World War. *History of Psychiatry, 10,* 491–510.

Shephard, B. (2000). *A war of nerves: Soldiers and psychiatrists 1914–1994.* London: Jonathan Cape.

Shorter, E. (1992). *From paralysis to fatigue: A history of psychosomatic illness in the modern era.* New York: Free Press.

Shorter, E. (1994). *From the mind into the body: The cultural origins of psychosomatic symptoms.* New York: Free Press.

Solomon, Z., & Benbenishty, R. (1986). The role of proximity, immediacy, and expectancy in frontline treatment of combat stress reaction among Israelis in the Lebanon War. *American Journal of Psychiatry, 143,* 613–617.

Southard, E. (1919). *Shell-shock and other neuropsychiatric problems presented in five hundred and eighty-nine case histories from the war literature, 1914–1918.* Boston: W. M. Leonard.

Southworth, S., & Kirsch, I. (1988). The role of expectancy in exposure-generated fear reduction in agoraphobia. *Behaviour Research and Therapy, 26,* 113–120.

Spiegel, H. (2000). Silver linings in the clouds of war: A five-decade retrospective. In R. Menninger & J. Nemiah (eds), *American psychiatry after World War II: 1944–1994.* Washington, DC: American Psychiatric Press.

Summerfield, D. (1999). A critique of seven assumptions behind psychological trauma programmes in war-affected areas. *Social Science and Medicine, 48,* 1449–1462.

van Emmerik, A. A. P., Kamphuis, J. H., Hulsbosch, A. M., & Emmelkamp, P. M. G. (2002). Single session debriefing after psychological trauma: A meta-analysis. *The Lancet, 360,* 766–771.

Werner, E., & Smith, R. (1982). *Vulnerable but invincible: A longitudinal study of resilient children and youth.* New York: McGraw-Hill.

Werner, E., & Smith R. (1992). *Overcoming the odds: High risk children from birth to adulthood.* Ithaca, NY: Cornell University Press.

Yehuda R., & McFarlane, A. C. (1995). Conflict between current knowledge about posttraumatic stress disorder and its original conceptual basis. *American Journal of Psychiatry, 152,* 1705–1713.

12 Cross-cultural Perspectives on the Medicalization of Human Suffering

DEREK SUMMERFIELD

Institute of Psychiatry, Kings College, London, UK

The roots of contemporary mental health practice go back to the valorization of reason and science ushered in by the European Enlightenment. The search for scientific accounts of the mind and its disorders started from Cartesian assumptions that the inner world of the mind had a realm separable from the outer world of the body, and was available for study in a comparable way. With this came an assertion of the causal nature of psychological events and a reliance on positivism to guide theory and research on the singular human being as the basic unit of study. Psychiatric science sought to convert human pain, misery, and madness into technical problems which could be understood in standardized ways and which were amenable to technical interventions by experts. Psychiatric knowledge was to be understood as neutral, objective, disinterested, and universally applicable (Bracken, 2002).

Illich (1975) saw the secularization of life in Western society, a waning of the power of tradition and religion, as an essential pre-condition for this philosophical development. Human suffering, until then accepted and explained as the will of God, had become a problem for scientists to solve, an undesirable condition. Thus, a major feature of twentieth-century Western culture—gathering pace in the past two decades—has been how medicalized ways of seeing have displaced religion as the source of everyday explanations for the vicissitudes of life, and of the vocabulary of distress. The impact of violence and other morally shocking types of suffering are now framed through the (morally neutral) sciences of memory and psychology (Hacking, 1996).

There is nothing quintessential about a particular traumatic experience. The attitudes of wider society (which may change over time) shape what individual victims feel has been done to them, and shape the vocabulary they use to describe this, whether or how they seek help, and their expectations of recovery. The more a society sees a traumatic event (rape, for example) as a serious risk to the present or future health and well-being of the victim, the more it may turn out to be. In other words, societally constructed ideas about outcomes, which include the pronouncements of the mental health field, carry a measure of self-fulfilling prophecy.

Posttraumatic Stress Disorder: Issues and Controversies. Edited by G. M. Rosen.
© 2004 John Wiley & Sons, Ltd.   ISBN 0-470-86284-X/0-470-86285-8.

PERSONHOOD AND THE FOCUS ON EMOTION

Underpinning the constructs of, say, "mental health" or "trauma" is the concept of a person. This embodies questions such as how much or what kind of adversity someone can face and still be "normal"; what is reasonable risk; when is acceptance or fatalism appropriate and when a sense of grievance; what is acceptable behaviour at a time of crisis (including how distress should be expressed and help sought), and whether restitution is due. Western citizens now of older age grew up in a society that emphasized stoicism, composure, and self-sufficiency. Broadly speaking, a person, adult or child, was assumed to be reasonably resilient in the face of life's vicissitudes (Summerfield, 2001).

But ideas about personhood do not stand still. When a psychiatrist or psychologist attests that an unpleasant but scarcely extraordinary experience has caused objective damage to a psyche, with effects that may be long-lasting, a rather different version is being posited. In what is in many respects a momentous shift, the concept of a person in contemporary Western culture now emphasizes not resilience but vulnerability (Pupavac, 2001). There is a focus on emotion as the touchstone of personal authenticity, a reflection of the "real" person, but also a cultural preoccupation with emotional trauma and the language of emotional deficit. What has been described as a culture of therapeutics has demonized silence and stoicism, and invites people to see a widening range of experiences in life as inherently risky and liable to make them ill. This involves a blurring between unpleasant but everyday mental states and those suggesting a clinical syndrome. The conflation of distress with "trauma" has acquired a naturalistic feel, part of everyday descriptions of life. Terms like "stress" and "emotional scarring", which like "trauma" started out life as metaphors, have hardened (the concrete thinking of a technocratic age!) into actual entities signalling candidature for professional help. So too "low self-esteem", which has acquired extraordinary explanatory power for problems at any stage of life, and as a point of reference for education policy. One telling pointer to these trends comes from newspaper citations. A search of 300 British newspapers in 1980 did not find a single reference to self-esteem; in 1990 there were 103 references; in 2000, no less than 3,328. Citations of "trauma", "stress", "syndrome", and "counselling" all rose by ten- to twenty-fold during the 1990s (Furedi, 2004).

An expansive mental health industry has in effect promoted the idea that the trials of life represent noxious influences easily able to penetrate the average citizen, not just to hurt but to disable. This is to endorse a much thinner-skinned version of a person than previous generations would have recognized or respected.

People are educated into accepting that experiences like bereavement, receiving the diagnosis of a serious medical condition, marital problems, bullying, sexual harassment (even if only verbal), an overbearing employer, giving birth, and many others (the list grows) may well require professional intervention even when the person concerned has lived a competent life to date and has never demonstrated vulnerability to mental disturbance. Medically authenticated "stress" or "work stress" is now epidemic, the number one cause of sickness absence in Britain (Wainwright & Calnan, 2002). Increasingly the workplace is portrayed as traumatogenic even for those just doing their jobs; ambulancemen, police officers, soldiers, teachers, and others now sue their employers on the grounds that they acquired PTSD on duty, presenting it as an industrial injury akin to pneumoconiosis in coal miners.

It is because medicalized and psychologized thinking is now so embedded in popular constructions of "common sense", and in the aesthetics of expression, that not to automatically use the language of trauma can make it sound as if what someone has gone through is being minimized. Thus, it is instructive to review responses to a disaster a few decades ago in the light of what would have happened today. In 1966, in a tragedy that shook the nation, a coal waste tip engulfed a school in a Welsh village called Aberfan, killing 144 schoolchildren and teachers. There was no counselling and the surviving children resumed school two weeks later so that their minds would be occupied. There were no demands for compensation and the victims' relatives refused to pursue a prosecution against the National Coal Board or Government because this would have seemed vengeful. A child psychologist noted some months later that survivors appeared normal and well-adjusted, and newspaper reports commended the villagers for rehabilitating themselves so admirably with little outside help. After such an incident today, the assumption would be that survivors were inevitably deeply traumatized—some for life—and needing the expert intervention of an army of counsellors and other professionals (Furedi, 2004).

The phenomenal rise of "trauma", both as cultural idiom and as psychiatric category, may be linked to the emergence of this expressive and individualistically minded version of personhood, connected to the hopes and fears of modern life. We live in brittle times, with social vitality dependent on ever-widening patterns of consumption (which include commodified "health"), requiring identification of new needs and desires. A nation is judged as if it is primarily an economy rather than a society and the lexicon of commerce increasingly regulates social relationships and responsibilities. The gap widens between winners and losers. On the one hand, the "modernization" of society has seen a loss in the binding properties of its fabric, and, on the other, there has been a promotion of personal rights and the language of entitlement. This climate fosters a sense of personal injury and grievance, and a demand for restitution, in situations that would formerly have been experienced as bad luck and the ordinary trials of life.

It has been argued that the concept of honour (which is oriented outwards towards social roles and community) has given way to the concept of dignity (oriented inwards towards an autonomous self). There has been a withering of our belief in the comfort of religion or other transcending meaning systems, including politics. Has this eroded our belief in a coherent and ordered world, and left us feeling on our own? If so, unpleasant experiences, which we now label "traumatic", may be more likely to leave us shaken and doubting. PTSD seems a tailor-made diagnosis for an age of disenchantment and disillusionment (Bracken, 2002; Summerfield, 2001).

MEDICALIZATION AND IATROGENESIS

The medicalization of life denotes the growth of the use of ideas about illness and disease to make sense of everyday experience. As medicalization has grown, so too have the number and authority of its practitioners. In Britain, the total number of consultant psychiatrists has doubled in 22 years, despite the closure of many of the old asylum-based psychiatric institutions. There has been a 50% increase in the past five years in the number of clinical psychology staff, and a tripling in ten years in membership of the British Association for Counselling (Appleby, 2003). In 1962 the USA spent 4.5% of its gross national product on health; 8.4% of GNP in 1975; and it is projected to spend 17% of GNP on health care by 2011. In Britain more than 2.7 million people of working age (7.5% of the working age population) are now claiming doctor-attested disability benefits, more than treble the number in the 1970s. Can the population really have grown so much more unhealthy? What has been described as a steadily mounting epidemic of low back pain and resultant work incapacity seems to reflect a greater willingness by people to report pain and to see themselves as incapacitated and requiring sickness certificates. Rising unemployment rates and changes in social security provision have doubtless also played a part (Croft, 2000).

Medicalization is also driven by an emphasis on instrumental reasoning: a particular experience is judged as a function of the quantifiable effects held to flow from it. In relation to claims making, it is not enough to have distress, one must have disability—a medical category. In Britain the number of prescriptions written for anti-depressants rose from 9 million to 21 million during the 1990s. Can anyone seriously argue that this merely reflects better recognition of a true epidemic of depression? (Double, 2002). The rise is even greater in the United States—a near doubling in the past five years—mirroring the production and marketing of SSRI anti-depressants. The first edition of the *Diagnostic and Statistical Manual of Mental Disorders* (DSM) of the American Psychiatric Association, in 1952, carried 104 psychiatric categories; the fourth edition in 1994 had 357. In the fourth edition the stressor criterion for PTSD was widened so that second-hand shocks now counted and many more people were diagnosable. It has been argued that as many as 1 in 4 of the US population could at any time be diagnosed with one or another DSM category. Is this remotely meaningful? DSM categories are the products of vested interests, a major use being communication with insurers and other third parties. The American Psychiatric Association reportedly makes US$60 million per year from selling the DSM.

There is persuasive evidence that the pharmaceutical industry is in a position to set research agendas and to promote expensive treatments for non-diseases. Industry strategies include casting ordinary processes as medical problems (e.g., baldness), casting mild functional symptoms as portents of serious disease (e.g., irritable bowel syndrome), casting personal or social problems as medical ones (e.g., social phobia), casting risk factors as actual diseases (e.g., osteoporosis), and using misleading disease prevalence estimates to maximize the size of a medical problem (e.g., erectile dysfunction; Moynihan, Heath, & Henry, 2002). Some commentators see the pharmaceutical industry as having influential segments of the psychiatric profession virtually in its pocket. For example, there is a clear association between sponsorship and reported findings in research on anti-depressants. Published studies sponsored by the manufacturers of SSRIs favoured these medications over other (and much cheaper) anti-depressants significantly more often than did studies sponsored in other ways (Baker, Johnsrud, Crismon, Rosenheck, & Woods, 2003).

How much extra "health " or "mental health" have these endeavours produced? Are there as yet uncounted costs? Clinical iatrogenesis is the injury done by ineffective or toxic treatments: a 1999 US Institute of Medicine report estimated that about 100,000 Americans a year died from preventable errors in hospitals. But this is not all. In a brilliant and prophetic analysis, Illich (1975) described the pervasive but largely unrecognized consequences of what he called social and cultural iatrogenesis. Health care consumed an ever-growing proportion of the national budget, and with unclear benefits for patients or society as a whole. Above all, Illich pointed to the implications of a longer-term destruction of time-honoured ways of dealing with pain, sickness, and death. Can we observe this today?

The more the mental health field promotes its technologies as necessary interventions in almost every area of life, and the more people pick up that they are not expected to cope through their own resources and networks, then the more that socioculturally constructed ways of enduring and coping may wither. As more resources are provided for mental health services, more are perceived to be needed—an apparently circular process. Has the mental health industry become as much a part of the problem as of the solution?

WESTERN MENTAL HEALTH: UNIVERSALLY VALID KNOWLEDGE?

The globalization of the Western order continues apparently irresistibly, accompanying the huge and widening disparities of power between the dominant institutions of the West, and those of the rest of the planet. Western ideas about suffering and its antidotes have been globalizing too: what claim to universal validity do they have?

In its development, Western psychiatry has tended to naturalize its own cultural distinctions, objectify them through empirical data, and then reify them as universal natural science categories (Littlewood, 1990). This is an achievement but it is not a discovery. There are many true descriptions of the world and what might be called psychological knowledge is the product of a particular culture at a particular point in its history. Western psychiatry is merely one among many ethnomedical systems. Thus, it is depressing that, to give but one example, an editorial in a major psychiatric journal can still maintain that "there is no solid evidence for a real difference in the prevalence of common psychiatric disorders across cultures" (Cheng, 2001). The socioculturally determined understandings that people bring to bear on their active appraisal of their predicament, and on their expressions of distress and help-seeking, are here being regarded as mere packaging. The (Western) psychiatrist is to see through this packaging to the psychopathology within, which he knows to be universal and the "real" problem.

All of psychiatry is culture-bounded, not just a few exotic syndromes in the DSM or the *International Classification of Diseases* (ICD). Organic brain disorders might seem most obviously to refute this statement—because of their biological basis—but even they will present in ways shaped by local lifeworlds and forms of knowledge. A psychiatric diagnosis is generally handled by doctors, by the medico-legal system, and indeed by wider society, as if it were synonymous with a disease—but it is not. The ICD and DSM categorize phenomenological constellations but this is not synonymous with scientific validation. A diagnosis can be seen as a point of reference, a way of seeing, a style of reasoning, and—in compensation suits and other claims-making—a means of persuasion. A diagnosis carries no deeper understanding of what is really wrong. Hacking (1996) commends the nineteenth-century philosopher William Whewell on this point. Whewell wrote that it was easy to generate true statements about a dog, but who could define a dog?

These classifications are also not atheoretical and value-free; for example, they contain ontological notions of what constitutes a real disorder, epistemological notions of what counts as scientific evidence, and methodological notions about how research should be conducted. They are contemporary cultural documents par excellence (Mezzich et al., 1999).

The psychiatric literature on the application of quantitative research methods to non-

Western settings largely founders on the rocks of what Kleinman (1987) called a "category fallacy". The fallacy is the assumption that because phenomena can be identified in differing social settings, they mean the same thing in those settings. The histories of terms like "depression" or "posttraumatic stress disorder", and the particular meanings and responses they mobilize in contemporary Western culture, are simply not straightforwardly reproduced elsewhere. There is no equivalent to these terms in many cultures (Pilgrim & Bentall, 1999). The history of depression reveals the gradual incorporation of the Western cultural vocabulary of guilt, energy, fatigue, and stress (Jadhav, 1996). Thus, depression or PTSD, as they stand, simply cannot be universally valid diagnostic categories. Yet the World Health Organization (1996) is claiming that "depression" is a world-wide epidemic that within twenty years will be second only to cardiovascular disease as the world's most debilitating disease. This is a serious distortion, which could serve to deflect attention away from what millions of people might cite as the basis of their misery, like poverty and lack of rights. The UN Food and Agriculture Organization says that the number of chronically hungry people in the world is rising by 5 million a year. Labelling these individuals as depressed would produce one clear-cut beneficiary, the pharmaceutical industry, with its vested interest in the biologization of the human predicament.

Many ethnomedical systems have taxonomies that range across the physical, supernatural, and moral realms, and do not conceive of illness as situated in body or mind alone. The body is seen to be susceptible to the actions and wishes of ancestors, and to spirits. Distress is commonly understood and expressed in terms of disruptions to the social and moral order, while internal emotional factors are not seen as able to cause illness (Kirmayer, 1989). The Western individual is seen as disengaged and free to the extent of being fully distinguishable from the natural and social worlds. If a patient's cultural background attributes more importance to causation than to the presenting clinical features, DSM categories, which work the other way, may violate that person's state of mind (Eisenbruch, 1992).

Higginbotham and Marsella (1988) studied the impact of Western psychiatry in Southeast Asia, noting a number of unanticipated and indirect effects: professional elitism, institution-bound responses to distress, and undermining of local traditional healing systems. Psychiatric universalism risks being imperialistic, reminding us of the colonial era when what was presented to indigenous peoples was that there were different types of knowledge, and theirs was second-rate. Sociocultural phenomena were framed in European terms and the responsible pursuit of traditional values was regarded as evidence of backwardness. Said (1993) noted that a salient trait of modern imperialism was that it claimed to be an education movement, setting out consciously to modernize, develop, instruct, and civilize. This echoes the earlier writings of such as Césaire and Fanon, who commented on the surreptitious incorporation of the ideologies of colonial dependence and racial inferiority into modern psychological discourse.

PERSONHOOD AND EMOTION IN NON-WESTERN WORLDS

My intention is not to cast "culture" as a monolithic bloc, nor to efface the differences between citizens of a particular society that relate to social or economic status, education, and urbanization. However, the dissemination of Western mental health practice introduces elements that are not mere surface phenomena but core components of Western culture: a theory of human nature and development, a definition of personhood but also of "childhood" and "family", a secular source of moral authority, a sense of time and a theory of memory. As already noted, any discussion about mental health or ill-health cannot but invoke the concept of a person current in that cultural setting. Consider the emphasis Western personhood gives to a deep, hidden, private self, and to emotion and vulnerability as described above. How congruent is this with non-Western definitions, in which the self is largely interpersonal and consensual, more orientated to key roles and relationships than to what is deeply private? Social connectedness, not personal depth, is the measure of the moral value of the self. In many cultures the harmony of the family or group matters more than the autonomy of the individual, who is not conceived of as a free-standing unit. Indeed, many African languages have no word for the self. Thus, containment of emotion and adaptation to social circumstances are viewed as signs of maturity.

Cultural worlds may differ so dramatically that translation of emotional terms means more than finding semantic equivalents. Describing how it feels to be aggrieved or melancholy in another society leads directly into an analysis of a radically different way of being a person (Kleinman & Good, 1985). A culture that does not embody a dualistic view of individual and "society" will have little time for the very category of "psychological states", and for the distinction between "emotion" and "cognition" (Ingleby, 1989).

As an example, for Somalis, emotional experience and expression are understood (by the individual concerned and by those around him or her) primarily in terms of what they say about sociopolitical, not intrapsychic, processes. This does not mean that an individual psychological dimension is not recognized, merely that the organizing framework is collective and sociopolitical, rather than medicopsychological. Expression of distress, particularly anger, is a communication about a moral injury, an appeal for validation and practical action (Zarowsky, 2000).

THE GLOBILIZATION OF "TRAUMA"

The most spectacular facet of the globalization of Western trends towards the medicalization of distress has been the "trauma" discourse. Over the past 15 or so years this has reshaped the way the experience of war, atrocity, or natural disaster anywhere has been seen (by the West), and responded to as a health or humanitarian issue. Expansive claims by Western health professionals—many working as consultants to UNICEF, WHO, and other major agencies—have promoted the idea of war as a sort of public mental health emergency, and of "posttraumatic stress" as a "hidden epidemic". "Trauma" has become a point of reference in Western countries for the appraisal and reception of asylum-seekers from war zones.

I have critiqued at length elsewhere the assumptions underpinning the globalization of "trauma" as a supposedly valid and relevant framework for capturing and addressing human response to extreme events (Summerfield, 1999a). Put briefly, these assumptions are that the experience of war routinely generates not just suffering or misery but "posttraumatic stress", a pathological condition affecting large numbers of those exposed and who need attention for this; there is basically a universal human response to such events, captured by the PTSD model; Western mental health technologies are universally valid, and victims do better if they "work through" their experiences; timely intervention can avert later mental disorders, violence, and wars. All these assumptions are highly problematic and the last one is preposterous.

In this new language, the emotional reactions of people affected by war are perceived as harmful to themselves ("traumatized") or as potentially dangerous to others ("brutalized"). War-affected children are also portrayed as "brutalized", and thus likely to grow up and start new "cycles of violence" in vengeance. This paints a picture of damaged psychologies and moral norms, of diminished humanity. UNICEF (1996) has stated that "time does not heal trauma" for millions of such children, who are often described as a "lost generation". The medical literature is replete with similarly sweeping statements which lack validity, and are pathologizing and stigmatizing. They seem a form of medical imperialism. Moreover, these subjects have not given consent for their mental lives to be objectified (typically from afar) and characterized as unhealthy: this seems an ethical question (Summerfield, 2002).

Studies of non-Western asylum-seekers in flight from violent conflict, seen in clinics in Western countries, have been highly prominent in the cross-cultural mental health literature in recent years. Yet, it is in clinical work that the lack of coherence and generalizability of the PTSD model is apparent at close range. PTSD criteria distinguish poorly between the physiology of normal distress and the physiology of pathological distress, so that over-diagnosis is easy (Summerfield, 2001). To give as an example the work of a much published authority in the field, Mollica et al. (1998) compared a group of Vietnamese refugees with a history of torture, newly arrived in the United States, with a control group of non-tortured Vietnamese refugees recruited in the local community. Fully 90% of the tortured group satisfied criteria for PTSD, but so did 79% of the control group.

Further, questions of validity and explanatory power came through strongly in a personal series of over 800 asylum-seekers or refugees, most with a history of torture or other forms of political persecution, whom I assessed as principal psychiatrist at the Medical Foundation for the Care of Victims of Torture, London, during the 1990s (and in previous research on war-wounded ex-soldiers and peasant survivors of atrocities in Nicaragua). Using PTSD checklists, a considerable proportion of these might have been diagnosable as "cases", but this was belied by their capacity to function. While there were a few whose despondency had dulled them to their immediate situation (and who merited more attention), the vast majority were as active and effective as opportunities in their new environments allowed. They were upset but not ill.

To understand this better we need a nuanced view of the construction of psychiatric facts in the clinic. First, what a patient brings to a medical setting is what he sees as appropriate to bring to such a setting. This generally means bringing symptoms. What he presents may not be what is troubling him most, or indeed at all, but it allows engagement with the doctor and what may flow from this. This is especially relevant to the asylum-seeker, for whom medical services are an early point of reference. This leads on to the demand characteristics of the medical interview itself. The asylum-seeker may have picked up that doctors are interested in the psychology of those who have survived war and other disasters, and that particular questions tapping psychology are asked regularly. He wants to be interesting and intelligible to the doctor, for he hopes for an ally or advocate with authority at a time when his social situation is precarious. Thus, the questions put to him become important precisely because it was the doctor who asked them. There would be additional medicalizing impetus if the asylum-seeker understood that his answers to the doctor's questions could form the basis of a psychiatric report in support of his asylum claim. The interview might elicit, say, low mood, disturbed sleep, or jumpiness, and in some cases a request for sedatives or sleeping tablets. But for many others, these features would be understandable by-products of their situation, and not what they were attending to. If we define a symptom as basically something a patient complains of, these were not symptoms but epiphenomena—incidental reactions to a stressful situation.

Thus, the process by which the answers to a doctor's questions are rendered up as "symptoms" (potential contributors to a psychiatric diagnosis) is as much the product of the mindset of the doctor as of the patient. It does not follow that the asylum-seeker's atti-tude to or handling of his mood, sleep or edginess when at home, or at the refugee com-munity centre, would be the same as it is formulated in the clinic. In a psychiatric interview the doctor is looking for patterns, and especially if he is primed by the assumption that survivors of traumatic events generally carry psychological effects (a cultural assumption, as outlined above), he is likely to find what he is looking for. For my part, I found that a diagnosis of PTSD in particular was poorly predictive of an individual's capacity to pay the psychological costs of what had happened, to function well despite hardship, and to keep going; nor was the diagnosis a reliable indicator of a need for psychological treatment.

Medicalized constructions of the experience of war posit an unduly mechanistic view of human experience, one that suggests that the traumatic effects of war are to be found inside a person (between his or her ears), and that a person recovers as if from an illness. In fact, there is a singular dearth of data suggesting that mental health morbidity is higher in populations exposed to war or other complex emergencies than in those not exposed. One interesting example is Northern Ireland, since it is one war zone where comprehen-sive health records covering the past 30 years of civil conflict are available. During this period there has been no evidence of significant impact on referral rates to mental health services (Loughrey, 1997). Indeed, several million civilians in Europe were exposed to events during World War II which would have rendered them liable to "post-traumatic stress" by the standards applied in Bosnia, Rwanda, and other conflict zones, let alone Western civil society in recent years. So where did this veritable epidemic go?

We must realize the limitations of a discourse in which the effects of collective violence and social upheaval are represented as individual illness and vulnerability. The medical-ization of distress entails a missed identification between the individual and the social world, and a tendency to transform the social into the biological (the mere machinery of the body). The objectification of understandable distress or misery as a pathological entity, a technical problem to which short-term technical solutions like counselling apply, is a serious distortion. This is not, of course, to play down what people may suffer, but to emphasize that suffering is not psychopathology. For the vast majority, "posttraumatic stress" is a pseudocondition.

The fundamental relativity of human experience, even in extreme conditions, and the primacy of the subjective appraisal and social context, mean that there can be no such thing as a universal trauma response. Human responses to aversive experience are not anal-ogous to physical trauma: people do not passively register the impact of external forces (unlike, say, a leg hit by a bullet); rather, they engage with them in an active and problem-solving way. Suffering arises from, and is resolved in, a social context: shaped by the meanings and understandings applied to events, evolving as the context evolves. It is subjective appraisal that determines what a stressful event means: one man's trauma is another's heroic sacrifice.

Health professionals have a duty to recognize distress, but also to attend to what the people carrying this distress want to signal by it. War-affected populations, for example, are largely directing their attention not inwards, to their mental processes, but outwards to their devastated social world. They know that they will stand or fall by what they do in and about that world. For them the key question is not "How am I feeling?" but "What can I do to bolster my situation?" The refugee literature highlights the pivotal role of family and social networks in exile. Among Iraqi asylum-seekers in London, current poor social support was more closely related to low mood than was a history of torture (Gorst-Unsworth & Goldenberg, 1998). In the longer term, it is socioeconomic and sociocultural factors that are major determinants of outcomes. Is the suffering of the world's hungry and undernourished children less of a "trauma" than that occasioned by bombs and bullets (Summerfield, 1999b)?

Medicotherapeutic ways of seeing assume moral and political neutrality. But all suffering evokes questions of values and morality, and the experience of war and social upheaval is bound up with notions of responsibility, accountability, and restitution. Medicotherapeutic interventions will not work when a morally blind technical fix is besides the point. There is no evidence that victims of such events, even in Western cultural contexts, do better if they undergo counselling to emotionally ventilate their experiences (Wessely, Rose, & Bisson, 1998). Further, the very idea of Western talk therapy or counselling, with its focus on detached introspection, is alien in most non-Western cultures.

In, perhaps, the first ethnographic account of its kind, Argenti-Pillen (2003) queries whether imported Western trauma work could contribute to a destabilization of culturally specific forms of post-war organization in southern Sri Lanka. She describes a linguistic discourse of "caution" that engendered a particular flow of knowledge about past violence, and which acted to curtail cycles of violence. "Cautious" talk used euphemism, indirect and imprecise speech, and minimized accusation. A folk ailment like "terrified heart" was only ambiguously attributed to human agency, and was treated by ritual cleansing ceremonies. Following the arrival of 30 non-government mental health organizations promoting Western-type counselling, "terrified heart" was liable to be recast as a war-related illness ("trauma"), with implications for a much less "cautious" understanding of events and their legacy. Elsewhere, the notion that "traumatic stress" causes psychological disruption may be invalid in cultures that emphasize fate, determinism, and spiritual influences. We need more ethnographic work of this kind in other parts of the world (like Rwanda) where imported trauma programmes and counselling have had high profile.

THE PROBLEM OF HUMAN PAIN AND "RECOVERY"

Human pain and suffering, and how it was to be understood, have always been central to the relationship between human consciousness and the material world. In the twentieth century, orthodox psychological science sought to conceptualize this conundrum as ulti-mately residing in the way the brain was wired and memories stored. The meaningful nature of reality was seen in cognitivist terms, as something arising from programmes or schemas running in individual minds. It is questionable how much such systems can capture universal truths about distress and suffering when they largely ignore the socio-cultural and situational forces which shape the active appraisal a particular subject brings to bear on what has happened. There is an ethical dimension to this (Bracken & Thomas, 2001).

There are dysfunctionally distressed and mad people in every society, as well as local forms of understanding, accommodation, and healing. To assert this is not to assume that such forms are at all times humane and effective, or that "culture" can always cope. There may be aspects of Western psychiatry or psychology, including medication, which are useful in some situations. The problem is the overall thrust that comes from being at the heart of the one globalizing culture. It is as if one version of human nature is being pre-sented as definitive, and one set of ideas about pain and suffering is being applied. These are ideas that go to the heart of the human condition, making it ever more difficult to prop-erly acknowledge difference and diversity (and not just pay lip service to it). A wiser and truer definition of "psychology" would be as the expression of a background intelligibil-ity comprising a system of thought and practice based on the day-to-day behaviour and points of view of the members of a particular group or people. There is no one definitive psychology.

It would carry us rather further to see meaning not as software in an individual mind, but as something generated through practical engagement with the world—through a lived life with all its complexity and capacity for multiple interpretations. These influences are not merely secondary, as Western psychological thinking asserts, but the very stuff of this background intelligibility against which distressing experience can be set (Bracken, 2002).

Psychiatry and psychology cannot use their methodologies and ways of thinking to critique their methodologies and ways of thinking. To get "outside" the problem requires a much broader sweep. Human pain is a slippery thing, sitting in sociomoral and philo-sophical domains which themselves are variable and slippery. Nowhere, no more in Western societies than elsewhere, is it straightforwardly subject to technical interventions in isolation from other aspects of life. This point seems ever more resonant at a time when, as outlined earlier, Western culture has moved towards a view of the human condition that is defined by vulnerability, with the professionalization of everyday life and "emotion" as its currency. Ironically, in such an environment it may be harder to reconcile to the losses and pain, and to life as a vale of tears, which is part of our common lot.

Health professionals should beware the limitations of looking at the world through a medicotherapeutic prism. The idea that "recovery" from an aversive experience (or "pro-cessing" or "healing" or "closure") is a discrete thing is again a legacy of the Cartesian assumptions that launched psychiatry and psychology—that the mental world is separable from the material world and can be instrumentalized. In the real world, "recovery" is even more slippery than "suffering", and as subject to sociomoral and philosophical considera-tions. Its setting is people's lives rather than their psychologies. It is an unspectacular and even banal matter, grounded in resumption of the ordinary rhythms of everyday life—

family, sociocultural, religious, economic—which make the world intelligible. Perhaps the imperatives of life leave little choice, that this is the lesson of history (Summerfield, 2002).

Naturally this is not to say that simply getting on with life ablates the suffering that has come from one experience or another. What people may carry in their hearts, or indeed take to their graves, is another matter; indeed, some would see it as morally important after terrible events not to "recover" or "come to terms with it". Such trajectories are not typically visible from the clinic: tracking them is the work of historians, sociologists, journalists, poets, religious and political leaders, and via the output of the actors themselves.

To conclude, the Western mental health field can seem to propagate a rather misanthropic view of mankind—as more or less damaged goods—and to neglect the sensibilities essential for more humanistic perspectives. The alternative, shaped by broader visions, is to see human nature—for all its inconsistency and ambiguity—as basically sturdy and resourceful, and as tending towards intelligent and progressive responses to the trials of life.

REFERENCES

Appleby, L. (2003). So, are things getting better? *Psychiatric Bulletin, 27,* 441–442.

Argenti-Pillen, A. (2003). *Masking terror: How women contain violence in Southern Sri Lanka.* Philadelphia, PA: University of Pennsylvania Press.

Baker, C., Johnsrud, M., Crismon, M., Rosenheck, R., & Woods, S. (2003). Quantitative analysis of sponsorship bias in economic studies of anti-depressants. *British Journal of Psychiatry, 183,* 498–506.

Bracken, P. (2002). *Trauma: Culture, meaning and philosophy.* London: Whurr.

Bracken, P., & Thomas, P. (2001). Post-psychiatry: A new direction for mental health. *British Medical Journal, 322,* 724–727.

Cheng, A. (2001). Case definition and culture: Are people all the same? *British Journal of Psychiatry, 179,* 1–3.

Croft, P. (2000). Is life becoming more of a pain? *British Medical Journal, 320,* 1552–1553.

Double, D. (2002). The limits of psychiatry. *British Medical Journal, 324,* 900–904.

Eisenbruch, M. (1992). Towards a culturally sensitive DSM: Cultural bereavement in Cambodian refugees and the traditional healer as taxonomist. *Journal of Nervous and Mental Disease, 180,* 8–10.

Furedi, F. (2004). *Therapy culture: Cultivating vulnerability in an uncertain age.* London: Routledge.

Gorst-Unsworth, C., & Goldenberg, E. (1998). Psychological sequelae of torture and organised violence suffered by refugees from Iraq: Trauma-related factors compared to social factors in exile. *British Journal of Psychiatry, 172,* 90–94.

Hacking, I. (1996). *Rewriting the soul: Multiple personality and the sciences of memory.* Princeton, NJ: Princeton University Press.

Higginbotham, N., & Marsella, A. (1988). International consultation and the homogenisation of psychiatry in Southeast Asia. *Social Science and Medicine, 27,* 553–561.

Illich, I. (1975). *Limits to medicine: Medical nemesis, the expropriation of health.* London: Marion Boyars.

Ingleby, D. (1989). Critical psychology in relation to political repression and violence. *International Journal of Mental Health, 17,* 16–28.

Jadhav, S. (1996). Cultural origins of Western depression. *International Journal of Social Psychiatry, 42,* 269–286.

Kirmayer, L. (1989). Cultural variations in the response to psychiatric disorders and mental distress. *Social Science and Medicine, 29,* 327–329.

Kleinman, A. (1987). Anthropology and psychiatry: The role of culture in cross-cultural research on illness. *British Journal of Psychiatry, 151,* 447–454.

Kleinman, A., & Good, B. (eds) (1985). *Culture and depression: Studies in the anthropology and cross-cultural psychiatry of affect and disorder.* Berkeley, CA: University of California Press.

Littlewood, R. (1990). From categories to contexts: A decade of the "new cross-cultural psychiatry." *British Journal of Psychiatry, 156,* 308–327.

Loughrey, G. (1997). Civil violence. In D. Black, M. Ewman, J. Harris-Hendriks, & G. Mezey (eds), *Psychological trauma: A developmental approach* (pp. 156–160). London: Gaskell.

Mezzich, J., Kirmayer, L., Kleinman, A., Fabrega, H., Parron, D., & Good, B. (1999). The place of culture in DSM IV. *Journal of Nervous and Mental Disease, 187,* 457–464.

Mollica, R., McInnes, M., Pham, T., Fawzi, M., Murphy, E., & Lin, L. (1998). The dose-effect relationships between torture and psychiatric symptoms in Vietnamese ex-political detainees and a comparison group. *Journal of Nervous and Mental Disease, 186,* 543–553.

Moynihan, R., Heath, I., & Henry, D. (2002). Selling sickness: The pharmacological industry and disease mongering. *British Medical Journal, 324,* 886–891.

Pilgrim, D., & Bentall, R. (1999). The medicalisation of misery: A critical realist analysis of the concept of depression. *Journal of Mental Health, 8,* 261–274.

Pupavac, V. (2001). Therapeutic governance: Psychosocial intervention and trauma risk management. *Disasters, 25,* 358–372.

Said, E. (1993). *Culture and imperialism.* London: Chatto & Windus.

Summerfield, D. (1999a). A critique of seven assumptions behind psychological trauma programmes in war-affected areas. *Social Science and Medicine, 48,* 1449–1462.

Summerfield, D. (1999b). Sociocultural dimensions of war, conflict and displacement. In A. Ager (ed.), *Refugees: Perspectives on the experience of forced migration* (pp. 111–135). London: Gaskell.

Summerfield, D. (2001). The invention of post-traumatic stress disorder and the social usefulness of a psychiatric category. *British Medical Journal, 322,* 95–98.

Summerfield, D. (2002). Effects of war: Moral knowledge, revenge, reconciliation, and medicalised concepts of "recovery". *British Medical Journal, 325,* 1105–1107.

United Nations Children's Fund (UNICEF) (1996). *The state of the world's children.* Oxford: Oxford University Press.

Wainwright, D., & Calnan, M. (2002). *Work stress: The making of a modern epidemic.* Philadelphia, PA: Open University Press.

Wessely, S., Rose, S., & Bisson, J. (1998). *A systematic review of brief psychological interventions ("debriefing") for the treatment of immediate trauma related symptoms and the prevention of post traumatic stress disorder.* (Cochrane Review). In The Cochrane Library, Issue 2. Oxford: Update Software.

World Health Organization (1996). *Investing in health research and development: Report of the Ad Hoc Committee on Health Research relating to future intervention options.* Geneva: WHO.

Zarowsky, C. (2000). Trauma stories: Violence, emotion and politics in Somali Ethiopia. *Transcultural Psychiatry, 37,* 383–402.

Index